Edwin E. Bobrow CMC is President of Bobrow Consulting Group, Inc., a management consulting company specializing in marketing and marketing management to such clients as Honeywell, Dow Corning, Gillette, Norelco and many others. He is accredited by The Society of Professional Management Consultants and certified by The Institute of Management Consultants.

Edwin is also an Adjunct Assistant Professor at New York University and lectures extensively to businesses, trade associations and universities. He has written over 100 articles and 4 books on sales and marketing. He is the co-editor of *The Sales Manager's Handbook* (Dow Jones-Irwin).

Mark David Bobrow is a writer of fiction and essays, and has been a writing instructor at Empire State College and New York University. He is currently a Graduate Fellow in Writing at the City College of New York.

Marketing Handbook

Volume II: Marketing Management

Marketing Handbook

Volume II: Marketing Management

Edited by
Edwin E. Bobrow
Mark David Bobrow

DOW JONES-IRWIN Homewood, Illinois 60430

ISBN 0-87094-524-6

Library of Congress Catalog Card No. 85–70440

Printed in the United States of America

1 2 3 4 5 6 7 8 9 0 K 2 1 0 9 8 7 6 5

Dedicated to the memory of
Abraham D. Bobrow.

PREFACE

This book is about marketing management. If you are looking for guidance, information, and counsel from proven professionals, the *Marketing Handbook, Volume II: Marketing Management* provides the state of the art in applied marketing. It is a companion book to the *Marketing Handbook, Volume I: Marketing Practices*. Together they could prove to be the most inclusive set of references on applied marketing available today.

The strategies that one company uses to achieve its marketing goals will probably not be the same that another company would use, even under similar circumstances. In order to help you develop the strategies that are responsive to your company's particular needs and to the peculiarities and changes in the marketplace, fresh ideas, new concepts, and, most important, "how-to applications" to help develop your unique approach are provided in these books by proven practitioners. With the shifts that are going on in virtually every area of marketing in America today, it is vital for each company to develop strategies that will give it a differential advantage in the marketplace. Contributors to this practical, state-of-the-art marketing management manual are all authorities in their area. Each chapter sets forth their ideas, their views. You may agree with them—you may not agree with them. The important thing is that they will provoke your thinking and perhaps bring you new insights.

We have done our best to select topics that cover every aspect of marketing. We did not want to put together a tome that would serve only as a reference book. Rather, our aim was to offer a work in which you can selectively find practical, solid thinking on the subjects most vital today. We did not even want this book to be in one voice. Rather, we wanted each of the authors' writing styles and approaches to the subject to come through loud and clear, as their method of presenting the material is sometimes as important as the material itself. There are even cases where the same subject is covered in several chapters.

Where this is done, you will find that the subject is being approached from different views, and therefore it gives you a fuller understanding of the subject matter.

Some profess marketing to be a science . . . others, an art. In our view, marketing is an art that uses the latest scientific tools for its successful practice. We hope this book will be a well-used tool for you as you practice the art of marketing.

Edwin E. Bobrow
Mark David Bobrow

Editorial Advisory Board

ACKNOWLEDGMENTS

Special thanks must be given to the outstanding group of individuals who contributed so much through their service on our Editorial Advisory Board. Not only did they present us with ideas and concepts, but they reviewed the works of the contributors and, in many instances, made suggestions that added dimension to these works. Some had the interest and took the time to contribute chapters of their own to the book.

The content of any written work is enhanced by good editing. We believe (and hope you will agree) that this book has been well-edited by our staff and that of Dow Jones-Irwin. For this reason, we particularly single out Gloria Bobrow and Maura Tobias for the help that they gave us in the compilation of the manuscripts.

We thank all the authors for their dedication, for meeting deadlines, and for giving us the kind of cooperation that made the compilation of this book a pleasure.

Edwin E. Bobrow
Mark David Bobrow

CONTENTS

Part 1
MANAGING FOR SUCCESS

1 Approaches to Today's Marketplace: Sales Driven, Production Driven, and Marketing Driven   Leah S. Tarlow and Boris M. Krantz   3

Introduction. I. Sales Driven Approach. II. Production Driven Approach. III. Marketing Driven Approach.

2 Managing Change   Joseph T. Plummer   14

Appendix: Managing Change Exercises.

3 Responsibilities of the Marketing Manager   Steve Power   31

Organize: *Establish Marketing Plan. Policies and Procedures. Train and Develop.* Manage: *Select Channel. Determine Product and Package Specifications. Establish and Monitor Pricing. Formulate Budgets. Set Forecast. Manage. Order Processing. Execute Plans.*

4 Setting Up a Product Management System   Ardis Burst   40

I. The Product Management System: Organization and Structure. II. When to Use the Product Management System. III. Duties and Reporting Relationships in a Product Management System. IV. Selecting the Product Management Team.

5 Selecting and Retaining Top Producers
Herbert M. Greenberg and Jeanne Greenberg   53

Psychology of the Top Producer. Sources of Productive Talent. Legal Aspects of Hiring. The Selection Process. Administration of a Psychological Test that Uncovers Basic Personality Dynamics.

6 Selecting the Marketing Management Team   John Burns, Mark Kelly, and Dan Ciampa   **74**

Introduction: *Factors to Consider*. Determining How Big a Team Is Needed: *Guiding Principles*. *Case: CAD/CAM Manufacturing Company*. Determining the Expertise Required: *Guiding Principles*. *Case: Cable Connector Company*. Assigning Responsibilities: *Guiding Principles*. *Case: Monitoring Systems, Inc*. Setting Up the Selection System: *Guiding Principles*. *Case: Richardson Rubber Products*

7 Eliminating Turnover in the Sales and Marketing Department   Lynn Tendler Gilbert, Janet Tweed, and Ann Hammer   **91**

Reward and Recognition. Promotions. Communication. Sensitivity. Growth and Development. Creativity.

8 Managing the Pricing Function   Kent B. Monroe and John T. Mentzer   **97**

Importance of Price Decisions. The Environment for Price Decisions. Pricing Decisions. Pricing over the Product Life Cycle: *The Experience Curve*. *Pricing a New Product*. *Pricing a Growth Product*. *Pricing a Mature Product*. *Pricing a Declining Product*. Product-Line Pricing: *Principles for Product-Line Pricing*. *The Problem of Pricing Multiple Products*. *Determining an Appropriate Pricing Rule*. *The Problem of Common Resources*. Price Administration: *Developing a Price Structure*. Who Should Set Prices?

9 Management Consulting: Help Is on the Way! John F. Hartshorne   **122**

Who Are Management Consultants? What Management Consultants Do. How to Tell if You Need a Consultant. How to Select a Management Consultant. How to Assure Successful Completion of the Projects. Project Planning. Confidentiality and Conflict of Interest. How to Evaluate a Project's Success. The Importance of Professional Credentials.

10 Training and Developing the Marketing Manager Robert F. Vizza   **132**

The Job of the Marketing Manager. The Need for Training and Developing the Marketing Manager. Designing a Training and Development Program for Marketing Managers. Evaluating the Training and Development Program.

11 Who Manages the Marketing Program   Bruce S. Fisher   154

Functions to Be Managed. Marketing Management for the
Multidivisional Companies. General Responsibilities of
Corporate Marketing Group. The Need for Teamwork. The
Role of the CEO. Procter & Gamble: An Important Lesson.

12 Managing and Improving Marketing Productivity
Dale P. Hugo   164

Introduction. Putting It Together: *Company Philosophy.
Management Style. Charting the Course.* Who Does What?
The Marketing Organism. Direction and Flexibility. Product Management. Market Management. Responsibility, Rewards, and Recognition. Improving Marketing Productivity: *The Market Perspective. Creative Communication.
Internal and External Strengths. Nonduplicative Effort. Innovation Can Work Wonders.* Paying the Piper: *Developing
the Goals. Do a Few Things Well. Balance the Checkbook
Periodically.* Doing It Better the Next Time: *Chart a Clear
Course. It's a People Business. Encourage a Boundless
Outlook.* The Loctite Way: *Statement of Loctite Corporation's Business Philosophy.*

13 Managing the Company-Owned Sales Force
Daniel K. Weadock   178

Establishing the Sales Force: *Channel of Distribution Consideration for Establishing the Sales Force. Objectives and
Goals for the Sales Force. Recruiting the Sales Force.*
Training the Sales Force: *Face-to-Face Sales Techniques.
Account Distribution in a Sales Territory; Time and Territory Management. Particulars about Prospects in a Territory. Training in Product Knowledge. Competition in a
Sales Territory.* Managing the Sales Force: *Operating-Line
Organizational Structure for the Management of the Sales/
Marketing Department. Staff-Line Organizational Structure for the Management of the Sales/Marketing Department.*

14 Managing the Sale versus Managing the Sales Force
Jim Rapp   202

Role of the Sales Manager. Position (Job) Descriptions.

15 How to Manage a Branch/District Sales Office
Arnold L. Schwartz   207

I. Establish a Personal Set of Leadership Values. II.
Goals and Expectations. III. Recruiting and Selection:

Recruiting and Interviewing Tips. IV. Training and Development: *1. New Salesperson Branch Indoctrination and Orientation Program. 2. New Salesperson Branch Training Program. 3. Continually Conduct Product and Sales Skills Training Classes. 4. Do Field Coaching and Training.* V. Motivation: *Principles for Motivating Salespeople.* VI. Field Coaching: *Some Key Tips for Field Coaching.* VII. Appraisal and Evaluation. VIII. The Branch Manager as a Business Person. IX. Personal Development.

16 **Alternative Channels of Distribution   Robert La Rue**   **221**

Case History 1. Case History 2. Case History 3: *A Look at the Case Histories.*

17 **After-Sale Strategies: A Perspective on Product Support
Dick Berry**   **232**

Product Support and After-Sale Strategy. The Search for Customer Satisfaction. The Insurance Perspective of Service. What Is the Opportunity? Service Support Level. Strategic Perspective for Service Support. Integrated Marketing Strategy. Service-Requirements Planning. Formulas for Estimating Service Requirements. Alternative Approaches to Product Support. Keys to Growth in After-Sale Service.

18 **Establishing and Managing Telemarketing
Stephen D. Boudreau, Jr.**   **244**

A Strategy of Communications. The "Abominable No-Man Syndrome." Setting Up a Telemarketing System: *Cost Is the Key. Customer Classification. Designation of Telemarketing Accounts. Organizing the Telemarketing Department. Selection of Telemarketing Personnel and Training. Record-Keeping and Monitoring Results.*

19 **Sales Measurements   Charles W. Stryker**   **268**

Background. Tracking Methods—Overview. Tracking Process—Implementation Details: *Prospect File. Response File. Call Report File. Customer File. Attrition File.* Tracking Results. Evaluation System Requirements: *Segment 1: Nonrespondents to Direct Marketing Program. Segment 2: Respondents/Nonbuyers. Segment 3: Buyers. Segment 4: Cancels.* Measurement System Management.

20 Computers in Marketing   Roberts A. Moskowitz   282

Computers Handling Sales Leads. Computers at the Point of Sale. Computers for Market Analysis. Computers for Sales Tracking and Control. Computers in Sales Calls. Computerized Customer Support. Computers in Politics.

21 Traits of a Good Manager   Marvin Rafal   308

Overview. Research Findings: *Results of Study. The Study of Values. The Interest Inventory. A Competency-Based Approach.* Self-Evaluation.

Part 2
NEW PRODUCT DEVELOPMENT AND MANAGEMENT

**22 Introduction to New Products Management
Larry Wizenberg   321**

**23 Finding and Launching Successful New Products
Stewart A. Washburn   326**

Introduction. Developing Strategic New Product Guidelines: *High Product Quality. Broad Product Offerings and Markets Served. Serve Narrow Market Segments. Secure a Healthy Market Share of Served Markets against Few Competitors. Healthy Margins. Marketing Efforts Stress Direct Sales and Minimize Advertising. Moderate New Product Activity. Low-to-Moderate Investment Intensity. High Value Added by Each Employee. Vertical Integration. Moderate R&D Aimed at Product and Process Improvement.* Finding New Product Ideas: *Invention. Acquisition. Evolution. Rejects and Failures. Customer Requests.* Conducting Market Audits and Market Research: *Market Audits. Market Research.* Selecting New Products for Development. Managing a Successful New Product Launch.

24 New Product Development   Steve Power   363

Need for New Product Development. Definition. Setting the Stage. The System: *I. Definition Phase. II. Design Phase. III. Development Phase. IV. Production Phase.*

25 Determining User Needs for New Product Development
Bruce Fisher   372

Types of New Products. Market Needs: The User. When
Will Users Innovate? Finding Innovators: *Key to Success.*
Listening to the Voice of the Marketplace. In-House or Out-
House: *Developing an "In-House" Capability. The Role of
the Marketing Department. Teamwork. How to Identify Po-
tential New Product Winners.* Researching for New Product
Development: A "Market Orientation."

26 Establishing a New Product Development Team   Jim Betts   383

The New Product Effort Is Vital to Business Growth. Setting Up the New Product Team. Before the Team, There Is
the Mission. Selection of New Product Team Members: *The
Team's Goals. The Team's Restraints.* Do What Works
Best.

27 Planning the Payback of a New Product
Angelico Groppelli   391

Estimating the Initial Investment Costs. Forecasting Revenues. Projecting Cash Inflows. Pro Forma Income Statement. Techniques for Planning Payback. Monitoring the
Payback Results.

28 Development and Marketing of a Nonconsumer Product
Ronald N. Paul   421

Background. Organizing for New Product Development. A
Strategic Approach to New Product Development: *Steps
One and Two: Marketplace Observations and Idea Genera-
tion. Step Three: Screening Step. Step Four: Preliminary
Evaluation Step. Step Five: The Prototype Development
Step. Step Six: Market Testing Step. Step Seven: Marketing
Launch Step.*

Part 3
LEGAL ASPECTS OF MARKETING

29 The Law's Impact on Marketing   Ray O. Werner   437

Using Marketing Laws to Gain a Market Advantage. History and Background of Laws on Marketing: *The Statutes
Regulating Marketing.* Current Impact. Future Impact.

30 **Layman's Guide to Contracts   Paul E. Saunders**   457

What about Forms? How to Get the Most out of Your Lawyer. Some Self-Help Ideas.

31 **Using Marketing Research in Litigation   Jeffery T. Wack and Steven E. Permut, Jr.**   463

Anticompetitive Practices. Trademarks and Brands. Deception in Advertising. Trial Process. Product Liability.

Biographies   480

Index   491

Part 1

MANAGING FOR SUCCESS

1

APPROACHES TO TODAY'S MARKETPLACE: SALES DRIVEN, PRODUCTION DRIVEN, AND MARKETING DRIVEN

by
Leah S. Tarlow
and
Boris M. Krantz

Krantz Associates, Inc.

INTRODUCTION

These are exciting, dynamic times in which to be a manager! Management responsibilities, however, come with no guarantee of success. The 1980s are an unsettled and transitional era for businesses.

There have been many business failures during the past few years, both of new companies and established ones. Acquisitions and mergers are extremely common. High-technology tools have changed forever the way companies operate. Many key products in today's economy were unheard of until recently.

Yes, managing today is a complicated combination of activities, with no guarantees of success. Managers who understand their marketplace and find a niche for their products or services increase their probability of remaining profitable—the measure of achievement.

Three management orientations are widely used today—sales driven, production driven, and marketing driven. Each has its own strengths and weaknesses, and the alternatives must be carefully weighed by top executives. The choice should reflect management's assessment of the market and of how to gain business.

I. SALES DRIVEN APPROACH

Definition: A sales driven approach to the marketplace focuses on gross sales; sales revenue is the measure of success.

In a well-run sales organization, products are moved efficiently to customers and sales revenue reaches an acceptable level. Products are eliminated when their contribution to gross profit fails to meet the established criteria. Customers are served well if they are satisfied with the company's product line. A good monitoring system highlights the products that are declining. Management can then study the situation and react appropriately.

Weaknesses to the sales driven approach are numerous. First, management is not focusing on the customer and his or her changing needs. Sales figures show current activity; they confirm which items are selling and which aren't. When effort is invested in understanding customers and their evolving needs, changes in demand can be spotted before earnings drop; the R&D department would have time to design or modify goods to meet market needs.

Second, sales figures reflect sales, not profit. When performance is measured by sales volume, salespeople often concentrate on selling easy-to-sell items, not necessarily the profitable ones. Sometimes highly profitable items compete with many others; after all, most companies in an industry recognize opportunity! Salespeople avoid competition and concentrate on products they know they can sell. Also, some products are more costly to sell than others. Some require numerous meetings with buyers, others require demonstrations and expensive training. When a salesperson sells products with high selling costs, the sales figures remain high, but profits sink.

Third, the sales figures don't always indicate market share, a key measure of success. In a vibrant economy, sales revenue can rise, while competitors gain more of the available business, either by attracting current buyers or by reaching new market entrants. A company that measures performance by sales dollars might be in serious trouble long before the financial statements reflect the situation. Management gains nothing when caught off guard. Knowing of potential difficulties gives one preparation time.

Examples of sales driven organizations are quite common. Many people—students, professionals, and those not currently in the work force—are suddenly interested in becoming computer literate. Computer schools are springing up everywhere, but often these schools are in existence only a few months. Why?

One explanation is that people with computer skills and the financial capability of buying several terminals aren't necessarily managers. They can find a few students to sign up for various courses, but they have not planned an entry into a very crowded market. In effect, they are sales oriented. Signing 50 students for a course does not mean that a business will be sustained. Immediate short-term revenues are encouraging, but other factors have been ignored.

The market share might be an extremely small one and become even smaller as local universities and adult education centers attract more students. Such a small business can thrive if it carefully targets a market segment that is not served well by current schools, but jumping into the high technology business without a plan almost assures failure.

Many companies do focus on sales revenue. They reason that if they can sell a product they will have the basis for sustaining a business. For example, a foreign manufacturer wanted to expand into the large market in the United States with a line of industrial equipment. He hired a sales manager to begin establishing a presence and to get the equipment into use. The reports sent abroad were encouraging: sales volume was slowly rising and new outlets were signing up to carry the products.

When a representative from abroad arrived to perform a periodic review of operations, he was shocked at what he found. The sales manager had moved much product to customers, but the recipients of the merchandise believed that they had the merchandise on consignment. Some of the sales that were true sales were finalized at extremely low rates; no profit was earned.

Unfortunately, this business closed. Management was too far removed to spot problems while they could still be corrected. They relied solely on sales figures with no understanding of the U.S. market, product mix, pricing, competition, and so on. A quality product didn't guarantee success!

II. PRODUCTION DRIVEN APPROACH

Definition: A production driven approach to the marketplace focuses on standard products and producing them in large quantities. Emphasis is on economies of scale and physical production.

The production driven orientation offers distinct advantages. Production costs are usually lowered and result in more competitive selling prices because of:

- Economies of scale, including efficient purchasing of raw materials.
- Steady production, eliminating overtime, and using the full capacity of the plant.

Also, deliveries to customers should be timely since steady production keeps inventory levels high enough to serve market demand. Reliability of shipment encourages buyers to continue ordering. A steady flow of orders makes the manufacturer streamline his system even more to fill demand. Truly a profitable cycle!

Some problems exist with the production driven approach. First, a production driven company is not responsive to customer needs. The emphasis is on production, and the products might lose their desirability before management is aware of changing needs.

Second, capital investments are usually too long-term. Management can easily find itself locked into an old technology and lose flexibility. When management becomes aware of required changes, fast response is often impossible.

Third, because the goals of a production driven organization are increasing the rate of production and are decreasing costs, the marketplace can become saturated with product. The company can quickly be faced with lowered demand for its merchandise and no way to switch to products for which there is current need.

A successful manufacturer of machinery has achieved a large share of his relevant market by perfecting production. His advanced technology encourages volume production, and the fabricated equipment has a quality reputation. Sales volume is high, and the cycle of efficient production continues. Refined production techniques—high-quality products—large sales volume: this is production orientation at its most successful.

Another manufacturer has concentrated on producing a quality product, unlike any other available publicly. People are not buying these improved items. Why? The market is not really aware of their existence. The most perfect product will not sell if potential customers don't know of its availability. Time and energy have been invested in product design and streamlining production, but without a marketing program the public will turn to other, lower-quality products. The production orientation doesn't answer two very basic questions:

— What should someone buy from you?
— How will potential buyers know that you want their business?

III. MARKETING DRIVEN APPROACH

Definition: The marketing driven approach is a well-planned program that focuses on the customers and on satisfying their wants and needs.

A properly designed marketing approach involves the total coordination of company activities with the goal of serving buyers. For a marketing orientation to be maximally effective, all top managers must be fully committed. If the buyers' needs are met, sales volume and profits will rise as customers continue to purchase goods and services.

The marketing driven approach forces management to understand the marketplace and to find a market niche. If management can identify a vacant niche that the concern can competently fill, the company has increased the probability of success. One importer of European goods, for example, recognized that other European manufacturers were having difficulty entering to trade in the United States. He expanded his company into a multimillion-dollar concern by helping others gain access to this market. He gets his client's goods through the physical entry process, warehouses inventory, prints literature, and even introduces manufacturers to reliable salespeople.

Before a meaningful marketing plan and schedule of activities can be formulated, management must know:

- Products.
- Target customers.
- Company—strengths and weaknesses.
- Competition—strengths and weaknesses.
- Business environment.
- Pricing and profitability.

Checklists I–V at the end of this chapter will help you to evaluate your understanding of your market and to highlight areas in which you should improve.

A marketing driven approach results in a concrete marketing plan. This plan should be in writing, because of the discipline involved in putting thoughts on paper. Management must get the thoughts of all departments involved in implementation. They should be encouraged to express opinions and challenge each other's ideas. The term *management team* is more than an idiom; everyone must work together.

Four separate activities are involved in developing a realistic marketing program.

1. Market research. This research can be as sophisticated or as simple as management chooses. Research provides management with much information: market size, market share, market potential, how the company and its products are perceived, knowledge of competition, market trends, and so on.

Marketing research should fill in the basic marketing equation:

$$(\text{Number of units} \times \text{Selling price/unit}) - \text{Cost} = \text{Profit}$$

Additional facts learned must increase the chance of success; otherwise, the investment of time and human resources isn't worthwhile. Impartial quantitative data are best but, at times, management needs to be aware of the attitudes and opinions of buyers. All facts must be digested by management and used in decision making—management is not relieved of responsibility. Sometimes market research will confirm management's intuitive thinking. This confirmation is valuable; then a new venture can be started with confidence.

2. Market planning should be based on all available information learned from market research, financial statements, employees, and other sources. First, long-term objectives are decided. "We want to increase market share by 10 percent in the next five years"; "We want to acquire a new business to give us vertical integration"; "Our product mix must be revised—we have too many mature products."

3. Specific, measurable, quantifiable short-term goals must be defined in every operating area. These short-term goals lead to the overall objectives. Specifying these goals includes deciding who is responsible and when the action should be completed. For example, the long-term goal is: increase market share by 20 percent. The near-term goals would be: each salesperson in territory 1 must open three new accounts by June and stock each of these new customers with $1,000 inventory per month.

Set goals for:
— Sales volume.
— Profitability.
— Production efficiency.
— Individual productivity.

Those actually having responsibility for implementing must be involved in setting the goals. Professionals become more determined to reach objectives they help set; in effect, they have put their necks on the line and don't want to fail.

If objectives aren't realistic, they are meaningless. Top management would love 100 new customers in each sales region, but the sales staff should really know their territories and be able to set achievable targets. Goal setting is a "give and take" process; many salespeople, if left on their own, might set low, easily reached goals so they won't have to work too hard or risk failure.

4. Constant reevaluation and setting of new goals complete the marketing cycle. When a program is functioning, "surprises" will always happen. The whole program might have to be reexamined. Perhaps a return to the marketplace is necessary to check basic assumptions. Slight adjustments in short-term objectives might be all that is required. Goal setting is an on-going process! Goals must reflect a realistic appraisal of the marketplace.

CONCLUSION

The marketing driven approach to today's marketplace increases the probability of success. Managers who constantly examine the business environment, seek out market niches, carefully develop a strategy designed for their target customers, and implement their plan thoroughly are generally the winners.

The checklists included in this chapter might highlight areas in which you and your management team have weaknesses. Learn about your market, set goals, implement, reevaluate, and GROW.

CHECKLIST I
Understanding Customers

Managers must understand their customer base, both overall and in specific large accounts.

1. What are your three best-selling products or services?

  1.   2.   3.

2. Why?
  a. These products fill my customers' needs.
  b. These are the products presented, even though others would benefit them more.
  c. Pricing is well below that of our competitors.
  d. Other_____.
  e. Don't know.

3. What are the benefits of our three best-selling products?
  Product 1_____
  Product 2_____
  Product 3_____

4. Does our sales staff understand these benefits and how to present them?
  Yes_____ No_____ Don't know_____

5. Is management aware of problems with customers?
  Always_____ Rarely_____
  Usually_____ Never_____
  Sometimes_____

If these questions were difficult for you to answer or if you were unable to answer them, you must learn what customers need. Companies who understand the market will attract orders.

CHECKLIST II
Knowledge of Specific Accounts

Managers in some organizations keep responsibility for several of the largest company accounts themselves. Whether or not this is the case in your company, you must keep up to date on account activities.

1. Name three large customers.
    Company 1 _____
    Company 2 _____
    Company 3 _____

2. Who are the buying influences in each of these companies?
    Company 1 _____   _____
    Company 2 _____   _____
    Company 3 _____   _____

3. Which products do they buy from you?
    Company 1 _____
    Company 2 _____
    Company 3 _____

4. Who else do they buy from? What percent of the business do you have?

	Supplier	Supplier	Percent Total Business
Company 1	_____	_____	_____
Company 2	_____	_____	_____
Company 3	_____	_____	_____

5. Do you know firsthand if the buyers are pleased with:

	Products	Service	Salesman	Competition
Company 1	_____	_____	_____	_____
Company 2	_____	_____	_____	_____
Company 3	_____	_____	_____	_____

You cannot rely on your sales staff to give you all the feedback you should have. They might be afraid to bring bad news. You must make time to keep in touch with your major accounts. If you could not answer these questions easily, then you must give customers more attention.

— You can't afford to neglect your customers!
— Where would your business be without them?

CHECKLIST III
Business Environment

A decision maker who grasps the environment in which his or her company functions has the best chance to succeed. Be aware of opportunities, technological advances, new products, and the like.

1. Name two general business-oriented publications you read on a regular basis.

   _____   _____

2. Name two trade journals you read at least once a month.

   _____   _____

3. Think of one technological change in the past year that might affect your market, either positively or negatively. How have you gone about learning more about it?

4. Has your labor supply been changing over the past few years? What are your sources today? What will be your source next year?

5. Are new competitors entering your market? What will happen to your market share?

6. Are competitors leaving your market? What will be your response?

You should know the most probing questions to ask in your particular industry. Don't let yourself be caught off guard by change. Those who see changes coming can prepare and often strengthen their market position.

CHECKLIST IV
Company Strengths and Weaknesses—Yours and Your Competitors'

Who responds best to customers? How do buyers select suppliers? Managers who have few illusions about their resources can steadily improve their market position.

1. Think of an account you lost in the past six months (every company has them). Why did you lose it? If you don't know, FIND OUT. Avoid the same mistakes next time!

2. How do you rate your company in the following categories?

	Excellent	Good	Average	Below Average	Poor
Product line					
Customer knowledge					
Delivery					
Human resources					
Product quality					
Retaining accounts					
Acquiring new business					

3. Repeat question 2 for at least three competitors.

Look closely at each area in which you rated your company "average" or less.

Next, look at the categories in which you rated competitors "Good" or "Excellent."

Do your competitors have an advantage over you? Do you see common problems that affect your whole industry? Awareness of a problem is the first step to finding a viable solution!

CHECKLIST V
Profitability

Every business has multiple goals, but the most basic underlying focus must be PROFITABILITY.

The following questions are key:

1. What are the gross profit margins of three products you sell heavily?
    Product 1_____
    Product 2_____
    Product 3_____

2. Have you investigated methods of cutting production costs?
    ___Constantly   ___Regularly   ___Occasionally   ___Rarely   ___Never

3. Do you analyze your general selling and overhead expenses?
    ___Constantly   ___Regularly   ___Occasionally   ___Rarely   ___Never

4. List three areas in which you can comfortably reduce costs:
    #1 _____
    #2 _____
    #3 _____
    Profitability will rise when expenses are lowered or when prices rise. Examine your pricing policies:

5. How does your pricing compare to the rest of the market?
    ___Very high   ___Above average   ___Competitive   ___Lower   ___Very low

6. Do your salespeople really understand the relationship between selling price and profitability?
    ___Yes   ___No   ___Don't know

7. Do they quickly reduce prices to get an order?
    ___Yes   ___No   ___Don't know

8. Does the sales staff sell solely on the issue of pricing or do they sell your company's total value?
    ___Price   ___Value   ___Don't know

Nobody wins a price war! Your company probably can't rely on low-margin business as a base. Management must know how the sales staff handles the price issue, and it must work on selling your company's value to the sales staff so they, in turn, can sell the value to customers.

2

MANAGING CHANGE

by
Joseph T. Plummer

Young & Rubicam

Change is in the air in America. You can feel it—like the first porten-
tous whiff of springtime. America and its people are:

— Changing from a nation dominated by the mass-production
  smokestack industries to one dominated more and more by
  service, information, and high-technology industries.
— Changing cultural and social norms.
— Changing economic conditions and our nation's demographic
  makeup.
— Changing from an isolated marketplace into a global marketplace.
— Changing pace of change.

It is somewhat disconcerting to reflect that less than 20 years ago
black people couldn't attend certain schools, join many fraternities, or
even vote in some states. Twelve years ago there was an ordinance in a
major city which prohibited women from shopping in shorts downtown. Less than 10 years ago there was no electronic game market or a
personal computer market. Less than eight years ago Luke Skywalker
and Darth Vader captured the imagination of people around the world.
What is going on? Who is in charge here?

One of the most astute and articulate observers of what is going on
and who is in charge, John Naisbitt, author of *Megatrends,* offers a
basic premise for this chapter:

Centralized structures are crumbling all across America. But our society
is not falling apart. The people of this country are rebuilding America from
the bottom up into a stronger, more balanced, more diverse society. The

decentralization of America has transformed politics, business, our very culture.[1]

We can see support for this premise all around us. In Westchester County and Fairfield County, a group of citizens with a "war chest" of over $50,000 is set to do battle with the EPA, FAA, and State of New York over the Westchester County Airport. In Madison, Wisconsin, the City Planning Department no longer asks for a rubber stamp on the master plan it creates. Instead, city planners first present citizen groups with an array of alternatives in informal neighborhood sessions. Iowa has developed a statewide town meeting system on issues and long-range planning. And in Columbus, Ohio, Qube is used to take "instant votes" on local issues.

In the city, county, or state, decentralization empowers people to tackle problems and create change on a small scale. Because political power is being decentralized, people can now make a difference locally. In fact, that might be the only way people can make a difference in our complex society. Decentralization has become the great facilitator of social change in politics today.

Decentralization and experimentation are also taking place in many business organizations today, and new management theories once relegated only to academic literature are now being practiced by more and more American corporations.

Examples of the new management theories include:

1. *Theory Y.*
2. *Networking* derived from cybernetics.
3. *Theory Z* and *Quality Circles* (borrowed from the Japanese companies who currently have over 6 million workers in 600,000 QCs throughout industry).
4. *Heterarchical* organization versus *hierarchical* organization structure has become a new trade-off decision.
5. *Matrix management* and venture group theory.

In addition there are some prominent examples of corporations practicing decentralization or new management theories:
An example of hetarchical theory and networking:

Intel—Robert Noyce—"What we have tried to do is put people together in ways that they make contributions to a wider range of decisions and do things that would be thwarted by a structured, line organization."[2]

---

[1] John Naisbitt, *Megatrends: Ten New Directions Transforming Our Lives* (New York: Warner Books, 1982), p. 97.

[2] Naisbitt, *Megatrends*, p. 199.

Theory Z and Quality Circles:

Honeywell has been working with Quality Circles since 1974. They now have 350 Quality Circles in operation throughout the company.[3]

An example of Venture Groups and Matrix Management:

3-M—Edward B. Roberts—"From top to bottom, 3M's management provides active, spirited encouragement for new venture generation. . . . The work environment within the company is distinctly favorable to entrepreneurial activity. In part this environment is the result of promoting top management from within, frequently from successes in venture management."[4]

From another perspective, Donald N. Michael, Brian Van der Horst, Meredith Larson, and Ian Wilson, authors of *The New Competence,* describe the need for new management *skills* beyond organization theories for succeeding in turbulent times:

The deliberate application of these new skills—such as multiple views of the present and the future, changing value patterns, and a wide variety of *qualitative data*—are seen as a necessary contribution to the process of transforming the conventional corporate organization into the *learning system* it must become if it is to survive and prosper under persisting conditions of great uncertainty.[5]

Many corporate observers have suggested that large hierarchical structures are becoming outdated in an "Information Environment" where speed, synthesis, and flexibility are critical factors—not order, repetition, and stability.

Roy Amara, director of the Institute for the Future, has stated that another crucial factor having an impact upon hierarchical structures in the 1980s is the size of the group of young people born in the 1950s entering the white-collar work force. These young people have been entering the work force in huge numbers, with very sophisticated educational backgrounds and high expectations. Amara forecasts that there will be 20 candidates vying for every managerial position in 1990 versus 10 candidates in 1980. Amara asks: "What will we do with all these well-educated Indians with Chief-like tendencies in the classic hierarchical organizations?"[6]

---

[3] Ibid., p. 201.

[4] E. B. Roberts, "New Ventures for Corporate Growth," *Harvard Business Review,* July–August 1980, p. 139.

[5] Donald N. Michael, Brian Van der Horst, Meredith Larson, and Ian Wilson, *The New Competence: The Organization as a Learning System* (Menlo Park, Calif.: SRI International, 1980), p. 36.

[6] Naisbitt, *Megatrends,* p. 199.

Are these observations merely academic theory about new organizational trends, or are there more basic social, demographic trends, and people changes occurring in America at large supporting this call for organizational change to better meet competitive and environmental challenges? Well, let us look briefly at some of the crucial factors that our research at Young & Rubicam (Y&R) suggests are underlying this need to change how we work, market, and innovate in business today—how we manage people and the resulting innovation.

I hope to demonstrate through this analysis that business *was* structured to succeed at stability and mass production because the mind set of people and our culture *was* different 15, 20, and 30 years ago. All that has changed in the past decade and will continue to change at a rapid pace in the 1980s. A "happy marriage," if you will, is *emerging* between the needs of organizations to change and innovate and a new mind set among Americans which has come about as a result of three critical areas of impact:

1. Societal changes since World War II.
2. Sociodemographic trends.
3. The resulting values change in response to environmental factors and a rapidly changing world in the past 10 years.

First, let's consider a brief historical perspective on contemporary American society since World War II that "sets the stage" for the sociodemographic and value changes.

1950–1967: *A Unique Period in American History*
Stable and rapid growth of industrialized America for mass production and mass marketing.

— Agreement on the American Dream.
— Political stability and the Great Society.
— Television becoming the centerpiece of leisure time.

1968–1974: *The "Trauma" Period*

— Vietnam War.
— Nixon and Agnew resignations.
— Oil crisis.
— Drug culture.
— Floundering economy.
— Questioning of and search for heroes.

1974–1984: *The Transitional Search*

— Search for new economic models.
— Experimentation in politics; primarily back to grass roots and nontraditional politicians.

— Sorting out old values and new values.

— Recognition of new age in energy and information.

— Recognition of the global marketplace.

D. Yankelovich, in *New Rules,* articulates this transitional search America has been going through in the past 10 years:

> We now find our nation hovering midway between an older postwar faith in expanding horizons, and a newer sense of lowered expectations, apprehension about the future, mistrust of institutions, and a growing sense of limits.[7]

Underneath these dramatic historical social periods affecting the mind set of people have been long-term and profound demographic trends which have dramatically altered the sociodemographic makeup of our country today and which will persist throughout the 80s. The major ones based upon our research at Y&R are shifts in geography, the changes in the work force and household composition, the new distribution of spending power, and *most important of all,* the impact of the "Baby Boomers" cohort group. Most people are familiar with these trends and the underlying causes; but it may be instructive to briefly highlight them in this context of the need for a new approach to managing change.

The significant geographic shifts have been the migration and population shifts from the Snow Belt to the Sun Belt, the growth of new cities and nonmetropolitan areas at the expense of rural America and the old central cities, and housing patterns which continue to show growth in multifamily housing over traditional single-household dwellings.

Closely tied to the geographic patterns is a long-term trend of workers moving out of the smokestack industries into service and high-technology industries. In addition, the severe economic crunch and new technology in manufacturing has caused the loss of 1 million blue-collar jobs since 1978. On the other hand, the robotics industry is forecast to be a $4 billion business by 1995. Thus, more and more blue-collar workers need to be retrained or stay forever "obsolete." The impact of these factors on the working class has been devastating.

Coupled with these trends is the continuing entry of women into the work force, creating a new phenomenon of dual-income households and putting strain on the traditional sex roles of husband and wife. This growth of women in the labor force is especially dramatic among women 20 to 44. There is little question today about the value of women gaining a college education.

---

[7] D. Yankelovich, *New Rules, Searching for Self-fulfillment in a World Turned Upside Down* (New York: Random House, 1981), p. 24.

The dual-income household is becoming the norm, rather than the exception. Currently, dual-income households are estimated to number about 24 million, which is over half of the husband/wife families. In 40 percent of these, both spouses are full-time workers. The median income of these dual-income households is over $30,000, compared with $25,000 for the part-time working wife and $19,000 where the wife doesn't work at all.

The key, however, is that the vast majority of dual-income households is young—70 percent are baby boomers and 60 percent have at least one child. These factors have had an enormous influence in the workplace *and* in the marketplace.

The most profound effect, probably the driving force behind the geographic, work force, household, and value shifts, has been this large baby boom cohort group that has been moving through our society since World War II like a "pig through a python." Figure 2–1 charts the impact of this group over time. The baby boom cohort group is that "Brady Bunch" who joined the population between 1949 and 1964—73 million strong—who are now beginning to dominate our adult population.

This baby boom bunch has influenced the child orientation and growth of schools in the late 1950s and early 60s. They filled our colleges, armed forces, and the work place in the late 1960s and 70s. Today they represent the largest adult segment of the population. This group, due to its historical upbringing and size, influenced the suburban family focus: the civil rights, peace, ecology, and free love movements of the late 1960s and the "age of me" of the middle 1970s. This group has had a dramatic impact on the following markets (among others) in the past decade:

— Jeans.
— High-tech entertainment.
— Beer, wine, and soft drinks (the decline of coffee).
— Foreign cars.
— Active sports.
— Gourmet and "good for you" foods.

As adults, they represent greater diversity in lifestyles than ever before in our history. Acceptable alternatives include postponing or never marrying, delaying children, new outer-directed values, new inner-directed values, dual-career households, single-parent households, exploring new career patterns, and a multitude of new products.

They are also unique in terms of higher education—half have been to college—and higher income—controlling nearly half of all aggregate income today. To have so much spending power concentrated among the younger age groups has never happened before. Thus, they are at

FIGURE 2–1
The Baby Boom Impact

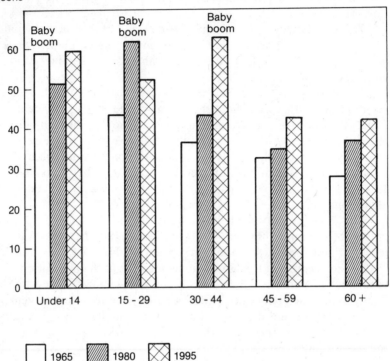

Millions
of
persons

Source: U.S. Bureau of Census; for 1965: "Estimates of the Population of the U.S. Including Armed Forces Overseas," Series P-25; for 1980: unpublished revisions to population estimates; for 1995: "Projections of the Population of the United States 1982–2050" (Advance Report), Series P-25, No. 922, and supporting unpublished detail tables.

the leading edge of forging a New American Dream or at least several new "value portfolios" for the 1980s.

Most of these inner-directed or new achievers of the baby boom group are seeking more out of life than a 9 to 5 job with security and classic upward mobility. They want a better quality of human experience than their parents had and the *real* freedom to pursue ideas and opportunities. They believe in an open democracy. They are far more comfortable than older generations with computers, experimentation, and the speed of change. They don't seem to accept the Old World model that world affairs, political or economic, must be on a win/lose basis all the time.

But, as Bill Huckabee states in his classic work, *Managing in Diversity,* this emergence of the baby boomers into the work force is bringing serious problems for corporate America:

> The most eminent clash is occurring inside major corporations between the more traditional Outer-Directed managers and the newer breed of Inner-Directed managers. Both are "right" but they disagree with one another, creating a potential for personnel tension and low productivity.
>
> The solution for pulling this diversity together has to do with the skills of the Integrated Manager. At the heart of the Integrated Manager's abilities are two skills: dropping assumptions and enlarging the context to incorporate diverse viewpoints into a new "unity" for the betterment of both employees and the corporation.[8]

A principal need for management in tomorrow's world will be to take an "integrated" approach: harnessing a diversity of value systems that continue to evolve both inside and outside the company.

Traditionally, the predominant management style in a large organization could be characterized as that of "outer-directed achievers," as indicated in column 1 of Table 2–1. The traits of outer-directed managers are familiar to most corporate officers. In recent years, however, the ranks of inner-directed people have been expanding rapidly. Many are now at an age where they are assuming managerial responsibilities. We can expect a sharp increase in the number of managers holding inner-directed values in the near future. These values of the inner-directed manager differ in many critical respects from the values of the outer-directed achievers. At an advertising agency like Young & Rubicam, this can be represented by creative types (more inner-directed) and management types (more outer-directed). The emergence of these two managerial patterns with distinct sets of values and traits clearly suggests that many management teams at more and more companies will be a mixture of both. The resulting managerial environment could be one of high turbulence and low productivity. But the integrated manager (described in column 3 of Table 2–1) possesses traits of both, and thus will be better able to lead increasingly diverse teams toward innovation and new growth.

Another useful concept to aid in the managing of change is to examine these three managerial or leadership modes within the context of the corporate life cycle, shown in Figure 2–2.

---

[8] B. Huckabee, *Managing in Diversity* (Menlo Park, Calif.: SRI International, 1980), p. 41.

TABLE 2–1
Outer-Directed, Inner-Directed, and Integrated Traits

Outer-Directed	Inner-Directed	Integrated
Individual traits:		
Pragmatic	Idealistic	Practical visionary
Self- and system-oriented	Person-oriented	Society-oriented
Materialism	Conservation	Sufficiency
Science/technology	Science/intuition	Wisdom/science
Commercial	Artistic	Effective
Independent	Self-reliant	Interdependent
Management style:		
Elite control	Elite control	Integration
High consensus	Low consensus	Consensus on critical issues
Centralized organization	Decentralized organization	Selective decentralization
Quantitative goals	Qualitative goals	Quantitative/qualitative trade-offs
Work in the system	Work around the system	Work to improve the system
Production for corporate profit	Production for personal satisfaction	Production for society
Emphasis on production	Emphasis on people	Emphasis on quality of life

Source: Bill Huckabee, *Managing in Diversity, Values and Lifestyles Program* (Menlo Park, Calif.: SRI International, 1980), p. 1. Reprinted with permission.

It is becoming accepted that a company, like a product, can have a definite life cycle. When a company is new, it has an exhilarating, all-consuming quality, and its focus is on its innovation and struggle to build a business. To this extent it is easy for management to be fairly single-minded. In its next stage, however, once its survival has been established, the company usually begins to concentrate more and more on market share and sales growth and solidifying a highly centralized organization. The third stage is the maturation of the original concept. Growth has made the company larger, its focus is on operational efficiency and it becomes more functional and bureaucratic in its orientation. Often the primary market for its product or service has begun to stabilize, as well. The battle for market share becomes intense and very competitive. Innovation tends to be thwarted or, at best, very "risk averse." The direction of the fourth stage depends significantly on the

FIGURE 2–2
Corporate Life Cycle

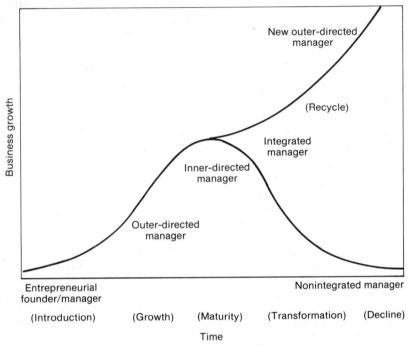

Source: Bill Huckabee, *Managing in Diversity, Values and Lifestyle Program* (Menlo Park, Calif.: SRI International, 1980), p. 19. Reprinted with permission.

company's leadership. The company may begin to decline when it coasts on its reputation while competitors and changing markets erode its base, *or* it may evolve to a new professional, entrepreneurial level by focusing more on problem solving and innovation. Such evolution is generally done by diversifying under leadership by new integrated managers. This need for new kinds of leadership is also supported by Naisbitt:

> At a time when decentralist and networking values are becoming more accepted and when businesses must do the hard work of reconceptualizing what business they are really in while facing unprecedented foreign competition, it is not the ideal time to be a traditional-type leader, either political or corporate.[9]

---

[9] Naisbitt, *Megatrends,* p. 204.

The best insight, I believe, on the possible leader of the future, comes out of the latest work by Arnold Mitchell, director of social research at SRI International. In a recent manuscript, called *Ways of Life,* Mitchell describes the leader of the past as "A Maker" and the new leader of the future "A Mover".[10]

Mitchell describes the "Mover" as a leader who will shun hierarchical methods of control for the excellent reason that they increasingly will not work. But without hierarchy, many say, there is anarchy. Organizations for centuries from the Roman army forward have depended upon a hierarchical organizational structure with strong dominating leaders at the top.

Yet, happy families are a good example of successful heterarchy. R&D laboratories, universities, creative companies like advertising agencies, and "think tanks" are other examples of successful heterarchy. Mitchell describes the new leader as follows:

> The Mover will be, almost surely, intensely person centered as an individual and yet society-oriented as a political being. The emphasis will be on issues of quality of life, but the definition will be large enough to embrace the physical, the secular, and the spiritual. As a person the Mover is likely to be in touch with himself or herself, trusting of inner response yet shrewd about the motives of others. If the Mover is to lead in the complex world of tomorrow, he or she must combine the pragmatic and the idealistic into what might be called the "practical dreamer." The Mover will not be a pushover but, rather, will be powerfully mission-oriented with a clear set of priorities enabling him or her to act decisively and with the self-assurance to hold fast against opposition. These capacities imply that the Mover will possess a keen sense of risk, a sensitivity to change, and an appreciation—indeed, love—of differences. This love of difference seems to us crucial to the success of Movers, for without it they can attract or understand only limited numbers of the other life ways and will be unable to learn as much from tradition as from the insights of the "New Age" and the "consciousness revolution."[11]

For certain, the world around us is changing at a rapid pace with an uncertain future. Such change is graphically represented in Figure 2–3. Some of the dimensions of change are rather clear and others remain to be discovered, researched, and articulated.

The critical perspective to keep in view is that in less than 30 years, we as a country have enjoyed the longest, most stable, and highest industrial growth in the history of America, going through enormous contemporary political and social traumas in the early 1970s and pass-

---

[10] A. Mitchell, *Ways of Life* (Menlo Park, Calif.: SRI International, 1982).

[11] Ibid., pp. 47–48.

FIGURE 2–3

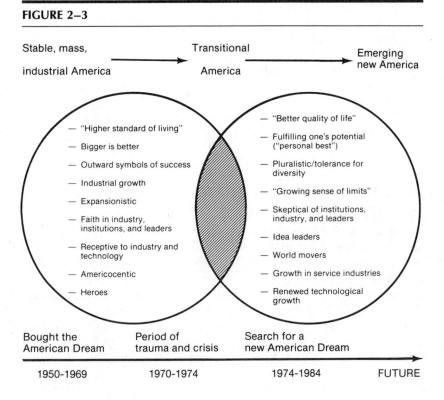

Stable, mass, industrial America → Transitional America → Emerging new America

- "Higher standard of living"
- Bigger is better
- Outward symbols of success
- Industrial growth
- Expansionistic
- Faith in industry, institutions, and leaders
- Receptive to industry and technology
- Americocentric
- Heroes

- "Better quality of life"
- Fulfilling one's potential ("personal best")
- Pluralistic/tolerance for diversity
- "Growing sense of limits"
- Skeptical of institutions, industry, and leaders
- Idea leaders
- World movers
- Growth in service industries
- Renewed technological growth

Bought the American Dream | Period of trauma and crisis | Search for a new American Dream

1950-1969   1970-1974   1974-1984   FUTURE

ing through a transition into an exciting future. As shown in Figure 2–3, our people have gone from a fairly clear set of agreed-upon values built around a common American Dream with all its outward symbols of success, an ever-increasing standard of living, an unfailing belief in industrial technology, and our major institutions usually led by clearly identified heroes emulated by the majority. . . . to a new set of values and expectations in an age of information and diversity. The search today by more and more people is for a better quality (not quantity) of life, the desire to fulfill one's potential, a growing sense of limits, healthy skepticism of institutions, tolerance of diversity, and the emergence of new types of leaders—the movers or those who can inspire us rather than command us. Therefore, because more and more people are concerned about themselves and *their* values, the organization must start there to gain commitment and innovation for the long-term good of the organization.

Within this bubbling mosaic of social, economic, and human change, corporate America is searching for *the* answer—wanting to change but finding old habits difficult to break and the risks rather frightening. We all should be encouraged, however, that change, evolution, and innovation have become an accepted pattern of life in America by most people, particularly the young. The change in people and values should make a change in leadership—the manager of ideas, a mover—easier to accomplish in most organizations. As Naisbitt points out, the people of this country are rebuilding a new America from the bottom into a stronger, more balanced, more diverse society. The boldness of a new enlightened leadership can mobilize this new energy of human capabilities and creativity into a rewarding future for all.

APPENDIX: MANAGING CHANGE EXERCISES

Since the new leader is not a son of the Pharaohs and is merely a first among peers, we believe that *personally* being creative is a critical element for leadership in the future. While no "trick" will make one a creative genius, the "exercises" listed here can be useful to a manager in developing fresh perspectives on a problem, encouraging innovation among employees, and becoming more open-minded in the search for fresh solutions to complex problems. The exercises or ideas are grouped by "types" of exercises based upon their value to you. All of these are more art than science and some will work well for you while others will not. Initially try all of these suggestions for sensitizing yourself to be more creative.

I. Exercises in Eccentricity to Help You "See" New Solutions

- Search for breadth as well as depth. You may need to specialize, to dig deeply into a subject, but you should also occasionally expand your horizons—read widely, let your curiosity take you wherever it will. Often a new idea, a new connection will emerge from "different worlds."
- Develop a honeybee mind. Gather your ideas everywhere. Don't be afraid to associate ideas fully. Let your mind buzz freely from one idea or source to another. Be open to experience and to stimuli of all sorts—both from within and in the world around you.
- Sharpen all of your senses. Schedule frequent practice sessions to see how vividly you can recall interesting faces, images, sounds, smells, factual experiences, tastes, and so on.
- Exercise your imagination. Guided imagery or guided daydreams are very useful exercises. Fantasy is not only for children. It is highly important in helping adults to "break out of the box" and "think beyond the edges of the familiar."

- Find new ways to change your point of view. Use Synectics, excursions through use of word imagery, analogies, and "upside-down" thinking—anything you can to help you see your perplexing situation in a different light, to restructure your perceptions, and to color your imagination to make new, possibly remote, connections.
- Seek dissimilar responses. The general semanticists remind us that often "advantageous vagueness" encourages "dissimilar" responses (as in brainstorming) and this helps us to avoid the "signal" (or obvious) response.
- Investigate parasensory experiences. A parasensory event is one leading to perception of knowledge not gained through the ordinary five senses. Much new research is opening up in this area. Some of the more promising nondrug procedures seem to be various forms of meditation (transcendental meditation, Yoga, Zen, and the like) and alphawave biofeedback training.

II. The Confidence Build: Help Encourage Ideas in Others

- Be optimistic in your approach. Remember that, for most things, somehow, somewhere there is a better way.
- Look for the "elegant" answer—don't be satisfied with just any solution to a problem.
- Be enthusiastic, confident. Your willpower controls your imagination and is affected by your emotions. So build faith in yourself by scoring successes on little problems before you tackle big ones.
- Don't kid yourself with vague ideas. Force yourself to do a little better each time. Strive for a set number of workable solutions to every problem. A deadline keeps you from putting things off from day to day.

III. Listening for Whispers: Help Yourself Follow "Hunches" in Yourself and Others

- Sharpen your nose for problems. Be curious about things that seem wrong or inadequate. Listen to the complaints of others. Jot down your own dissatisfactions with things and situations. Develop an attitude of constructive discontent—welcome problems as opportunities not only to accomplish something but to sharpen your creative abilities.
- LISTEN to small voices in yourself; half-spoken sentences sometimes contain the germs of big ideas. Learn how to take a "hunch break" when working very hard on a specific problem.

- Be alert for the welcome "hunches." When you get them, do something about them. Keep track of how your hunches work out. If you're right more than half of the time, that is a sign it's your intuition talking—not just your prejudgment.
- Be alert for the unexpected. Serendipity, or the "happy discovery," happens only when you are actually seeking something. As Pasteur said, "Inspiration is the impact of a fact on a prepared mind."
- Watch for the "quiet person" in a group. Often he or she may be thinking about a solution while others are making noise.
- Do not be afraid to speak out loud about your inner hunches or to write them down. This will not only strengthen your self-confidence about the small inner voices but could be a springboard for other ideas.

IV. Idea Practice to Help You Demonstrate to Others Your "Idea Leadership"

- Consider yourself a thinker. It's good to be a learner and a doer, but be an idea man or woman as well as a man or woman of action.
- Learn to play with ideas. At times you must "regress"—back off from the problem and try to think about it with the naiveté and freshness of a child. Even Einstein felt it was often useful to take a few steps backward in order to leap forward.
- Continue to acquire a growing body of knowledge about your field—and don't hesitate to challenge "sacred cows" (i.e., long-standing but possibly outmoded or erroneous concepts).
- State your problem carefully. Don't let the statement suggest the answer. For instance, if you ask a man to think up a new way to toast bread, you've already suggested a toaster. What you really want is a new way to dehydrate and brown the surface of the bread. State it this way, and you open up new idea opportunities.
- Schedule practice sessions—with yourself, that is. Conduct your own private brainstorming session each day. Come up with ideas—good, bad, and mediocre. Never mind the duds. Accept all ideas from yourself; don't reject any. Write them down. Unless you drill your mind regularly to produce a bag full of ideas, you haven't really decided to be creative.
- Carry your idea trap around. Keep a pad and pencil with you all the time. Why? Because ideas are elusive. They will drive out of your grasp as readily as they drift in. Better trap them on paper, in black and white.
- Use idea banks and idea museums. Ideas don't fall out of the

blue. Keep an idea bank—a dream file of clippings, notes from your idea trap, pamphlets, and so on, even if you can't work on them right now. Your idea museum is your reference library. Keep scanning it for ideas. Store them up to solve future as well as present problems.

- Relax your mind. After a hard day's work, let it wander. Free-associate while you walk or drive to and from work. Try a hot bath or shower, restful music. After a good night's sleep, get up an hour early, take a long walk, meditate. Take an airplane ride, play golf, or go fishing. Use the two-day formula: set your problem aside for a day, then hit it hard after a day's rest. Or plan to work on two projects alternately. Often when you are actually working on one, a new idea for the other will pop into your conscious mind. In a sense, this is planned incubation.
- Find the right time of day, the time of day when you're most creative. You know when you're full of drive. That's the time to build up a stockpile of ideas. The time for "red light" thinking comes when your mind isn't running creatively.
- Set a quota—and a deadline, too. Force yourself to do a little better each time. Strive for a set number of workable solutions to every problem. A deadline keeps you from putting things off from day to day.
- When evaluating, ask "What's good about it?" Often with a little work a strange idea can become a great idea. In the Synectics process, the evaluator is asked to suggest several good points about an idea before indicating its shortcomings, thus closing the gap and allowing a panel to concentrate on the latter. Whatever procedure you use, remember to consistently ask, "What's good about it?"
- Set your own mood by starting. The best method is not to wait for a proper mood but to pick up a pencil and start writing down the different parts of your problem and the different approaches you might use. The creative mood will come when you are actively engaged in writing things down.

SUGGESTED READINGS

Bouvier, Leon F. *America's Baby Boom Generation: The Fruitful Bulge.* Population Bulletin, vol. 35, no. 1. Washington, D.C.: Population Reference Bureau, 1980.

Broder, David S. *Changing of the Guard.* New York: Simon & Schuster, 1980.

Buzan, T. *Use Both Sides of Your Brain.* New York: E. P. Dutton, 1976.

Fordyce, J., and R. Weil. *Managing With People.* Menlo Park, Calif.: Addison-Wesley Publishing, 1971.

Gordon, T. *Leadership Effectiveness Training.* New York: Wyden Books, 1977.

Garreau, Joel. *The Nine Nations of North America.* Boston: Houghton Mifflin, 1981.

Hawken, Paul. *The Next Economy.* New York: Holt, Rinehart & Winston, 1983.

Jones, Landon. *Great Expectations.* New York: Coward, McCann & Geoghegan, 1980.

Koestler, A. *The Act of Creation.* New York: Macmillan, 1964.

LeBoeuf, Martin. *Working Smart.* New York: McGraw-Hill, 1979.

Mitchell, Arnold. *The Nine American Lifestyles.* New York: Macmillan, 1983.

Nicholson, J. *Habits.* London: Pan Books (Macmillan & Co.), 1977.

Reich, Robert B. *The Next American Frontier.* New York: Times Books, 1983.

Watzlawick, P., J. Weakland, and R. Fisch. *Change.* New York: W. W. Norton, 1974.

White, Theodore H. *America in Search of Itself,* New York: Harper & Row, 1982.

REFERENCES

Huckabee, B. *Managing in Diversity.* Menlo Park, Calif.: SRI International, 1980.

Michael, D. N., M. A. Larson, B. Van der Horst, and I. Wilson. *The New Competence: The Organization as a Learning System.* Menlo Park, Calif.: SRI International, 1980.

Mitchell, A. *Ways of Life.* Menlo Park, Calif.: SRI International, 1982.

Naisbitt, J. *Megatrends: Ten New Directions Transforming Our Lives.* New York: Warner Books, 1982.

Roberts, E. B. "New Ventures for Corporate Growth. *Harvard Business Review.* July–August 1980, pp. 134–142.

Yankelovich, D. *New Rules, Searching for Self-fulfillment in a World Turned Upside Down.* New York: Random House, 1981.

3

RESPONSIBILITIES OF THE MARKETING MANAGER

by
Steve Power

Thermo-Serv., Inc.

The scope of the marketing manager's role varies considerably from one company to another. Markets served, products manufactured, competitive climate, and myriad other factors influence the duties that must be carried out by the top marketing executive. Whether a company manufactures and distributes consumer goods, industrial products, or provides a service, it is up to the marketing manager to determine the needs of the consumer and to effectively regulate the activities of the company to meet those needs in a framework that will accomplish the company's goals and profit objectives.

In simple terms . . . it is up to the marketing manager to *organize* and *manage* all of the planning and administration activities that fall under the marketing umbrella. The specific responsibilities outlined in Figure 3–1 are based on the premise that the company embraces the marketing concept.

ORGANIZE

Establish Marketing Plan

Short-Range Plan. There are basically three ways to establish a plan. First, top management can set the corporate goals and develop the plans for all of the lower levels of management to administrate. This form of planning, obviously, does not take advantage of the best thinking of the managers who are most often closest to the business and competitive climate.

FIGURE 3–1
Responsibilities of the Marketing Manager

Organize	*Manage*
• Establish marketing plan.	• Select channels.
• Set strategies and tactics.	• Determine product and packaging
• Policies and procedures.	specifications.
• Train and develop.	• Establish and monitor pricing.
	• Formulate budgets.
	• Set forecast.
	• Manage:
	—Sales.
	—Advertising and sales promotion.
	—Order processing.
	• Executive plans.

The second form of planning takes exactly the opposite approach. It provides lower levels of management the opportunity to prepare their own goals and to submit their plans to top management for approval. Although this approach provides total involvement for all levels of management, it may not comply with top management's desire for the direction of the company.

A third and more practical form of planning involves good participation of both upper and lower levels of management. Top management evaluates the various opportunities available for growth. Goals are then established and given to lower management who, in turn, develop the plans for accomplishing them. This is the most common form of marketing planning and historically has provided the best results.

It is up to the marketing manager to monitor the success of each manager's performance toward accomplishing the plan.

Long-Range Plan. It is important that every marketing manager take the time to get away from the day-to-day tasks and pull together a long-range marketing plan to provide overall direction for the company. Care should be taken that the short-range plan fits into long-range (three- to five-year) objectives.

The most effective way to approach a long-range plan is to ask three simple questions:

1. Where are we?
2. Where are we going?
3. How are we going to get there?

Once these questions are answered, they will provide direction for evaluating potential acquisitions and help to guide the new product development activity.

Set Strategies and Tactics

It is important that a marketing manager establish a good understanding with all other managers within the department about how responsibilities break down and what is expected of each member of the marketing team.

Once the marketing plan is established, each manager should provide the marketing manager with a written summary of personal objectives toward accomplishing the plan. These should be broken down into strategies of how each aspect of the plan will be approached, as well as specific tactics on how they will be achieved. For example, a local soft-drink bottler, in an effort to improve sales, may define as a strategy the attempt to get more free-standing display space in convenience stores. A tactic used to achieve this strategy could be to provide a large colorful umbrella as a part of the display, which would be kept by the store manager when the product is sold out.

During the planning process, it is up to the marketing manager to weigh the merits of all of the strategies created to accomplish the plan. All of the costs associated with accomplishing these programs need to be evaluated in terms of their potential for achieving the overall objectives. At times, the marketing manager must make tough decisions on where the limited resources of the company will be applied. Good judgment and sound reasoning are important during this exercise.

Policies and Procedures

A tremendous number of questions arise in running any business. Someone must evaluate each situation individually and arrive at the most practical solution. Within the marketing area, for instance, the turnaround time from the point at which an order is received until goods are shipped must be defined. Policies must be established and procedures put in place to accomplish the desired service level.

Train and Develop

Regardless of how talented and ambitious a marketing manager is, he or she cannot lead a company to success without a reliable and dedicated marketing staff. Dartnell's *Marketing Manager's Handbook*[1] defines two classic structures for a marketing organization.

---

[1] Stewart H. Britt, *Marketing Manager's Handbook* (Chicago: Dartnell, 1973).

The simplest form is the *functional marketing organization* (see Figure 3–2). Within this organization, each functional specialist reports to the marketing manager.

In a small to medium-sized company with a somewhat homogeneous product line or market base, a single organization such as this can

---

FIGURE 3–2
Functional Marketing Organization

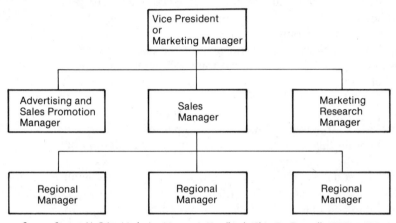

Source: Stewart H. Britt, *Marketing Manager's Handbook* (Chicago: Dartnell, 1973), p 130.

---

accomplish the marketing task. In a large and more diversified corporate situation, several autonomous divisions organized in this manner may exist. Each market manager or vice president would report to a divisional manager or to a president.

Under this structure, a company with a multitude of products or brands may be better served by a marketing organization comprised of several product managers (see Figure 3–3).

Each product manager is responsible for planning sales strategies, formulating advertising campaigns and sales promotions, tracking competitive activity, and the like. The market manager's primary responsibility is to continually weigh the opportunities presented by each product manager and allocate an appropriate amount of financial and human resources to maximize these opportunities.

Regardless of the organizational structure, it's essential that each member feels a part of the overall marketing team. Each manager should have an accurate and up-to-date job description outlining responsibilities and specific duties within his or her functional area.

FIGURE 3–3
Product Manager Marketing Organization

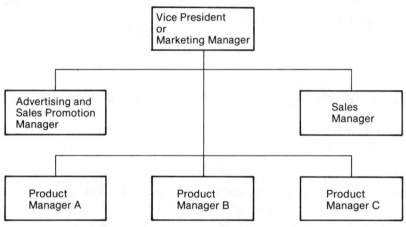

Source: Britt, *Marketing Manager's Handbook*, p. 131.

Periodic performance evaluations should be given so that there is a clear understanding of how each manager is measuring up to expectations.

MANAGE

Select Channel

"How" the company takes its products to market is oftentimes as important as the products themselves. Individuals or marketing organizations that help facilitate the flow of goods from the manufacturer to the end consumer are called "marketing intermediaries." Whether a manufacturer sells direct to retailers, moves its goods through wholesale distributors, or does a combination of both is an important strategic decision. It is up to the marketing manager to evaluate all of the options and make sure the marketing programs are set to carry the company in the desired direction.

Marketing intermediaries provide important services. When many stock-keeping units are involved, for instance, the role of a distributor is essential. The distributor will stock the goods and break master cartons to supply smaller retail dealers with a lesser quantity of a wider range of items.

Another aspect of channel selection involves staying abreast of retail trends and taking advantage of new opportunities as they arise.

The tremendous growth of the home center industry in the early 1970s provided an entirely new means to reach the do-it-yourself consumer.

For companies with mature product lines, good-quality merchandise, but a flat sales curve, new channels of distribution can provide growth opportunities for a stagnant product line. There is far less risk involved by pursuing new channel opportunities, compared with the investment required in machinery and tooling for the development of new products.

In addition to the opportunity of opening new channels of distribution, it is important that the marketing manager keep up to date on changes within *existing* channels of distribution to take advantage of new opportunities as they arise.

Determine Product and Package Specifications

Marketing management has total responsibility for both new and current products in the company's line. New product development, as discussed in another chapter, is a tremendously important element in the growth equation. The difference between the sales volume that can be realized from existing products three years out and a desired projected sales volume at that time is known as the "new product gap." That is, incremental sales above those that can be realized with products that are in the line today must come from products that currently don't exist.

Another method to give sales a boost is to make product improvements. Changes, regardless of how minor, oftentimes can be promoted efficiently to provide a competitive advantage.

It's imperative that the marketing manager stay in touch with current fashions and with changing consumer needs so product alterations can be made or packaging revisions can be put into place on a timely basis to take full advantage of changing market trends. In some instances, product changes are not even required; new packaging graphics can merely call out features that have been in existence all along.

Establish and Monitor Pricing

Perhaps the most challenging aspect of a marketing manager's responsibility is the establishment and revision of pricing. There are so many variables that enter into the process that it is impossible to do justice to this topic in the short amount of space allowed here.

It should be mentioned, however, that the marketing manager is charged with the task of meeting the company's profit objectives. While the manufacturing executive strives to achieve the lowest possible cost of the goods-sold figure, the marketing manager must forecast sales and establish a pricing structure that will provide the desired net profit.

A close eye must be kept on competitive activity with regard to pricing. With the recent use (according to many, overuse) of consumer rebates, marketing people must always be poised to take swift action to offset the aggressive moves of their competitors.

Formulate Budgets

As a result of the market planning process, sales projections are established and an estimated cost of manufacturing is determined. Once profit objectives are factored in, an overall dollar figure surfaces as the framework of a budget to operate the business. The marketing manager must make the difficult decisions on what portion is applied to advertising, sales promotion, new product development, and so on.

Depending upon the makeup of the product line, it's generally advisable to apply a disproportionate amount toward the promotion of new products and improved established items that offer long-range potential. Those items, at the peak or postpeak of your product life cycle, should be used to help fund the promotion of these new items.

Budgeting is also an area where consideration should be given to how much promotional effort will be applied to each channel of distribution. Here again, where future growth relies upon the development of a new channel, it is sometimes advisable to apply more money here, even though it is sometimes difficult to justify based upon current volume.

To insure that all budgets stay in line, the marketing manager should approve all purchase requisitions that affect the marketing budget and monitor disbursements on a monthly basis. This will safeguard against any misapplications of payments that may accidently occur.

Set Forecast

Manufacturing relies heavily upon marketing's input on what products will be produced. Typically, the marketing department will provide an annual forecast broken down on a monthly basis.

The forecast must be reviewed on a weekly to monthly basis, depending upon the nature of the business. Unusual sales trends should then be analyzed, and the forecast should be revised to reflect the current situation.

Since marketing creates all of the advertising and sales promotion campaigns that affect the demand for certain items, it stands to reason that marketing should project the results of these campaigns in terms of additional demand by month. This information should be given to manufacturing as far in advance as possible so additional materials or manpower, or both, can be added to support the influx of orders. It's equally important that, when these promotions are completed, forecasts are adjusted to reduce the demand to normal levels.

Manage

There are three primary areas that fall under the marketing management responsibility.

1. Sales. Although sometimes sales management is a line position reporting on the same level as a marketing manager, in many cases it reports to the marketing manager. Within this structure, the marketing manager must work with sales to establish sales goals by geographic area and to provide a great deal of motivation to the sales personnel to encourage them to meet established objectives.

2. Advertising and Sales Promotion. All companies, especially those involved in the sale of consumer goods, must spend a tremendous amount of money on advertising and sales promotion. Marketing management in this area must concentrate primarily upon the content of the message and upon the image of quality that it projects. Product catalogs and sales literature also fall under this category of responsibility. Management of this area is especially difficult. While one should not stifle the creativity of the advertising and sales promotion specialist, it's often necessary to revise and rework suggested campaigns so the desired message gets through to the consumer.

Order Processing

At a recent advertising specialty show, sales consultants were seen wearing buttons that read "I ♡ companies that ship." Every Monday morning buyers at Sears Tower in Chicago receive a computer printout entitled "Blue Monday Report," showing those suppliers that have promised merchandise and have failed to ship. These are only two examples to illustrate the importance of processing orders quickly, accurately, and completely so the retailer and industrial user ordering the merchandise get what they ordered on time. The marketing manager is charged with establishing guidelines for reasonable performance levels and then following through with the order processing personnel to insure that these levels are maintained. Recent progress in this area has been made through the introduction of electronic equipment that permits the linkup of suppliers and users computer equipment so the orders can be submitted during off hours over telephone lines. This eliminates all of the previously needed manual steps, reducing significantly the turnaround time from receipt of order to shipment.

Execute Plans

This final segment of the management responsibility is perhaps the most important and the most difficult to describe. For a marketing plan to work, an individual must follow up each element on a consistent basis to make sure these strategies and tactics are carried out as planned, and that advertising and promotional programs dovetail with the availability of products and packaging revisions. This is a continuing process that at times is very demanding.

The marketing manager, in this context, can be viewed as the choir director, with the various department managers as the members of the choir.

4

SETTING UP A PRODUCT MANAGEMENT SYSTEM

by
Ardis Burst

Burst-Lazarus Associates, Inc.

Any company that is organized with a major emphasis on marketing is repeatedly exposed to the idea of the product management system as a possible way of organizing its marketing effort. Although product management can be described in fairly simple terms, such a description does not provide a manager with a true understanding of a system that is, in fact, complex and subtle.

The following article is designed to help a general manager or marketing manager, who has not had firsthand experience with product management, develop a working knowledge of the system. The ultimate objective is to provide enough information for the manager to decide whether product management might be an appropriate organizational structure for his or her organization to investigate further, or whether it is a system best left to others.

The following topics will be covered:

I. The product management system: organization and structure.
II. When to use the product management system.
III. Duties and reporting relationships in a product management system.
IV. Selecting the product management team.

I. THE PRODUCT MANAGEMENT SYSTEM: ORGANIZATION AND STRUCTURE

The product management system is basically a matrix organization. That is, reporting relationships are established both vertically, as in

FIGURE 4–1
Organization and Structure

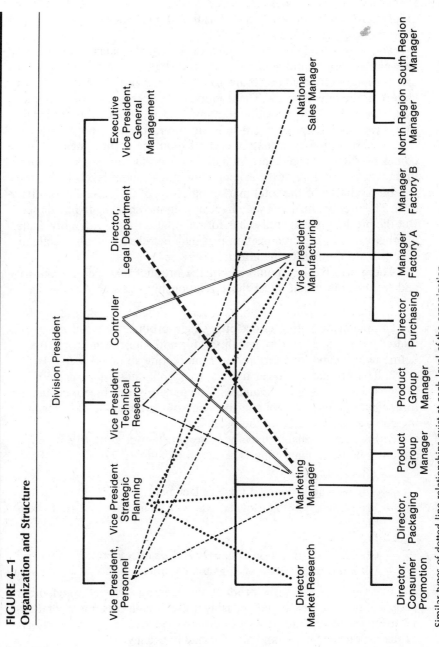

Similar types of dotted-line relationships exist at each level of the organization.

traditional organizational structure, and also horizontally. A matrix organization chart looks like a grid, rather than like a branching tree or an inverted pyramid (see Figure 4–1).

The vertical relationships indicate the usual chains of command between superiors and subordinates. But the horizontal relationships are between individuals who are roughly equal in title, function, and stature in the organization. These individuals operate in different functional areas of the organization that must act in a cooperative manner. Thus, the lines between them indicate interaction but not authority.

As constituted in a matrix organization, marketing logically becomes product management. An individual product manager is located in the linear structure of the organization one or more levels below the person in charge of the total marketing effort of the company or division. The product manager may have assistants reporting to him or her. But the product manager also has formal relationships with individuals in other areas of the organization that may be related either directly or indirectly to the marketing effort.

There are five key points about the product manager's authority and responsibility that make these relationships clearer.

1. The product manager has, at least in theory, responsibility for the complete marketing effort of a single product or small group of related products. This responsibility is for both short-term efforts (marketing tactics) and long-term efforts (marketing strategy).

2. The product manager usually has profit-and-loss responsibility for the business he or she manages. The person's job objectives, therefore, center on meeting volume and share of market goals while managing certain costs related to the product.

3. Product managers usually have substantial authority in areas directly related to marketing. These can include:

— Advertising copy.
— Advertising levels and media placement.
— Promotion type and levels, for both consumer and trade promotion.
— Packaging.
— Choice of distribution channels and balance between them.
— Ultimate price range of consumer purchases.

But even in these areas, the product manager must work through other people. For example, the advertising copy, media placement, and advertising levels are almost always determined through the joint efforts of the product manager and an advertising agency.

4. The product manager does not have authority over some areas which are key to meeting his or her business objectives. These usually include:

— Manufacturing.
— Sales.
— Purchasing.
— Corporate financial management.

For example, a product manager may find it necessary to achieve a certain distribution level in grocery stores if the product is to meet its share and volume objectives. The field sales force actually works to obtain these distribution levels. But the field sales force does not report to the product manager. Rather, the salespeople report to the national sales manager who has a dotted-line or horizontal-line relationship with the product manager (i.e., the national sales manager and the product manager have no authority over one another but must work together to meet the product manager's objectives).

5. The product manager's job is usually described as similar to that of the manager of a single-product company. But since the product manager is actually part of a large organization, often one with many divisions, there are overriding issues which can and do effect the product manager's day-to-day business decisions.

For example, the product manager may have established advertising levels for the last quarter of the fiscal year which will assure a certain share and volume range for the first quarter of the next fiscal year. But the corporation finds that some other divisions are not going to meet their fiscal objectives for the year, and a certain earnings level is important to the corporation in order to maintain its stock prices.

The product manager is directed by the marketing manager to cut the fourth-quarter advertising budget in order to contribute additional short-term profits to the total corporation, even if this jeopardizes future volume objectives on the product manager's business. Usually, in such a case, the product manager is no longer held accountable for his or her original objectives. However, such occurrences do point up the fact that the product manager's role is not purely that of an independent entrepreneur.

To summarize, the product manager's role is filled with paradoxes and imbalances. Obviously, this is not the type of structure that is attractive to all corporations or to marketing-oriented managers. When can it be well used? That is the next question to be considered.

II. WHEN TO USE THE PRODUCT MANAGEMENT SYSTEM

First, a company should consider using a product management system only if marketing is, or should be, very important to the success of the company. In many companies, "marketing" is really sales, and this is appropriate to the company's business. In other companies, the key to success is being first in research and development or in maintaining status as the low-cost producer. For any of these companies, introducing a product management system, with its complex reporting relationships and often aggressive managers, would be like giving experimental drugs to a well person. Hopefully, it will do no harm; certainly, it will do no good.

To return to the type of company for whom this organizational structure would be an asset, it is usually a company selling products that must have a clear image and marketing position in the marketplace. Putting the entire marketing effort for the product in the hands of a single individual can help insure that this image and position are maintained. To enlarge:

1. Usually such companies are primarily oriented toward consumer products, rather than industrial products. This is because consumer products often require complex marketing programs that meet consumers' psychological and concrete needs. These marketing programs, which include advertising, consumer and trade promotion, frequent packaging reformulation, and so on, often require coordination by a single individual. Thus, they are quite appropriate for organization into the product management structure. A good example of a situation of this type is a cosmetics company where the products must meet a wide range of consumer needs, from those verging on medical (e.g., dry skin) to those which are almost purely psychological (e.g., perfume).

2. These companies usually operate in markets where the action is lively and fast-paced. Thus, marketing plans must change frequently to meet competitive actions, and changes must take place quickly, since even a temporary advantage can have long-lasting repercussions. In such situations, it is very desirable to have one person, such as a product manager, who can coordinate responses and see that they take place quickly. Companies selling packaged grocery items, such as soap powder, cereals, and coffee, are prime examples of this type of organization.

3. Often these companies market products that are very similar to those marketed by their competitors. Thus, each product must have its own image that differentiates it from similar products. When all of the marketing efforts for a given product are coordinated by one individual (the product manager) this can help assure that the product's image will be clear and consistent across advertising, promotion, pricing, and the like. Soft drinks are a good example of this type of product. Mountain Dew and 7UP may have very similar tastes; but their total marketing effort is directed toward differentiating them from one another and from all other soft drinks that could be purchased in their place.

Besides making sure that a company sells the type of products that are appropriate for the product management organizational structure, a manager who is considering looking into this system should also take into account two other things before making even a preliminary commitment to product management.

First, product management usually is an expensive investment. Because each product manager by definition focuses on only one or a small group of products, an organization may have to add people when moving to this type of structure. These people will each command a substantial salary and must be organized in groups with possibly additional levels of supervision.

Furthermore, each of these people will be eager to expand the market for his or her product in ways that often include increasing total marketing expenditures. While these increases are expected to pay back in volume and earnings growth, these do represent a real cash outlay with no positive guarantee of returns.

Second, expenses aside, the company must be sure that it is able to cope with the complexities and pressures of the matrix organizational structure and, also, that it is prepared to manage the upwardly mobile, entrepreneurially-oriented managers who will be attracted to the product management system. A company, for example, that has traditionally promoted slowly from within, with many managers who are satisfied with remaining at the middle-management level throughout their entire careers, might be torn apart by the demands of a group of young, aggressive product managers as they charge through the organization acting as adversaries for their own products.

With these caveats in mind, let us now turn to the actual duties and relationships of the typical product management group.

III. DUTIES AND REPORTING RELATIONSHIPS IN A PRODUCT MANAGEMENT SYSTEM

A typical product management system consists of the following levels within the marketing organization.

1. *VP Marketing* (or in a very large company maybe a lesser title, such as *marketing manager*). Responsible for all marketing planning, long and short term. Interacts with vice presidents from other functional levels in making business plans for corporation or division.

2. *Product Group Manager.* Manages the work of a group of product managers, usually all of whom work on products that are similar in content, distribution channel, or in some other way. For example, a product group manager might manage a group of bath soaps.

3. *Product Manager*. Manages a given product. May supervise one or more subordinates.

4. *Assistant Product Manager*. An entry-level position, reporting to a product manager. Usually responsible for some aspect of the product's marketing effort, such as promotion.

There may be some differences in this basic structure, depending on the size of the organization or the size of the products being managed, or both. Some very lean organizations have product managers reporting directly to the marketing VP and have no marketing people below the product manager level. At the opposite end of the spectrum, some companies with very high-volume products, like General Foods and Procter & Gamble in their coffee divisions (where leading brands can have sales in the $1 billion range), have an additional level between product group manager and the marketing VP and also have a level between assistant product manager and full product manager.

In addition to the vertical reporting relationships just described, the product manager also has horizontal relationships. Generally these are with organizational peers in areas which are independent functionally but which provide support to the marketing area.

First, there are the "close-in" support areas which provide services to help the product manager perform day-to-day marketing work. These include the following areas:

1. *Sales*. The relationships between the field sales force and product managers are extremely important. This is because the field sales force is responsible for a marketplace implementation of the product manager's plans. These include executing trade promotion programs for wholesale customers, obtaining distribution at retail, setting up and managing special displays and events in the marketplace.

In addition, the field sales force provides feedback to the product manager on what is going on in the field from the competitive point of view and also on the responses of wholesale customers to various aspects of the marketing plans.

2. *Manufacturing*. The product manager works closely with manufacturing managers in order to do volume planning, to identify manufacturing problems that might affect product availability, to plan for special manufacturing needs, such as promotional packaging, and to monitor product quality as it relates to consumer satisfaction.

3. *Promotion*. Many companies have in-house promotion areas. In these companies, the product manager works with the promotion area to develop ideas for specific consumer promotions, such as couponing, games, special packs, and so on. The promotion area provides technical expertise on promotion effectiveness, testing, and promotion execution. The product manager retains responsibility for setting the ultimate strategic objectives for consumer promotion campaigns and also makes the final choices between promotion options.

4. *Packaging.* The product manager usually works with the packaging area in the same way that he or she works with the promotion area. The packaging experts know the ins and outs of packaging design, testing, and manufacturing. The product manager makes the strategic packaging decisions, such as how many different size packages to offer, what should appear on the package, what the basic visual message of the package should be, and so on.

5. *Market research.* Market research plays a major role in marketing management in most companies which are organized around the product management system. The product manager is usually responsible for working with those experts in market research design, implementation, and interpretation who make up the market research department. Again, the strategic decisions are in the hands of the product manager: what products to test, what markets to monitor, what competitors to follow, and so on. But often the ideas of the product manager are tempered by input from the market researchers in such areas as size of market research projects and which specific testing techniques to use.

Besides the horizontal relationships with the close-in support groups, the product manager usually has similar relationships with other areas that, while not related to the day-to-day marketing effort, are nonetheless important in implementing marketing plans. These typically include the following groups:

1. *Legal department.* This department often is involved in many aspects of marketing decision making. The lawyers usually review all advertising, promotion, and packaging copy to identify direct or implied claims regarding product content and performance. They review promotion plans to make sure that they favor all wholesale and retail customers equally, not passing on uneven prices, for example. They supervise contractual relationships with outsiders who supply packaging, promotion, advertising, and market research services. They also consult with the product managers on such issues as ingredient and packaging safety as these relate to corporate liabilities.

2. *Technical research.* In highly competitive marketing environments, the product manager usually has an ongoing relationship with the tech researchers. They work together to develop new products, also to reformulate existing products to improve quality or reduce costs, or both. Technical researchers also can keep product managers informed on what is happening in their area that might have competitive implications. For example, they might be aware of new patents being taken out by competitors, academic research that has implications for manufacturing techniques, and so on.

3. *Finance department.* Because the product manager is operating in a large corporation, there are usually sophisticated financial analyses that are applied to individual products, their levels of marketing expenditures, their raw material costs, and so on. Often the product manager does not actually perform this kind of financial analysis directly but works with a divisional or product group financial analyst who uses the product manager's input to perform the analysis.

The product manager has one other important working relationship: with the outside advertising agency that handles his or her product. A typical advertising agency has an organizational structure parallel to that of the marketing area, with junior and senior account executives equal to product managers and their subordinates, and account supervisors equal to product group managers.

The advertising agency is hired by the company for whom the product manager works to provide such services as developing advertising campaigns, recommending advertising levels and placement, and advising the marketing organization on consumer issues, such as promotion, packaging, and product development. While the responsibilities of the agency are fairly clear-cut, the relationship between individual product managers and account executives is often ambivalent. Agency people are expert in advertising issues, while product managers may have very little specific advertising experience. But the product manager knows his or her brand better than the account executive. Because the product manager and the account executive work for two different organizations, there are often more problems in developing compromises between these two groups of experts than there are, for example, between product managers and sales managers.

The situation is further complicated by the fact that the advertising agency is employed by the product manager's company, rather than by the individual product manager. Thus, the product manager is never in a position to fire an agency. At most, a product manager can ask that personnel assigned to his or her product be rotated off of the assignment.

These, then, are the many and varied organizational relationships of the product manager. Following is a discussion of the product manager's job from the point of view of areas of responsibility and day-to-day activities.

The main responsibilities of the product manager can be divided into three areas: organizational, analytical, and managerial.

The product manager's *organizational responsibilities* have already been described. It should only be added that, in many organizations, high value is placed on the ability of the product manager to manage, train, and motivate his or her subordinates.

In the *analytical area,* the product manager is usually responsible for analyzing the following areas:

1. *Product environment.* What is happening in the marketplace? What are consumers' or potential consumers' attitudes toward the product? The product manager usually answers these and related questions by using field data on product sales, such as sales records and syndicated data from A.C. Nielsen or other services, and by using information from certain types of market research that focus on consumers, their behavior, their attitudes, and the like.

2. *Competitive environment.* Using these and other sources, the product manager constantly follows and tries to understand the behavior of his competitors.

3. *Business analysis.* The product manager is responsible for performing certain types of internal analysis on his or her product and relating this information to the product and competitive environments. For example, the product manager might develop internal statistics on coupon redemption for his or her product or might do a breakeven analysis as a justification for increasing advertising expenditures.

The product manager is expected to use the results of the analytical work to keep volume and profit and loss projections up to date.

The product manager's *managerial responsibilities* focus on managing the elements of the marketing plan on a day-to-day basis, including updating plans in light of analytical findings, as described above. Working with support groups, the product manager oversees these areas:

— Advertising copy and levels.
— Media selection and placement.
— Consumer promotion programs: selection, level of expenditures, execution.
— Trade promotion programs: development and execution.
— Packaging.
— Price: wholesale and target retail.
— Distribution.
— New-product development.

In summary, the duties and responsibilities of the product manager are easy to list but hard to execute, since the reporting relationships and interactions that he or she must maintain are complex and rarely straightforward.

IV. SELECTING THE PRODUCT MANAGEMENT TEAM

In selecting people to serve on the product management team, general managers should look at two different areas: the skills of the people being considered and their personalities.

There are four sets of skills that are important to product management. First, in order to design and manage marketing programs, the product manager must have a marketing perspective. But the product manager must also have a management perspective in order to relate to the problems and points of view of the other functional areas with which product management must work closely. Many companies staff their product management areas primarily with MBAs, because MBA training at least theoretically is heavily oriented toward the general management perspective.

Second, the product manager must have good analytical skills. There are many things that must be monitored, evaluated, and weighed in overseeing a product and its marketing. These are both numerical and qualitative. Therefore, the product manager must be able to manipulate numbers quickly and correctly but must also be able to organize and evaluate soft data.

Third, the product manager needs some creative skills. Advertising, promotion, and packaging all have strong aesthetic aspects, and the product manager must be able to evaluate these things accurately. However, it is also important for the product manager to see these things as consumers see them. It is not enough for a package to have artistic validity; it also must have the universal appeal that will enable the product within to sell well.

Fourth, the product manager needs well-developed skills in self-expression. Because he or she interacts with so many different people in such a variety of situations, it is essential that a product manager be able to write clearly and to make oral presentations which are succinct and convincing.

An individual with all of the above skills is not guaranteed success as a product manager, however. There are certain personality traits that also are generally necessary for success in this area.

First, the person must have "people ability." Subordinates must be brought along, superiors must be kept happy, and peers in other areas must be managed tactfully. Furthermore, the successful product manager must have a true respect for these other individuals, because they are all so essential to the successful functioning of the business. A subordinate may have detailed knowledge of some aspects of the marketing effort that the product manager lacks; the superior may have a broader perspective that is important; and the peers undoubtedly have essential skills that the product manager must draw upon.

Next, the product manager must have a unique blend of entrepreneurial and corporate instincts. Because, in many respects, he or she does run a small business, entrepreneurial instincts are vital to build and continually refresh the business. On the other hand, as described above, the product manager must function in a large organization with multiple levels of management and complex reporting relationships. The pure entrepreneur would find such an organization very frustrating and constricting.

Third, the product manager must be ambitious. Most product management jobs require long hours, hard work, and frequent frustration as the product manager interacts with others in the company. Rarely are product management jobs permanent positions. It would be almost impossible to keep a fresh marketing perspective year after year while managing the same product or even operating at the same general level of management. Most companies have found that it is more productive to bring marketing people into the organization in product management, rotate them through various products and levels of responsibility, and then move the successful individuals into general management.

If product managers are constantly being moved around and promoted, how can an organization successfully keep up its product management team? In general, organizations follow one of two approaches.

Some organizations have an ongoing in-place recruiting system for attracting entry-level product management people, usually with the title of assistant product manager. These are frequently large organizations that need many people in the product management area. They are willing to spend the money to recruit and train individuals for several reasons. First, individuals who enter in this way are usually young and are easy to integrate into the organization, in terms of internalizing the corporation's attitudes and approaches to management. They quickly become part of the team. Second, these organizations need a number of people to handle detailed and narrow aspects of product management of very large brands. So an assistant product manager might begin by being responsible only for trade promotion and then go on to manage consumer promotion, jobs which take a lot of time but are not appropriate to a more experienced manager.

Other organizations, usually those with fewer products or levels of management, hire from outside the product management area (e.g., from sales, the promotion area, and the like) or from outside the company. In the latter case, these companies hire product managers who have already been trained in the essentials of product management but who have chosen to leave the larger companies for whom they have worked. For example, some product managers get impatient with the speed of promotions in their original companies and look for greener pastures. Others choose to move to new geographic areas where their employer does not have offices. And still others turn out not to fit into the original organization or to have exactly the set of skills or kinds of interests required. Yet these people can often be extremely successful in another organization.

Product management as described above is obviously a complex, sometimes frustrating organization structure. But when it is appropriate to an organization and its products, it can be a valuable asset. Any organization seriously interested in considering moving to a product management form of organization is well advised to call in a team of experts in organizational behavior. They will help evaluate the organizational climate and needs and ultimately help set up a product management system. Many large national consulting companies have divisions which work in the area of organizational structure. Also, professors of organizational behavior often work as management consultants, either alone or with consulting companies.

While product management should never be viewed as a panacea for marketing problems, it can be a valuable asset. Its benefits can even be sufficient to offset the complexities and frequent difficulties encountered in using this structure.

5

SELECTING AND RETAINING TOP PRODUCERS

by
Herbert M. Greenberg
and
Jeanne Greenberg

Personality Dynamics, Inc.

Whenever sales and marketing executives get together, poor productivity and high turnover are invariably key topics for discussion. These executives are constantly seeking ways to reduce the incredibly high cost, in both time and money, of recruiting, selecting, and training salespeople, only to have the majority be poor or, at best, mediocre producers. While striving to solve these problems, they nevertheless seem to accept as a fact of business life that 80 percent of what is sold is done so by 20 percent of the sales force. The obvious waste and staggering costs stemming from this 20/80 situation are accepted as inevitable. In addition, the high turnover, which is directly traceable to the 20/80 ratio, is also accepted as a necessary cost of managing a sales force. The fact is that neither the 20/80 nor the high turnover need be accepted as inevitable.

Based on our studies of thousands of sales forces across many different industries for more than two decades, we have found that 55 percent of the people earning their living in sales do not have the personality attributes or dynamics that would allow them to sell successfully. Another 20 to 25 percent have sales dynamics but are selling the wrong product or service. In other words, they could be successful in certain selling situations, but they are marginal in their current sales position. This leaves approximately 20 percent of salespeople who genuinely possess the personality dynamics to sell, and who are selling precisely what is best suited for their personality. It is this 20 percent of properly placed people who are responsible for selling 80 percent of what is sold. It follows, then, that if a higher percentage of each sales force were made up of these appropriate people, a company's sales force could more nearly approach what is obviously desirable—50 percent of the people selling 50 percent of what is sold. With a more scientific approach to the recruitment and selection of sales personnel, more productive people can be selected and retained, with the result of increasing overall productivity and drastically reducing turnover.

Before we discuss the process by which the productive salesperson should be selected, it is important to understand something about the psychological characteristics that make up the potentially successful salesperson.

PSYCHOLOGY OF THE TOP PRODUCER

When we examine the psychology of the successful salesperson, we must begin by asking what kind of a human being would be motivated to expose themselves to the rejection, the risk, the abuse, and sometimes even the hostility that salespeople must subject themselves to? Our research led us to the discovery of three central qualities that an individual must have for any sales job. It is important to note here, however, that someone may have these precise personality qualities but may not necessarily perform successfully in every sales position. There are many reasons why this is so, but mostly it is attributable to the fact that each sales job has its own unique requirements which necessitate additional qualities for success. Therefore, for someone to succeed in any kind of selling situation, the individual should begin by having three basic qualities: *empathy, ego drive,* and *ego strength.*

The first quality we found to be of major importance is *empathy.* Empathy is defined as the ability to sense the reactions of another person. It is the ability to pick up the subtle clues and cues given by another person in order to accurately assess how the person is feeling. Empathy does not necessarily involve agreeing with the other person's feelings, but it does involve knowing what another person's feelings or ideas are.

Empathy is not sympathy. Someone once said that "empathy is placing oneself in the other person's shoes, but sympathy is putting them on and feeling the pinch." Objectivity is lost in sympathy. Sympathy involves the overidentification with another person and, thus, the loss of objectivity. If you are really feeling the emotion of another person, you cannot view him or her in a sufficiently dispassionate way to be objective and helpful. In order to sell, an individual must understand how the other person is feeling, while still maintaining one's own sense of identification, one's own purpose, and one's own objectives. All of this is in order to maximize upon the powerful feedback that empathy provides.

It used to be felt that the successful measurement of empathy would be sufficient to predict sales success. Indeed, there proved to be a high correlation between empathy and sales success. However, as we ran studies in company after company, a pattern began to emerge indicating that, although empathy was clearly essential for sales success, empathy alone was not enough. In case after case, the majority of successful salespeople in an organization possessed fine empathy, but invariably situations would arise where the chief executive officer agreed that certain other individuals were accurately assessed as possessing empathy but nevertheless producing poor sales results. Often we were told that these individuals presented a product or service well, developed excellent relationships with customers and associates, possessed strong technical ability, maintained existing accounts, but rarely brought in new business. The simple fact was that they could not "close" the sale. We concluded that, although an individual definitely needed empathy in order to sell, he or she also had to possess the motivation to utilize the empathy as a tool for persuasion. It was not enough to understand and get feedback from another individual, but rather one also had to want to persuade another person in order to close a sale.

We term this motivation to persuade and close a sale as *ego drive*. Ego drive is the second personality quality essential to sales success. Ego drive is the inner need to persuade another individual as a means of gaining personal gratification. The ego driven individual wants and needs this victory—successful persuasion—in an intensely personal way as a powerful enhancement of his or her ego. Ego drive is not ambition, aggression, energy, or even the willingness to work hard. The ego driven individual wants and needs to persuade, not primarily for the practical benefits which might be gained (i.e., money, promotion, or other rewards) but for the feeling of satisfaction that comes from the victory. Successful persuasion, then, is the particular means through which the ego driven individual gains pleasure and ego gratification. Everyone works hard to enhance their own ego—to do things that make them feel good about themselves. For the real salesperson, that satisfaction comes from the successful one-to-one persuasion of another person. The ego driven person feels nine feet tall when he or she receives that "yes" from the customer. The "yes" and the "I agree" to the ego driven person is much the same as applause is to the actor, the published book to the author, or a respected title "Mr. Senator" to the politician. To the truly ego driven individual the "yes" provides the incentive, regardless of whether a commission or any other financial remuneration is involved. The money is a symbol of success—the reward for getting to the "yes."

Although for purposes of clarification we have discussed empathy and ego drive as separate characteristics, and indeed they are separate insofar as someone can have a good deal of empathy and any level of ego drive, nonetheless these dynamic factors are inseparable as determinates of sales ability. In fact, empathy and ego drive act on and reinforce each other. Empathy alone cannot achieve the close; and ego drive without empathy could irreparably burn territory.

When looking at the combination of empathy and ego drive, one can think of ego drive as the motive force launching the salesperson toward the target customer, and of empathy as the guidance mechanism allowing the salesperson to follow the prospect through evasions and objections until he or she homes in on the real needs of the prospect and closes the sale. The individual with a great deal of ego drive and not much empathy will knock over a certain number of victims through the sheer force of their drive, but one side step on the part of the customer will result in the sales person hitting the wall or plowing through the plate glass window of the showroom. The lack of empathy deprives that salesperson of information about what is really going on in the environment. These salespersons do not have the feedback necessary to make adjustments, and so they drive ahead, missing more closes than they achieve. On the other hand, the salesperson with a great deal of empathy and not much ego drive is probably a nice person, gets along well with others, services well, and may even take a few orders because they are so nice. But, fundamentally, these people will not close new sales because they lack the ego drive—the real motivation necessary to close. Then there are the 55 percent of the people now attempting to sell across industry who possess neither the empathy nor the ego drive necessary for sales success. The unfortunate aspect here is that these people for the most part might be extremely effective in many positions but they simply should not be selling.

We discussed earlier how selling is an occupation with a lot of built-in rejection. Rare indeed is the salesperson who can close one in two contacts. Regardless of industry, the person who is attempting to persuade another individual is more likely to be rejected than to be accepted. What happens then to the persuader when the inevitable rejection occurs? The obvious answer is that the individual feels diminished. If they feel nine feet tall when they succeed, they feel three feet tall when they fail. But the key here is that they must never feel totally diminished. When anyone fails, she or he obviously does not feel too good, but the essential question is: Do they have the resiliency—or what we call "ego strength"—to bounce back from that rejection? Will they be even more motivated, more charged, for the next try?

Someone with ego strength feels as bad as anyone would with failure, but reacts to that failure much as the hungry person does to missing a meal—he or she is all that much hungrier to eat (close) at the next opportunity.

When a person does not have sufficient ego strength to react with such resiliency, they take the rejection personally. They feel that the "no" is a "no" to them personally, and are, therefore, very hesitant to expose themselves to any situation that could incur yet another rejection. The person lacking ego strength cannot deal with rejection and avoids conflicts. They have the problem of being so occupied with their own conflicts, with the job of simply accepting themselves, that they cannot work in a consistent way, especially when there is any pressure involved.

Ego strength is quite simply an individual's feeling good enough about herself or himself to accept rejection not as a personal affront but as part of life. The individual with ego strength has the ability to leave the rejection behind and to go on from there. Those who accept themselves, who possesses ego strength, operate freely and fully and allow themselves to function at or near the top of their capacity.

It is important to repeat that, as each individual is being evaluated for a company's specific sales position, the possession of these three key personality qualities cannot guarantee success in every sales role. Other qualities besides the central dynamics of these three must be examined in order to match the person to the specific job, company, and industry.

One case history will illustrate this point. We recommended to one of our clients that a young applicant be hired for a sales role. This person possessed the empathy, the ego drive, and the ego strength necessary to become a top producer. Although this person had little experience and lacked knowledge of the industry, the capacity to learn quickly was evident in the individual's personality dynamics. The individual was hired and proved to be as successful as was predicted. Three years later the client contacted us and asked us to review this individual's psychological test, because the company was considering moving this person into another sales role with considerably more responsibility. After reviewing the personality profile derived from the results of the individual's test, we suggested to the client that, despite this person's phenomenal success in the first position, they should not move this person into the new position. After much discussion, the client felt that, given the track record, this person should be given the new opportunity. Six months later we received another call indicating the move to the new job was a total failure, and that our concerns proved justified. Why?

Why will a successful salesperson fail selling the same product and service for the same company in a new environment? The reason is that the new situation contained a major psychological ingredient absent from the first position. The original position involved working out of the home office under close supervision of top management in a totally structured and planned environment. All this person had to do to be successful was to follow through on what was structured and use his very powerful, effective sales personality. By contrast, the new situation involved being sent to a virgin territory where this person would be the only representative of the company within a radius of 500 miles. The new position called for an individual who possessed excellent self-starting ability—the ability to plan and organize one's work and time effectively. This person lacked these particular attributes and so, even though the individual possessed the empathy, ego drive, and ego strength to sell effectively, his inability to be a self-starter and to manage time competently kept him from having enough opportunities to meet potential customers.

Unfortunately for the company, the result was the loss of an excellent salesperson, because, as is all too often the case, the individual would not return to his previous lower-status position, despite having achieved great success in the position. We have seen that, besides empathy, ego drive, and ego strength, other qualities must be assessed to determine whether an individual will succeed in the specific sales job for which he or she is being considered.

Here are just a few examples of what is meant by "other qualities": the larger the ticket of the item being sold and the more complex the technical nature of the product, obviously the more conceptual intelligence is needed by the salesperson. The ability to deal with complex ideas and concepts is as important in certain sales situations as empathy, ego drive, and ego strength. On the other hand, in straight sales, where there are tangible smaller-ticket items, this type of conceptual ability is more than likely not critical. The ability to think on one's feet, to negotiate, and to make quick decisions could, again, be vital to success in some sales situations but may be far less important in others. The ability to prospect systematically and with persistence can be as critical to sales success as was seen in the case study and in many other sales situations. But where the sales job calls for being in a facility where customers come in, such ability may not be important. Thus, depending on the specific sales job, such attributes as self-starting ability, time planning, detail ability, patience to prospect and follow through, and more, could have considerable impact on the success or failure of the individual in the specific role.

To evaluate sales personnel effectively requires an understanding of the real functional requirements of the specific sales job and a matching of those requirements to the personality attributes possessed by an individual. If the personality strengths of the individual match what is required for the specific job, and there are no weaknesses precluding success, success then can be predicted.

This obviously raises the question that, if a specific job can be analyzed and an individual's sales potential can be evaluated, where can a company find prospective salespeople?

SOURCES OF PRODUCTIVE TALENT

The first place to look for potentially successful sales talent, the most constructive and probably the most productive, is within one's own company. Our studies have revealed that, in most industries, four out of five people are doing jobs for which they are not best suited. This probably means that some employees who may be marginally successful, or who are even at the edge of being terminated from their present position, could be highly productive if moved to a more appropriate spot within the organization. It could be that the technician who keeps making those mistakes could be your best field salesperson . . . or that secretary, who is always late and just not good enough at detail, is functioning poorly because she is better suited to sales than to secretarial work.

In any event, there is a great deal you already know about the people in your employ, and so some of the steps to hiring can be skipped if you take a close look at home before you seek people from outside the organization. In addition, much more important than the economy of time and money is the fact that there is nothing finer for company morale than giving employees the opportunity to grow and to fill positions that better tap their potential.

Assuming that the position cannot be filled from among current employees, the best place to seek personnel is the whole world. Our studies have shown that the typical hiring criteria most frequently used (or really abused) by industry in the selection process simply do not work. Age, sex, race, and even experience and formal education are not predictors of success for most occupations. Obviously, there may be certain requirements absolutely essential to the job, but be sure, before you impose these, that they are actually prerequisites to doing the job, rather than the kind of product knowledge or skill that can easily be taught once someone is hired.

One out of every four people in all segments of the population possess the dynamics which would enable them, if given the opportunity, to sell successfully. Many of them would be well suited to the job which you are attempting to fill. When you advertise for people, you should cast the broadest net possible to attract applicants. Imposing artificial restrictions based on old stereotypes can only serve to limit the number of people from whom you can choose. Imposing these stereotypes can, and often does, weed out some of the best potential people for your positions. As will be discussed in the next section, this is not only good business practice but also conforms to the law.

LEGAL ASPECTS OF HIRING

Before turning to the selection process, it is important to understand the legal pitfalls that employers could stumble into in their hiring procedures.

Employers must be aware of the need to recruit and select employees in a manner that is free from discrimination. State and federal officials will look to an employer's basic hiring procedures to assure themselves that the employer is in full compliance with all applicable nondiscrimination laws. It is important that an employer's inquiries do not intentionally, or even inadvertently, restrict or deny employment to minority or female group members, or both.

Title VII of the Civil Rights Act of 1964 forbids employment discrimination on the basis of race, color, religion, sex, or national origin. Additional federal statutes forbid discrimination on the basis of age and require equal pay for equal work. Moreover, many states have enacted their own "fair employment regulations." These often exceed federal regulations. Even with these restrictions in mind, it is clear that an employer is permitted to seek any information which is essential to effectively evaluate a person's qualifications for employment. Questions which would tend to screen out or disqualify members of minority groups or persons of one sex are permitted, provided the employer can substantiate that these inquiries or qualifying factors are valid criteria for determining successful job performance or can be justified by "business necessity."

The concept of business necessity was first enunciated by the U.S. Supreme Court, which held that, if an employer's action or policy, although neutral on its face, is discriminatory in effect, the policy is unlawful, unless the employer can show there is a substantial business justification for that policy. However, business necessity does not include inconvenience, annoyance, or expense to the employer. A policy with a discriminatory effect could be tolerated only if it was related to "job performance."

In some instances, a discriminatory policy may be justified by showing it is essential to the safe and efficient operation of the business and that no acceptable alternatives would serve the same purpose. The burden is on the employer to prove the justification for discriminatory policies.

In addition, an employer is permitted to seek and obtain information needed for implementation of affirmative action programs. Caution is advised, however, when collecting this data. The employer must be able to show that the information was collected for legitimate business purposes. We suggest, therefore, if this information is obtained for affirmative action programs or other legitimate reasons, that it be recorded and filed separately from regular employee documents to avoid the appearance of discrimination.

With regard to specific preemployment questions and qualifications, the following should be considered:

The EEOC regards questions concerning race, color, religion, age, or national origin as irrelevant to an applicant's ability—except in a very few limited circumstances where it is a bona fide occupational qualification or is required by some affirmative program or regulation.

Unless the employer is able to show that the educational requirement was somehow related to the performance of the job applied for, questions regarding an applicant's educational level may be discriminatory; they could serve to eliminate from consideration a disproportionate number of members of protected groups.

Questions concerning pregnancy, future child-bearing plans, or the number and age of children should be avoided. The questions could be used to deny or limit employment to women and, are seldom, if ever, job related. Questions regarding child-care plans are permitted if asked of both men and women.

Often employers ask seemingly innocuous questions regarding an applicant's physical condition, such as height and weight, but a word of caution: Unless these questions are related to job performance (which in most cases they are not), they should not be asked.

Arrest and conviction inquiries are another area where caution is advised. For example, questions regarding arrest records are generally held unlawful, because a disproportionate number of members of minority groups have arrest records. Refusal to hire an applicant because of an arrest record may be held unlawful, *unless* the reason for rejection is job related. In addition, the *mere request* for this information, without disqualifying an applicant, may discourage minority applicants and, hence, may be illegal on its face.

Also, positive conviction inquiries should not be used as a basis to disqualify applicants, unless the conviction was very recent, perhaps within five years. More important, there must be a relationship between the safe and efficient operation of the employer's business and the employee's past conviction. If the employer does make the inquiry, he or she should include a statement that a conviction is not an automatic disqualification and that other factors, such as the seriousness of the offense and rehabilitation, will be considered in all determinations. Inquiries concerning credit and credit references also fall into this category.

Questions regarding availability for Saturday and holiday work are permitted. Employers, however, are required to make reasonable efforts to accommodate employees who, for religious reasons, are unable to work on Saturdays, Sundays, and holidays, unless it would cause undue economic hardship to the employer or to other employees. Minimal inconvenience to the employer may not be enough reason to disqualify the employee.

It is extremely important that you, the employer, preserve employment applications for a period of not less than six months from the date of the application or from the date that action was taken, whichever is later. However, various factual circumstances may obligate employers to retain applications and other employment records for several years. This requirement applies to application forms and records related to hiring, promotion, demotion, transfers, layoff or termination, rate of pay or other terms of compensation, and selection of training or apprenticeship. This requirement does not apply to temporary or seasonal employment. However, we suggest that all records be maintained for substantial time periods.

Additionally, the employer is not required to offer job applications to anyone at any time, unless the employer's policy is to offer these applications whether there is a job opening or not. If you permit an individual to fill out an application, then you must receive it from him or her and file it as you normally would. But you are not required to inform the applicant why he or she was hired or rejected unless that is your general policy.

What we have set forth are examples of some preemployment inquiries and how the EEOC or various courts interpret their effect. They are offered as guidelines in determining the appropriateness of preemployment questioning.

The most important consideration is whether the questions to be posed to the applicant verbally or on your application form can be justified by business necessity as being job related. Any interviewing process that disproportionately screens out members of minority groups or members of one sex is vulnerable to discrimination charges. You must, therefore, determine in advance whether the answers to questions will really assist you in predicting successful job performance.

There should be a job analysis performed to discover what information is needed to properly judge an applicant's competence or qualifications for that particular job. Past experience in hiring for the same type of job is the best guide in performing this analysis. Certain obvious considerations include what type of skills, training, education, and other specialized or general talents are required to perform the job well.

Based upon the job analysis, the interview questions should be framed to get at the information that is objectively necessary to the hiring decision.

THE SELECTION PROCESS

By turning to the procedures for screening applicants and understanding the steps leading to the final hiring decision, we can begin with the preliminary interview.

The preliminary interview should be designed to quickly and efficiently screen out those candidates who lack the basic requisites for the position—in effect, those individuals who are obviously inappropriate. This initial interview should not take much time. Most often, 10 or 15 minutes should be sufficient to determine if the applicant meets minimum professional requirements for the position. You can learn quickly whether the individual has the licenses, technical knowledge, or other background qualifications required to permit him or her to be considered further. In addition, a quick judgement can be made about whether the applicant's appearance, demeanor, and overall attitude is sufficient for further consideration of their application. For example, if the position involves a great deal of phone work and the applicant has a harsh, shrill, or otherwise unpleasant voice, the person could immediately be screened out as being inappropriate for the particular position.

When this first interview is begun, it should be made clear right away that this is a preliminary interview and that only a few minutes will be spent with the applicant. An applicant frequently expects a long interview and might view 10 or 15 minutes the equivalent of an outright rejection. A simple statement, that you plan to spend only a few minutes at the initial interview, will remove some of the natural anxiety every applicant feels. It also serves the purpose of getting both you and the applicant to be as specific as possible much more quickly in an initial conference.

Be sure that, as part of the interview, you at least glance at any documents the applicant has—for example, an application form, a résumé, letters of reference, and the like. You are not going to have the time to study these in detail, but a quick glance might bring some omission or questions to your attention that might be usefully probed on the spot. Furthermore, the review of the papers provides the applicant with the feeling that, regardless of the brevity of the interview, you are genuinely interested in him or her.

The preliminary interview is the first step of what is essentially a "pyramid-building" process. Through your recruitment effort, you start off at the base with a pool of job candidates and methodically narrow the field until the best candidate or candidates reach the top. The process is designed so that you will spend very little time with the large base of applicants but rather invest your time where it counts, near the top of the "pyramid" during the final steps of the selection process.

Do not assume that an individual who projects the best image at the first interview will necessarily be your final choice, or that an applicant who makes a less-favorable impression will not be. Today, people are extremely sophisticated in dealing with interviews. Very often such a sophisticated person can mobilize sufficiently to make an excellent impression in the first interview, but that may or may not represent the person's ability to do the job. The preliminary interview should only determine an applicant's basic suitability. Its purpose is to help the employer decide if an applicant should or should not move to the next step in the selection process. It is a process designed to screen out, on the basis of obvious "knock-out" factors, and never to screen in.

Step two in the process is a review of employment history. In reviewing a résumé, it is important to remember that the aim of any résumé is to present the applicant in the most favorable light. Information provided on a résumé is a one-sided version of the individual's accomplishments, described in the most flattering and laudatory terms. Avoid being influenced by the one-sided picture. Look for patterns in the job history. Have job changes tended to result in increasing compensation or responsibilities and/or in bringing the applicant closer to his or her stated career track? On the other hand, is there any evidence of frequent job changes without any apparent career direction? Bear in mind that job-hopping, though it can be an important negative indicator, is not necessarily so. For some, job-hopping may be a courageous attempt to really find their proper niche. Use job-hopping, then, not as a red flag but as a yellow blinker light warning you that, at some point in the interview process, this is one area to be investigated more fully. As you review a résumé, keep in mind that it is but a piece of paper prepared by the applicant. It is important that all aspects of the résumé be verified.

Even after the résumé is verified, it still provides insufficient information on which to base a hiring decision. Although a résumé or job application can tell you what a person has done in the past, it rarely tells you anything about his or her real success or failure at these jobs—or about fundamental suitability for the jobs he or she happened to have had. On the other hand, the fact that an applicant has not held precisely the same position for which each is being considered does not necessarily indicate that they are any less suited for the position at your firm. Much of this vital information can be obtained through the next step—checking references.

A review of references from past employers or supervisors will provide an informed, though highly subjective, evaluation of the applicant's performance, specific functions, attitudes, and ability to work with others. It is only logical that the applicant will provide you with the names of references that he or she is confident will speak highly of them. It is important then, to probe a little bit deeper. If the applicant provides you with the names of two references, ask for one or perhaps two more. If the person is currently unemployed and references do not include an immediate supervisor, ask why not, and try to get the name of such a supervisor, or the names of a couple of past immediate supervisors. In short, begin the reference check by being satisfied with the quality of the references themselves. It is difficult enough to gain objective, totally truthful data from references; but if they are of so little importance to you that you pass them off with a form letter, you will almost invariably get nothing but a glib, form response.

It is critical that you or someone in a responsible position personally telephone the reference and open the call by making it clear to the person from whom you are seeking information that the information is important to you, and that you are counting on the individual to give you important input. Doing this still guarantees nothing, but not doing it guarantees a useless exercise.

Most people will go out of their way, from their own perspective, of course, to help someone by saying only good things about them. You must, in effect, give them permission to say something negative. You can often achieve this by listening to a whole series of complimentary things about the individual and responding, "That's great! Can you point out any weak areas that we should know about so we can help him or her on the job? Are there any specific kinds of functions where he or she might need some extra training or supervision?" What you are doing here is asking the reference to help the person by suggesting ways you can help the applicant. Consequently, you are getting the information about weak spots that otherwise would never come out in the standard reference check. When you have called on the reference, it is likely you will have some information about the working relationship between the applicant and the references. If it is not clear, begin by asking the reference to spell out that relationship: How much time did they work together? How often did they see each other? What was the nature of the reporting process? Even before you ask questions about the applicant, you want to ascertain the position of the reference in order to establish his or her validity as an information source.

Bear in mind that a reference is, nevertheless, a subjective evaluation of the applicant's ability and must be weighed accordingly. Every employer's standards are different. What might be considered outstanding performance by one supervisor may be considered less than satisfactory by another. References must be viewed as part of a total picture. Therefore, references are a useful part of the screening process, and, although they yield some relevant information, they have to be integrated with an objective evaluation of the applicant.

Despite certain obvious limitations, at the completion of this step in the selection process you have substantially reduced the number of candidates worthy of further consideration.

ADMINISTRATION OF A PSYCHOLOGICAL TEST THAT UNCOVERS BASIC PERSONALITY DYNAMICS

What is needed now as the next step in the selection process is an objective evaluation of the applicant's personality strengths and weaknesses to determine which of the personality qualities specifically match the functional requirements of the position for which the individual is being considered. In the previous steps, you have eliminated numbers of people on the basis of other observations and criteria. Now it is time to begin the "screening-in process" to determine by objective means if the applicant is or is not for you.

But, before we discuss this, first let's look at why so many psychological tests used over the past decade have failed to do the job of helping to predict sales performance. Why is it that most tests simply do not work? The first, and perhaps the most important reason for tests misfiring—for their inability to predict job success—is their obvious ability to be faked. People applying for a sales job who are asked, "Would you rather be a forest ranger or a salesperson?" or "Would you rather stay home reading a good book or go to lively parties?" or "Do you blush easily?" or "Do you go out with members of the opposite sex?" will obviously and easily be able to give the responses the tester is seeking. The only screening that these tests are likely to do is to screen out people who are so trusting and naive that they do not know how to "psych-out the test" and, therefore, do not know what answers are being sought. The irony is that some of these very people might have the capacity to do the job.

The reason many tests are so obviously fakeable often relates to the reason these tests were developed in the first place. Most of the tests now used for predicting job success were initially developed for clinical purposes. They were developed as diagnostic tools for use in mental institutions or by colleges for vocational guidance. Each of these situations is one in which people would tend to be quite truthful, since, after all, they were seeking help. When a person is applying for a job, he or she is going to tell the tester what the person thinks the tester wants to know, in order to sell the tester on the fact that he or she is good for the job.

Perhaps a good parallel might be seen in a medical examination. If you are going for a physical that you are paying for, you are obviously going to tell the doctor everything you know about symptoms you have—to help the doctor find out what may or may not be wrong with you. If you are going for a medical examination to obtain a life insurance policy, you are hardly likely to ask the doctor about that lump or to describe in vivid detail the pains you feel in your chest. On the contrary, you will do your best to cover up those symptoms.

It is the same way with psychological tests. If you are taking a test because a psychiatrist has asked you to, or for vocational guidance, naturally you are going to tell the truth in the hope that the tests will provide useful information. On the other hand, if you are taking a test which is easily fakeable to get a job, you are going to put your best foot forward and fool the test to the best of your ability. The more transparent the test is, the less effective it is in predicting whether you can do that job. Unfortunately, most tests offered on the market today are easily fakeable.

The other, and perhaps second most important, reason for test failure is that many tests have been based on the naive assumption that interests equal aptitude. In other words, if the test taker has the same interest pattern as successful people in the job, then that test taker will also be able to do that particular job well. The methodology utilized is to run tests of the interest of engineers, or salespeople, or managers, or whatever the occupation, next find out the norms of their interest pattern, then run the same test for applicants for that job, and those applicants who have the same interest pattern would be defined as being suited for that particular job.

Interest is really only a matter of exposure. Any interest test that purports to predict aptitude on the basis of interest pattern alone is failing to acknowledge the fact that interest does not, and cannot, equal aptitude. There are, of course, some cases where people who have a particular interest also happen to have an aptitude for that interest. If this sounds too simplistic to you, you are right. Loving football does not ipso facto make you a football player. People who have not been exposed to a particular kind of work or kind of activity can have no interest in it, and yet, given that exposure, they can potentially have enormous ability and, in the long run, develop interest. Simply, interest tests do not work to predict job success.

The third reason that tests have problems in predicting success is the very basis on which they are constructed. What is typically done is the tester—the psychologist—will give a number of questions to individuals holding a particular job—managers, salespeople, engineers, teachers, whatever. The people will then be looked at, comparing the "successful" or "unsuccessful" people in those particular occupations. Any item that separates successful from unsuccessful people would be considered a good item and would be used in the test which is ultimately developed. There are a couple of problems with this approach. First, who is to define success or failure? Second, again very similar to our discussion of interest, the fact that successful people answer particular items in a particular way does not necessarily mean that, if you answer the item in the same way, you are going to be successful in a particular job.

How often have you seen an award given for the most successful salesperson of the year? You might anticipate seeing a strikingly handsome young man stride up to the microphone and give his acceptance speech. But what do you see? More often than not, you see an ordinary-looking person say how delighted he or she is to have broken every sales record for the company. In other words, successful people can be any shape, size, or description, and yes, with different overt characteristics.

Any belief that a particular response to a given question, or even a small cluster of questions, can predict success, on the basis of the fact that successful people respond similarly, is incorrect. The human machine is much too complicated for such simplistic approaches. Finally, all tests that do not identify the central dynamics required for sales successes will fail to predict sales performance.

More than two decades have passed from the time our information was gathered about why most tests cannot predict sales, or, for that matter, performance, in almost any job. Once the reasons for test failure were understood, ways to solve this complex problem were undertaken, starting from an entirely different premise. We formulated our concepts by first asking ourselves (and many others) what constitutes the psychological makeup of the successful salesperson. When these characteristics were identified—empathy, ego drive, ego strength, and the like—we then were able to develop testing which would identify these qualities and which would overcome the failings of previous tests.

The test we developed indicates the individual's specific strengths and weaknesses for the position, and whether they can sell your product(s) in your particular market and in the context of your company's environment. This test has no biases. It is blind to color, sex, age, education, and experience. Its results are neither influenced by the applicant's appearance or conduct during an interview nor by an impressive résumé or glowing references. It is free of subjective impressions and helps the employer focus on the objective question: Can the person do the job for which he or she is being considered?

Any good psychological test goes beyond surface characteristics to reveal the applicant's basic personality dynamics: leadership and decision-making ability, organizational talent, capacity to handle detail work, and much more. It can also give you important insight into an individual's ability to learn and grow on the job and to work for extended periods without ongoing supervision. It is also designed to ascertain whether an individual possesses the basic dynamics necessary for sales success. It can determine whether an individual has empathy—the ability to sense the reactions of another person; ego drive—the need to persuade as a means of gaining personal gratification; and ego strength—the ability to take the inevitable rejection involved in sales and to come back for more work.

It can answer such additional questions as: Are the individuals good self-starters? Can they think on their feet? Are they service-oriented? Can they plan and organize their work and time? These questions are virtually impossible to answer without an objective measure.

There are literally thousands of tests on the market which measure various personality traits, some of which claim to draw a profile of these traits for specific jobs. As you are determining what test to use, you should answer a number of questions before making your selection of the most appropriate instrument. If the answer to any of the following questions is no, the test should probably not be used.

1. Do the publishers of the test present proof that it does not discriminate against individuals by sex, age, race, or national origin?

2. Do the publishers present convincing statistical evidence that the test is effective in predicting success in the job for which you are considering its use?

3. Are trained personnel used to evaluate the test?

4. Are the results of the test related specifically to your company, or do you receive some computer write-up which has nothing to do with your specific situation?

5. Can the test publishers give you the names of 8 to 10 companies in your industry or in a related industry that have had at least one to two years of successful experience with the instrument?

6. Is the test simple to administer?

7. Are the test publishers providing you with interpretation, support, and ongoing help in the use of test evaluations?

8. Is reporting time fast enough for your needs?

9. Do you have the opportunity to speak with the publisher's evaluators to discuss the person being considered, or do you merely get a written report or printout?

Be certain that the test is designed to evaluate basic personality and not simply the superficial attributes that you were able to observe in the preliminary interview or through résumé and reference checks. Be extremely wary of inexpensive screening and self-scoring devices. As we discussed previously, people are complex, and the complexity becomes even greater when attempting to predict performance in a specific role. Simple, "speedy devices" can only produce trivial information irrelevant to job performance.

After you have reviewed the results of a valid test, you will have both an objective and subjective assessment of the applicant. These now need to be integrated to form a total picture of the individual. You should have narrowed the applicants down to those few who obviously should receive a full in-depth interview.

The purpose of the in-depth interview is to supplement, fill in, or clarify the information already obtained through the previous steps of the selection procedure. All the information and data collected in steps 1 through 4 should form the framework of the interview and, in fact, direct the course it should take. It is during the exchange, this in-depth interview, which should be held in privacy and without interruptions, that you should utilize the results of the psychological test to prove those areas of weakness and strength uncovered by the test. For example, if the test shows that a person is dogmatic or rigid, question him or her about opinions or observations. Present alternatives to see if the applicant clings to a point of view or opinion.

The same thing can go for many other key personality attributes in which the test indicates the applicant might have a problem. Probe carefully and make the applicant discuss that area, and question his or her responses carefully. The final interview is the opportunity to verify the information, or any doubts, that the test has revealed about the person's basic personality dynamics and see how it relates to your own impression of the applicant.

The in-depth interview is also the time to seek answers to questions that arose as a result of employment or reference checks and of observations made during the initial interview. Make a real attempt in the final interview to put the applicant at ease. If there are gaps in the résumé, ask the applicant to fill them in—and make sure those gaps are filled in to your satisfaction. If the jobs held as presented in the résumé are unclear, make the applicant explain carefully what each job entailed, including a thorough description of what he or she actually did in the course of doing the work. Do not let the individual say, for example, "I manage a department." Ask the individual to tell you how he or she went about it, what the problems were—in effect, what the individual did in the course of a day's work.

You can follow this by probing what aspects of the work the individual did or did not like, and very simply tie his or her reactions back to the nature of the work situation involved in your position. If, for example, the individual indicates that he or she did not like the routine aspects of the former position, try to get each to describe honestly the routine involved in their former position. Question the individual about how the routine work involved in your position differs from the former job, and ask why he or she might like this one more. Listen carefully to the individual's response to learn if he or she is confronting the real question of routine work and the ability to cope with it. As the individual is discussing the job, you might even refer to the results of the test to see what indications it provides about his or her willingness to deal with routine.

Another important focus of the in-depth interview should be reconciling any discrepancies between the résumé and the reference checks. For example, the résumé may indicate that an individual managed a territory, while the reference check reveals that the individual was selling in a particular territory. Is the problem just one of terminology? Was there an exaggeration? Again, make the applicant discuss it. Along the same lines, clarify relationships between the applicant and the references you spoke with about the applicant. Make the applicant describe the precise working relationship and the extent of involvement with the reference. Check this feedback against the information provided by the reference; and if the references give any negative information about the applicant, so far as you can, confront the applicant with it. Let him or her deal with it. As all this is occurring in the interview, you should be checking the information and the applicant's responses against the insights into the person provided by the psychological test.

There are a few mistakes commonly made during the final interview that you should work hard to avoid. One is "browbeating" or putting the applicant on the defensive. Ideally, the final interview is a time for applicants to open up and discuss frankly their strengths and weaknesses. You do not want to stifle discussion, but rather to encourage it. The so-called stress interview forces discussion into one channel; and though it may reveal some things about the applicant—his or her ability to function under stress—it probably blocks a great deal of other important information.

Do not use the final interview to secure information you have already obtained. This is the time to tie down loose ends, to confirm or reject tentative information, and to clarify confusing or contradictory results from the earlier steps in the process.

Do not talk too much. Too many interviewers use the interview as their therapy. The interview must be focused on the applicant. You want to hear what the applicant wishes to say, rather than the sound of your own voice. A good rule of thumb here is that you should speak no more than one word to every four spoken by the applicant. Too many interviewers try to sell the firm or the job to the applicant. Obviously, you should answer any questions about the job, but the applicant should be "selling" you on what he or she can contribute to your organization. The fact that the individual is there for the final interview should indicate that he or she wants the position. You are the buyer; the applicant must be the seller.

The hiring process we have discussed, through its series of inter-locking steps, has provided you, by the end of the in-depth interview, with all the information necessary to make the best-possible hiring judgment. Each of the steps has a unique and integral function neces-sary to the process. Because each step reveals specific information, no one step can substitute for another. For example, a psychological test cannot tell you the type and duration of the individual's past jobs any more than the applicant's work history can give you a definitive assess-ment of his or her basic potential. A reference from a previous em-ployer cannot substitute for a personal history or a face-to-face obser-vation of the individual. Furthermore, just as a psychological test cannot describe how a person looks or speaks, an interview cannot really tell you much about a person's basic personality. At best, the interview can only reveal how a potential employee reacts in this type of stress situation. This may (and quite often does) differ substantially from how the individual functions on a day-to-day basis in a given job. Basing your hiring decision on impressions made during the interview alone will lead to some disappointment. How many times have you thought, "But he or she looked so good in the interview"?

Not only is each step an essential part of the process but the order of the steps is also significant in terms of obtaining essential informa-tion at the proper time, at the least cost, and in a manner that makes the best use of the executive's time.

This pyramid approach suggests recruiting among the largest possi-ble population and stimulating the maximum response. Little executive time should be taken with the earlier steps. How often do managers spend large percentages of their day talking to people who are not in the least qualified for a position? The short screening-out interview should reduce considerably this waste of executive time. Every step screens out more people, narrowing the field to those who should be tested, and then further narrowing the field to the final interview. Skipping any step could eliminate the piece of information that might screen-in a strong performer or prevent you from hiring a guaranteed loser. Trying to save money by not telephoning references, by using an inexpensive but nonpredictive test, or by short-circuiting the in-depth interview could lose your company thousands of dollars as a result of a wrong decision.

The scientific approach to recruitment, selection, and hiring outlined in this chapter is designed to avoid the costly hiring mistakes caused largely by the use of invalid hiring criteria and inappropriate recruitment and selection techniques. Thousands of companies, across industry, have successfully utilized the approach outlined here, with the result of substantially increasing productivity.

6

SELECTING THE MARKETING MANAGEMENT TEAM

by
John Burns, Mark Kelly, Dan Ciampa

Rath & Strong, Inc.

INTRODUCTION

Selecting a marketing management team is not a "cookbook" exercise. There is no universal 10-step process which, if followed, will always produce an effective management team.

Each industry, firm, and collection of marketing executives is different. Even the same firm will have differing needs from one point in time to another. In short, the process of selecting a marketing management team can be described as being:

1. Dynamic—changing over time.
2. Situational—depending on circumstances.
3. Subjective—relying on judgement.

Factors to Consider

Yet, despite the variability, a number of important factors remain as consistent considerations when selecting a team.

At the top of the list is: What era of evolution the company is in—start-up, growth, maturity, decline, or renewal. A new era, by definition, is a time to arrive at a new perspective about the essentials of running the business.

To make an effective era assessment, you need to examine the following:

1. *Market:* Is it growing or declining?

Are competitors entering or leaving?

Are customer needs changing?

2. *Product:* Is the technology changing?

Is the production process changing?

Are other products filling the same need?

3. *Organization:* What are the values and goals of top management?

Does the culture of the organization reflect those values and goals?

Is the company structured to respond effectively to the marketplace?

Different company and product eras require different competencies from the marketing management team. A company just starting up requires people with different skills than a well-established and mature firm that is highly knowledgeable about its markets, customers, and competition.

The start-up company needs a marketing management team that is capable of educating the marketplace about the company and its product and is skilled at spotting and quickly exploiting new business opportunities. The mature company needs a team experienced in maintaining sound working relationships with established customers.

The creativity needed for a start-up operation where, typically, resources are limited is reflected in the example of a West Coast firm. Operating with meager dollars to support a marketing program for a new microchip design, the founder and several other members of the company visited trade shows and routinely spent time in areas frequented by trade journalists. The firm's members were able to establish interest with some journalists and industrywide articles began to appear praising the new product's performance.

The skills these managers displayed were appropriate for the embryonic position their firm occupied. The skills are not necessarily the ones that would be critical to the successful management of a company entrenched in a mature and less-dynamic market.

A second factor to consider is the history and structure of the existing marketing organization. Few managers have the opportunity to "cut from whole cloth"—to build a new marketing organization from the ground up. Rather, they inherit an organization, its people, its history, and a structure that has been in existence for some time.

The new management team must be able to fit into the existing organization, draw upon existing resources, and gain the loyalty required for leadership. It must be sensitive to the culture and adept at initiating change with a minimum of resistance from current employees.

Balance is required between stressing the need for change and improvement in the way the business is operated and insuring that the strengths and attributes of the business are not lost and denigrated in the eyes of customers and employees alike. If a new management team has been brought in or is in the midst of being created, it is likely the owners have determined that something is wrong and corrective action is required. Such a change can communicate to members of the old marketing and sales organization that they have failed, and that their plans and programs are without merit. The message of change may have wrapped within it the seeds to create a "we/they" environment made up of "winners and losers."

In many instances, implementation of the new, creative marketing strategies will be the role of the old marketing and sales team members who remain. Their support and cooperation in helping the new team to avoid the pitfalls resulting from inexperience with the market, product, or customer base is invaluable. Sensitivity to these issues on the part of new management is primary.

A third factor to consider is the norms and practices of the industry. These norms will play a large part in influencing how the marketing organization will be structured. For example, if dealers are the industry's major method of distribution, the marketing organization must have expertise in developing effective dealer distribution strategies.

Many industries are going through revolutionary changes in their norms and practices. The transportation industry, for example, is operating in a new, deregulated environment. This requires leadership from the marketing management team to guide the organization in developing new norms for the emerging environment.

Industrial marketing teams that sell directly to original equipment manufacturers will find the character of the sales environment different in important ways from the environment which exists in sales to distributors and dealers. The nature and frequency of sales calls, the size of orders, lead times, and stocking and inventory programs are among the variables influenced by these differences. The experience and skill required to successfully market and sell in a particular environment are factors to consider when structuring and staffing the marketing team.

A fourth factor to consider is the financial constraints of the company. Decisions about the size of the marketing organization and the price of the expertise required will be heavily influenced by available dollars in the budget and by projected return on investment. These financial constraints should be balanced against the demands of the marketplace and the relative strength of the competition.

Case: CAD/CAM Manufacturing Company

CAD/CAM Manufacturing Company makes and sells computer-aided design (CAD) and computer-aided manufacturing (CAM) systems on a worldwide basis. Sales in 1983 were $500 million and the company employs 7,000 people with 10 manufacturing plants around the world.

The company is in an era of rapid growth. The market is diverse and growing; the products are complex and changing. Management has set aggressive market share goals, the organization is technology driven, and innovation is rewarded.

Bill Roberts is president of CAD/CAM Manufacturing. He is 48 years old and a design engineer. In talking about the size of his marketing management team, Bill is clearly focused on the needs of his market:

> To stay competitive in this business, we have to stay at the leading edge of technology. The three major products we built five years ago now account for only about 25 percent of our current sales. Our customers are becoming more sophisticated. They know what is possible, and they have high performance expectations for their CAD/CAM systems. The rate of change is fast and dramatic.
>
> Our strategic advantage is our ability to perceive new customer needs and build new products that meet those needs faster and better than our competitors. Our markets cut across a variety of industries and countries. The key to our ability to respond quickly is a broad-based sophisticated marketing organization—and that requires a lot of good people.
>
> I realized that the standard formula for determining size simply did not apply to us. The cost to our company of missing a shift in the market is our survival. A shake-out is already beginning. So I decided that we would have as many people as it takes to maintain a worldwide presence and continue to grow.
>
> If you fall behind in product development or in improving your niche in the market, it becomes incredibly expensive to regain the lost ground. I'm not certain that you can ever buy back that lost opportunity in this business.
>
> As our industry has become more technically sophisticated, we've seen greater segmentation of the market. We've developed a vertical alignment where we have whole marketing groups which specialize in industry segments. For example, architects have distinct needs, and the building design and construction industry needs to be tackled by marketing people who speak the industry language and know the needs of that specific group. Having a good understanding of the needs of the packaged goods industry isn't all that helpful when anticipating products that will tap into the needs of architects. How can you effectively deal with such segmentation by relating your marketing organization's costs (which translate into numbers of people and ultimately into structure) to some fixed percentage of the total amount of sales you do, say 6 to 8 percent?

Each of these factors will vary by company and each will change over time. Those responsible for selecting the management team should evaluate each factor carefully before making plans or taking action.

What follows is a series of principles that apply to the major questions one needs to address in establishing a marketing team. Each set of principles is highlighted by a case example, which serves to illustrate those principles and provide insight into how, in an actual instance, one company responded to the major question confronting it.

DETERMINING HOW BIG A TEAM IS NEEDED

Guiding Principles

Size is relative—big to company A is small by company B's standards. Many companies determine the optimal size of the marketing team based solely on financial constraints—for example, if the marketing budget is 2 percent of sales and compensation dollars are a certain percent of the total marketing budget, then we can hire so many people at each level. (When sales go up, we can justify more people.)

The problem with this approach is that size is pegged only to internal factors (available dollars) and not to the needs of the market. Two percent of sales may not be enough to meet the expectations of the marketplace or match the performance of the competition.

The size of the team should be the number of people required to make the company's influence felt in the marketplace. This will depend on the size and complexity of the market, the number and complexity of products, and the market share goals a company sets for itself.

The size and mix of the marketing management team of a company that makes and sells jet fighters around the world will be different than that of a company that distributes snack foods in five states.

Thoughtful companies ask themselves what key functions have to be performed to participate in new markets. These functions may include research, product development, planning, administration, advertising, pricing, sales, distribution, and customer service.

The size of the marketing management team is then based on the number and variety of tasks required in each function. These tasks might be divided into "essential" tasks and "desirable" tasks. Essential tasks are those that if not done will result in loss of market share.

The key point to remember is that there must be a "critical mass" of management people to perform the essential tasks in each key function. The "critical mass" is determined by the needs of the marketplace.

We now have just over 200 people in the marketing organization—that is 3 percent of our work force. By the end of next year we will probably be up to 4 percent. That is high compared to our competition. But then, we intend to take away a lot of their business and eventually be the market leader.

If we were in a mature business, having a marketing organization of 50 to 70 individuals would probably be enough, somewhere in the neighborhood of ¾ of a percent to 1 percent of our work force. In our business we're growing at an exponential rate, and I for one plan for us to remain the leader. I guess if you were willing to settle for less, to be somewhere back there in the pack, you would use a fixed percentage figure and allocate staff to the market segments by some rigid dollar equation.

The top level of the marketing management team now stands at 11 people. That's about three more than I would like to have. The problem is that I cannot find enough people with the right mix of education, experience in this industry, and management skills. So we have to split up the work a bit more. Besides, we'll need them by the end of next year.

DETERMINING THE EXPERTISE REQUIRED

Guiding Principles

The marketing management team needs three types of expertise:

1. Knowledge of the key marketing functions.
2. Experience in the industry.
3. Ability to lead and manage people.

The knowledge of key marketing functions and experience in the industry can be determined by interviewing the candidates and investigating their prior work experience. These two types of expertise are "content" issues, and a candidate's relative strength can be assessed fairly easily. The ability to lead and manage people is more of a "process" issue, and determining a candidate's relative expertise is more difficult than with the other two. Those responsible for selecting the marketing management team should look for evidence of the following behavior profiles in making their evaluation.

First, an individual should be achievement-oriented, with a strong will to win. The ideal candidate would view his or her personal goals and achievements in close alignment with the organization's goals and achievement. The company's success is his or her success.

Second, an individual should possess an ability to generate a clear vision about where the organization needs to go. This vision should be balanced by a pragmatic and flexible attitude toward planning and problem solving. The ideal candidate would persevere to reach individual goals but adapt strategy and tactics when circumstances change.

Third, an individual should possess a high degree of personal intelligence, integrity, and maturity. She or he must be able to gain the loyalty of the employees, to make responsible judgements, and to live in an environment of ambiguity and change. An ideal candidate would provide intellectual leadership to the marketing organization and manage with a style that elicits support from employees in times of change and uncertainty.

The expertise required will depend on the era the company is in. The management team should include a mix of those with competence in the era they are leaving and those with competence in the next era they are entering. The relative mix will depend on how far along the company is in the current era. For example, a company moving from a mature to declining era will need people with good product and key account expertise as well as those who can move the company into new products and markets. The management team must be able to balance the need to generate revenues today with the need to free up resources for new ventures.

The key point to remember is that expertise, like size, should be determined by the needs of the marketplace. The mix of expertise depends on the company's era.

Case: Cable Connector Company

Cable Connector Company (CCC) makes and sells custom-molded cable connectors to customers who manufacture computers and instrumentation devices. Sales in 1983 were $25 million within the continental United States. The company employs 400 people in two plants in the Chicago area.

The company is now in an era of slow decline. Sales have been flat for the last five years. The company's principal product is being challenged by an improved patented competitor's product, and the top five management people are all over 60 years old.

Dan Wilson, the president of CCC, founded the company in his basement in 1948. Dan talked about the issue of expertise:

> In the beginning, the person who made the product sold it—me. Each person I hired had to be a jack-of-all-trades. To pay them for their sales effort, they got a straight commission on whatever they sold.
>
> As we continued to grow, I turned the people who were best at selling into full-time account representatives. They knew the product well and could sit with the customers and figure out exactly what was needed. I saw each of these account representatives as handling accounts as if it were their own business. That way I knew they'd put forth the energy and commitment needed to make them a success. With their being successful, I and the company would be a success.

In the early days, there was no such thing as marketing. And since we only serve two primary markets, the only key function of salesmen has been to get more sales. I've talked to several people over the years who said they were marketing specialists, but they hadn't ever really sold anything themselves. So I didn't hire them.

Everything went along fine, and we were slowly growing until about five years ago. Our industry was in a recession then, and I figured we would come back when the economy did. Then our competitor came out with that new product about five years ago, and we began losing a lot of our old customers.

I asked everyone who was selling what they thought we should do. We jointly agreed we would have to simply work harder and generate more prospects. But eventually they were all working 80-hour weeks, and we were barely holding our own.

It was really strange. There I was, heading up a business that had done well, particularly considering that it started in my basement. I had account representatives, five in all, who were making excellent incomes. More than one of them was earning over $100,000 a year. And that was several years ago!

Yet we were in an incredible squeeze. One of my top account representatives—he made over $90,000 this particular year—came in to see me and told me he was quitting. I was stunned. I asked him what he was going to do, and he said he wasn't sure, probably work in the construction business. It was incredible. He told me he couldn't take the pressure and confusion anymore. The number of accounts he was handling was numbing. He had some on the East Coast, some on the West Coast where we had added two manufacturer's representatives to help out. To ensure our quotations were complete and accurate, I had established the practice years ago of having the account representatives track down the bill of materials and walk the design aspect through engineering, checking each step of the process. That way, when a customer needs a status update or wants detail information about the part, the account representative is able to give them the right information. Our customers welcome the way we stay close to their order. This particular account representative was under intense pressure from some of his West Coast accounts, where our lead times had lengthened to 14 to 16 weeks.

I didn't think about it at the time, but we were developing individualized quotations on every inquiry we received, whether it came in over the transom or through one of the account representatives. This was the case even though a good percentage of the requests for quotation could be met by a fairly standard set of parts. Our costs continued to climb, and, while we had an excellent reputation for our technical excellence, we were constantly being pressured by competitors who came in with a lower price.

Dan finally hired a marketing consultant to help improve their situation. The consultant quickly realized they did not understand the composition and dynamics of their market. He immediately started collecting data on the source of current sales. The data showed that almost 30 percent of sales came from a standard product with minor modifications. The consultant recommended the company change its product quotations and costing systems, improve its production efficiency, lower the cost of making the standard product, and offer a pricing discount to customers.

Since a good percentage of quotations would be handled by a range of standard products, time and costs of generating these quotes became critical. A standard operating manual was constructed with cost ranges for each segment of the part based on known parameters. These parameters were determined by an intensive industrial engineering study, which isolated the standard part into six major segments. In this way, the costing function for a standard item (although still not an "off-the-shelf" item) could be greatly simplified. Pricing responsibility was assigned to a newly created position—marketing director. Engineering and manufacturing were to be assigned critical cost reduction goals. The new marketing director would head up a product cost improvement task force, with members coming from sales, engineering, manufacturing, purchasing, and accounting.

The marketing director was chosen from inside the organization. Dan weighed the need for marketing know-how and expertise against the need to know the industry, product line, and customer base. Dan's belief was that "the foundation of our business and the main profit area will be in customer applications. That's the part of the business I want us to concentrate the most on. Over time a customer application will probably shift to a more standard item. I think we can teach our internal choice for marketing director enough about marketing. He has the basic savvy to do the job. By separating the marketing function from sales, I think we'll begin to pay more attention to where we are taking this business. The boom in personal computers has opened up a whole new opportunity for us, and I want someone who knows our company to help me think through our plans for that market."

Dan continued: "Our internal candidate has excellent rapport with both the manufacturing and engineering staffs. He's a hard worker who meshes well with others. He doesn't bulldoze his way through the organization. Instead he takes the time to explain to folks why it's important to do such and such. People trust him. This is a home-grown organization, and we have a lot of managers who have developed from within. It's important we don't introduce too much change too fast."

The consultant also recommended that the sales organization reorganize along industry lines instead of geographical territories. This allowed the company to bring in some new people to sell the standard products, reducing their need for in-depth technical expertise. The technical salesmen could then concentrate on the custom business, where understanding customer needs is critical. Industry managers have been added to manage sales efforts into select industry groups. While reporting to the director of sales, they work in close coordination with the marketing director. This structure has allowed the proper concentration on growth markets and highlighted the need to develop and maintain a high level of industry specific product knowledge.

Sales have started slowly to grow again, and standard product sales now account for 45 percent of the business. Their renewed growth resulted from segmenting the market, competing aggressively on price, and adding people who were better salesmen than they were technical specialists.

ASSIGNING RESPONSIBILITIES

Guiding Principles

Assigning responsibilities requires the dividing up of the work to be done. But, before you can divide up the work, you must first:

1. Look to the marketplace and identify which key functions are required.
2. Evaluate the company's present and emerging era to determine the expertise-required to execute key tasks.

You are now in position to assign responsibilities. Work should be assigned to those most competent to do it. In short, structure follows competence. This does not mean that you do not chart out the ideal structure first, develop a set of required competencies, and then seek to hire or develop people who demonstrate those competencies. Rather, it means that you must make modifications in the structure to ensure that people are placed in positions that take best advantage of their competencies.

Many companies assign responsibilities based on a structure that is outdated. As people leave and new people are hired, they are selected and assigned the responsibilities of the person they are replacing. The company tends to perpetuate a structure and a group of competencies that may have been appropriate 20 years ago but are not the competencies needed now. This makes it difficult for companies to make successful transitions from one era to another.

Rather than automatically perpetuating an inherited, existing organization, it is important to redefine and, when appropriate, reassign responsibilities. In the CCC case, responsibilities were changed from territorial to industry-based to allow people with more sales competence to enter the organization. Responsibilities of those with technical product expertise were redefined. A marketing director's position was established to allow the appropriate concentration on development of markets and products.

The key point to remember is to let the assignment of responsibilities flow from the competence of people, as well as the present and emerging needs of the marketplace. Don't feel constrained by how the blocks on the organization chart are currently drawn.

Case: Monitoring Systems, Inc.

Monitoring Systems, Inc. (MSI), develops and sells computer software systems for monitoring government productivity improvement programs. Sales in 1983 were $10 million, and the company employs about 100 people.

In 1982, MSI developed a new hardware and software product for monitoring productivity programs in manufacturing companies. The company is in a transition stage from a start-up to a growth era. Management has high expectations that their new product will double their sales in three years.

Although they had never sold to manufacturing companies in private industry, they were confident that their product could speak for itself. All they had to do was get their foot in the door with the right people.

The responsibility for developing this market was assigned to Dr. Adam Starski, MSI's best salesman and contact man in the government market. Adam is a physicist who joined MSI from NASA and who initiated the action that resulted in several of MSI's biggest government contracts. He was well respected by his customers and trusted by the chairman.

Adam was appointed as a general manager on a part-time basis, and limited funds were earmarked as start-up money. Six months later, not one significant contract had been closed.

The chairman soon realized he had placed the right man in the wrong job. Although Adam was technically competent and quite successful in the government arena, his strengths did not transfer to the private sector. Industrial executives perceived Adam to be too theoretical and out of touch with the practical day-to-day problems of productivity improvement. They complained of his overemphasis on the paperwork and documentation instead of on getting the job done. He also had no network of industrial contacts to tap into to generate new business.

The chairman also realized that funding a new project like this on a piecemeal basis sent a mixed signal about its importance—a signal that could indefinitely delay getting results.

The chairman then took a dramatically different approach. He split the new products into a separate division. He went outside the firm to hire a new general manager from private industry who had been responsible for his prior employer's rapid growth. He hired a director of sales, also from private industry, and he offered both men significant stock options for achieving aggressive sales targets. He also capitalized the new division with $1 million, a sum equal to the entire profit from the previous year.

Immediately upon arrival, the new general manager began a series of in-depth, one-on-one interviews with each member of his staff. Besides wanting to get to know each individual, he was interested in obtaining their views about how key responsibilities were being carried out. Since the business was in an embryonic stage of development, the general manager soon learned of the confusion that existed.

Much of the business was sold on a custom basis. MSI was, in a sense, a job shop. The technical group spearheaded the decisions on product development; marketing played a more passive role and engaged in pricing and promotional activities. Cost overruns were frequent.

The general manager decided on a three-day planning session which was aimed at sorting out responsibilities and assigning clearer roles to each major department. He had the functional head of each department review that department's major tasks and identify how those tasks related to that department's role. They also identified other departments that were primarily impacted by their department's key task performance. The overlap among responsibilities soon became apparent. During this session, the general manager worked deliberately to reassign the product planning responsibilities to a task force consisting of staff from the marketing, technical, and finance departments. The task force was to be chaired by a market manager. Decisions and agreements reached during the meeting were recorded and responsibility charts were constructed. Each major decision area needing to be addressed was identified in terms of which function had primary responsibility, what groups shared joint responsibility, which decisions were to be "one alone," and which were to be made in consultation with other departments.

At subsequent staff meetings, the responsibility charts were used as a frame of reference to review plans and actions and to provide further clarification of responsibilities based on actual operating experience. The responsibility charter served to provide a structure. Yet since it was always under some degree of modification, it provided flexibility to adapt to changing business conditions.

Concerning the chairman, he did a number of things right the second time around:

- He recognized the different dynamics of the private industrial market.
- He realized that the expertise required in the government market did not (in this case) transfer into private industry.
- He hired people who had demonstrated competence in the market and era MSI was about to enter.
- He changed the structure and assigned responsibilities in a way which allowed the new expertise to be successful.
- He hired a critical mass of people to perform the key tasks, with enough money to support the venture on an aggressive growth curve.

SETTING UP THE SELECTION SYSTEM

Guiding Principles

Setting up the selection system is probably the most clear-cut stage in the process of assembling a management team. The following five steps, if adhered to, will increase the odds of building an effective team.

First, involve both the president and other top management in the selection process. In the three cases presented so far, the chief executive took the lead in selecting the marketing team. The personnel department played only a supporting role.

Second, set up a screening process that gives both the company and the candidates several good long looks at each other before a decision is made.

Third, look for significant examples of prior success—the best predictor of future leadership.

Fourth, look for people who have been through the era you are entering next. This becomes critical if the company is in transition.

Fifth, examine issues of style as well as content in prior experience. It is important to select people with a management style that can gain acceptance from the organization as well as provide leadership through periods of change.

The key point to remember is that the selection system should be set up to provide a thorough and exploratory examination of the candidates. In the end, the decision is a subjective judgment made by top management. The more data they can get, the better-quality judgment they can make.

Case: **Richardson Rubber Products**

Richardson Rubber Products (RRP) makes and sells engineered rubber products to major industrial manufacturers (primarily auto makers).

Sales in 1983 were $50 million. The company employs 800 people and has three plants.

The company is in an era of decline. Being dependent on the automobile industry, sales began to fall in 1978 as the recession progressed. Although RRP's products were competitive in quality and price, there were simply too many competitors for a shrinking market.

Frank Richardson, the son of the founder and president of the company, was forced to rethink the business and find ways to grow again. His first decision was to hire a new vice president of marketing from the outside and give him the mission of "shaking the place up" and leading the company aggressively into new products and markets. He fired the new vice president nine months later for nonperformance.

He also hired and fired two more marketing VPs from the outside within a three-year period. In the first case, the new VP could not gain the acceptance of the sales organization when trying to initiate change.

The sales force was conservative and traditional. Salesmen were knowledgeable about the products, worked in geographical territories, and were paid on a commission basis. If the sales force did not understand the changes the VP wanted to make, or if they thought the changes were too radical, they ignored directives and sabotaged new projects.

Frank concluded he had been leading Richardson Rubber through a major organizational change. The company had been going through a process of renewal, and early efforts had been aimed at the manufacturing and technical departments. Substantive progress was made in upgrading these functions and strengthening the leadership and functional competence of these groups. What Frank realized was that the balance of competencies had shifted to manufacturing, and what was needed in a marketing leader was someone who could function in a team environment and, with credibility, build a marketing organization.

As Frank conducted reviews on the failure in marketing management leadership, he realized that both the manufacturing and technical departments were much further ahead in coalescing into a team. He also realized that, on paper, the second vice president of marketing—an MBA graduate of a prestigious business school, with over 15 years of industrial sales and marketing management experience—had looked like an excellent choice.

Frank had been actively involved in the search for the marketing vice president. He personally interviewed and spent time with the finalists. He was familiar with the job specifications. In fact, he had helped to draw them up. After considerable deliberation, he concluded that the major reasons for past failure had to do with the new era upon which Richardson Rubber was embarking. The second vice president of marketing, Greg Holland, had no experience with and little under-standing of the type of dramatic change Richardson was going through. Greg's past success was clearly related to the fact that he was in positions that were fairly well defined, with clear sets of expectations. His rather structured approach to managing and, in particular, to estab-lishing relationships with peers was a key reason for his failure to perform within Richardson Rubber. Greg's style simply was never ac-cepted by other members of the top management team.

Frank now believed that marketing know-how was perhaps a less important issue. The primary issue revolved around the need for an individual to have an understanding of how to develop and grow a competent management team. While Frank was convinced that the marketing knowledge he ideally would like the candidate to have wasn't likely to be found inside the organization, he became more convinced of the need to put an "organization builder" in the market-ing role. The risks were high. With three failures behind him, Frank decided he needed to place someone in that position who would enjoy the respect and support of his manufacturing and technical counter-parts. He also decided to look inside the company to see if someone could do the job. He found Jim Barnes. Jim was currently the director of human resources but also had production experience. He had been with the company for five years.

While Richardson was considering Jim's background and mix of skills, he learned that Jim had been on several cross-functional task forces. He talked to some of the other members and all agreed Jim had been instrumental in leading the group to high-quality decisions. Al-though Jim did not have any marketing experience, the president felt that Jim's competence at working with other people in the company was a more important strength. After several sessions of talking with Jim, he was selected to be the new VP of marketing.

Jim's mission was to renew the marketing organization and bring a multidisciplinary approach to the marketing issues. After an initial period of orientation, Jim began, quietly, to make some innovative changes:

- He convinced Richardson to set up an internal consulting depart-ment with responsibility for identifying and addressing cross-functional issues.
- He divided the product lines into major product groups and es-tablished group incentives for each area.
- He introduced the concept of business planning, so that each department began to think about the future in a consistent and systematic way. He made planning a "bottom-up" exercise, so that everyone was responsible for developing their own goals.

- He established a market research function and helped educate the sales force to be market researchers, so that they became aware of marketing issues and participated in collecting data for their own business plans.
- He held regular off-site planning sessions, using team-building techniques to foster trust and cooperation. After initial success within the marketing group with these techniques, Jim began to hold joint sessions with the manufacturing and technical staffs as a way to include them in the planning for new products and in identifying cost reduction methods for mature products.
- Jim developed a plan for his own education in marketing principles. He visited other firms to witness firsthand how they were staffed, and he attended several university-sponsored industrial marketing programs.

As groups became skilled at the market research and planning skills, they began to identify new areas of opportunity for existing products as well as product modifications that would open up new markets. Jim worked closely with the internal consulting team to anticipate problems and get company-wide cooperation for new projects.

Since Jim took over a year and a half ago, the company has entered two new markets which are generating 20 percent of sales. Some new faces have been added to the sales force, all of whom were well accepted by the organization. Although Frank Richardson took a risk in selecting Jim, he recognized the need to rejuvenate the culture of the organization and selected someone with proven success in getting people throughout the company to work together.

SUMMARY

The process of selecting a marketing management team is a dynamic, situational, and subjective exercise. Some factors to consider in selecting a team include:

1. The company's present and emerging era—start-up, growth, maturity, decline, or renewal.
2. The history and structure of the existing marketing organization.
3. The norms and practices of the industry.
4. The financial constraints.

Each of these factors will vary by company and each will change over time.

The size of the team should be the number of people required to make the company's influence felt in the marketplace. There must be a "critical mass" of management people to perform the essential tasks in each key function. That critical mass is determined by the needs of the marketplace.

The expertise of the marketing management team should include knowledge of the key marketing functions, experience in the industry, and the ability to lead and manage people. As individuals, they should be achievement-oriented, have a clear vision of where to take the organization, be adaptable to change, and have a high degree of personal intelligence, integrity, and maturity. The expertise required depends upon the needs of the marketplace and the company's present and emerging eras.

The assignment of responsibilities should flow from the competence of people as well as the present and emerging needs of the marketplace. Top management should be careful not to perpetuate a structure that is outdated and no longer appropriate.

The selection system should be set up to involve the president and other top management, to provide sufficient screening time for both the company and candidate, to identify candidates who have had prior success in the era the company is entering, and to identify individuals with an appropriate management style.

In the end, the selection of the marketing management team is a subjective decision that relies on the judgment of top management. The quality of their judgment can be improved if they carefully consider the needs of the company and the market, and if they collect sufficient data on each candidate.

7

ELIMINATING TURNOVER IN THE SALES AND MARKETING DEPARTMENT

by
**Lynn Tendler Gilbert, Janet Tweed, and
Ann Hammer**

Gilbert Tweed Associates, Inc.

For a corporation to thrive and grow, it must manage its human resources carefully. Marketing and sales professionals, in particular, must be painstakingly selected, trained, motivated, and nurtured, for it is through them that a company's destiny, in large measure, lies. Their analytical, creative, and persuasive skills are crucial to the development and implementation of a successful marketing plan . . . one which will capture a hefty share of the marketplace. If treated insensitively, rewarded inadequately, or challenged insufficiently, they will move to a more rewarding environment. Their loss, disruptive and costly to a corporation, can lead to severe problems on the bottom line. It is in a company's best interest, therefore, to formulate and implement strategies that eliminate turnover in its sales and marketing department.

Like everyone else, sales and marketing professionals have a few key, very human needs which must be satisfied in order for them to work happily and productively. Recognition, both financial and psychological, is crucial. Knowledge about the workings of the company, its strategies, the impact of sales and marketing on those plans, and what an individual's contribution means to the total picture are all essential to enhance an individual's feelings of "corporate worth." An atmosphere of good, open communication is paramount. License to be creative, a degree of freedom regarding sales and marketing strategies, and the opportunity to develop and expand one's particular skills are also extremely important. With forethought and planning, a corporation can create an environment that meets all these needs. This will result in its having a marketing department that is committed to furthering company goals, one in which individuals of ordinary ability may achieve extraordinary results.

REWARD AND RECOGNITION

Perhaps the most obvious way for a company to win the allegiance of its sales and marketing professionals is to reward them. Without a doubt, financial rewards in the form of salary, incentive, benefits, bonus, and profit sharing have considerable influence on a professional's performance and that person's desire to remain with a company. Naturally, those programs with deferred benefits that increase with length of stay or which are forfeited with departure, or both, provide particularly strong incentives to stay. Hence, it is crucial that a company look critically at the monetary package it offers to ensure that it is to some degree generous and, at the very least, competitive.

Perquisites are another way to attract and retain valuable professionals. A company that offers perks, such as country or athletic club memberships and cars or travel opportunities, demonstrates how important its employees really are. Some companies offer the opportunity for low-rate home mortgages through cofinancing, almost a gift in these days of high interest rates. Service-oriented programs are also an asset and indicate a company's willingness to take care of its employees. Company day-care centers are a real boon, as more and more couples work. The high cost of education today makes college scholarships, perhaps awarded on a regional sales basis, extremely attractive. Financial planning services, stress management courses, and counseling programs in nutrition, fitness, and alcoholism are other ways to increase allegiance. Gould Corporation near Chicago offers its people bonuses for participation in its in-house fitness programs. As a result, it finds its employees to be happier, healthier, and more productive. Another incentive can be regular meetings with a "party" atmosphere, particularly for salespeople who work out of their homes. Meetings and social events at corporate headquarters or resort facilities provide an important connection with the company and an opportunity to socialize with other salespeople. Spouses should always be invited so that both family members feel like part of the company.

Just as important as financial rewards are those of a subtler, more psychological nature. Praise and recognition are essential to any professional's self-esteem and job satisfaction. The feeling that skills and accomplishments have been recognized by superiors and that they have been singled out as a valuable member of the department is essential. Old theories in psychology held that praise leads to worker complacency and poor performance. On the contrary, new studies indicate that the most effective style of management is one that is built on mutual trust and understanding and on consistent praise for jobs well done.

Praise can be transmitted to the professional in a number of ways: when given knowledge that others seek advice and solicit opinions; when praised verbally or in writing for a job well done, a problem overcome, or for an improvement in performance; when permitted a degree of freedom and autonomy in work; and when needs, problems, and frustrations are taken seriously. Public recognition is particularly important for the salesperson. Although sales success is quantitative and easy to see, reputation and ego are constantly on the line. Therefore, articles in company newsletters, "salesperson of the month" awards, and other such signs of public recognition can be excellent vehicles for transmitting praise and appreciation. In contrast, the marketing professional is less able to track his or her successes. For this reason, there is a strong need for acknowledgement. Marketing professionals feel particularly appreciated when they are given the opportunity to be creative, when they are listened to in a conceptual way, when they are made part of management committees, and when resources are made available to them whereby they can utilize their abilities to the utmost.

PROMOTIONS

A company striving to eliminate turnover would do well to give its sales and marketing people a clear picture of its organizational structure. They will want to see a clear track for growth and promotion— visible ladders by which they can pace themselves as they seek increasing levels of responsibility. Is there a fast track to promotion, and, if so, what does this entail in terms of performance? Most people will want to know where they are in the corporate hierarchy and whether their goals are reachable. In the same vein, it is important that promotions are real and distinct. One large company in the Midwest "promoted" six district managers by sending them to manage "geographies" with larger sales volumes. Although it may have been meant as a promotion, most of the district managers did not feel that bigger numbers meant a promotion, and four of the six managers saw through the sham and left the company. Obviously, it was a most costly and misguided attempt at recognition and "promotion."

COMMUNICATION

Paramount to winning the allegiance of its marketing department is the company's commitment to open communication. Good communication should begin with a clear statement of corporate goals. It is essential that sales and marketing professionals understand both short-term and long-term corporate objectives, and equally important, what is expected of them in terms of meeting these objectives. They must understand where the company's priorities currently lie. Is it putting an emphasis on new product development? Research? Market expansion? Such knowledge will help individuals understand corporate decision making and help them channel their work in the most productive direction. Additionally, good relationships must be established between marketing and sales and all other departments—manufacturing, engineering, R&D, finance, and human resources should have input into the marketing area and vice versa. The free flow of ideas and information can result in new strategies and product ideas and a real spirit of cooperation.

Within the sales and marketing department, communication in the form of brainstorming sessions can increase productivity and innovation. It seems there is often a rather tenuous relationship between sales and marketing professionals, and such sessions can reduce competitive feelings and foster cooperation, as well as provide an excellent opportunity for exchanging ideas. A company should strive to combine the expertise of the salespeople, who are in constant touch with the vagaries and fickle nature of the marketplace, with the marketing staff, who are equipped to create solutions for these problems. The result will be the development of a flexible and profitable marketing plan that can have an impact on corporate profits. Regular and timely reviews are another important element of good communication. Professionals should have an ongoing sense of their performance level. Managers should keep the tone of these reviews positive, with an emphasis on accomplishments and progress, as well as on ways to improve. A manager can create a spirit of "we're all in this together" by taking some responsibility for problem areas and offering constructive suggestions and assistance. Additionally, there should be both formal and informal opportunities for frank discussions between subordinates and their superiors regarding job satisfaction. Professionals must feel that they can share their concerns with those higher up, and that their needs and frustrations are at least understood, if not always accommodated. Regular meetings should be scheduled to provide an opportunity for managers to help the department live with its problems or to institute change. On a more ad hoc basis, people should feel free to voice their feelings and thoughts on any issue without fearing retribution.

SENSITIVITY

A company should be sensitive to the individual personalities, goals, and abilities of its employees. What are the career objectives of its sales and marketing people? If a person strongly desires to stay in the same geography, it is fruitless to develop that person in a direction that will land him or her in another part of the country. If a salesperson wants focused product experience, he or she should be exposed to that marketing area. All in all, it behooves a company to develop its employees in ways that are compatible with their overall goals. How much responsibility can the individual handle? It is not unusual that, during periods of rapid growth, companies promote individuals too quickly, thereby drowning potential with too much responsibility too soon. Be careful to assess capabilities; and discuss these capabilities, as well as goals and objectives.

A company must also be sensitive to the salesperson's accomplishments. One company pushed its salespeople to develop their territories to the $2MM level, and then rewarded them by cutting the territories in half. The salespeople were then expected to bring their smaller territories back up to the same level. As could be expected, the salespeople became disgruntled after awhile, and, because the compensation plan did not accommodate these changes, the company suffered significant losses.

GROWTH AND DEVELOPMENT

As much as possible, a company should strive to provide a rich and varied experience for its sales and marketing department. Individuals should be encouraged to attend seminars and courses, at company expense, as a way to improve job performance and to expand job responsibility. The course material should be relevant to the job and usable on a day-to-day basis within the company so that the individual can bring something new and important to his or her job.

Cross-pollinization is yet another tool for growth. For example, Burroughs has found it beneficial to take selected salespeople out of the field and bring them into headquarters for product management experience before returning to the field as district managers. Corning has a similar system which seems to have served it very well, whereby certain selected high-performance individuals are routed through many departments. For example, after being in sales for two years an employee can be brought into the corporate personnel office before being promoted to district manager. Later, the employee is brought back to gain experience in the production area before becoming a regional sales manager. Not only does this provide a rich experience for the person but it creates a cadre of Corning people who identify with many aspects of the company and who are very unlikely to leave.

It is also important that a company be a facilitator for sales and marketing people to do what they do best. A salesperson should be out in the field selling, not bogged down with paperwork in the office. A company should not be pennywise and pound foolish—CRTs, word processors, and home computers can, with the touch of a button, provide salespeople with information they need regarding the state of their orders, the marketplace, and the competition. Archaic support systems should be abandoned in favor of newer time-saving systems that free professionals to perform their jobs.

CREATIVITY

It is imperative that a company not be overly directive, and that it encourages creativity in its sales and marketing professionals. Within broad guidelines, marketing people should be encouraged to use various approaches to define and capture the marketplace, to package, advertise, and distribute the product, as well as develop new products. Given the capricious nature of the marketplace, they should feel free to discuss needed changes in strategies at any point. Strict adherence to a rigid marketing plan simply will not be productive in the long run. Salespeople, too, should be permitted some degree of freedom, particularly in the selection and maintenance of their customers. Salespeople in a small California company were frequently forced to drop or exchange customers with whom they had developed long-term relationships as territorial boundaries continuously changed. The company president permitted them so little input in this area that, eventually, several salespeople left—a most significant loss.

CONCLUSION

In summary, there are many methods a company can utilize to increase the tenure of its sales and marketing professionals. None are particularly difficult or costly to implement. In fact, most of the strategies mentioned cost nothing and are merely reflective of a certain overall corporate philosophy. This philosophy is one which places a high value on individual worth and, therefore, strives to create an environment in which individual growth and corporate prosperity flourish. Ultimately, management's investment of time and energy in these areas will result in the creation of a healthy and highly profitable corporation.

8

MANAGING THE PRICING FUNCTION

by
Kent B. Monroe
and
John T. Mentzer

*Virginia Polytechnic Institute
and State University*

IMPORTANCE OF PRICE DECISIONS

Pricing a product or service is one of management's most vital decisions, yet it has often been the most neglected marketing decision. When prices are based on a markup over costs, management is left with decisions related only to product, promotion, and distribution. However, pricing is crucial to all marketing-mix activities. In effect, pricing is the company's statement of value for the rest of the marketing mix.

Behavioral price research suggests price does communicate information to buyers and is not simply a measure of sacrifice.[1,2] Beyond this literature, price is an important decision variable due to its effect upon volume. This volume effect consequently affects revenues and costs and, therefore, profitability. For example, if the price of an inelastic product is raised, revenue will increase despite the relatively small drop in volume. However, this loss of volume may raise costs

---

[1] Kent B. Monroe, "Buyers' Subjective Perceptions of Price," *Journal of Marketing Research* 15 (February 1973), pp. 70–80.

[2] Kent B. Monroe, *Pricing: Making Profitable Decisions* (New York: McGraw-Hill, 1979).

(through loss of some economies of scale, for example) and, thus, offset the effect upon profits caused by the increase in revenues.

Moreover, the interaction of price with other marketing mix variables is considerable. The product mix and how that mix is perceived by customers is influenced by product-line pricing decisions, which, in turn, implies a product-market positioning strategy.[3,4] The success of new products is definitely linked to the introductory pricing strategy.[5,6]

Although a manufacturer cannot legally control prices through a marketing channel, channel member prices are influenced by the manufacturer's prices, discount structure, and credit policies. Indeed, the theoretical reason for offering functional or trade discounts, quantity discounts, or cash discounts is to enhance the distributor's motivation to provide superior service for the manufacturer.

Distribution costs and the necessary price that can be charged are inextricably linked. The manufacturer may offer channel members superior distribution service—for example, a faster mode of transportation or assuming the burden of carrying inventory. However, this service may increase the manufacturer's cost structure and necessitate charging a higher price. This higher price will be successful only if the distributor perceives that the extra benefits exceed the extra cost. It is necessary to measure the value and costs of changes in distribution service before making price adjustments.

Communication strategy must recognize that price is also a message. The product's price must be consistent with the quality. Prices, advertising, and salespeople must convey a consistent message. A product promoted as a relatively high-quality product at below relative market prices is not likely to be perceived as a high-quality product. Both industrial buyers and consumers judge quality partially by price, and the message conveyed by the entire marketing mix must be consistent.

THE ENVIRONMENT FOR PRICE DECISIONS

The pressures of adapting to today's changing environment are placing additional burdens on the management of business firms. In some

---

[3] Kent B. Monroe and Susan M. Petroshius, "A Theoretical Approach for Determining Product Line Prices," in *Theoretical Developments in Marketing,* ed. Charles W. Lamb, Jr., and Patrick M. Dunne (Chicago: American Marketing Association, 1980), pp. 21–24.

[4] Benson P. Shapiro, "Common Fallacies," in *Pricing Practices and Strategies,* ed. Earl L. Bailey (N.Y.: The Conference Board, Inc., 1978), pp. 29–33.

[5] Anthony Doob et al., "Effects of Initial Selling Price on Subsequent Sales," *Journal of Personality and Social Psychology* 11 (1969), pp. 345–50.

[6] Monroe, *Pricing.*

cases, the burden on profits might be eased if more attention were given to determining relevant prices.

The need for correct pricing decisions is becoming ever more important as competition is becoming more intense and public and governmental concern more profound. Because of the increasing rate of technological progress, the time lag between invention and commercial innovation has shortened the average life of new products and provided for quicker competitive imitative responses. Technological progress has widened the alternative uses of buyers' money and time and has led to a greater density of substitute products and services. The demand for pure and product-attached services has exceeded the supply of these services, resulting in rapidly increasing prices and increased public concern. Foreign competition has shown that there is demand for lower-priced products, particularly as buyers' priorities shift to leisure and recreational activities. A major impact of these environmental pressures has been to make product and service pricing more delicate, more complex, and more important.

PRICING DECISIONS

Our purpose here is to describe the major price decisions, their complexities, and how to administer the price throughout the marketing channel. Pricing decisions for a modern business organization are complex and important. In the past, however, such decisions tended to be passive, with firms following the pricing practices of a competitor or the pricing practices established many years earlier. Today, businesses compete with firms that may have more efficient methods of production and lower labor costs—for example, foreign firms that can set prices below those charged by American business. Thus, pricing based upon competition is not relevant when the competition has a substantially different cost structure. As a result, more and more firms are rediscovering price as an active determinant of demand and are making more aggressive pricing decisions.

There are many kinds of pricing decisions, including the specific price to charge for each product or service marketed. However, a specific price depends on the type of customer purchasing the firm's product or service. If different customers purchase in varying quantities, should the seller offer a discount for volume purchases? If so, at what volume points should a discount be offered? How much of a discount should be offered? If the firm markets through a mixed-distribution channel, what prices should be charged to wholesalers who, in turn, distribute the products to their retail customers? What prices should be charged to retailers who buy direct from the manufacturer? The setting of prices to charge channel members involves determining functional discounts, or margins, allowed to the middlemen for distributing the firm's products.

The firm must also decide whether or not to offer discounts for early payment. If the firm decides on a cash discount policy, it must then determine when a customer is eligible for a cash discount and how much to allow for early payment. Should the firm attempt to suggest retail prices?

Normally, the firm sells multiple products, and the pricing questions just posed must be answered for each product. Making the pricing problem even more complex is the need to determine the number of price offerings per product and the price relationship between the products offered. For example, should a camera manufacturer produce and sell only one camera model or should several cameras be sold? Usually, the decision to sell several models of a product means the seller is attempting to appeal to several market segments for the product. Once it is decided to offer a number of models at different prices, the seller must decide what the lowest price should be and the price differentials between each alternative price offering.

Additionally, the management of a multiproduct firm should be concerned with pricing products over their life cycles. Thus, plans must be developed that consider the life cycles of sales, product contribution to profits, and direct variable and separable fixed costs. At the same time, a plan for managing marketing costs as well as production costs must be developed. Although the concept of the experience curve suggests costs and prices decline over the life cycle, this phenomenon does not occur automatically. Hence, all costs and activities must be controlled so the direct cost reductions due to accumulated experience can be realized.

PRICING OVER THE PRODUCT LIFE CYCLE

The analysis and planning for pricing a product should begin at the start of the development stage of a new product. One of the primary considerations for accepting a new product proposal and initiating the developmental investment is the rate of return on investment expected during the product's life. However, the investment analysis requires estimates of revenues and expenditures over time for each alternative under consideration. There is an explicit price/volume/cost relationship that influences both revenues and expenditures. Consequently, the analysis must project estimated cash flows over the entire investment life cycle. Therefore, it is necessary at the outset to have some preliminary price/volume/cost estimates for the different stages of the product life cycle. One approach to obtaining volume/cost estimates is to utilize the experience curve concept.

The Experience Curve

According to the experience curve, prices and costs decline by some predictable amount each time accumulated experience is doubled. Indeed, many companies have developed successful marketing plans using this relationship among costs, prices, and accumulated experience. However, this cost/price relationship to accumulated experience does not occur by accident, and there are some disadvantages to an uninformed use of this phenomenon.

Costs and Experience. For many companies, costs tend to decline by a predictable amount each time accumulated experience is doubled. This phenomenon makes it possible not only to forecast one's own costs, but also to forecast competitor's costs. *In constant dollars,* this decline goes on without limit as long as demand for a product is growing. If demand for a product is not growing, then the rate of cost decline slows down and approaches zero. When accumulated units of a product are increasing at a constant percentage rate, then each year of product experience produces about the same percentage effect on cost.

Three key points must be understood about the cost/price experience phenomenon. First, we are talking about *accumulated experience* (volume) over time. Hence, we are not talking about a doubling of the production rate between two points in time.

The second point is that costs are measured in constant dollars. Hence, cost data must be deflated through the use of an appropriate economic deflator. Because inflation primarily serves to mask the true price or cost effect of product or marketing improvements, price and cost data should always be developed on a constant dollar basis to enable management to determine actual cost or price effects due to volume changes.

Finally, management must be careful about what costs are included in the analysis. As much as possible, costs that vary with activity levels are the relevant costs, since any arbitrary cost allocations will tend to hide the real changes in costs. Hence, the emphasis should be on out-of-pocket costs or cash flows.

The Volume Trap. Firms utilizing the experience curve when developing their long-term pricing strategy tend to fall into the trap that more volume (or market share) is inherently better. Hence, they price the product so as to build volume. However, two problems may develop from such an orientation.

The first problem occurs when it is believed that volume and market share have *inherent* advantages for the company. It has become fashionable to suggest that there is a direct and positive relationship between market share and profits. These profits supposedly derive from improved economies of scale, the "experience curve," market power, and quality of management. While the plausibility of the experience curve will be explored below, let us first examine the strategy of using a low price to build volume and market share. Here the real issue is the value of additional volume and the feasibility of achieving the desired volume. Since the value and feasibility of additional volume will vary over businesses, products, markets, and competitive situations, the essential starting point is to assess the specific price/volume tradeoffs.

To illustrate, assume management has a product designed to sell for $40, with variable costs of $30 per unit, fixed costs of $2,000,000, and a profit objective of $10,000,000. Management is considering lowering the price to $36 in an attempt to gain additional volume and market share.

To evaluate this decision, the profit/volume ratio at each price is needed:

$$PV = P - VC/P$$

where: PV = Profit/volume ratio

P = Price

VC = Variable cost

For the $40 price, the PV ratio is:

$$PV = (\$40 - 30)/40 = 0.25$$

or 25 cents from every dollar of sales is available to cover fixed costs and contribute to profit. For the $36 price:

$$PV = (\$36 - 30)/36 = 0.167$$

To meet the profit objective at the $40.00 price, the firm must sell: ($2,000,000 + $10,000,000)/.25 = $48,000,000, or 1,200,000 units. To meet the same objective at the $36.00 price, the firm must sell: ($2,000,000 + $10,000,000)/.167 = $71,856,287, or 1,996,008 units. Thus, lowering price by 10 percent *must* result in a volume increase of 66 percent to maintain the profit objective. Only very price-elastic products could accomplish this volume expansion.

If the increased volume resulted in unit variable costs falling to $28.00, then the necessary volume would be ($2,000,000 + $10,000,000)/.22 = $54,545,454, or 1,515,152 units. Thus, a 10 percent price reduction—causing a volume increase that results in a 6.7 percent unit variable cost reduction—must still result in a volume increase of 26 percent to maintain the profit objective.

When considering a price reduction to enhance a volume-oriented pricing strategy, the firm must consider the incremental profit leverage from the additional volume. In the above original example, with variable costs of $20 per unit, the PV would be 0.50 and the firm would need to sell 600,000 units to achieve its profit objective. A 10 percent reduction to $36 would require an increase in sales volume of 150,751 units, or a 25 percent volume increase. Clearly, a high contribution-margin product is a better candidate for a volume-oriented pricing strategy than a low contribution-margin product, even when unit cost reductions result from the volume increase. For a low-margin product, the firm will need to protect price levels, even at the expense of market share.

The second problem arises when it is believed that increased volume provides for *automatic* cost reduction opportunities as volume grows. It is logical to expect unit cost reduction through the learning curve, value engineering, and product process improvements. However, these cost reduction opportunities are not automatic. Management must be devoted to a concentrated effort of improving efficiency in manufacturing and marketing a product. In addition, cost reduction opportunities are not necessarily similar from one situation to another. In fact, leaders in cost reductions from one product often cannot make the transition with other products. Further, a low contribution margin product must have a relatively large cost reduction before the experience factor is profitable.

In many cases, a product's costs may not be under management control. For example, a company with a labor-intensive product may have rigid union work rules and, thus, not be able to realize experience curve savings, or a material-intensive product's costs may be controlled by a vendor. Since the proportion of controllable costs varies widely over products, so will opportunities for reducing costs. Management should not assume that a cost reduction will automatically accompany volume/market share increases.

Pricing a New Product

One of the most interesting and challenging decision problems is that of determining the price of a new product. New product pricing decisions are usually made with very little information on demand, costs, competition, and other variables that may affect the chances of success. Many new products fail because they do not possess the features desired by buyers, or because they are not available at the right time and place. However, a number of new products fail because they have been priced wrong and the error can as easily be in pricing the product too low as in pricing it too high. One of the reasons for new product pricing errors is the paucity of knowledge on how these decisions should be made. Thus, the decision maker often relies on intuition, and experience does not appear to improve measurably the chances of success.

The difficulty in pricing a new product depends on the relative "newness" of the product. Some products are new in the sense that a product which already exists in the market is offered by a company that is new to the market. Generally, the price of such functionally identical products is determined by existing prices of competing products. That is, the new product's price is likely to be similar to existing products' prices. Depending upon features offered and the quality image the new company wishes to project, the new entrant may be priced at, below, or above the competitive norm.

Other new products are new both to the company and to the market, but they are functionally competitive with established products. Pricing these new products is more difficult, but the prices of similar products influences the decision. Perhaps the critical question to be answered is how much buyers will be willing to pay for perceived differences in function, utility, or appearance.

The most difficult new product pricing problem occurs when the product is unique (i.e., functionally dissimilar to any other product). If the product is a major innovation in the market, there is much uncertainty surrounding the pricing decisions. Essentially, the market is undefined; that is, demand is unknown, and not all potential uses of the product are known. There are no comparable market experiences—no existing channels of distribution, no existing markups, no production and marketing cost experiences. Potential customers will be uncertain about the product in terms of its functioning, its reliability, or its durability. They may be concerned whether improvements will be made later and what the effects of these improvements will be on the product. Customers may also wonder whether prices will be reduced later when more sellers are distributing the product and when mass production techniques lower production costs.

Estimating Demand for a New Product. The demand estimation problem can be separated into a series of research problems. The first research problem is concerned with whether the product itself will fill a need or want and, therefore, will sell if the price is right. The second research problem is to determine the range of prices that will make the product economically acceptable to potential buyers. Third, at feasible price points in the acceptable price range, expected sales volumes must be estimated. Finally, potential competitive reaction must be determined.

Alternative Strategies for Pricing a New Product. It has been generally presumed that there are two alternatives in pricing a new product: "skimming" pricing, calling for a relatively high price, and "penetration'' pricing, calling for a relatively low price. A *skimming price* may be appropriate for new products if: (1) demand is likely to be price inelastic; (2) there are likely to be different price/market segments, thereby appealing to those buyers first who have a higher range of acceptable prices; (3) little is known about the costs of producing and marketing the product; (4) a capacity constraint exists; and (5) there is realistic value (perceived) in the product/service. A *penetration price* may be appropriate if: (1) demand is likely to be price elastic in the target market segments; (2) competitors are expected to enter the market quickly; (3) there are no distinct and separate price/market segments; and (4) there is the possibility of large savings in production and marketing costs if a large sales volume can be generated (the experience factor).

A caution is suggested in any selection of a skimming or penetration pricing strategy. Generally, there may be at least one current product that will serve as a frame of reference to potential buyers. They are likely to use this product to form their opinions of the value and price of the new product. Where such a reference product exists, the price setter must determine the price differential (higher or lower price than the reference product) and fit the new product into the established population of existing products.

The factors mentioned above may suggest an overall pricing strategy for a new product. However, *these two alternative strategies should not be viewed as either/or alternatives*. Rather, they merely reflect two opposite strategy extremes. Therefore, considerable latitude exists in choosing the specific price level for a new product.

Pricing a Growth Product

If the new product survives the introductory period, demand typically increases. At the same time, however, the nature of the marketplace and the rate of profits change. Competitors producing and selling a similar product usually enter the market and serve to establish a market price. Although there is a wide range of market prices early in the growth stage, the price range narrows as the product approaches maturity.

At least three price-related changes should be noted: (1) the range of feasible prices will have narrowed since the introductory stage; (2) unit variable costs will have decreased due to economies of scale (experience factor); and (3) fixed expenses will have increased because of increased capitalization and fixed marketing costs. Subject to competitive conditions, pricing decisions during the growth stage focus on selecting a particular price or prices which will help to generate a sales volume that enables the firm to realize its profit or sales goals.

Pricing a Mature Product

As a product moves into the maturity stage, it is necessary to review past pricing decisions and determine the desirability of a price change. Replacement sales now constitute a major share of demand, and competition from private-label products typically increases. When market conditions do not appear to warrant a price increase, the pricing decision is to reduce price or stand pat.

When is a price reduction profitable? We know that, when demand is price elastic, it is profitable to reduce prices if cost increases do not exceed the increase in revenues. The number of close substitutes in the maturity stage probably means that the firm's demand curve will be elastic. However, if all sellers match the price reduction, then the firm's market share remains relatively constant, and any increase in the firm's demand will result from the increase in industry demand. Therefore, to reduce price for a mature product, industry demand must be elastic, the firm's demand must be elastic, and the marginal revenues associated with the increased volume must be greater than the marginal costs of producing and selling the additional volume.

As an example, assume a firm is currently selling 1 million units at $75 per unit and that both the industry and firm's demand is price elastic with an elasticity value of -1.5. Further, assume that a price reduction by the firm is exactly matched by rival sellers, such that relative market shares remain constant. This means that an industry-wide price reduction will increase industry demand, but that each firm's demand increased only in direct proportion to its market share. The firm is considering reducing its price to $72, or 4 percent. Because demand price elasticity is -1.5, a 4 percent price reduction will increase demand by 6 percent (-4 percent $\times$ $-1.5 = 6$ percent). The comparative effect of the price reduction in the firm's revenues is shown in the first part of Table 8–1. With a price of $72, revenues will increase by $1,320,000.

However, although revenues have increased, profits have not necessarily increased. To determine the effect of the price decrease on profits, assume that variable costs per unit are $55.50 and that the firm has fixed costs of $8,600,000. Table 8–1 also shows the effect of a 6 percent increase in volume on costs, as well as the comparative effect on profits. Thus, while the price reduction produced a revenue increase of $1,320,000, profits were reduced by $2,010,000. Expressed in unit terms, revenues were reduced by $3.00 per unit, while the total cost per unit was reduced by only $0.4868, not a marginally profitable situation.

At the maturity stage of the life cycle, the firm probably should attempt to maximize short-run direct product contribution to profits.

TABLE 8–1
Effects of a 4 Percent Price Reduction on Revenues, Costs, and Profits

Effect	Before	After
Revenues:		
Demand, units (Q).	1,000,000	1,060,000
Price (P).	$ 75	$ 72
Revenues (PQ).	75,000,000	76,320,000
Costs:		
Fixed.	8,600,000	8,600,000
Variable ($55.50Q).	55,500,000	58,830,000
Total costs.	64,100,000	67,430,000
Profits:		
Total revenues.	75,000,000	76,320,000
Less: Total costs.	64,100,000	67,430,000
Net profits.	10,900,000	8,890,000

Hence, the pricing objective is to choose the price alternative leading to maximum contribution. If competition reduces prices, the firm may, however reluctantly, match the price reduction. On the other hand, the firm may try to reduce costs by using cheaper materials, eliminating several labor operations, or reducing period marketing costs. All or any of these actions may allow the firm to match competitively lower prices and still maintain target contributions to profit.

For example, assume a competitor has reduced price to $72. Since the firm wishes to meet that $72 price, it attempts to maintain profitability by modifying production procedures and reducing marketing period expenditures. The effects on costs and profits are shown in Table 8–2.

TABLE 8–2
Effects of a Change in Cost Structure and Price

Effect	Before	After
Revenues	$75,000,000	$76,320,000
Costs:		
Fixed	8,600,000	8,100,000
Variable (unit)	55.50	51.00
Profits:		
Total revenues	75,000,000	76,320,000
Less: Total costs	64,100,000	62,160,000
Net profits	10,900,000	14,160,000

Pricing a Declining Product

During the declining phase of a product's life, direct costs are very important to the pricing decision. Normally, competition has driven the price down close to direct costs. Only those sellers who were able to maintain or reduce direct costs during the maturity stage likely remain. If the decline is not due to an overall cyclical decline in business, but to shifts in buyer preferences, then the primary objective is to obtain as much contribution to profits as possible.

As long as the firm has excess capacity and revenues exceed all direct costs, the firm probably should consider remaining in the market. Generally, most firms eliminate all period marketing costs (or as many of these costs as possible) and remain in the market as long as price exceeds direct variable costs. These direct variable costs are the minimally acceptable prices to the seller. Thus, with excess capacity, any market price above direct variable costs would generate contributions to profit.

PRODUCT-LINE PRICING

From a market perspective, many firms have discovered that there are specific price/market segments for their products, and that determining prices to differentiate these products is a complex decision. Whether to add a middle-priced product or change the number of price offerings depends not only on the number of price/market segments, but also on clearly differentiating the products in the minds of buyers.

Generally, the firm has several product lines—a group of products that are closely related either because they are used together, or they satisfy the same general needs, or they are marketed together. Within a product line, some products are usually functional substitutes for each other, and some products are usually functional complements to each other. For example, a photographic product line would include cameras, film, flashbulbs, projectors, screens, and other accessories. Because of the demand interrelationships inherent within such a product line (as well as the cost interrelationships) and because there are usually several price/market targets, product line pricing is a major challenge.

Although the organization may wish to pursue a pricing policy of high prices only (or low prices only), the firm must still decide how high (or low) its prices should be and the differentials between different products in the line. It must also set the lowest (or highest) price so as to maintain a consistent price policy. Thus, three types of pricing decisions are required: (1) determine the lowest-priced product and its price; (2) determine the highest-priced product and its price; and (3) set the price differentials for all intermediate products.

LE 8–3

uct	PV	Plan Proportion of Total Volume	Weighted PV	Actual Proportion of Total Volume	Weighted PV
	0.50	0.45	0.2250	0.20	0.0100
	0.30	0.30	0.0900	0.30	0.0900
	0.20	0.15	0.0300	0.30	0.0600
	0.15	0.10	0.0150	0.20	0.0300
posite PV			0.3600		0.1900

36 cents of each sales dollar to cover fixed costs and contribute to fits.

Suppose, however, the actual data at the end of the planning period as provided in the fifth and sixth columns of Table 8–3. The comite PV shows that in actuality the product line contributed, on the rage, 19 cents of each sales dollar to cover fixed costs and contrib to profits, a decline in gross margin of 47 percent. If the target sales lar volume of $6,000,000 is reached and fixed costs remain at 0,000, then actual profits will be 57.9 percent less than planned 40,000 actual versus $1,360,000 planned). To maintain profits of 360,000, sales would have to increase 63.2 percent to $9,789,474— without costs changing.

The point of this example is that product-line profitability is af ted by the price, costs, and relative volume of each product in the e. In the example, profit declined because of a shift in the product e mix from the more profitable product A to the less profitable prod ts C and D. This shift may reflect shifts in customer demand, in ased competition with respect to A, or different stages of the oduct life cycle (growth for C and D and maturity for A).

termining an Appropriate Pricing Rule

tablishing gross margin goals for products is a common practice, pecially in times of strong market demand. These goals, however, ore such factors as the buyer's willingness to pay, relative price nsitivities across product/market segments, different stages of the e cycle, the product/sales mix, or relative capacity utilization.[7]

---

[7] James P. Nault, "Common Fallacies," in *Pricing Practices and Strategies*, ed. rl L. Bailey (New York: The Conference Board, Inc., 1978), pp. 3–6.

Compounding the pricing problem is that comple
exist even if the products are functional substitute
substitute relationship exists for the product-line bra
itors' brands, but a complementary relationship exis
within the product line. By adding new items or
prices, a firm may increase demand for already-exist
example, the new products may make it easier to
products because the seller has a wider assortment.
that the lowest- and highest-priced products are reme
ceived more frequently, implying a further compleme
end price usually is the most frequently remembered
bly has considerable influence on the marginal buy
buyer who is still seriously considering making the pu
the lowest-priced product is often used as a traffic buil
hand, the highest-priced product also is quite visibl
through quality connotations, may also stimulate dem

Principles for Product-Line Pricing

The correct pricing of a product line should follow thr

1. Each product should be priced correctly in relat
   products in the line. Specifically, perceptively no
   ences in the products should be equivalent to p
   differences.
2. The highest and lowest prices in the product line
   complementary relation to other products in the li
   be priced so as to facilitate desired buyer percep
3. Price differentials between products in the produ
   get wider as price increases over the product line.
   follows the behavioral finding that price percept
   logarithmic scale rather than an arithmetic or line

The Problem of Pricing Multiple Products

In a multiple product business, different products prod
profit volumes. That is, each product has a different amou
it generates, a different cost structure, including variab
costs, different types of competition, and, of course, diff
and revenues.

Assume the planning data for a product line are given
and fourth columns of Table 8–3. As the data illustrate, e
has a different PV value and different volume levels. The
PV shows the plan calls for the product line, on the average.

Compounding the pricing problem is that complements are likely to exist even if the products are functional substitutes. For example, a substitute relationship exists for the product-line brand versus competitors' brands, but a complementary relationship exists between brands within the product line. By adding new items or reducing certain prices, a firm may increase demand for already-existing products. For example, the new products may make it easier to sell the existing products because the seller has a wider assortment. It is also known that the lowest- and highest-priced products are remembered and perceived more frequently, implying a further complementarity. The low-end price usually is the most frequently remembered price and probably has considerable influence on the marginal buyer (the doubtful buyer who is still seriously considering making the purchase). Hence, the lowest-priced product is often used as a traffic builder. On the other hand, the highest-priced product also is quite visible and, possibly through quality connotations, may also stimulate demand.

Principles for Product-Line Pricing

The correct pricing of a product line should follow three principles:

1. Each product should be priced correctly in relation to all other products in the line. Specifically, perceptively noticeable differences in the products should be equivalent to perceived value differences.
2. The highest and lowest prices in the product line have a special complementary relation to other products in the line and should be priced so as to facilitate desired buyer perceptions.
3. Price differentials between products in the product line should get wider as price increases over the product line. This principle follows the behavioral finding that price perception follows a logarithmic scale rather than an arithmetic or linear scale.

The Problem of Pricing Multiple Products

In a multiple product business, different products produce different profit volumes. That is, each product has a different amount of volume it generates, a different cost structure, including variable and fixed costs, different types of competition, and, of course, different prices and revenues.

Assume the planning data for a product line are given in the third and fourth columns of Table 8–3. As the data illustrate, each product has a different PV value and different volume levels. The composite PV shows the plan calls for the product line, on the average, to contrib-

TABLE 8–3

		Plan		Actual	
Product	PV	Proportion of Total Volume	Weighted PV	Proportion of Total Volume	Weighted PV
A	0.50	0.45	0.2250	0.20	0.0100
B	0.30	0.30	0.0900	0.30	0.0900
C	0.20	0.15	0.0300	0.30	0.0600
D	0.15	0.10	0.0150	0.20	0.0300
Composite PV			0.3600		0.1900

ute 36 cents of each sales dollar to cover fixed costs and contribute to profits.

Suppose, however, the actual data at the end of the planning period are as provided in the fifth and sixth columns of Table 8–3. The composite PV shows that in actuality the product line contributed, on the average, 19 cents of each sales dollar to cover fixed costs and contribute to profits, a decline in gross margin of 47 percent. If the target sales dollar volume of $6,000,000 is reached and fixed costs remain at $800,000, then actual profits will be 57.9 percent less than planned ($340,000 actual versus $1,360,000 planned). To maintain profits of $1,360,000, sales would have to increase 63.2 percent to $9,789,474—all without costs changing.

The point of this example is that product-line profitability is affected by the price, costs, and relative volume of each product in the line. In the example, profit declined because of a shift in the product-line mix from the more profitable product A to the less profitable products C and D. This shift may reflect shifts in customer demand, increased competition with respect to A, or different stages of the product life cycle (growth for C and D and maturity for A).

Determining an Appropriate Pricing Rule

Establishing gross margin goals for products is a common practice, especially in times of strong market demand. These goals, however, ignore such factors as the buyer's willingness to pay, relative price sensitivities across product/market segments, different stages of the life cycle, the product/sales mix, or relative capacity utilization.[7]

---

[7] James P. Nault, "Common Fallacies," in *Pricing Practices and Strategies,* ed. Earl L. Bailey (New York: The Conference Board, Inc., 1978), pp. 3–6.

TABLE 8–4
Contributions and Profits for a Product Line

Item	A	B	C	D	Total
Unit variable cost	$ 18	$ 24	$ 30	$ 36	
A Before					
Selling price.	$ 30	$ 40	$ 50	$ 60	
Contribution	$ 12	$ 16	$ 20	$ 24	
Units sold (000's)	50	60	40	30	180
Total revenue (000's)	$1,500	$2,400	$2,000	$1,800	$7,700
Total contribution (000's)	$ 600	$ 960	$ 800	$ 720	$3,080
B After					
Selling price.	$ 28	$ 40	$ 54	$ 70	
Contribution	$ 10	$ 16	$ 24	$ 34	
Units sold (000's)	70	60	38	25	188
Total revenue (000's)	$1,960	$2,400	$2,052	$1,750	$8,162
Total contribution (000's)	$ 700	$ 960	$ 912	$ 850	$3,422

Table 8–4 illustrates a situation where a firm sets a pricing goal of 40 percent gross margin for each product. However, after examining the pricing decision, they discovered that product A was price-elastic—implying a price reduction would lead to a greater percent change in sales volume. Product B was priced correctly, and products C and D were found to be price-inelastic. As shown in Table 8–4 (B: After), after adjusting the prices for A, C, and D, contributions increased by $342,000 on increased revenues of $462,000, substantially more contributions than the firm's original objective.

Further, a manufacturer utilizing gross margin to set prices ignores the goals of channel members. A retailer is motivated by profit and volume. Although a manufacturer can attempt to project the retail price down the channel, it is the retailer who makes the final decision based upon the company's volume and profit expectation, merchandise philosophy, and competition.[8] The key point is that the manufacturer's price must be set with not only the manufacturer's goals in mind but also the goals of the other channel members.

The Problem of Common Resources

Often, joint or common resources are used to produce different product lines. The same physical facilities may be used in the production of

---

[8] Ibid.

these product lines; similar research and development facilities may be used; and selling, administrative, and warehousing facilities may be commonly used in the production and sale of these products. Moreover, a critical or scarce resource may be used in the production of these products.

Because product prices must reflect the competitive situation, the reactions of buyers, as well as costs and corporate objectives, not all products make the same use of resources per dollar of revenue or per dollar of out-of-pocket costs. However, when determining prices it is important to consider the degree that the products (or special orders) use available facilities (capacity) and consume available resources. Otherwise, the firm may be short of the necessary resources to obtain the desired level of contribution.

Indeed, the pricing of special orders or the composition of the product line strictly on contribution (gross margin) may result in the exhaustion of available resources without obtaining the target contribution. In Table 8–5A, the basic price and cost data for a product line are provided. Table 8–5B provides the demand forecasts, cost estimates, and required supply of a common resource material to meet the demand forecast.

TABLE 8–5
Product-Line Contribution Analysis

A. Unit Data

	Product A	B	C
Price	$6.60	$9.00	$12.00
Variable costs:			
Direct labor	$3.60	$2.10	$ 1.80
Direct materials.	1.23	4.62	7.20
Total	$4.83	$6.72	$ 9.00
Contribution (1–4)	$1.77	$2.28	$ 3.00

B. Data for Planning Period

	A	B	C	Totals
Demand (units)	$ 6,200	$ 8,100	$ 5,000	—
Revenue	40,920	72,900	60,000	$173,820
Direct labor	$22,320	$17,010	$ 9,000	$ 48,330
Direct materials.	7,626	37,422	36,000	81,048
Contribution	$10,974	$18,468	$15,000	$44,442
Pounds of material				
required	1,000	5,000	4,800	10,800
Units per pound	6.2	1.62	1.042	—
Pounds per unit.	.161	.617	.960	—

As shown in Table 8–5A, product C contributes $3 per unit sold to cover fixed expenses and profits. This unit contribution by product C is $0.72 larger than B's unit contribution, and $1.23 larger than A's unit contribution. However, in Table 8–5B it can be seen that, because of total expected demand, the total dollar contribution is larger for product B, with product C ranked second, and product A ranked third.

Now suppose this common material resource currently is scarce, and the firm has been advised that it can acquire no more than 5,000 pounds during the planning period. Furthermore, the supply of this material is expected to be below demand for at least several years. The firm must now consider the alternatives of reducing production of each product, eliminate a product and reduce production of the other products, or some reasonable derivation of these two choices.

Pricing a product line strictly on gross contribution or margin may result in the exhaustion of available resources without obtaining the largest contribution to profits possible. Essentially, the margin approach does not consider how much of the scarce resource is consumed per unit of output.

The data in Table 8–5 demonstrate that a pound of the resource material is necessary to produce 6.2 units of A, 1.62 units of B, and 1.042 units of C. Thus, what is necessary is to develop a decision rule that utilizes the information on how products consume scarce resources.

As the data in Table 8–5B indicate, it requires .161 pounds of the scarce resource to produce a unit of product A, .617 pounds to produce a unit of product B, and .96 pounds to produce a unit of product C. At current prices each unit of A produces $1.77 contribution. Thus, .161 pounds of scarce material help produce a $1.77 contribution. Therefore, a pound of the material produces $10.99 contribution. Similarly for product B, the contribution per pound is $2.28/.617, or $3.70. For product C, the contribution per pound is $3.00/.96 or $3.12.

Thus, the first 1,000 pounds of the scarce material should be allocated to product A, since each pound used in product A contributes more to profits and covering fixed costs. This allocation procedure is followed because product A has the highest *contribution per resource unit* (pound). When the resource is in limited supply, the decision criterion is to allocate resources to the profit segments with the highest contributions per resource unit (CPRU). This illustration provides a fundamental principle: *When the volume of products that could be sold is greater than the resource capacity to produce those products, the largest contribution (and profit) results from producing those products and orders that generate the greatest contribution per resource unit used.* The resources that cause the bottleneck could be machines, equipment, time, skilled labor, materials, cash, or storage capacity.

PRICE ADMINISTRATION

Price administration includes deciding (1) the appropriate discounts to offer middlemen, buyers, and volume purchasers; (2) the kind and amount of credit to offer to middlemen and to the ultimate consumer; and (3) the monitoring of pricing policies and programs to ensure compliance with the organization's marketing plans and legal constraints. These are the problems of administering the basic prices throughout the channels of distribution and the markets in which the products are sold.

Price administration deals with price adjustments for sales made under different conditions, such as: (1) sales made in different quantities, (2) sales made to different types of middlemen performing different functions, and (3) sales made with different credit and collection policies. Another problem is that of determining the amount of control the manufacturer wishes to exert over the prices at which the products are sold at various levels of distribution. Thus, we shall discuss determination of discount and credit decisions and methods of controlling resale prices throughout the channels of distribution.

Developing a Price Structure

Our discussion of pricing so far has been oriented toward determining what may be called a base or list price. It is this price, or some reasonable deviation therefrom, that consumers normally encounter. However, there is a second vital dimension to prices called price structure. *Price structure* involves determining when and the conditions of payment, the nature of discounts to be allowed the buyer, and where and when title is to be taken by the buyer. In establishing a price structure, there are many possibilities of antagonizing distributors and even incurring legal liability. Thus, it is necessary to avoid these dangers, while at the same time using the price structure to maximize profits.

Trade Discounts. Trade or functional discounts are based on a distributor's place in the distribution sequence and represent payment for performing certain marketing functions. Although we are accustomed to thinking of price as a single number, price is usually quoted to distributors as series of numbers, for example, "30, 10, 5, and 2/10, net 30." The first three numbers represent successive percentage discounts from the list or base price. The "2/10, net 30" part of the quotation reveals that a further 2 percent discount is allowed if payment in full is made within 10 days, but the full amount is due within 30 days. The list price usually designates the approximate or suggested final selling price of a product and represents the price usually referred to when discussing the methods of price determination. The list price is used to quote and figure the discounts.

The justification for trade discounts is that different distributors perform different functions within the distribution channel and should be compensated accordingly. It is often difficult to identify fully the various functions that middlemen perform, and, therefore, it is difficult to determine a trade discount structure that reflects the services performed. Much of this difficulty stems from the fact that some distributors are combination wholesalers and retailers, and that many different kinds of wholesalers and retailers exist.

Since trade discounts are not mentioned specifically in the Robinson-Patman Act, their legality has not been completely resolved. However, it has been generally interpreted that these discounts are lawful as long as they are offered to all competing buyers of the same distribution class on the same terms, and as long as the discounts accurately reflect cost savings to the seller. The difficulty arises when a retailer in direct competition with other retailers who buy through a wholesaler buys directly from a manufacturer. Although the direct-buying retailer is, in effect, performing all or most of the wholesaler's function, it could be construed that competition would be impeded if he set lower prices because of his more favorable discount.

The policy of offering price concessions to members of the distribution channel can be cumbersome and legally involved. It should be clear that tradition is not a defense for a discount policy. Today, with the additional complexities of vertically integrated distribution systems, it is important that sellers carefully analyze functional discount policies.

When establishing a functional-discount pricing structure, the seller should determine: (1) the functions the distributors should perform for the seller; (2) the costs to the distributors for performing these functions; (3) the relative costs of selling to different types of distributors; (4) the trade status of each buyer—that is, the buyer's position in the distribution sequence; (5) the extent of competition among buyers at all levels in the distribution sequence; (6) for combination wholesaler-retailer buyers, the sales that are wholesale and the sales that are retail (by segregating the wholesaler-retailer's purchases between the wholesale and retail function and allowing a wholesale discount only on legitimate wholesale purchases, the seller is demonstrating compliance with Section 2(a) of the Robinson-Patman Act.); and (7) the savings in costs of serving the different distributors.

Promotional Discounts. A promotional discount is given to distributors as an allowance for the distributors' efforts in promoting the manufacturer's product through local advertising, special displays, or other promotions. These allowances may take the form of a percentage reduction in the price paid, or they may be an outright cash payment either to the distributor or to the promotional vehicle (e.g., a local newspaper). Promotional discounts, as well as the costs of special price deals, are not normally thought to be aspects of the overall pricing framework. However, promotional discounts serve as price reductions and should properly be construed as pricing decisions. According to the Robinson-Patman Act, promotional discounts are illegal if they discriminate, tend to lessen or harm competition, or create a monopoly.

Cash Discounts. A cash discount is a reward for the payment of an invoice or account within a specified time. In our example earlier, 2 percent may be taken if payment is made within 10 days, though the account must be paid in full within 30 days. Many firms even quote an interest rate that will be charged if payment is delayed after 30 days. Cash discounts are lawful under the Robinson-Patman Act, provided they are offered under the same terms to all buyers.

The cash discount is intimately tied to the firm's credit policy and represents both a financial as well as a marketing decision. From the financial viewpoint, the extension of credit involves two basic costs: (1) the risk of bad debt losses and (2) resources embedded in accounts receivable foregoing alternative uses. The gains from extending credit revolve around the increase in demand because of this pseudoreduction in price. From a decision perspective, the seller must decide on: (1) the amount of cash discount, (2) the length of the credit period, (3) the amount to spend attempting to collect overdue accounts, (4) the customers to whom to offer credit terms, and (5) the magnitude of the line of credit.

Cash discounts and credit policy have traditionally been considered the purview of finance. However, analysis of the elements of credit policy decisions suggests that demand is affected by these decisions and that a more active decision approach can have positive effects on the firm's product demand. An active approach to determining credit policy requires analyzing the relationship between demand and (1) the credit period, (2) the amount of the cash discount, and (3) collection expenditures. Other things remaining the same, we would expect demand to increase with a lengthening of the credit period— that is, for a given list price, shifting from an "all sales cash" policy to allowing purchases "on account" should result in an increase in demand as the number of days an account is allowed to be outstanding is increased. Increasing the amount of the cash discount or lengthening the time period that the discount applies will normally result in increases in demand as well. In either decision, the key information is to know the elasticity of demand with respect to changes in these variables.

Suppose a company offers a 2/10, net 30 policy to all customers. Since the company is willing to take 2 percent less money to receive payment 20 days earlier, the per annum interest rate is 36 percent (360 days/20 days × 2 percent = 36 percent). Unless the company has a hurdle rate (investment potential) of 36 percent, it is worse off offering the discount. For example, a customer owing $1,000 takes advantage of this offer and pays $980 on day 10. If the company could invest the money at 24 percent (more than twice the prime rate), on day 30 they would have accumulated $13.10 interest or a total of $993.10—$6.90 less than if the discount had not been offered. More sophisticated models of cash discount policy have been developed,[9] but, as with a price reduction, an increase in demand must accompany a cash discount for the company's profit picture to improve. However, how much must sales increase to make a cash discount profitable? Mentzer and Monroe[10] have demonstrated that the equation to determine the new total sales volume necessary to maintain profitability (when a discount is offered for paying in 10 days or payment in full on day 30) would be:

$$Q' = (P - V)Q/(P(1 - d) - V - 2/3\,iP(1 - \%) \\ + 2/3\,iP(1 - d)\%)$$

where:

Q' = the new total sales volume resulting from the cash discount
d = the cash discount expressed as a percent of the price
PR = profits
P = price per unit
Q = quantity sold
V = variable costs per unit
F = fixed costs
$\%$ = the percent of sales which take the cash discount
i = the company opportunity cost per month

To illustrate, suppose the price of a particular product was $1,000, variable cost was $650, fixed cost was $1,000,000, and unit volume was 3,000; then the original profit was:

$$PR = PQ - VQ - F$$

---

[9] Michael Levy and Dwight Grant, "Financial Terms of Sales and Control of Marketing Channel Conflict," *Journal of Marketing Research* 17 (November 1980), pp. 524–30.

[10] John T. Mentzer and Kent B. Monroe, "Some Common Misconceptions About Price," *Working Paper* (Blacksburg, Va.: Virginia Polytechnic Institute and State University, 1983).

or

$$PR = \$1,000(3,000) - \$650(3,000) - \$1,000,000 = \$500,000$$

If a cash discount of 2/10, net 30 was offered, 55 percent of the new total sales volume was expected to take advantage of it, and the company opportunity cost was 1 percent per month, the new total sales volume (to maintain profitability) would have to be:

$$Q' = (\$1,000 - 650)3,000/(\$1,000(.98) - \$650 - 2/3(.01)\$1,000(.45)$$
$$+ 2/3(.01)\$1,000(.98).55)$$
$$= 1,050,000/(980 - 650 - 3.0 + 3.593) = 3,176$$

or sales will have to increase 176 units (5.87 percent) from a 2 percent cash discount, implying a product with an elasticity of 2.935, quite an elastic demand. However, Anderson[11] demonstrated that cash discount demand will normally be inelastic. Thus, in many situations elastic demand is required when, in fact, inelastic demand is more likely. Such a potential situation necessitates careful analysis of required and actual elasticity before implementing a cash discount policy. A cash discount should not be solely a financial decision or a competitive reaction, but a decision made in conjunction with marketing.

Quantity Discounts. Perhaps the most common type of discount is the quantity discount, granted for volume purchases (measured in dollars or units) either in a single purchase (noncumulative) or over a specified time period (cumulative, deferred, or patronage). The discount schedule may specify a single product, a limited number of products, or a complete mix of products ordered in a single purchase or over a period of time.

Noncumulative quantity discounts encourage larger and fewer orders over a given time period, which means the seller has fewer orders to process, ship, and invoice and, thus, reduces his total cost for these activities. Cumulative discounts lack these cost-related benefits, but they tend to tie a buyer to a seller over the discount period. Moreover, the nature of the product can make it advantageous to place small orders—for example, perishable products, large consumer durables, or heavy equipment and machinery. For these kinds of products, buying in small quantities is practical, and a cumulative discount schedule is beneficial to both parties.

Decisions to be reached in setting a quantity discount schedule are: (1) the minimum quantity to be purchased before any discount is ap-

---

[11] Paul F. Anderson, "The Marketing Management/Finance Interface," *Educators' Conference Proceedings* (Chicago: American Marketing Association, 1979), pp. 325–29.

plied, (2) the number of breaks or additional discounts for larger purchases, (3) the maximum quantity qualifying for any additional discount, and (4) the amount of discount to offer at each quantity level.

Quantity discounts are offered on the assumption that ordering in large quantities saves the seller money, part of which can be passed on to the buyer in the form of a price discount. Although the goal of such a discount may be to increase demand, demand does not have to increase in the long run if the seller's profit picture improves from cost savings in filling quantity orders.

The potential problem in quantity discounts lies in basing the discount on traditional quantity breaks and, in turn, ignoring the buyer's cost structure. It is necessary to develop a quantity discount structure that saves the seller sufficient money to offer a discount sufficient to offset the buyer's additional costs. In other words, the discount should leave both buyer and seller better off. Methods for examining buyer and seller quantity costs and appropriate discounts can be found in Crowther,[12] Mentzer and Monroe,[13] and Monroe and Della Bitta.[14]

By looking at changes in quantity, the savings (increases) in costs for both buyer and seller can be determined. If the seller's costs decrease more than the buyer's costs increase, the seller's savings can be so split that both parties are better off. The exact split (discount) will be a function of the costs involved, the seller's perceived value of selling in quantity, and the buyer's perceived value of different magnitudes of discounts. However, without such prior analysis, discounts may be offered which do not benefit the seller, are not sufficient to entice the buyer to quantity purchases, or both.

WHO SHOULD SET PRICES?

Who determines price may range from an executive level committee to a price manager to the comptroller's office to the sales force. The pricing decision may be centralized with top management or decentralized to the individual salespeople. While there is rationale to support either approach, it is unlikely that either will effectively relate price to the core marketing strategy. While upper management lacks the firsthand knowledge of the market, salespeople lack an overall knowledge of corporate goals and strategies. Both lack the integrated approach to reaching the corporate markets afforded by the marketing organiza-

---

[12] John F. Crowther, "Rationale for Quantity Discounts," *Harvard Business Review* 42 (March–April 1964), pp. 121–27.

[13] Mentzer and Monroe, "Some Common Misconceptions About Price."

[14] Kent B. Monroe and Albert J. Della Bitta, "Models for Pricing Decisions," *Journal of Marketing Research* 15 (August 1978), pp. 413–28.

tion. In most companies it is virtually impossible to define who has responsibility for setting prices and the process which is followed.[15]

A formal approach which integrates input from all levels of marketing, finance, and corporate planning should be used to set price. Finance must provide accurate and informative analysis of costs and cost structures. Corporate planning should provide input on future capacity and corporate plans and goals. Although the final decision-making authority for price should rest with marketing, information must also be gathered and analyzed on sales force pricing information, promotional plans and costs, product design and tests, distribution configuration, and market and competitive reactions before an intelligent pricing decision can be made. Everyone in key information positions should be involved in a formally defined information-gathering and decision-making procedure before prices are set.

Careful analysis of alternatives is critical when setting prices. To develop profitable pricing strategies, it is imperative to know competitive prices and possible reactions, cost structures, levels of capacity utilization, customer reactions to price and discounts, and corporate objectives. It is important, also, that pricing be an integral part of a consistent marketing strategy. Unless the pricing process is integrated within a dynamic long-run marketing strategy and developed by the marketing organization, a pricing policy unrelated to the marketing strategy will probably evolve.

SUGGESTED READINGS

Anderson, Paul F. "The Marketing Management/Finance Interface." *Educators' Conference Proceedings.* Chicago: American Marketing Association, 1979, pp. 325–29.

Crowther, John F. "Rationale for Quantity Discounts." *Harvard Business Review* 42 (March–April 1965), pp. 121–27.

Doob, Anthony, et al. "Effects of Initial Selling Price on Subsequent Sales." *Journal of Personality and Social Psychology* 11 (1969), pp. 345–50.

Levy, Michael, and Dwight Grant. "Financial Terms of Sale and Control of Marketing Channel Conflict." *Journal of Marketing Research* 17 (November 1980), pp. 524–30.

Mentzer, John T., and Kent B. Monroe. "Some Common Misconceptions about Price." *Working Paper.* Blacksburg, Va.: Virginia Polytechnic Institute and State University, 1983.

Monroe, Kent B. *Pricing: Making Profitable Decisions.* New York: McGraw-Hill, 1979.

_____. "Buyers' Subjective Perceptions of Price." *Journal of Marketing Research* 10 (February 1973), pp. 70–80.

_____, and Albert J. Della Bitta. "Models for Pricing Decisions." *Journal of Marketing Research* 15 (August 1978), pp. 413–28.

---

[15] Shapiro, "Common Fallacies," pp. 29–33.

_____, and Susan M. Petroshius. "A Theoretical Approach for Determining Product Line Prices." In *Theoretical Developments in Marketing,* eds. Charles W. Lamb, Jr., and Patrick M. Dunne. Chicago: American Marketing Association, 21–24.

_____, and _____. "Buyers' Subjective Perceptions of Price: An Update of the Evidence." In *Perspectives in Consumer Behavior,* eds. T. Robertson and H. Kassarjian. 3d ed. Glenview, Ill.: Scott, Foresman, 1981, pp. 43–55.

_____, and Andris A. Zoltners. "Pricing the Product Line During Periods of Scarcity." *Journal of Marketing* 43 (Summer), 49–59.

Nault, James P. "Common Fallacies." In *Pricing Practices and Strategies,* ed. Earl L. Bailey. New York: The Conference Board, 3–6.

Shapiro, Benson P. "Common Fallacies." In *Pricing Practices and Strategies,* ed. Earl L. Bailey. New York: The Conference Board, 29–33.

9

MANAGEMENT CONSULTING: HELP IS ON THE WAY!

by
John F. Hartshorne, CAE

Institute of Management Consultants, Inc.

- A steel service center serving a regional market, primarily in the construction industry, saw its sales drop from $8 million to less than $3 million in two years because of a steep decline in local construction business. Seeking to diversify out of the construction market, it set out to sell out steel plate to manufacturing companies, but soon realized that it didn't know how to market that service professionally. The company called in a management consultant. The consultant developed a sophisticated marketing program to sell cut plate to industrial customers but, in the process, discovered there was an even bigger market for pipe products. So the company entered the industrial pipe distribution business and within three years became the largest distributor of this product in the region.
- A chemical manufacturer, packaging and selling commodity and specialty chemicals through distributors, found itself after several years with an unchanging share of market, inadequate profits, and a growth rate that only matched the industry average. A management consultant was asked to audit the company's overall marketing strategy and operations. The consultant's recommendations formed a blueprint for a two-year program of sales force reorganization and development. Implementation steps, in which the consultant participated, included: restructuring the sales management organization, realigning sales territories, redirecting the sales effort and incentive compensation

system to stress the sales training for the company's and distributors' sales staff, and establishing effective management controls over the selling effort. During the first year of the program, total company sales volume increased 15 percent and profits rose 31 percent, despite the fact that all expenses for developing the program were charged to that year's budget. The second year, sales volume increased 22 percent and profits rose 28 percent. These increases did not include the contributions made by new products. Needless to say, the chemical company is gratified by the return on its investment from outside help.

These two real-life cases are typical of literally thousands of client engagements performed by management consultants every year for marketing managers in the United States and abroad. They illustrate the tremendous leverage that is available to the alert manager who knows when outside help is needed, where to find it, and how to work with management consultants to get the greatest benefit from the knowledge and services available. That is the purpose of this chapter: to tell you who management consultants are, what they can do and how they do it, how to find and select the right consultants for your needs from the bewildering number and variety available, how to work with your consultant to assure the successful outcome of your consulting engagement, and how to evaluate the project and measure its success.

Those things are important for the business manager to know—for the manager of a smaller business as well as a large corporation. The scope and complexity of business today is such that no one person can master all the information, tools, and techniques that are required to make sound plans and informed business decision. Successful business managers are those who are aware of the limits of their own knowledge and who are skilled in the use of outside expertise.

In years long gone, calling in a management consultant was considered to be a move of desperation by a business in trouble. Consultants in those days were known as "doctors to sick businesses." Not so today. Today, the large majority of management consulting assignments are for successful companies, and the "problems" consultants solve are, more often than not, growth opportunities: finding ways to capitalize on new products and new business ventures.

"But how can I, a small businessman, afford to hire a management consultant?" you may be asking yourself, thinking consultants are a luxury only the *Fortune* 500 can afford. "How can I afford not to?" might be a better question. First, consultants' fees may not be as enormous as you think. Consulting fees are almost always based on person-days of work multiplied by a per diem rate. The smaller the business, the smaller the project, usually, and the fewer person-days involved.

Second, the payout can be many times your investment. When you consider the long-range impact on your company's financial performance of choosing the right marketing strategy, or of establishing the best distribution network, or of organizing the most effective sales force, your original investment in consulting help to plan these vital steps may appear small by comparison.

WHO ARE MANAGEMENT CONSULTANTS?

There are many consultants *to* management; there are not so many *management* consultants. By this we mean to clarify the distinguishing attribute of management consultants: their expertise in the process of management. Some consultants to management are experts in insurance or advertising or telephone rate structures. Management consultants are experts in the management process, which essentially consists of planning, organization, direction, and control, as applied to the total enterprise or to individual functions within it, such as marketing, manufacturing, or finance. Management consultants are skilled in applying that knowledge to the solution of problems in the management of an enterprise.

By this definition, there are some 30,000 management consultants practicing professionally in the United States today. Approximately two thirds of these consultants are on the staffs of large management consulting firms—the "management services" arms of the "Big 8" and other CPA firms, and such free-standing generalist firms as McKinsey & Company; Booz, Allen & Hamilton, Inc.; and Arthur D. Little, Inc. The remaining third of the consulting population are in smaller firms or in solo consulting practice. The larger firms have hundreds of consultants on their staffs and are organized to perform a broad range of services using teams of two, four, or a dozen or more consultants. Smaller firms tend to specialize in one functional area, such as strategic planning, data processing, or physical distribution. Sole practitioners may be either specialists or generalists. As a rule (with its exceptions), they work for smaller clients.

Management consulting traces it origins to the 1890s and the pioneering concepts of "scientific management" as first propounded by Frederick W. Taylor. Taylor and his disciples were called on by company after company to apply the principles of industrial engineering and time-and-motion study to the production process. Thus, they became the first management consultants (or "management engineers," as they were then called). Industrial engineering continued as the primary focus of consulting practice until the 1930s, when the Great Depression shifted the focus to finance and the rescue of bankrupt business. World War II forced the need for increased manufacturing productivity, and "efficiency expert" became the consultant's sobriquet. Marketing came to fruition as a major consulting function following World War II, when companies vied with each other to fill pent-up consumer demand. Then, in the 60s, came the computer, and with it revolutionary changes in data processing and management information systems. The impact of computer technologies continues to be a major stimulant to management consulting practice.

WHAT MANAGEMENT CONSULTANTS DO

A management consultant is an independent professional who, for a fee, helps the management of client organizations define and achieve their goals through a better utilization of resources. The consultant may do this by helping to identify and define current or future problems or opportunities. Management consultants are change-agents; they not only propose change but help implement it, as well.

Management consultants supplement—they do not supplant—management. They don't make decisions for their clients, because they have no such authority. They do try to persuade their clients to act, but only by the force of the information and logic behind their recommendations. "Transfer of confidence" is the name of the game. The successful consultant instills confidence. Often it is the consultant's own assurance and professional expertise that gives the client confidence to sail uncharted waters.

The end product of a management consulting assignment is usually more than a report of survey findings, although in some instances, such as a marketing research study, that may be all that is required. It is more, even, than the installation of a new system or a revised organization structure. The end product, in addition to these elements, will usually include new knowledge on the part of people in the client organization about how to handle the same or similar problems themselves in the future. The professional consultant will always try to leave the client organization stronger, more capable of solving its own problems, than he or she found it. Thus, the consultant is a teacher as well as a problem solver.

The management consultant brings four unique attributes to each client engagement. These are objectivity, analytical skill, comparative knowledge, and full-time attention to the problem. There is no substitute for objectivity—the independent, unbiased point of view. The ability to see the forest for the trees is often the most valuable ingredient in solving a client problem. Analytical skill is the knack of taking things apart and putting them together in new ways to reveal new meaning. The consultant is naturally good at this and practices the skill to a higher degree of perfection with every assignment. Comparative knowledge is the accumulation of experience with other client situations that is applicable to the problem at hand. Lastly, the consultant's ability to devote full-time attention gets the client's problem solved expeditiously.

Beyond these basic attributes, the management consultant brings technical knowledge and skill, usually in several—but never in all—specialized functional areas. Some of the more common consulting specialties include the following:

— Strategic planning.
— Diversification—mergers, requisitions, and joint ventures.
— Organization design.
— Manpower planning.
— Executive compensation, wage and salary administration.
— Financial planning and control.
— Management information systems and data processing.
— Production planning and control.
— Materials management.
— Marketing and sales management.
— Physical distribution.

Within the marketing management area, the following are among the more common subjects of study by management consultants:

Marketing strategy—broad objectives and coordinated plans for establishing a successful niche in the marketplace.
Product-line planning—rounding out the line with a view to life cycles of present products.
Marketing research—measuring the acceptance and sales potential for existing or contemplated new products.
Sales management—planning, organization, direction, and control of the sales force.
Pricing policies—balancing sales volume with profitability.
Distribution channels—selling through wholesalers versus selling direct.
Physical distribution—balancing customer service with manufacturing, warehousing, and shipping requirements.

HOW TO TELL IF YOU NEED A CONSULTANT

There are no hard and fast rules for deciding if and when a management consultant should be brought in. However, a few common situations suggest that a consultant may be helpful or necessary. These are:

— When management does not have the specialized knowledge or skill needed to solve a problem it has identified.

— When management has the needed knowledge and skills but not the available time or personnel to solve a problem.

— When management's persistent efforts are unable to produce the long-term improvements that are desired.

— When management requires an independent third-party opinion, either to confirm a decision or to provide an alternative.

— When management feels that things could be better but does not know where to act or what to do.

Equally important is to be aware of when *not* to hire a management consultant. Here are three key rules:

1. Never hire a consultant unless management clearly understands what the objectives of the assignments are. It may be that the consultant's first assignment is to define the objectives for subsequent work. The most common source of dissatisfaction with consulting engagements is the absence of clearly defined and agreed-upon objectives.

2. Never hire a consultant unless management is fully committed to support the program that results from the consultant's recommendations. This means organizational and financial support. Nothing will happen unless there is evident commitment from the top down.

3. Except in those rare instances where it is clearly recognized as a temporary expedient, never hire a consultant to run your business. It is the consultant's responsibility to recommend a course of action and to give management adequate information on which to decide to act. Responsibility for the consequences of action can never be delegated to the consultant. The consultant can design new systems and help management install them, but only management can exert the authority needed to put the systems into operation.

HOW TO SELECT A MANAGEMENT CONSULTANT

Assuming the need for outside help is recognized and the objectives of the consulting assignment are at least preliminarily defined, the next most important step is to select the right consultant for the job. This means the right consulting firm and the right individual within the firm to perform the assignment.

You should make your choice from at least three written proposals from qualified consultants, and probably no more than five. To arrive at that point you should meet personally with those three to five consultants, and possibly a few more.

There are several sources of referral to competent consultants. Your company's attorney, accountant, or banker probably can recommend reliable firms and individual consultants, as can trade or professional associations to which you or your company belong. Executives of other companies with similar interests can also provide leads. However, the usefulness of these referral sources is only as good as their personal experience. For a broader view of the possibilities, you should turn to the major associations representing the management consulting profession itself:

Institute of Management Consultants
19 West 44th Street
New York, New York 10036
(212) 921-2885

which certifies the professional competence and conduct of individual management consultants.

ACME Inc.
The Association of Management Consulting Firms
230 Park Avenue
New York, New York 10017
(212) 697-9693

which accredits the professional competence of some of the larger consulting firms.

Association of Management Consultants
500 North Michigan Avenue
Chicago, Illinois 60611
(312) 266-1261

which accredits the professional competence of some of the smaller consulting firms. All of these organizations will gladly furnish names of qualified consultants for you to contact.

In screening recommended consultants, three considerations are involved: (1) the consultant's experience in handling similar situations, (2) what the consultant's references say about his or her ability to achieve desired results within time and budget targets, and (3) your personal rapport with the consultant during initial interviews. In interviews, you should determine whether the consultant displays a thorough familiarity with the situation and can suggest a few other possibilities or points of inquiry regarding the problem. The consultant should furnish references (people within client firms) for whom he or she has performed similar assignments. These references should be checked thoroughly. Of special interest should be the results obtained, the honesty and tact with which recommendations were made, and the ease with which the consultant worked with people in the client organization.

When these considerations have been carefully evaluated, the consultants of choice should be asked to submit a written project proposal. The proposal should define in as much detail as needed such things as:

— The objectives and scope of the assignment.
— The approach the consultant plans to take in gathering facts and performing the analysis.
— The nature of the final report and interim progress reports.
— The anticipated professional fee and expense charges, basis of fee estimate, and terms of payment.
— Conditions under which client or consultant may cancel the agreement.

The most-favored proposal should be reviewed with the consultant and all questions about it resolved. Portions may have to be rewritten to provide necessary assurances and explanations. Only when the terms and conditions are thoroughly understood and agreed to should the proposal be accepted.

HOW TO ASSURE SUCCESSFUL COMPLETION OF THE PROJECT

There are several things management can do to help assure successful completion of the consulting project. At the outset, it is important to ensure the cooperation of all company people with whom the consultant must work to develop inputs and recommendations. Recognize that there is always individual anxiety when people learn that a consultant has been engaged. Anxiety is best allayed by information. Even before the consultant steps in the door, it is desirable to call a general meeting or to issue a memorandum announcing that a consultant has been engaged and explaining the nature and purpose of the engagement.

The consultant must be given ready access to necessary background information about the company and the situation under study. This will be obtained from documents and personal interviews. The data-gathering process, which is often the most time-consuming (and, therefore, the most expensive) part of the project, can be expedited by assigning one of your key executives as liaison to the consultant, if you cannot perform this role yourself. Your liaison officer can help the consultant gather necessary documents and arrange interviews.

PROJECT PLANNING

A key step to assure the successful outcome of a consulting project is the development of a detailed project plan. This is the responsibility of the consultant, of course, but management must be actively involved in the process. A little time invested here, in assuring yourself that the consultant's workplan covers all the essential bases and leads to the end product you desire, will save a lot of time and cost over the life of the project.

A schedule of progress reports is normally part of the project plan. Progress reports are key to project quality assurance. They give you the chance to see that the project is proceeding according to plan and schedule (or to help the consultant make mid-course corrections if it is not), to verify information that is being developed, and to react to preliminary recommendations as they emerge. A byword in good consulting is "No surprises." Management should be made aware from the earliest possible stages the direction in which the consultant's study is trending and its probable outcome. Indeed, management may actually participate in the development of the recommendations. When the study is completed, then, its outcome is a foregone conclusion. It does not have to be "sold" to management.

CONFIDENTIALITY AND CONFLICT OF INTEREST

In the course of their consulting studies, consultants often must acquire a great deal of knowledge about a client's operations and personnel. Sometimes this information is sensitive, competitively or otherwise, and clients are understandably concerned about its possible misuse. Be assured that all reputable consultants regard such inside information as strictly confidential and not to be disclosed to, or discussed with, a third party without the client's express permission. Further, no ethical consultant will work with two competing companies without the permission of both. These are requirements of the codes of ethics to which all reputable consultants subscribe.

HOW TO EVALUATE A PROJECT'S SUCCESS

The success of a consulting project can be measured in many ways. Frequently, the change that results from an engagement is obvious; for example, measurable savings being realized, new business being generated, delays eliminated, and so on.

Some projects, however, may not produce immediately measurable results, their payoffs being realized gradually, over a long time. However, in such situations, there should be a clear sense of direction and observable movement toward the achievement of goals or the solution of problems identified in the consultant's final report.

Finally, and beyond such objective measures, there is one measure of a more subjective nature. Ask the question, "On balance, and considering everything, would I hire the same consultant again?" If the answer is "Yes," the project can generally be considered a success. Three quarters of the consulting work of most reputable management consultants is repeat or continuing business for clients they have served in the past. This fact suggests that the odds on the successful outcome of a consulting project are favorable indeed.

THE IMPORTANCE OF PROFESSIONAL CREDENTIALS

Note that statements in the paragraphs above are often qualified as applying to "reputable" management consultants. Unfortunately, not everyone who carries the name "management consultant" meets the same minimum standards of competence and conduct, as would be required if management consulting were a licensed profession. However, professional credentials do exist in management consulting. A consultant who has met rigorous requirements for membership in the Institute of Management Consultants, is accorded recognition as a Certified Management Consultant (CMC). When you see those initials following a consultant's name you can be assured that he or she has met high standards of professional competence and conduct. These standards include long experience as a full-time practitioner (at least five years), a record of more than satisfactory client relationships, as verified through extensive client reference checks, technical competence evidenced in detailed written descriptions of five representative client assignments, and in an oral interview with three professional peers. CMCs also sign a pledge to abide by the institute's strict Code of Professional Conduct, which is enforced.

SUMMING UP

In today's sharply competitive economy, chief executives and marketing managers, particularly, must seek out every means at their disposal to assure business success. One such means—and not to be overlooked—is the professional management consultant. Here is a ready source of new ideas and of new tools and techniques for solving problems and improving profits. The manager who knows how to choose and use management consultants effectively will have definitely gained a competitive edge.

RECOMMENDED READINGS

Greiner, Larry E., and Robert O. Metzger. *Consulting to Management.* Englewood Cliffs, N.J.: Prentice-Hall, 1983.

Kubr M., ed. *Management Consulting: A Guide to the Profession.* Geneva, Switzerland: International Labour Office, 1980.

Fuchs, Jerome H. *Making the Most of Management Consulting Services.* New York: Amacon, 1975.

"Code of Professional Conduct." New York: Institute of Management Consultants.

Drucker, Peter. "Why Management Consultants?" In *The Evolving Science of Management,* ed. M. Zimit and R. Greenwood. New York: Amacon, 1979.

Turner, A. N. "Consulting Is More Than Giving Advice." *Harvard Business Review,* September–October 1982.

Bower, Marvin. "The Forces That Launched Management Consulting Are Still at Work." *Journal of Management Consulting,* Fall 1982.

10

TRAINING AND DEVELOPING THE MARKETING MANAGER

by
Robert F. Vizza

Manhattan College

It has been estimated that American industry spends approximately $40 billion a year on training and development.[1] Add to this the budgets of university executive development programs, and the deep concern for enhancing management performance through training and development becomes apparent. The development of human resources is one of management's most serious responsibilities. The organization has a serious moral obligation to develop its most important resource—people. But the need to train and develop executives is not simply a demand of social responsibility; it is also a demand of sound business practice. In the marketing area, the focus of this book, executive obsolescence and a shortage of managerial talent provide both opportunities and problems for managers and corporations. Recognizing the needs and opportunities in marketing, companies ask, "What can we do, and should we do, to develop the talent needed in marketing management?" This chapter will attempt to address that question.

It will first define the job of the marketing executive, next examine the need for training and development, then suggest guidelines for a company to follow in designing a training and development program, and conclude with suggestions for evaluating the development program.

---

[1] "National Report for Training and Development" (Washington, D.C.: American Society for Training and Development, 1983).

THE JOB OF THE MARKETING MANAGER

The term *marketing manager* means many things to many people. In some organizations, it refers to a staff person responsible for developing the marketing plan; in other companies, it refers to a line executive in charge of the entire marketing function. The title demands definition and, at the same time, defies definition. As one noted authority observes:

> It is surely a crying absurdity that the British Institute of Management, the Institute of American Management, and, indeed, all the national institutions have yet to agree on the concept of "manager." What are the students of management to make of the constant use of the term in such a way that everyone is left to put their own idiosyncratic connotation to it?[2]

In this chapter, "marketing manager" will be used to describe the executive with overall responsibility for the marketing activities of the firm. Many of the concepts will also apply to the executives responsible for the specific functions of marketing (i.e., sales, advertising, marketing research, product planning, distribution, and the like), although these jobs are not specifically the focus of this chapter.

Briefly, the job of the marketing manager is to plan, organize, implement, and control the marketing activities of the firm. In so doing, all of the functions of marketing must be coordinated into a cohesive program and be integrated with the other functions of the firm, particularly with production and finance. The responsibilities of the marketing manager are more fully covered elsewhere in this book, but for the purposes of providing a frame of reference for this chapter, include the following:[3]

    I. OBJECTIVE

        To plan, organize, and implement those activities necessary to develop and deliver need-satisfying products and services to the customer at maximum profits.

    II. PLANNING

        A. *Corporate Goals*

            1. Profit.

            2. Return on investment.

            3. Share of market.

            4. Image.

---

[2] Wilfred Brown, "Conceptualizing the Role of the Managers," *Management Education, A World View of Experience and Needs,* Report of the International Academy of Management (London, 1981).

[3] Robert V. Vizza, *Adoption of the Marketing Concept, Fact or Fiction* (New York: Sales Executives Club of New York, 1967), pp. 101–2.

B. *Market Intelligence*
1. Economic market factors.
2. Sociological market factors.
3. Psychological market factors—consumer motivation.
4. Political climate.
5. Ethical considerations.
C. *Marketing Objectives*
1. Sales.
2. Profit.
3. Share of market.
4. Market image.
D. *Marketing Departmental Objectives*
1. Advertising and promotion objectives.
2. Sales objectives.
3. Transportation and inventory policy objectives.
4. Product planning and innovation objectives.
5. Marketing research objectives.
6. Marketing personnel objectives.
E. *Marketing Planning*
1. Goods and services mix—including product planning.
2. Communications mix—including advertising and sales promotion.
3. Physical distribution mix—including transportation and inventory.

III. ORGANIZING
A. Coordinates the functions of marketing.
B. Integrates entire marketing function with production, finance and control, personnel, and legal functions.
C. Oversees departmental plans.
D. Structures and staffs the marketing organization.
E. Provides for marketing personnel development.

IV. CONTROL
A. Establishes criteria for marketing effectiveness measurement.
B. Gathers feedback on all aspects of marketing operations.
C. Takes corrective action to assure profit realization.
D. Supervises marketing and departmental budgets.

V. REPORTING RELATIONSHIPS
A. Reports to president or divisional head.
B. Supervises the sales manager, advertising director, marketing research director, product planning director, product managers, physical distribution manager.

C. Relates to executives in charge of research, production, finance and control, personnel, legal.

D. External relationships include trade and customer relations.

THE NEED FOR TRAINING AND DEVELOPING THE MARKETING MANAGER

Basically, the responsibilities of the job are clearly identifiable and appear to be rather constant from firm to firm and time to time. What does change, however, is the *environment* in which the job is performed, the *people* to be managed, and the *tools and methods* used by the marketing manager to do the job. It is this constant change that gives rise to the need for a *continuous* program of training and development. Let us look at these change agents in order to provide a foundation for designing the right education program.

I. Changes in the *environment*. There are at least six sets of environmental influences that have an impact on management:

A. *Political factors.* The all-pervasive role of government in management decision making, including, but not limited to, government regulations and the law, create an environment that places constraints as well as obligations on marketing management. Other political factors include the increasing demand for worker participation in management decision making, trade union power and its political involvement, and the increasing interdependence of employers, labor, and government.

B. *Economic factors.* Such serious economic factors as inflation and unemployment and the shift from an industrial manufacturing economy to a service economy, present many challenges for management decision making.

C. *Resource availability.* There appears to be considerable agreement that we are fast using up the world's irreplaceable resources and that, by the end of the century, the effects will be seriously felt unless substitutes have been found. Petroleum and other minerals are in short supply. Fuel and food are a constant cause of concern in most economies of the world. It may well be that the emphasis for management will increasingly turn from growth to the management of contraction and conservation.

D. *Technology.* Many of the technological innovations affecting managers in their work or as individuals have already taken place, and many are still in the process of development, and the full impact will not be seen for years. The areas in which radical developments have taken place in technology include agriculture, travel, communications, information, and automation. The evolving revolution brought about by the development of the microprocessor will have an impact on American industry that will be far greater than the Industrial Revolution. The ways that the computer will affect the methods that managers use to manage can scarcely be understood at this time. What is clear, however, is that present and future managers will have to be well attuned and constantly updated in their knowledge of this powerful tool of management.

E. *Social changes.* There are significant factors which affect management at all levels, and these include a greater degree of permissiveness, a generation gap and breakdown of traditional family life, married women in the work force, the aging population, changing attitudes toward work, a better-educated work force, a demand for greater worker participation and more meaningful jobs, consumerism, massive youth markets, and changing value systems.

F. *International factors.* It is clear that marketing in the future will have to be conducted in an environment of multinational dimensions. Some of the major influences on management due to these international factors include the population explosion in developing countries, the arms race, political instability, the formation of economic and commodity blocks (such as the EEC), the reentry of China into world commerce, the increasing penetration of world markets by industrializing countries, growing nationalism of developing countries, and the like.

II. Changes in the *people* to be managed. People to be managed in the future will be greater in number, younger, better educated, and espousing a set of values that replaces the Puritan work ethic with a value that is centered more in making a creative contribution than in making a living. The role of work in people's lives is changing, and today's young professionals have their primary commitment to their discipline, rather than to the organization. This type of employee will be less motivated by money and will look for work challenges and opportunities for education and self-development in selecting an organization. If a company is to attract, develop, and hold this type of employee, and it must in order to survive, it has to concern itself with the continuing education and development needs of personnel.

III. Changes in management *methods.* As suggested above, the information and telecommunications explosions are just beginning to be felt by management. The marketing manager of today, as well as of the future, will be more comfortable with a more scientific approach to management, based on analysis of fact and current information. This higher degree of sophistication requires constant training and development as technologies continue to advance.

Because of the constant and escalating pace of change described above, there is a need for a greater recognition and adoption of the idea of Life-Long Learning—L^3—for the manager. Our society has, for too long, embraced the front-end load model of education—that is, educate someone at the beginning of his or her life and then, education completed over 16 years, put them in the work force for 50 years! Occasionally, bring the manager back for a week or two of job training. This front-end load approach, along with a series of ad hoc educational experiences, *must* give way to L^3 that sees education as a *continuous* and *continuing* process over the life of one's career (or two careers). A phenomenon thoughtful business people perceive today is what might be termed a *knowledge-experience gap*. This is the gap that exists between new-hires, who are recent college or MBA graduates, and their managers. The grads' knowledge is current, but they lack experience; the managers are experienced, but their knowledge is not as current. Frustrations are built into this relationship for both the managers and the new-hires. Managing these people presents its own problems. The disturbing aspect of this gap is that it is self-perpetuating— by the time the grads gain experience and subsequently become managers, their knowledge is no longer current; they will experience the same gap with their new-hires, but from the other side. And thus the wheel turns again. Since there is no such thing as instant experience, this gap must be closed by making the managers' knowledge current. This can be accomplished, at least partially, by the company's training and development program.

DESIGNING A TRAINING AND DEVELOPMENT PROGRAM FOR MARKETING MANAGERS

In designing an educational program, it is important to keep in mind that all development is ultimately self-development. In the end analysis, it is the individual who accepts or refuses, responds to or rejects, efforts to develop his or her capabilities. What, then, is the corporate role if this assumption is true? It is simply this—to provide the environment and motivation for personal development and to make available the necessary guidelines, tools, and training programs. Development programs will succeed only to the extent that they are encouraged and supported by top management. In addition, since development is people-oriented, it must be geared to the individual. There are areas of learning common to all managers within a company, and these can be imparted to a group. But one person's weakness is another person's forte, and top management must help the individual assess strengths and weaknesses in order to capitalize on the one and to correct the other.

Basic to the individual's response to training is the degree to which the person finds his or her own goals compatible to the goals of the organization. The greater the degree of conflict, the more resistance will be exhibited toward development programs. People must be motivated to develop; they must recognize needs and realize that the development program will allow them to satisfy these needs. The program environment is the same as the climate required for sound and sincere human relations programs. This environment must exist in order for learning to take place.

An important aspect of this climate is the vertical relationship between superiors and subordinates in the organization. It is this relationship that predominates the environment. It interprets needs and supplies the guidelines and tools for development. It determines in large part the degree of acceptance or rejection of any development program. Risking oversimplification, it can be said that the necessary climate flows from the *attitudes* of top management. There must be a commitment to executive education, one that is based on a firm belief in the sound moral and business requirements of human resources development.

Just as there is a required environment for effective training and development to take place, the concept of Life-Long Learning requires that a distinction between training and development be understood:

— Training is imparting the knowledge and skills required to perform a task or to accomplish an objective; development is a broader concept that deals with attitudes and habits.
— Training is job-oriented; development is person-oriented.
— Training is temporary in duration; development is a continuous process.
— Training is concerned with the performance of a specific, present job; development is concerned with the future growth of the individual performing that job.

As such, training is one aspect of the broader concept of development. Development deals with the whole person and employs behavioral concepts to guide that person toward actualization of his or her capabilities and satisfaction of his or her needs. You can train people to run a machine, but you cannot train them to think—you must develop the ability and the desire to think.

Because development is a continuous and constant process, and is consonant with the concept of Life-Long Learning, it suggests the necessity for the organization to design a "career path" for marketing management. A *career path* is the description of the likely avenues of advancement for both line and staff positions in the marketing area. In addition, a complete career path indicates the qualifications for each job along the path and the responsibilities and expected achievements at each step. Achievement, not time, is stressed as a determinant of movement from one job to the next. Also, a complete career path will suggest the training available for each position. Additionally, it will recognize the reality that not all people will move into high executive positions and will make provisions for advancement within job classifications. Flexibility is a characteristic of an effective career path, so as not to lock either the company or the individual into a rigid step progression. The obvious use of the path as a means of communicating opportunities to employees is only one of its applications. Another is its use as a master plan for indicating checkpoints for personal appraisal and personal development planning.

The career path thus becomes a timetable for training and development. Figures 10–1 and 10–2 illustrate a typical career path actually in use in one company. The individual enters the marketing organization as a marketing trainee and then can either move up the sales management path or move up the product management path. In the course of upward mobility, the individual can cross over from sales management to product management, with marketing management as the ultimate path. The use of the career path concept does not imply that all people would move into high executive positions. Nor does its use imply a time-related seniority system for advancement. As it should be applied, the concept shows that the avenues are not mutually exclusive and that there should be mobility from one to another. Achievement is the prime criterion for advancement, and the career path is intended to be applied in such a way that each person will advance at his or her own pace and go as far as their capabilities and interests permit.

The career path is of immediate use as a framework in planning and timing specific training programs appropriate to the various job levels, as shown in Figure 10–2. The training programs that are available in-house for each job on the path are identified. In this way, individuals can be trained for their present job, as well as trained for their next job before actual appointment.

Given that the right environment exists for management education and development, how, then, can an organization go about designing a development program for marketing managers? Basically, development is a three-step process, as illustrated in Figure 10–3.

FIGURE 10–1
Career Path: Marketing Avenues of Advancement

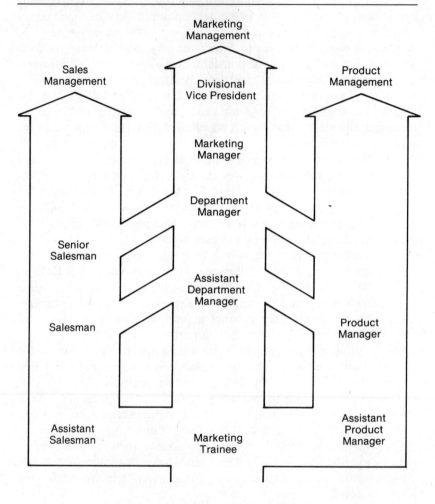

1. Identification of the attributes required for the job.
2. Assessment of individual needs.
3. Matching individual needs to available training resources.

Let us examine this process in more detail:

1. The first step requires that the attributes required for each job in the marketing career path be clearly identified. These attributes may be classified into three categories:

FIGURE 10–2
Career Path: Planning Individual Training

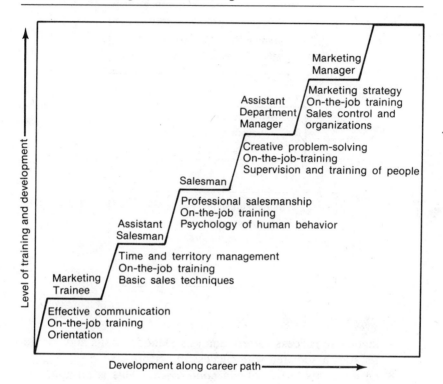

a. *Knowledge*—a body of facts, principles, definitions, and concepts in the cognitive, functional disciplines.
b. *Skills*—nonfactual dimensions required to perform a job.
c. *Personal characteristics*—traits and values required to perform the job.

Since these attributes are job driven, we begin by analyzing the job of the marketing manager. A good unit of analysis is the decision unit—that is, what decisions, both strategic and tactical, the individual will be called upon to make in the job. Together with the position description of required responsibilities, objectives, and duties, the attributes begin to emerge. Other techniques include:

A. *The difficulty analysis.* This is the identification of problems and stress points to be anticipated in performing a job. The approach is a refinement of the job analysis and indicates special knowledge and skill requirements of the job. Correspond-

FIGURE 10–3
The Training and Development Process

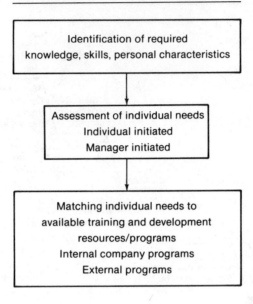

These analyses will uncover different attributes for different companies. The following list of attributes is intended to be illustrative (but is, in fact, the actual list developed by a major corporation).

ingly, the success pattern analysis identifies traits and characteristics associated with successful performers.

B. *Group problem-identifying conferences.* This is an approach whereby the incumbents meet to discuss the problems they face in doing their job. It is advisable to consider using an outsider to moderate such sessions in order to elicit more open feedback from employees.

C. *Attitude surveys.* When the opinions of prospective trainees are solicited, training needs are often uncovered. The surveys also serve to involve the individual in planning training programs and, thus, contribute to the acceptance of subsequent programs.

D. *Drive pattern identity.* This involves determining the forces that cause a person to behave in a certain way. Such motivator identification suggests areas for personal development necessary to achieve satisfaction. Uncovering drive patterns is difficult and involves the use of behavioral sciences.

These analyses will uncover different attributes for different companies. The following list of attributes is intended to be illustrative (but is, in fact, the actual list developed by a major corporation).

A. KNOWLEDGE
1. *Pricing*—practices, policies, techniques.
2. *Marketing communications*—advertising, promotion.
3. *Marketing information*—types and sources of data; primary and secondary research techniques; marketing intelligence systems.
4. *Forecasting*—techniques, applications, concepts.
5. *Budgeting*—techniques, application, concepts.
6. *Marketing planning process.*
7. *Distribution channels*—types, characteristics, policies.
8. *Product knowledge.*
9. *Industry knowledge*—competitive intelligence.
10. *Market*—customer knowledge.
11. *Legal environments*—knowledge of and working familiarity; regulatory agencies; business law.
12. *Computer applications in marketing*—information theory.
13. *Company knowledge*—history, organization, structure, policies, personnel, procedures.
14. *Accounting*—financial statement analysis.
15. *Economics*—macro—national income analysis.
     micro —costs, demand, pricing.
16. *Finance*—money and banking institutions, instruments, methods of financing, investments, capital formation, reporting, markets.
17. *International marketing.*
18. *Government relations.*
19. *Social policy*—social responsibilities of marketing.
20. *Logistics*—inventory, transportation, distribution.
21. *Consumer behavior*—demographics, motives, buying patterns.

B. SKILLS—*Administrative and Interpersonal*[4]
1. *Organizing and planning.* Establishing courses of action for self or others, or both, to accomplish specific goals, which include planning proper assignments of personnel and appropriate allocations of resources.
2. *Decision making.* Choosing among alternative courses of action that are based on logical assumptions and available

---

[4] Many of the definitions come from the following sources:

Accreditation Research Project, Report of Phase 1, American Assembly of Collegiate Schools of Business, St. Louis, vol. 15, November 2, Winter 1980.

R. Boyatzes, *The Competent Manager* (New York: John Wiley & Sons, 1982).

Douglas Bray, Richard Campbell, and Donald Grant, *Formative Years in Business* (New York: John Wiley & Sons, 1974).

factual information; this includes a basic willingness to form judgments, to make decisions, and to take action or commit oneself to complex situations, or both.

3. *Leadership skills.* Utilization of appropriate interpersonal styles to stimulate and guide individuals or groups toward goal and task accomplishment.

4. *Oral and written communications.* Effective expression of ideas or viewpoints to others in individual or group situations (includes gestures, nonverbal communications, and the use of visual aids). Clear expression of ideas in writing and in appropriate grammatical form.

5. *Motivation.* Understanding individual behavior and providing appropriate stimulation to bring about goal achievement.

6. *Personal impact.* Creating a good early impression, commanding attention and respect, and showing an air of confidence through one's verbal and nonverbal presentation.

7. *Social objectivity.* This dimension has to do with a person's freedom from prejudices against racial, ethnic, socioeconomic, educational, and other kinds of groups.

8. *Recruitment, selection, training subordinates.*

9. *Supervision of subordinates.*

10. *Negotiation skills.*

C. PERSONAL CHARACTERISTICS[5]

1. *Analytical thinking.* Identifying the fundamental ideas, concepts, themes, or issues that help to integrate, interpret, and explain underlying patterns in a set of information or data.

2. *Range of interests.* Exploring to what extent the person is interested in a variety of fields of activity, such as science, politics, sports, music, and art.

3. *Behavior flexibility.* Modifying behavior to reach a goal; adapting one's behavior to respond functionally to changes in the situation or environment.

4. *Resistance to stress.* Stability of performance under pressure or opposition, or both.

5. *Tolerance of uncertainty.* Maintaining effectiveness when working in varying environments, on varying or new tasks or with a variety of people.

6. *Self-objectivity.* Realistic evaluation of one's own assets and liabilities; this includes insight into personal motives, skills, and abilities as applied to the job.

---

[5] Idem.

7. *Energy.*
8. *Self-discipline*—time management.
9. *Primacy of work.* Extent to which the person finds satisfaction from work more important than satisfactions from other areas of his or her life.
10. *Values.* The ideals to which one adheres that influence behavior.

This latter category of personal characteristics and some of the skill areas have been receiving increasing attention by the behavioral scientists of late. There is much research that suggests these skills and characteristics are measurable and teachable.[6]

2. The second step in the development process is the assessment of each individual's training and development needs. This should be accomplished through the individual's initiative and personal assessment, and through the manager's initiative and performance appraisal of the individual. It must be emphasized that, since training and development is an individual process, a personal training and development plan is necessary for each individual in the marketing organization. Many major companies utilize the assessment center concept, whereby individuals go through a battery of measurement and testing experiences.

These experiences include psychological tests, role-playing, projection techniques, in-basket exercises, simulation, and gaming exercises. The pioneering work of American Telephone & Telegraph in this area has been well documented.[7]

3. The third basic step in the development process is a matching of the educational needs of the individual to the educational resources and programs available, both those sponsored by the company and those available outside the company. The educational resources will include programs, job assignments, and self-development materials.

Let us turn our attention now to the design of specific internal training and development programs. This process includes the following steps:

1. Set *objectives* for each education program.
2. Design the *content* and *curricula* of the program.

---

[6] See, for example, the work of R. Boyatzis, *The Competent Manager;* the American Management Association's Competency Based Development program; the work of Douglas Bray et al. of A.T.T., *Formative Years in Business;* and William Byham of Development Dimensions, Inc., Pittsburgh, Pa.

[7] Bray et al., *Formative Years in Business.*

3. Determine the training *methods* to be used.
4. Decide *when* the programs will be conducted.
5. Decide *who* will do the training.

1. Set *objectives* for the development programs: Training and development program objectives should be specific and should evolve from the training needs of the organization and the individual—in our case, the marketing manager. To be clearly stated and understood, the objectives should be in writing. Formalized objectives also facilitate evaluation of the program. Whenever possible, program objectives should be measurable, or at least capable of estimated accomplishment. Objectives to be set fall into at least three categories:

   a. The knowledge, skills, and personal characteristics required for the job;
   b. Individual behavior (i.e., how one behaves in the performance of the job). The behavioral scientists have focused a great deal of late on the concept of behavior modification.
   c. Organization results (i.e., more efficient communications, coordination, planning, and the development of a corporate culture).

2. Design the program *content* and *curricula:* The program content must reflect the training and development needs of the marketing manager. The list of attributes, knowledge, skills, and personal characteristics described above suggest the areas to be included in the program content. An analysis of the qualifications required to be an effective marketing manager suggests that the following be included in the program content:

   a. The marketing manager must be quantitatively oriented to utilize the capabilities of the computer and to be compatible with it. The manager must have an appreciation for what the computer can do and how it can be used to assist in the larger job responsibilities. Decisions regarding pricing, advertising, the size of the sales force, territorial design and coverage, warehouse location, inventory and product planning, and many other areas should be based less on intuition and guesswork but more on fact and logic.
   b. The marketing manager must have a familiarity with and working knowledge of behavioral and humanistic concepts, which are absolutely necessary to manage the kind of employee described earlier in this chapter.
   c. The marketing manager's interactions with the changing

environment require an ability to apply the insights of the social sciences—sociology, cultural anthropology, demography, ecology, and social psychology.

d. The marketing manager's perspective must be worldwide as the barriers of time, distance, cultural differences, and trade regulations are removed. Knowledge of the social sciences should extend to other cultures.

e. The marketing manager must have an appreciation for learning and an ability to learn fast, because knowledge continues to proliferate. The effective executive operates under the concept of a lifetime of education and takes the necessary steps to keep current.

f. The marketing manager must be flexible and have the ability to manage change. He or she is responsive when necessary in adapting to change and is innovative at other times to cause change.

g. The marketing manager will tend to become more of a specialist as knowledge continues to develop and as the scope and complexity of business enlarges. But marketing managers must not be isolated specialists. They will have to relate to the rest of the business. As one progresses in his or her personal career, one will build on the base of this specialization—but will also become more of a generalist. The successful marketing manager can, therefore, best be described as a *generalized specialist.*

3. Determine training *methods:* In *what* is to be learned—knowledge, skills, personal characteristics—to *how* it is to be learned, it becomes apparent that these are multiple approaches to training methodology. The matrix illustrated in Figure 10–4 indicates that each area of learning can be learned/taught in a variety of ways through formal education in a classroom setting, or on-the-job experiences, or a combination of the two.

Formal education techniques are usually off-the-job and include:

a. Straight lecture. This involves a directive approach by a professional trainer.

b. Conferences, workshops, and seminars. These involve a pooling of thoughts and an interchange of ideas. The distinction is that in the conference technique, the trainer acts as the leader; in workshops, the trainer and participants alternate in leading the group; the seminar presents a panel of experts who discuss the material and entertain questions from participants.

c. Case method. This introduces a particular form to the conference technique. It concentrates on a situation and requires an analysis and a distillation of the principles illustrated by the case.

d. Simulation. These techniques attempt to approximate real-world conditions and require the learner to take some action under these conditions. Simulation grew out of army training techniques, whereby battle conditions were simulated with sound motion pictures and the trainee was instructed to react. Industry has adopted this approach, and a number of training techniques have evolved from it.

Business games are one such technique. Here, a hypothetical situation is structured to simulate a real-market situation. The participants are placed on competing teams and have to make a series of decisions. The decisions of one team are unknown to the other teams but have an effect on and are affected by the competitive decisions. The results of the first decision are made known to the team, and they go on to make the next decision. The decisions are scored by an umpire. Games are designed to be scored by computers which can be programmed to print out detailed financial and other reports as a result of actions taken. The computerized games are, of course, more complex and contain many more variables. There are many good noncomputer games, however, for those without access to a computer.

e. Role-playing. This is a form of simulation in which a situation is enacted by members of the group. Critical analysis is helpful in emphasizing techniques and principles. Videotape and other audiovisual devices are particularly useful here.

On-the-job techniques include:

a. Counseling and appraisal techniques. Almost every working contact between supervisor and subordinate provides an opportunity for training. Appraisal sessions offer an opportunity to suggest steps to be taken to improve performance.

b. Job rotation. This technique places the individual in a succession of jobs on a planned basis to provide him or her with the exposure and experience necessary to perform at certain levels. This rotation should conform to the career path described previously.

c. Manuals. These may take the form of programmed instruction, which has proven beneficial to individual learning.

d. Correspondence courses. These are useful for training in knowledge areas and do not require the person to leave the job to attend a training program.

The middle row of Figure 10–4, labelled *combination techniques,* is possibly the most important, since formal edu-

FIGURE 10–4

		What Is to Be Learned		
		Knowledge	Skills	Personal Characteristics
	Formal education	1	2	3
How Learned	Combination techniques	4	5	6
	Practice (on the job)	7	8	9

cation without application is futile, and application without education can be fatal. It is at this row—cells 4, 5, 6—that the continuous nature of education becomes apparent and requires the constant working relationship of supervisor and subordinate. These techniques include on-the-job coaching and supervision of the application of training material to the job. Performance appraisal programs, programs to set standards of performance, and management by objective programs all provide opportunities for combining formal education with practice. Internship programs for college students, as well as leave programs for marketing managers to attend a concentrated education program, are further examples of this approach.

4. Decide *when* the programs are to be conducted: Training and development programs are usually offered to individuals in a particular job to help their performance in that job. Some thought, however, must be given to exposing promotable candidates to training programs geared to their future jobs. The use of the career path suggests the points in an individual's

progression in the company at which they should be involved in formal educational programs. These might be laid out on a continuum that includes a series of formal educational programs, interrupted by on-the-job practice and then a subsequent return to formal programs at different stages of the individual's career.

5. Decide *who* will do the training: Here, again, as in determining training methods, there is a combination of individuals and institutions involved in conducting educational programs. Figure 10–5 describes a matrix of these relationships. Univer-

---

FIGURE 10–5

		What Learned		
		Knowledge	Skills	Personal Characteristics
	Universities and Professional Associations	Yes 1	Yes 2	Some 3
Who Provides	Overlap Zone: Joint Efforts	Some 4	Yes 5	Yes 6
	Employers: Inside staff Outside professionals Supervisors	Some 7	Yes 8	Yes 9

---

sities, through their MBA programs, executive development, and other nondegree programs, are particularly proficient in cell 1 and decreasingly effective in cells 2 and 3. Employers' programs concentrate on cells 7, 8, and 9, and they are particularly effective in cells 8 and 9. The overlap zone, the joint efforts of university programs and corporate programs, is especially effective in developing skills and personal characteristics (cells 5 and 6). These joint efforts might include internships, for example, or an individual enrolling in a formal program sponsored by a university and monitored in the application of the program back on the job.

This matrix, presented in Figure 10–5, provides a guideline for analyzing the various roles to be played in the training and development of the marketing manager. Regardless of who actually conducts the educational program, however, the role of the marketing manager's immediate supervisor cannot be overemphasized. The responsibility for training and development rests with the employee's immediate supervisor and cannot be shifted to corporate staff. The supervisor's role is to: *(a)* determine the individual's training needs; *(b)* select the formal and informal programs designed to satisfy those needs; *(c)* assist in conducting formal courses, where applicable; and *(d)* supervise the individual's progress on the personal development plan.

EVALUATING THE TRAINING AND DEVELOPMENT PROGRAM

There is no adequate theory of measurement of the effectiveness of training programs. However, this does not excuse management from attempting to evaluate the programs against the *objective established* for the programs. Basically, the following are areas for evaluation:

1. *Reaction*. How do the participants feel about the program—content, methods, facilities, lecturers? Questionnaire techniques are usually employed to evaluate reactions.
2. *Learning*. The knowledge and skills areas usually have learned objectives which can be measured through tests. The learning should be measured against what the individual knew *before* the course to determine the *value added* by the training program.
3. *Behavior change*. To evaluate behavioral change and relate the results to a training experience is difficult. However, a comparison of preprogram behavior and post-program behavior in specific areas can be revealing. Further, a comparison of a behavior trait exhibited by participants of a program against the same behavior pattern of a control group of nonparticipants is an important measure of program effectiveness.
4. *Organizational results*. As in all evaluation techniques, this area must be related to the objectives set and underscore the necessity to set thoughtful objectives for development programs. Again, the use of preprogram and post-program testing, and a control group, are advised. Some typical evaluation criteria that might be used in assessing organizational results include:
   a. *Turnover ratios*. Ratios kept before the institution of a training program may be compared to post-training ratios. Any improvement may be partly attributed to training.
   b. *Number of unfilled positions*. Since training should reduce turnover and provide a reservoir of managerial talent, a low

number of unfilled positions indicates that training is effective.

c. *Number of promotions.* Promotions, as they reflect satisfactory performance in prior jobs, reflect well on the training program.

d. *Performance appraisal.* This may reveal the impact of training on performance. Comparisons between different groups of personnel, one which has been exposed to training and one which has not, can provide meaningful evaluation of the program.

e. *Goal achievement.* This is often looked upon as a measure of training effectiveness. The difficulty is that the contribution of training versus other inputs to the accomplishment of a goal defies measurement.

It is obvious that there is no single, accurate approach to determining training effectiveness. The main difficulty is in isolating its impact on performance. What must be done is to establish clear-cut learning objectives for a training program in the areas of knowledge, skills, and personal characteristics. Then the measurement process should determine whether these attributes have been acquired and developed. Measurement methodology to do this has been developed by the behavior scientists.[8]

SUMMARY

This chapter ends where it began, with the notion that the development of human resources is one of management's most serious responsibilities. Success or failure in this area appears to be primarily a function of the attitudes of top management. In this regard, certain factors are relevant:

1. Management must recognize that there is a distinction between training and development. Training is only part of the overall concept of developing individuals. Development is person oriented.

2. Management must recognize that all development is self-development, and that each individual must be motivated to actualize his or her capabilities and realize their fullest potential.

3. Management must recognize that, since development is self-development, the role of the corporation is to provide the climate, guidelines, incentives, and tools necessary for training and development to take place.

---

[8] For example, the work of Bray, Bayatzis, Byham, and others cited previously.

4. Management must make a commitment of human and financial resources to the training function. Full-time training specialists should be considered captive consultants to the organization.

5. Management must recognize that the responsibility for training and development rests ultimately with the employee's immediate supervisor and cannot be shifted to a staff department. The role of the line executive in training and developing is to: *(a)* determine the individual's training needs, *(b)* select the formal training programs designed to satisfy these needs, *(c)* assist in designing and conducting formal training courses, and *(d)* supervise and control the individual's progress in his training program.

6. Methods for evaluating the effectiveness of training programs must be developed and implemented.

In the long run, there is a strong positive correlation between the standing and profitability of a company and its commitment to formal training and development. Investment in people is the most important investment for the future.

11

WHO MANAGES THE MARKETING PROGRAM

by
Bruce S. Fisher

Lightolier, Inc.

Companies which have adopted the marketing concept also have understood the importance of a coordinated, organizational approach to guarantee a strong and unified marketing effort. Rather than allowing sales, advertising, market research, product management, and other marketing functions to go forth in separate directions, these corporations have assigned key managers to be responsible for making sure that established goals and policies are carried out, with the customer's viewpoint always primary.

Depending upon the particular organization, the individual responsible for the marketing program could be one of the following:

1. Large, divisionalized company: Vice President–Marketing
2. Smaller company: Marketing Director

Integration is the key term, regardless of the size of firm, breadth and complexity of the product line, and sophistication of the organization.

If a company is operating in accordance with the marketing concept, all departments within the operation, not just marketing, must look to the external environment for direction. Organization, per se, won't necessarily create a viable customer-oriented approach. Just because one individual is given the responsibility doesn't mean success is guaranteed. In fact, in a survey of 464 companies completed by the Sales Executive Club of New York, only 60 percent had the sales manager reporting to the top marketing executive.

In summary, the marketing concept is a philosophy, not an organization chart. Every key departmental executive, as well as the CEO, has a tremendous interest in the marketing program. Success in the 1980s will, in many markets, depend on attaining greater share. Therefore, the ability of the marketing department to marshal all the strengths of a company becomes increasingly critical. In some cases, survival will be at stake.

FUNCTIONS TO BE MANAGED

In the expanded marketing department of the 1980s, a varied and long list of functions are being consolidated under this umbrella. Also, there are some problems which occur beyond the large number of activities involved. These include:

1. Communication between the marketing department and the rest of the organization.
2. Integration of all marketing activities into one cohesive plan.
3. Communication of this plan to widespread (worldwide) geographic areas and particular segments of the market.
4. Many functions cannot be separated easily due to personnel involved or corporate organizational structures.

Victor Buell attempted to list the key marketing functions and who was responsible for their management.[1] These are:

Function	Who Manages
1. Set policies and objectives.	1. Corporate and marketing management.
2. Identify markets for present and new products.	2. Marketing research
3. Measure company's and competitors' standing in market.	3. Marketing research.
4. Forecast sales.	4. Marketing research and sales.
5. Recommend product and package specifications.	5. Product manager, marketing research, marketing manager.
6. Select channels of distribution.	6. Sales, marketing research, marketing manager.
7. Determine strategy and tactics.	7. Marketing manager and department heads.

[1] Victor Buell, Editor in Chief, *Handbook of Modern Marketing* (New York, McGraw-Hill, 1970), pp. 8–9.

Function	Who Manages

8. Prepare short-range plans
  a. Sales plans
  b. Advertising and sales promotion plans
  c. Product introductions
	8. Marketing manager
	  a. Sales management
	  b. Advertising management
	
	  c. Product manager, advertising, and sales.

9. Prepare budgets.	9. Marketing manager and department heads

10. Recommend and set prices
  a. Administer prices
	10. Marketing manager
	  a. Sales or product manager

11. Execute plans
  a. Sales
  b. Advertising and sales promotion
  c. Introduce new products
	11. Marketing department
	  a. Sales
	  b. Advertising and ad agency
	
	  c. Sales and advertising

12. Manpower training and development.	12. Training department and all levels of supervision.
13. Arrange for order processing, field inventories, and shipments.	13. Marketing and traffic.

14. Recommend credit and collection policies and procedures
  a. Administer
	14. Sales and marketing management, finance
	  a. Finance and sales

15. Provide customer services.	15. Customer services, technical services, sales.
16. Establish and administer controls.	16. All levels of supervision.
17. Prepare long-range plans.	17. Marketing manager and department heads.

Source: Victor Buell, Editor in Chief, *Handbook of Modern Marketing* (New York: McGraw-Hill, 1970), pp. 8–9.

MARKETING MANAGEMENT FOR THE MULTIDIVISIONAL COMPANIES

Because corporate structures are becoming increasingly complex due to mergers and multiple-product companies, management of the marketing function becomes even more difficult. In fact, a third variable has come into play during the past few years—a market-oriented division. Products, per se, are no longer the key criteria but rather a specific group of end users; for example, residential versus commercial. Under the old system, products would be managed for all markets in a particular division. This resulted in a lack of focus on market segmentation and compromises in the product and marketing program. Bloated and unwieldy marketing organizations grew at the division and corporate level. Problems of reporting also surfaced, since the division marketing group had to contend with the general manager as well as with the corporate staff. In this mixed-up and complicated environment, the management of the marketing program got lost in a maze of organization and politics. Companies tended not to move decisively, no clear lines of responsibility existed, and firms which allowed these conditions to exist found themselves in real trouble during the recession of the early 1980s. Although never perfect, steps can be taken to minimize such blocks to corporate growth and profitability. When divisionalizing, agreement must be reached on which marketing functions should be assigned to a particular division and which, if any, should be given to corporate. Three areas need analysis:

1. *Profit responsibility.* One cannot hold a general manager accountable under a P&L system unless he or she has control over the key elements of the marketing program (i.e., sales, advertising, product management, pricing, and promotion).

2. *Costs.* Certain functions, such as market research, can be performed more economically at the corporate level. To this extent, significant analysis should be completed to determine which tasks belong in the division and which can be completed most effectively at corporate.

3. *Amount of corporate authority.* As a general principle, the divisions should retain as much authority over their own destiny as can be justified from a size and affordability point of view. This increases their effectiveness in managing the marketing program, since the division is closest to the market and should have the best feel for what is needed.

Because of overhead and organizational implications, the corporate marketing executive and staff have been subjected to increasing pressure. Many companies have abandoned the system altogether. If organized properly, though, they do serve a purpose. Criteria for placing key functions include:

1. Decentralization versus centralization of authority—in a highly decentralized company, the division should handle as many marketing functions as possible. In a centralized environment the opposite would be true.

2. Scope of division and period cost considerations—in small divisions with overhead pressures, the corporate staff plays a bigger role.

3. Ability of divisional marketing team—if limited, reliance will be placed on corporate staff.

4. Expertise of division general managers—if not in marketing, the same holds true as in point number three.

5. Comparison of products and markets between divisions—if similar, the corporate marketing staff has an important coordination and communication function. If different, the opposite would be true.

6. Advertising policies—staff usually plays a large role if there is one umbrella advertising contract for all divisions, since there would probably be significant economies of scale. Also, if a corporation needs an image campaign, this can best be accomplished at the corporate level.

GENERAL RESPONSIBILITIES OF CORPORATE MARKETING GROUP

In general, this group is responsible for establishing the overall corporate marketing objectives and policies, coordinating marketing activities throughout the divisions, and making sure these activities are integrated within the other functions of the company. Specific services include:

1. Leadership in the guidance and coordination of the marketing job.
2. Advisor to the CEO and division general managers on all marketing subjects.
3. Evaluation of the individual divisional marketing plans.
4. Short- and long-range planning in all areas of marketing.
5. Supervision and direction of all advertising programs at the corporate and divisional levels.
6. Provide marketing services to the divisions on an as-needed basis.

THE NEED FOR TEAMWORK

Because marketing has become the catalyst for growth and profitability in many companies, coordination between functional departments is very important. Everyone must feel as if they have a piece of the action. When asking, "Who manages the marketing program?" the answer should be, "We all do." Two examples of how this may be accomplished are:

1. Adding other functions, full time, to the marketing staff. For example, a product manager could have a factory engineer reporting to him or her so a strong technical assist is available during the idea formulation stage. This individual must also have a strong dotted-line relationship with manufacturing so each group maximizes available resources and increases productivity.

2. Establishing an action group, consisting of representatives from various functional departments to operate as a unified team in setting marketing objectives, strategies, and programs for a given project. This can also be done within the marketing department itself by taking members of sales, advertising, product management, and research, and creating an action team.

THE ROLE OF THE CEO

In 1980, a Dartmouth marketing professor, Frederick E. Webster, Jr., published a study on the attitudes of the CEOs about their marketing people.[2] In general, Webster found that top management does not feel that the marketing group has their act together. Conversely, current periodicals have repeatedly talked about the short-term view of most CEOs, and how this has gotten many companies in real trouble in the past five years. There seems to be a direct conflict between what each group is looking for.

According to Webster, the CEO's biggest complaint was "the lack of innovative and entrepreneurial thinking on the part of the marketing organization in response to a changing marketplace." Yet, we have received many unfavorable comments about the demands made by top management. Chris Argyris found that many CEOs are perceived as "encouraging conformity among their subordinates and discouraging others from taking risks."[3]

In the Webster study, CEOs felt that marketing was a key tactical function but were concerned about whether they challenged their people enough. There was also confusion over whether marketing was a staff planning function or a line sales-related function charged with meeting the current shipping budget. Professor Argyris observed: "They [CEOs] want innovation, but they want it their way. Thus, by setting tight managerial controls (especially financial) and by making highly detailed plans (especially in marketing, sales, manufacturing, and engineering), he [the CEO] may unwittingly encourage dependency, submissiveness, and lack of initiative among subordinates."[4]

On a different note, Webster found senior managers upset with marketing executives who were preoccupied with tactical problems,

---

[2] Frederick E. Webster, Jr., "Top Management View of the Marketing Function," *Marketing Science Institute,* November 1980.

[3] Chris Argyris, "The CEO's Behavior: Key to Organizational Development," *Harvard Business Review,* March–April, 1973, p. 56.

[4] Ibid., p. 57.

such as media selection, ad copy, sales administration, trade shows, and the like. They should be concentrating on broad strategic issues so that the entire business is pointed in the right direction. Yet, it is the responsibility of the CEO to create an atmosphere which encourages the proper focus by the marketing group. A good example of this issue involves advertising: setting objectives and objective measurement of results.

When the Marketing Communications Research Center (MCRC, now part of the Advertising Research Foundation) surveyed 30 CEOs of leading manufacturing companies, it found that most of them did not believe advertising was really measurable.[5] Only 25 percent of the respondents admitted to setting objectives to begin with; 44 percent cited image building as their primary focus, and only 14 percent said new product introduction was a critical function of advertising.

Because so few companies set goals for advertising, the results are not apparent. Therefore, top management's negative view of the function is reinforced. Another problem occurs because the same "bottom line" measures utilized in sales and manufacturing are forced into advertising. This just reinforces the misunderstanding between top management and marketing. There appears to be an unwillingness on the part of top management to judge advertising as a communication message (creative strategy and quality) as well as cost. Measures of ad readership scores and user awareness are utilized to judge effectiveness, but CEOs generally assume this is strictly commensurate with media cost-per-reader. Part of the problem, as raised by Rabin Research of Chicago in a 1981 study,[6] is the common complaint of "metooism" by the advertising fraternity. Instead of looking for a creative way to differentiate a particular brand, advertising agencies tend to take the easy way out and position products similar to competition.

The advertising scenario clearly demonstrates the general conflict between the CEO and marketing. Are agencies truly allowed to be creative? Or is the entire process just a microcosm of the bigger problem? We strongly believe it is. If the CEO understands the importance of establishing longer-term marketing strategies, he or she must encourage a different environment, one which values creativity, entrepreneurship, and the role of "champion" by the marketing group. The CEO cannot "manage" the marketing program through a rigid structure so disciplined that it stifles an individualized thought process by marketing executives. We do not discount the roller coaster economy forecast by many for the 1980s. Why not put the burden where it

---

[5] MCRC.

[6] Bob Donath, "Chief Executives and Marketers: Who's Doing It to Whom?" *Industrial Marketing*, November, 1982, p. 66.

belongs? Marketing people, if they are worth what they are being paid, should take these kinds of external factors into account during the establishment of overall strategies.

PROCTER & GAMBLE: AN IMPORTANT LESSON

Procter & Gamble, long recognized as one of the nation's most successful packaged goods company, is undergoing changes which would have been considered heresy a few years ago. *Business Week* chronicled the revised expectations of P&G's CEO, John G. Smale.[7] Besides placing greater emphasis on cost control, Smale seemed determined to push P&G managers to take more risks and exploit opportunities in the marketplace. Niche competitors had quietly carved out a share in some of P&G's best markets because of their ability to move decisively when action was warranted. Because the philosophy at P&G has been to make decisions based upon facts and not on educated guesses, speeding up decision making will be difficult.

The challenge is epitomized by the centralized and bureaucratic approach to marketing they've developed over the past 30 years. They have undercut their brand management system that developed product champions who felt they could really sponsor a particular piece of business. One group vice president, described in the *Business Week* article, had actually become involved in the detail of writing recipes for food products.[8]

Too many decisions are being forced up the organizational ladder to senior managers farthest away from the market. An example given involved the exchange of memos, and the decision to supply products in Japan only to supermarkets (and to avoid smaller retailers). P&G lost an estimated $100 million in sales because executives at headquarters did not allow this type of decision to be made locally. The principle of allowing those closest to the market to manage the marketing program is a valid and important business strategy.

SUMMARY

Business must have a marketing orientation in order to be successful in today's marketplace. But many companies are either sales or production-oriented and ignore the marketing concept. In effect, nonmarketing exec-

---

[7] "Why Procter & Gamble Is Playing It Even Tougher," *Business Week,* July 18, 1983.

[8] Ibid.

utives end up managing the marketing program. The following summarizes this phenomenon:[9]

Business Orientations

Production orientation

Focuses on:	What we can make.
Deemphasizes:	What we know how to sell.
Ignores:	Customer needs.

Sales orientation

Focuses on:	Pushing what we've got.
Deemphasizes:	Meeting customer need through product innovation.

Marketing orientation

Focuses on:	Meeting customer needs.	
Requires:	(1)	Precise definition of target markets.
	(2)	Detailed understanding of customer needs.
Results in:	(1)	All business functions oriented toward serving customers.
	(2)	Above-average long-run profit.

Dynamic, clearly defined signals must be given by the CEO regarding management of the marketing program:

1. Those closest to the market should have the most responsibility for decision making.
2. The responsibilities of division and corporate marketing groups should be established to avoid confusion, to increase productivity, and to maximize results.
3. A long-term commitment must be made to marketing strategies, avoiding the short-term return-on-investment mentality which discouraged creativity and differentiated programs.
4. A cultural environment must be encouraged, dedicated to a total involvement by all operating departments in the marketing program.

"Who manages the marketing program?" Answer: "We all do." The marketing department acts as a quarterback in developing a team approach so that everyone feels ownership of the marketing opportunity.

---

[9] Frank R. Bacon, Jr., and Thomas W. Butler, Jr., *Planned Innovation* (Ann Arbor: University of Michigan Press, 1981).

BIBLIOGRAPHY

American Management Association. *The Marketing Job: Responsibilities of the Top Man and His Staff.* New York: American Management Association, 1961

Argyris, Chris. "The CEO's Behavior: Key to Organizational Development." *Harvard Business Review,* March–April 1973.

Bacon, Frank R. Jr., and Thomas W. Butler, Jr. *Planned Innovation.* Ann Arbor: University of Michigan Press, 1981.

"Why Procter & Gamble Is Playing It Even Tougher." *Business Week,* July 18, 1983.

Carrood, Paul A., and Connie A. Carrood. "Strategic Interfacing of R&D and Marketing." *Research Management,* January 1982.

Corbin, Arnold. "Organization for Marketing." *Handbook of Modern Marketing,* 1970.

Donath, Bob. "Chief Executives and Marketers: Who's Doing It to Whom?" *Industrial Marketing,* November 1982.

"The Industrial Product Manager—General without an Army." *Marketing Forum,* October 1965.

Webster, Frederick E., Jr. "Top Management View of the Marketing Function." *Marketing Science Institute,* November 1980

12

MANAGING AND IMPROVING MARKETING PRODUCTIVITY

by
Dale P. Hugo

Loctite Corporation

INTRODUCTION

The three topics at hand are: defining, managing, and improving marketing productivity. Marketing productivity can be defined as getting the most value from the available economic, creative, and personnel resources. It differs from the numerical payback orientation of sales, in the general sense, because much of the payback cannot be easily identified or quantified. Productive marketing does not have an exclusive franchise on creativity, however.

Improving productivity is also a matter of relativity, inasmuch as the marketing output is the sum total of people and actions, plus resources employed. The difficulty of defining and measuring marketing productivity should not discourage the manager from the continuing goal of improving it.

Some concepts in this realm are explored in the following pages. Each of them is easily understandable, even though the end results may not be easily measurable.

PUTTING IT TOGETHER

Productive marketing first has to be considered in the context of company philosophy, management style, and the charting of the marketing course.

Company Philosophy

The marketing function has to be considered as a positive, contributing factor to the company's well-being. Too many companies have the marketing group reporting to sales management or positioned as a staff/overhead operation. It can be readily appreciated that such a structural positioning often places marketing in a secondary rank perception within the general organization and can reduce its effective contribution to the overall success of the company.

The sales function should utilize a great deal of creativity, but it is primarily concerned with the short-term generation of sales and profits (somebody has to keep the money coming!). Marketing, on the other hand, tends to provide short and long-term strategic planning, product and market development, and marketing programs—including advertising and sales promotion. Both sides of the equation are necessary to successfully operate in the marketplace. The more cohesive this joint operation becomes, the more effective it will be in the creative process and in the economic payback. Mutual respect and cooperation between these groups is essential.

Management Style

Organization charts are necessary to establish the formal chain of command and the authority relationships within the company. But a chart cannot reflect management style. Rigid insistence on the formalities of organization can easily stifle marketing creativity—exactly the opposite result desired. Lengthy project approval lists often serve the same negative function, albeit a necessary one in the case of legal clearances and overall approval requirements.

Two methods of enhancing management productivity are: (1) keeping the lines of authority clear but reasonably loose and (2) encouraging personal creativity at all levels. An open door and a cup of coffee can be very beneficial. Informal discussions and openness in communication provide a fertile bed for creativity, as well as promoting a desired group cohesiveness and esprit de corps.

Charting the Course

Management flexibility in the organization structure and outlook does not imply random freedom in the marketing effort.

There should be a clear corporate or division charter, or both, and a mission statement. The Loctite Corporation recently developed the corporate mission statement excerpted below. It clearly defines the corporate mission and management style; the complete statement can be found at the end of the chapter.

The Loctite Way[1]

Mission. We will be the #1 market share seller of high value, branded chemical products that help our customers assemble, seal, repair, and maintain things. . . .

We expect to be a growth company, and plan to grow at an above average rate. . . .

We are dedicated to the belief that our people are our most important resource. . . . We believe people respond positively when they feel involved, are free to participate, have their opinions considered, and see clearly the opportunity to develop. . . .

We are a market-oriented company that will always recognize that our customers are "all important." We will provide high customer value in product quality and service, and expect a fair price in return.

We seek a company that is flexible, innovative, responsive, and entrepreneurial in style. We are results-oriented, and favor substance over form, and quality over quantity.

The above addresses the overall mission of the corporate entity, its people, and its management style. The company's financial results, in good times and bad, reflect the positive impact of this statement. It took a group of senior management executives from each major division several months to develop it. The "Loctite Way" has been printed in the annual report and disseminated throughout the management structure to clearly chart the course and improve profitability in the sense of individual goal setting, style, and fulfillment—all with the proper focus on the marketplace and end user.

WHO DOES WHAT?

The most common answer to this topical question is the organization chart and position descriptions. While such charting is usually necessary, the creative and productive marketing organization transcends the rigidities of formal structure.

The Marketing Organism

Today's marketplace demands a fair amount of flexibility, as well as marketing creativity. A potentially rewarding organizational concept is that of the project team, or "marketing organism." It is so defined because the expertise of many different individuals and disciplines can be brought together, on an "as needed" basis. They can explore and

---

[1] "The Loctite Way," statement of Loctite Corporation's business philosophy. Approved by the board of directors February 26, 1982. Excerpted and reprinted by permission.

exploit new product and marketing opportunities without unduly infringing on anyone's time and without the need for standing committees.

The focus of the project will determine the makeup of the team. In the early stages, it will heavily involve R&D personnel, evolving through primary and secondary packaging, consumer/market research, graphics design and displays, sales promotion, and so forth. It provides the necessary focus of the various specialists along the way, and it keeps the creative enthusiasm generating by the evolutionary makeup of the group. In all cases, the project team should be limited in the number of participants at any one time. When the project is successfully completed, however, all the participants should receive appropriate recognition of their contributions.

Direction and Flexibility

As previously noted, the general direction of the company is found in the mission statement. Any such statement, however, cannot detail market, product, and other needs. This detailed direction is found in the company's annual business plan. Usually included are marketing, sales, research and development, manufacturing, distribution, and financial plans. Such plans normally cover a three to five year period.

Each product manager is responsible for defining the market and product needs, and the total brand requirements—including products, packaging, pricing, promotion, and so forth. When the market manager organizational structure is utilized, that individual is the one who groups together the various plans. The primary requirement is to have a well-coordinated market plan that has clearly defined objectives and has detailed plans and programs designed to reach those objectives, with stated financial rewards. The total market plans are then combined to make up the overall business plan.

The direction afforded by such planning varies widely, as a reflection of management style. Too often the planning involved is viewed as a time-wasting useless exercise. After completion, the annual plan is stored away for another year. The plan should be an action plan—minimum preamble and statistical examination, maximum action steps to be taken. And it should be reviewed quarterly or semiannually to determine what progress has been made or what changes are required because of changed conditions, or both.

Flexibility is a desirable component in all such planning. As noted, conditions can change rapidly in the marketplace—competition, consumer/user attitudes, or whatever. Not every contingency can be anticipated, but those that can be defined should be part of the planning process.

Flexibility can be considered as "bending without breaking." Plans can be modified to reflect changing needs, if necessary; but enough flexibility should be built into the plans to allow for some modification or alternative actions.

A flexible planning method is the use of the "go-ahead" plan to expand the planning horizon. The concept assumes that additional investment of resources will result in additional financial payback. Such investment can include additional advertising, incentive programs, or other alternatives. The basic plan is considered minimal goal achievement. The additional payback is to be funded by additional resource investment, however, not just higher management expectations.

Product Management

The product manager organizational structure is used by many companies. Some of the advantages of this concept include product focus, personal commitment, and market knowledge. The major problems include "technological tunnelvision," and "marketing myopia." That is, there is such a concentration on a short range of products and a few markets that coordination with other areas is difficult, and a disproportionate amount of the company's resources may be dedicated to these products or markets. Personnel turnover can also cause rapid changes in how the products are marketed, which dilutes marketing effectiveness. (More detailed analysis of the advantages and disadvantages of the product manager organizational can be found elsewhere in this book.)

Market Management

A more recent organizational concept is that of the market manager. The total marketplace, trade channels, and the end user are the focal points for the entire market and related product groups.

For example, a company serving the consumer household and automotive markets would assign them to a consumer market manager and an automotive market manager, respectively. Related product managers would report to each market manager so that planning, products, and programs would be coordinated, on one hand, and properly focused on the two marketplaces, on the other. Coordination between these market managers would occur at the next senior marketing or general management level.

The market manager is not only concerned with coordinating product manager activities but also with longer-range planning and special projects.

Responsibility, Rewards, and Recognition

The Loctite corporate mission statement, previously noted, describes the expectations for employee performance, and the ensuing rewards:

> We believe that people respond positively to recognition, involvement, courtesy, and appreciation of their efforts. We-believe decision making is best made by the competent person closest to the situation and to all the facts. Managers are expected to clearly communicate goals, to encourage people to make their "job-rightful decisions," and to support their people.[2]

The statement goes on to comment about "job security based on performance," and that "all employees should be compensated fairly, and in proportion to their contributions to the Company's success." As much time should be spent on the proper compensation incentives for inside management as to the sales force compensation method.

IMPROVING MARKETING PRODUCTIVITY

Marketing productivity and its improvement is the sum total of much planning and effort. Some of these concepts may be useful in developing concepts and successfully implementing the marketing effort.

The Market Perspective

The market perspective is an essential ingredient in managing and improving marketing productivity. Simply, it is determining the needs of the marketplace and the company resources required to fulfill those needs, and it starts with the end users.

The identity of the users, what they need, or think they need, and how their needs can be fulfilled are the three basic questions involved. A specific need is not necessarily the only consideration, either. For example, several recent advertising slogans have addressed the consumers' general needs:

— "The right thing to fix almost anything."
— "The right tool."
— "_____helps you do things right."

The point of these messages is, "Whatever your need, we have the answer." It is a particularly effective way for a multiproducts company to promote the usefulness of a number of products or services.

It also pays to have a listening eye; that is, reading consumer letters that outline needs and complaints derived from using the com-

---

[2] Ibid.

pany's products. An eyeglass repair adhesive was recently launched in direct response to numerous consumer complaints about the failure of other products to make this particular repair. Instructions were also changed on a number of products over time because of consumer confusion, or lack of clarity in the directions.

A growing information tool is the use of toll-free consumer information telephone numbers. This allows the consumer to secure instant help on product applications, or on general product/service information, without the long delays and bother of correspondence. It is a particularly useful concept in the world of consumerism.

Creative Communication

Communication seems like such an obvious need; but it is often stalemated by the formal organization or by the insulated individuals or departments. It is important to observe the formal organization; but formal and informal communication should be an integrated function, as well as management style.

A useful communications tool is the use of interdepartmental creative seminars. This concept has been used to revitalize product lines and to develop others. Individuals from various departments were invited and presented with a very sparse subject outline on easel charts. After each major topic was developed by the group, the filled-out chart was posted on the wall so the group could refer to the different points, as well as to see the progress of the discussion topic. It is suggested that such seminars be limited to a half day, with one major discussion covered. Participant fatigue can overcome protracted creative sessions.

Joint marketing conferences also are a useful communications device for company divisions. These conferences serve to acquaint the various individuals, provide information and idea exchanges, and promote the realization that most marketing challenges are common to seemingly diverse marketing groups. Such conferences can be a productive investment for the company.

Internal and External Strengths

Every business entity has some real or potential marketing strengths that are not necessarily related to size. For example, marketing flexibility can be practiced by anyone—and so can creativity.

Rather than assume that you know the strengths, take the time to list them. Afterward, determine which ones can be specifically exploited to enhance the marketing effort. It may be difficult to determine whether a strength is internal or external, but it doesn't matter as long as it can be exploited.

Some examples of these company strengths are listed below.

Strength	Advantage
Company/brand awareness.	Consumer preference. High market share. Strong distribution network.
R&D capabilities.	High product quality. New product development.
Manufacturing facilities.	Lower product cost. Competitive selling price or higher profit margin, or both.
Sales force.	Consistent trade coverage. Account programming.
Promotion investment.	Brand awareness. Point-of-purchase displays. Pull-through promotions.

Nonduplicative Effort

Duplication of effort can be a major contributor to negative productivity in the marketing effort. It can occur within a department or, more likely, between departments. Joint strategy sessions, creative seminars, and the like can be used to alleviate the situation. Continuing communication of plans and efforts will provide the various parties with the knowledge of progress made and additional help or information required.

The elimination of unnecessary effort can be visualized as a pie chart with the various functions grouped around the central objectives, as shown in Figures 12–1 and 12–2.

Productive effort starts with the common knowledge of the objectives and the resources required to fulfill those objectives. Clearly defining the responsibilities and timetables is also required, which will reduce or eliminate the overlap of activities. And, as you proceed from the broad planning base to the fulfilled project, the focus becomes more sharply defined. The end result of these efforts should be the optimization of time, effort, and resources.

The project manager should be sure that the project is not distorted by a dominant function (e.g., manufacturing needs, to the detriment of its successful completion). The basic needs of each area—and the proper balance—should be inherent in the planning process. Such

FIGURE 12–1   **FIGURE 12–2**

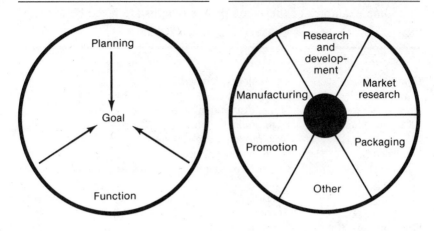

planning and coordination can result in positive synergistic effects, such as additional product benefits, lower costs, and the like. Every person involved should be given the opportunity to contribute and be appropriately recognized for their contributions.

Innovation Can Work Wonders

Encouraging and rewarding innovative marketing concepts is an excellent method of enhancing marketing productivity. It can keep the market leader outdistancing the competition, or help leapfrog the competition.

Here are some innovative marketing concepts that have helped to maintain one company's market leadership:

1. A rust treatment product that destroyed old rust and provided protection against re-rusting.
2. A plastic syringe applicator for adhesives that eliminated waste and allowed easier application.
3. A computerized planogramming service that not only provided recommended product assortments for retailers but also provided financial payback projections.
4. An electronic point of purchase display that helped consumers select the product(s) required to do the selected project.
5. A product that established a new market by fulfilling a long-standing consumer need for repairing laminate countertops.

Innovation spans products and services—and every aspect of marketing. It is the spark of creativity that provides positive use and convenience advantages for the end user and additional rewards for the innovator.

PAYING THE PIPER

Financial resources are always limited. It is extremely important to structure the marketing budget to efficiently and effectively attain the marketing goals. (Details of budget development are found elsewhere in this book.)

Developing the Goals

Attainment of the marketing goals requires that appropriate resources be allocated to each element. The axiom of the chain being as strong as its weakest link is particularly appropriate to the budgeting process. Products and services require adequate marketing budget support if they are to achieve their full market potential and financial payback. Underfunding critical areas can foredoom marketing success.

Some flexibility should be built into the budgeting process, as well as into the market planning. Unexpected opportunities or problems may require additional funding. The marketing budget should not be considered as a source of additional profits, however, to the detriment of the total marketing effort.

Do a Few Things Well

A few well-funded projects are usually preferable to the shotgun approach and the underfunding of critical areas. Clearly defining the project requirements will help to delineate the financial needs; that does not mean only one thing can be accomplished.

For example, one consumer goods company used the "star product" advertising approach for several years. It worked for one product but failed on a subsequent product. Inasmuch as the company had a broad line of products, it switched to a consumer-oriented approach of answering various needs with a variety of products (i.e., "the right thing to fix almost anything"). Either strategy can be effective.

New product development may need additional funding for a growth-oriented company that needs new marketing opportunities. Or, antiquated equipment may need upgrading to provide competitive costs, enhanced product quality—or what have you.

Balance the Checkbook Periodically

Periodic budget reviews provide not only continuing control of expenditures but also the opportunity to reassess goals and funding priorities. That is not to say that projects and priorities should be constantly shifted, because that will confuse issues and perceptions.

DOING IT BETTER THE NEXT TIME

Managing and improving marketing productivity is an ongoing process. It should be considered an active and positive goal by each of the participants involved in the process.

Chart a Clear Course

Setting clearly defined goals and articulating plans to attain those goals are the keystones to maximizing marketing productivity. Communicating those goals, plans, and procedures is also required. Creative seminars, joint department seminars, and periodic reviews are just a few of the methods of maintaining clarity of purpose.

It's a People Business

The computer age still relies on people. Their contributions need to be encouraged, recognized, and rewarded. The best-laid plans, carefully communicated, require the dedication and expertise of people to make them happen. Recognition can be an informal conversation, a lunch, praise in front of others, or a more tangible reward, but it will help to enhance marketing productivity through people. When they are successful, the project manager is successful. Enlarge their responsibilities and reward their efforts as much as possible; kind words cost nothing, but cash is always acceptable!

Encourage a Boundless Outlook

The closed mind is the antipathy of marketing productivity. The creative seminars work because they allow a creative platform beyond the normal job responsibilities for many of the participants.

Emerging industries, new technologies, and the changing world will continue to provide new opportunities. Encourage a boundless outlook of the present and the future. The future belongs to both dreamers and planners. New ways of enhancing marketing productivity will be found by inquisitive minds.

THE LOCTITE WAY[3]

Statement of Loctite Corporation's Business Philosophy

MISSION

We will be the #1 market share seller of high value, branded chemical products that help our customers assemble, seal, repair, and maintain things.

GROWTH AND PROFIT

We expect to be a growth company, and plan to grow at an above average rate, thereby protecting our assets against inflation and making possible job security and advancement opportunities for our people. We expect to earn above average profits and return on equity, thereby providing acceptable return to our shareholders and cash for investments in our future. We refuse to enter the "people first, or profits first" debate. People make our profits, and profits provide for our people. Profit is a good and worthy goal, for it is profit that fuels reward to employees and shareholders. Profit is the responsibility of everyone, and it is our day-to-day performance, including an appreciation of expense control and the need to spend the company's money wisely, that adds or subtracts from profitability.

PEOPLE

We are dedicated to the belief that our people are our most important resource. We believe that people respond positively to recognition, involvement, courtesy and appreciation of their efforts. We believe all Loctite employees should have the freedom to do their job. We believe decision making is best made by the competent person closest to the situation and to all the facts. Managers are expected to clearly communicate goals; to encourage people to make their "job-rightful" decisions; and to support their people.

We believe people respond positively when they feel involved; are free to participate; have their opinions considered; and see clearly the opportunity to develop. People must feel free to constructively expose problems, and to contribute to solutions.

Management is responsible for providing a sense of direction. Managers are responsible for individuals' development. Managers are expected to be self-critical, and to provide an atmosphere encouraging open, constructive confrontation. Managers are expected to face up to problems and make it safe for anyone to seek help in solving problems. Managers will be judged on these abilities.

We believe that everyone benefits when the most capable person "gets the job". We reward tenure and loyalty, and believe in job security based on performance. Office politics is a destructive activity and cannot be condoned.

---

[3] "The Loctite Way" is copyrighted, 1982, by the Loctite Corporation, Newington, Connecticut.

We want people who do their jobs well, and who expect their co-workers to do likewise. All employees should be compensated fairly, and in proportion to their contributions to the company's success.

We believe that a lean, hard working organization helps maintain stable employment, and provides greater opportunity for job enrichment and added responsibility. We believe in enthusiasm at all levels, and managers should be selected for this value.

We believe that all Loctite people are entitled to participate in setting their own goals, and judging their own performance. Every career employee is entitled to have their job performance reviewed at least once a year by their supervisor. Career people interested in other positions are encouraged to discuss job opportunities with their supervisors.

CUSTOMERS

We are a market-oriented company and will always recognize that our customers are "all important." We will provide high customer value in product quality and service, and expect a fair price in return. We maintain focus on our mission, and believe it is our responsibility to be leaders in our markets. We are sensitive to competition, and put the highest priority on new products. But we get our inspiration from our customers and from our evolving vision of the market, not from watching competition. We will constantly listen to the marketplace, responding quickly to our customers' current needs, and anticipating their future needs. We believe such a customer focus is absolutely necessary, and people will be judged on their demonstrated ability to provide and maintain this focus.

ORGANIZATION

We encourage voluntary cooperation over centralized control. We prefer less structured environment, rather than overly controlled, layered organizations. We encourage decentralized decision making, but with a great attendant accountability and responsibility to the remainder of the company. Decentralized groups are expected to put the overall good of the company above their interests. We believe in cross-group collaboration and shared goals. We prefer task teams to permanent structure. We encourage "project champions."

We seek to limit management levels, and push responsibility down into the organization. We prefer to rely on employees' honesty and good judgment, and discourage company-wide or group policies unless critical to running the business.

If policies are needed, it is the responsibility of the involved manager to create them, and for all employees to respect them. We expect conformance to corporate accounting and reporting systems, but we discourage the implementation of "over controls".

We seek a company that is flexible; innovative; responsive; and entrepreneurial in style. We favor simplicity. We want action. We are results oriented, and favor substance over form, and quality over quantity.

We believe in the free flow of information up, down and across organizational lines. We insist on "homework" and planning.

We seek an organization that understands the constant need to adapt to changing environments, and at the same time protects the stability of the organization.

COMPANY

We will remain an independent company. We encourage every employee to become a shareholder; to own a part of the company. We seek to be known as innovative in all areas; as quality-oriented in all areas; and as a high technology company. The company will act responsibly in each local community. We expect all employees to understand our codes of behavior. We encourage all employees to participate in community affairs. We believe firmly in the principles of the free enterprise system.

The Loctite Way expresses our shared values. It is the duty of every employee to keep and vigilantly defend these values. We want Loctite Corporation to be a good place to work, but we do recognize that our Company may not be best for everyone. We encourage individualism, but expect team players who subscribe to our values.

THIS IS THE LOCTITE WAY

Approved by The Board of Directors
Loctite Corporation
February 26, 1982

13

MANAGING THE COMPANY-OWNED SALES FORCE

by
Daniel K. Weadock

Matheson Gas Products, Inc.

ESTABLISHING THE SALES FORCE

The manufacturer of a product or the provider of a service must be concerned with the most efficient and effective way to influence the largest possible audience for each's product or service through a sales force. In order to do this, each must have a detailed knowledge of how the product or service it "sells" reaches the end user or consumer.

Thinking in terms of the flow of goods or services to the end user allows the provider of these products to begin to understand how best to influence the key-purchase control areas with its sales force. A producer of canned fruits or vegetables has a very complex channel of distribution to the end user. The producer might have to sell to wholesalers, distributors, and agents before it can even move its product into a "food store." It then has to influence the food store to purchase its product from the wholesaler, distributor, or agent. The producer then has to influence the "shopper" to "pull" the product off the shelf.

Channel of Distribution Consideration for Establishing the Sales Force

When a sales force is being established—or if it already exists and must be properly maintained and staffed—the flow of goods or services to the end user must be continuously studied by the provider of the goods and services to insure that their sales force is effectively used. An examination of the flow of an industrial product—specialty chemicals for example—from the manufacturer or packager to the end user will show how a sales force should be established and deployed.

Figure 13–1 shows the flow of specialty reagent-grade chemicals to the end user, in terms of producer cost in dollars. The total dollar

---

FIGURE 13–1
Flow of Goods Analysis

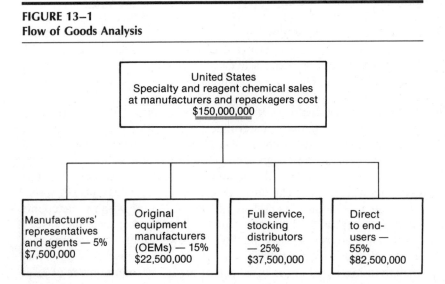

volume for these types of chemicals is shown as $150 million. Manufacturers' representatives account for 5 percent of the dollar volume of the industry, while original equipment manufacturers (OEMs) represent 15 percent. The full-service stocking distributor channel accounts for 25 percent of the industry's dollar volume. The most important channel of distribution for specialty chemicals is sales direct to the end user. This channel represents 55 percent of the industry's sales.

Objectives and Goals for the Sales Force

Considering the specialty chemical example, the initial sales goal might be to become the dominant supplier of specialty and laboratory chemicals. The company must then study in detail the different channels of distribution for its products, to determine how its products can best be sold by the sales force.

For the purposes of this example, assume that the company already has 10 percent of the specialty chemical market. In order to become the dominant force, the company would have to bring its sales from $15 million to $45 million per year (in terms of Figure 13–1), thereby increasing its market share to 30 percent. The company must increase its market share by 2 percent per year in real terms for 10 years to achieve this goal. This hypothetical company must set sales objectives and strategies on how its sales force is to achieve this goal.

Staffing Requirements. Referring to Figure 13–1, the most important channel for these chemicals is the "direct to end-user" class. It is responsible for consuming 55 percent of the product sold in terms of dollars. This company now has about 10 percent of this market. If it is to achieve a goal of increasing its market share to 30 percent, the company will have to grow at least to 30 percent or more of the direct to end-user class. The sales force must be large enough to achieve this goal.

Based on a knowledge of the specialty chemical industry, the management of this company determines that a salesperson can usually make 30 effective sales calls per week. However, the goal is a 2 percent growth in real market share per year. More new accounts must be called on and captured. To achieve this goal, a salesperson in this company's sales force can only make 25 effective sales calls per week. The salesperson must spend a great deal more time with new accounts in order to capture and maintain them if a real market share increase of 2 percent per year is to be achieved. However, the total number of sales calls made by the entire sales force must increase if the 2 percent growth in market share is to be achieved. If the total number of sales calls does not increase, new accounts will not be captured. The only way the total number of sales calls can be increased, when the number of sales calls made by individual sales people decreases, is to increase the number of salespeople.

The difference in average number of calls per week for the industry and the number of effective sales calls per week for the salesperson who must show 2 percent real market share growth can be related to the size of this hypothetical company's sales force in relation to the competition's. It must be about 20 percent bigger than what would be normal for a company with 10 percent of the existing market (30 calls per week minus 25 calls per week $\div$ 25 = 20 percent).

A company with 10 percent of the market for these chemicals in the direct to end-user channel would normally expect to have 10 salespeople servicing these accounts. To service its accounts and begin to gain 2 percent market share increases per year, the company would need 20 percent more salespeople. A similar analysis, as shown above, is used for determining the staffing levels needed for salespeople calling on the other channels: manufacturers' representatives, original equipment manufacturers, and full-service distributors. The company will need about 20 percent more salespeople than it would expect if it did not have such a strong growth goal.

This hypothetical company must create a field sales management structure that will allow it to operate in a high-growth mode. The geographic distribution of accounts by state will determine the concentration of salespeople. The average number of effective sales calls a salesperson can make in a week, month, or year and produce the 2 percent real growth in market share per year will determine the total number of field salespeople needed. The distribution and number of regional and district field sales managers will be directly related to the number and distribution of field salespeople. The actual location of regional and district sales managers should be sited to minimize the travel needed to work with their subordinates.

Industry, Customer Service Requirements. When a sales force is being established or maintained, the management of the company must determine if there are specific practices or customs in its industry that will influence the size and distribution of that sales force. In the example considered above, there are no unusual industry service requirements that a specialty chemical supplier must meet. However, there are sales situations that may influence the need for more or fewer salespeople and their geographic distribution. These situations are related to service requirements and they affect the amount of time a salesperson must spend with a customer. This can affect the total number of salespeople required. The point is that special time and service requirements must be considered when staffing at all levels in the sales force.

Specific customer needs also must be considered when establishing and maintaining a sales force. Not only are there industry considerations but some customers may have unusual service needs that could be very time-consuming for a sales person. Allowances must be made for the time requirements of these customers when staffing a sales force.

Competitive and Geographic/Economic Considerations. A company establishing or maintaining a sales force must plan sales strategies that deal with the competition's strengths and weaknesses.

When a sales force is established and goals are set, it is important to determine in what products the competition has particular strength. This strength can be in terms of patent protection or of manufacturing capabilities. In the specialty laboratory chemical example previously considered, it would be foolish for this firm to tell its sales force to push a product or group of products where the competition's cost structure or patent protection is much more favorable than its own. What the company must do is stress products or lines where it is better situated than or at least on a par with the competition.

Geographic considerations are important when establishing and maintaining a sales force. It is important to compare your own firm's sales force's strength and that of the competition in relation to where the customers are. In order for the sales force to beat the competition and show significant real growth, it must make more high-quality calls than competitive salespeople. The sales force can best do this if it is geographically closer to the customer than the competition is.

Economic considerations will affect decisions that influence the establishment of a sales force. In order to establish a sales force or increase its size, the profit margins on the products sold must be able to support the field sales efforts, cover the company's other expenses, and produce the necessary aftertax profits. Sales management must consider the importance of profit margins when a sales force is established. The accounts that consume products that produce the best profit margins must be given particular emphasis (targeted) when the goal is to increase market share. If a particular geographic area or region has a high concentration of accounts that consume a large quantity of high-margin products, then this area or region must receive more sales force coverage than an area of similar size not containing these types of accounts.

Recruiting the Sales Force

Before hiring someone, it is necessary to develop a "candidate profile," a description of the type of person you want to hire.

The actual face-to-face interview is the most important point in the hiring process. Procedures should be followed during the interview process that maximize the probability of hiring effective salespeople. The Ego-Empathy Grid and the Challenge-Response interview are concepts that are used during the interview of prospective sales candidates. Properly used, they greatly increase the chance of hiring successful salespeople.

The Candidate Profile. Any company hiring a salesperson should have a description, almost a checklist, that describes the ideal candidate. Having a profile of the ideal candidate will allow the company to screen many prospective candidates out of the interview process. This saves valuable interviewing time. The components of the profile should be numerically weighted so the most-promising candidates will receive the closest attention in the interviewing process.

Many of the characteristics on the candidate profile will be found in the Sales Position job description. These characteristics might be: educational background, prior sales experience, specific work experience, and the like. Educational background and other sales candidate characteristics should receive a numerical rating on the candidate profile. For example, the perfect sales recruit would receive a total rating of 100 on the candidate profile. Those characteristics which sales management feel are most important for the job would contribute heaviest to this rating.

Other characteristics can be listed on the profile. Work experience would be heavily weighted in the final score. Professional references, memberships in professional societies, and specialized training would be considered. Also, the personnel department of a company might administer or have administered objective tests to measure other important characteristics of a candidate. The results of these tests would also have a weighted value for the profile. Finally, the results of the initial interviews with the company's personnel department would receive a rating for inclusion on the candidate profile.

The company will already have successful salespeople working for it or it will know successful salespeople in its industry. These people can also contribute ideas about what characteristics should be included on the company's candidate profile. Again, these characteristics would be given a weighted numerical value.

The development of the profile should be as objective as possible. Only those things that reflect possible success in the sales position should be included.

After prospective candidates are found by either the personnel or sales department, the numerically weighted profile should be completed. The management of the sales department might determine that only candidates with a numerically weighted score of 75 or more on the candidate profile will progress into the actual sales interview process.

The Ego-Empathy Grid and the Challenge-Response Interview. Every sales position requires the salesperson to persevere over negative objections, rejection, competition, and possibly even irate customers. A company should know to what degree its salespeople will meet these adversities when selling the product or service.

Situations exist where a salesperson has almost no competition. If the company has strong patent or proprietary positions on its products, it probably will not have much competition. An example of this exists in the pharmaceutical industry, where exotic drugs are heavily protected by patents.

To the degree that objections, competition, and buyer resistance is met, the salesperson will have to use a more aggressive and persuasive sales approach. Also, the salesperson will have to continually come back to meet the buyer's resistance; he or she will have to persevere in the face of negative objection. In order to do this, a salesperson must have a strong ego. Each must be sure of themselves, have a sense of their own worth, and be able to accept rejection.

In some sales situations (e.g., maintenance selling, handling repeat orders), it is not likely that the salesperson will meet strong objections and literally be rejected by the customer. In these situations, as well as instances where little or no competition exists, the salesperson probably need not have such a strong ego. In these cases, objections and the sense of rejection in the sales situation will not be a recurring theme.

In order for salespeople to be successful, they need more than a very strong ego. They must be able to relate to the customer. In a sales situation, it is very difficult for a customer to like a salesperson who does not seem to understand and have feeling for the customer's position. In short, the customer wants salespeople to have empathy for his or her position. If the salesperson shows this empathy, it will be easier to "sell" the customer.

The sales management of a company must decide the degree of ego and empathy their salespeople must possess in order to be successful. If a lot of sales resistance is met, then the ego component of a candidate's personality is most important. If less resistance is met, then the empathy component is more important. The ego-empathy relationship can be called a "quotient,"[1] the degree of ego needed to succeed versus the degree of empathy needed to succeed in a given sales situation. The ego-empathy quotient is closely related to how hard or easy a sell is required to successfully sell a company's product.

For the purposes of helping to determine which sales candidate will meet the company's needs, the ego-empathy grid (Figure 13–2) can be constructed. It is simply a graph with a quantitative statement on each axis of ego and empathy. It is used to evaluate candidates in relation to what the sales management of a company feels is the proper ego-empathy balance required in its salespeople.

The **challenge-response interview** contains a series of questions relating to selling the company's product. These questions must solicit open-ended responses from the prospective candidate. The content of the interview questions and their numerical value is the critical issue that must be developed by the company. Some of the questions are used to develop the ego numerical rating; others are used to develop the empathy rating.

---

[1] The ego-empathy relationship can be expressed as a quotient: the numerical value for ego divided by the numerical value for empathy. However, it could also be stated in terms of E squared (E^2), where these numerical values would be multiplied. Also, other mathematical values could be used: addition, subtraction, and even logarithmic.

FIGURE 13–2
Ego-Empathy Grid

The best way to locate a person on an ego-empathy grid is
for a skilled interviewer (preferably several interviewers) to
have what is called a "challenge-response interview" with
the candidate. It will be most effective if more than one
interviewer has this type of interview with the candidate on
more than one occasion. This greatly enhances the objectivity and accuracy of the interview process.

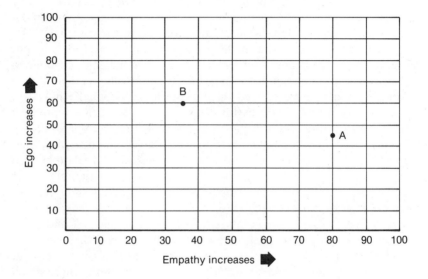

Perhaps 30 or more questions will be asked during the challenge-
response interview process. Every answer the prospective candidate
gives should be objected to challenged. The degree to which a salesperson will meet objections and rejections selling the company's product
determines how strongly his or her answers to these questions will be
rejected. If a hard sell is needed to sell a company's product, multiple
challenges must be made to the candidate's responses; in some cases,
the answers should be rejected outright.

If a less-hard sell is needed to sell a company's product, and sales
management feels the empathy component is more critical to the sale,
then questions that measure a candidate's empathy will be more important. The ego component still must be measured. However, it is less
critical than empathy in this case.

As difficult as this type of interview can be, it must be conducted in
a decent and fair manner. The questions asked of the candidate, and
the challenges to the responses, must be handled in such a way as not

to turn the candidate off. All questions and challenges must be objective and job-related. The questions, challenges, and their respective numerical ratings must be constructed by individuals who have in-depth experience with the company's product, customers, and industry. This will help insure that the challenge-response interview remains job-related.

All candidates for the sales position must be questioned and challenged in the same way in the interview process. The content of the questions, challenges, and their numerical rating should be developed in part by the sales management. Also, the existing sales force may contribute to this exercise. Finally, professional psychologists can develop questions, challenges, and ratings for use in the interview.

After the content of the challenge-response interview is developed, it remains only to quantify ratings for the way a candidate responds to questions and objections. Here sales management will give a numerical value to each response based on its knowledge about the industry. Again the firm's own successful salespeople can indicate numerical values for responses. As the questions and objections are raised during the interview, the candidates' responses are given a numerical rating. Approximately half the questions and challenges should relate both to ego and empathy. At the end of the interview, the numerical rating for each characteristic ego and empathy is arrived at by summing the numerical value for each response.

On Figure 13–2, two points are listed as examples: A and B. A person showing characteristics that placed him or her at position A would have shown an empathy component of 80 and an ego component of 45. This person would be suitable for sales situations where much more empathy was needed than ego. Sales management would have to decide if this type of person would be most suitable for the sales situation.

A person who showed characteristics that placed him or her at position B would have an ego component of 60 and an empathy component of 35. Again, sales management would have to decide if this type of person is most suitable to sell the company's products.

For both positions A and B, the numerical ratings are produced by the challenge-response interview. Each candidate responded to those questions and to challenges related to ego and empathy. Their individual responses were given a numerical value. At the end of the interview, the numerical ratings were added up and that produced the ratings.

TRAINING THE SALES FORCE

A training program for a newly hired salesperson should not be cluttered with a great deal of unnecessary information or emphasize product knowledge while neglecting other selling skills and necessary information. The sales training program should be structured in such a way that parts of it can be given at any time to one or more persons.

In order to sell a company's product or service effectively, skills in five areas must be perfected. A brief consideration of the sales position will show why this is the case. Sales is the most goal-oriented corporate function. Most professional sales job descriptions state a major corporate objective as part of the job description. Frequently, the corporate objective is stated in terms of market share growth, or in terms of growth in total sales dollars, or profit dollars. In any case, achieving a tangible objective is the requirement of a professional sales position.

In sales, unlike other line functions, individuals must achieve their goals while working almost independently from the rest of the organization. In general, the salesperson is not closely controlled by management in the day-to-day methods used to achieve their goals. At issue, then, is how to train a person who has a specific, visible, quantifiable objective. In order to sell a company's product effectively under these conditions, skills in five areas must be perfected. They are:

1. Face-to-face sales techniques.
2. The account distribution in a sales territory; time and territory management.
3. Particulars about prospects in a territory.
4. Training in product knowledge.
5. Competition in a sales territory.

Whether the salesperson is newly hired, or has several years experience with the company, each must master these five areas in order to sell a company's product successfully. A completely inexperienced recruit must receive in-depth training in all five areas. A more experienced sales person may already be skilled in several of them. They should receive training in the one or two areas where they are less effective.

Many sales trainees are frustrated in the training program long before they actually get into the field. This five-part compartmentalized program can be constructed in such a way that much of it is accomplished while the trainee is actually performing sales tasks. This will help minimize the frustration of goal-oriented sales trainees and minimize turnover in the sales trainee group in the early stages of their tenure with a company.

Face-to-Face Sales Techniques

Assisting a sales recruit or even a more experienced salesperson to become more effective at selling involves training them in one or more face-to-face sales techniques. One sales technique will not work with all customers. The many situations a salesperson confronts on a daily basis are too varied to be accommodated by one approach to the sales process.

Numerous sales techniques can be used in the face-to-face selling situation. These various techniques usually have some basis in psychology or sales philosophy. The responsibility of the sales management of a company is to see that its sales force is skilled in selling techniques most suitable for the company's customer base and product line.

The company's customer base and product line may require a very intensive hard-sell effort. This may be because of competition or simply related to the customer's idiosyncratic behavior. It might also be related to the product. Life insurance, because of its association with death, is a product that sometimes requires a very hard sell.

The needs of the customer and of the company's product line may sometimes require a much-less hard sell. In fact, it may involve a lot of technical-type, consultative selling where a hard sell might be inappropriate. In any case, the sales management of a company must determine, based on the customer's needs and knowledge of the industry, what types of sales approach is most suitable to sell the product. Management must then see that its sales force is trained to utilize one or more of these sales techniques. Two basic sales techniques are described below. One is probably more appropriate for the hard, tough-sell situation. The other would be more suitable for a soft-sell, consultative-type situation.

The *hot-button sales technique* would be most useful in a hard-sell situation. Basically, in this technique, the salesperson determines the dominant need of the potential customer. This need is called "the hot-button." Then, during the sales presentation, the salesperson continually refers to this hot-button and shows how his or her product or service fulfills the customers dominant need.

This sales technique is useful, is relatively simple, and can be effective in many sales situations. To be successful in using it, the salesperson must be skilled in asking probing questions, to determine the customer's principal need. However, once that need is determined, all that is necessary is a constant reference back to it showing how the product solves the need.

A second technique to selling can be called the *features, advantages, and benefits* approach. It can be used in a consultative-type of selling situation. In this situation, the salesperson will present the product in a much broader way. He or she will stress many features of the product will show the multiple advantages of the features. Finally, the salesperson will construct a model showing the benefits conferred on the customer by the features of the product. This approach would be more suitable to a soft-sell situation.

In features, advantages, and benefits selling, the salesperson must also ask probing questions. However, in this case, the salesperson determines the multiple needs of the buyer. These multiple needs are related to the benefits conferred by the product. In this type of selling, the salesperson creates the conviction and then the desire to own the product.

Asking for the order, called "closing," must correspond to the sales technique the salesperson uses. If the salesperson uses a hard and very intensive sales approach, he or she should be straightforward about closing. If a softer approach is used, he or she should be a little less direct in the close. In any case, when management is training salespeople how to sell, it should also teach them how to close the sale.

Account Distribution in a Sales Territory; Time and Territory Management

To increase the sales representative's effectiveness in a sales territory, the salesperson must know how to efficiently travel in it. Whether a territory is large or small, in a geographic sense, the salesperson must learn how to contact the largest number of customers with the least amount of travel. There are procedures and techniques a salesperson can learn for scheduling—to visit a specified number of accounts in a specified order. The schedule or itinerary a salesperson develops to travel a territory should minimize the time necessary to get to the customers. This will help maximize the time available for face-to-face customer contact.

The sales trainee must become skilled in the use of ZIP code account distributions and ZIP code maps to develop an efficient plan to cover a territory. If a ZIP code listing of all the accounts in a territory is not available, the sales trainee should be required to create one as part of the training process. The trainee should collect all the sales invoices that have been generated in the assigned territory in the previous 6 to 12 months. These invoices will show the ZIP codes for the accounts in the territory. Using ZIP code maps, the trainee arranges the accounts by distribution and account size in the various ZIP codes in the territory. If the territory is geographically small, then five-digit ZIP codes are used. If it is large, then three-digit ZIP codes should be used. When this project is finished, the trainee will have a ZIP code map and a listing showing the distribution of accounts in the territory.

The next thing the sales trainee should learn is how to lay out a daily, weekly, monthly, and quarterly sales-call itinerary. All he or she really needs to do is to learn how to lay out a daily plan. This can then be applied to the week, month, and quarter. The point the trainee must understand is the need to minimize travel time and to contact the greatest number of accounts with the least amount of travel. The largest travel area can be covered with the shortest amount of travel by moving in a circle or in an elliptical path. This is provable mathematically. A sphere (circle) contains the greatest possible volume to surface area of any form. Therefore, to cover the largest area with the shortest amount of travel, a circular path is most desirable.

The sales trainee should be shown why he or she should not become a "star" salesperson from a time and territory point of view. Normally, being a star salesperson is a compliment. In this case it is not.

Thinking in terms of making six or seven sales calls per day, the sales trainee should be shown, using a star concept, not to go back and forth over the same ground when visiting accounts. The accounts must be visited sequentially, as if they were on the perimeter of a circle or ellipse. If the salesperson travels in this circular way, travel time between sales calls will be minimized.

Another principle that can be used to assist the sales trainee in learning how to lay out a travel day can be taught in terms of an analogy with a tree and a menu. Every workday must contain one principle, most important sales call. This is a sales call at a large actual or potential customer. Thinking in terms of a tree, the tree has a trunk that supports branches. Thinking in terms of preparing an important dinner, it has a main entrée; the entrée supports the entire meal. In this analogy, the main sales call of the day is like the trunk of the tree supporting branches, or the main entrée supporting the other components of the meal. The salesperson knows the zip code for the account representing this main call for the day. He or she must then reference the previously constructed zip code listing and maps to determine the locations of other nearby accounts. The salesperson then adds branches to the tree or other parts of the meal. He or she adds other calls in the same zip code or nearby zip codes for that day, until he or she has the total number of sales calls established for the day. In this way the salesperson maximizes the sales calls for the day by bunching them geographically. Thinking in terms of the tree or menu analogy helps develop this daily call pattern as a matter of practice for the sales trainee.

Particulars about Prospects in a Territory

A great deal of information is available within a firm concerning its customers. The previous section, Account Distribution, contained a description on the use of invoices to locate customers by zip codes. Customer invoices contain additional information. While bunching accounts by zip codes from invoices, the sales trainee can also begin to list products purchased by customers in the trainee's territory, and other valuable information.

Most salespeople keep account profiles on customers in each's territories. Among other things, these profiles list key purchasing influences at each account. They also contain such information as phone numbers, days the client sees visitors, call history on the account, and competitive information. The sales trainee should have access to these profiles and other records that were kept by the previous salesperson in a territory. The trainee should have the opportunity to review all the accounts in a territory with the person who had previously been responsible for it. The previous salesperson in a territory is the best person to teach the trainee about customers in the territory.

If the previous salesperson responsible for a territory is not available to the recruit, then the appropriate district or regional manager should review account profiles with him or her. If account profiles do not exist for the accounts in a given territory, then the new salesperson must be taught how to gather this information by phone, and from in-house information, and construct the profiles themselves.

Training in Product Knowledge

A company's sales management must determine how much and what training the field salespeople should have concerning product knowledge. The degree of training management gives its people on products must be related to customers' needs and expectations. In order to be effective in the sales sense with customers, the salesperson needs to have product training.

Sales representatives should know the products they sell so well that they can converse intelligently about them with their customers. They should be able to service their customer's product needs to a reasonable degree. They should be able to answer most product questions and know how to get the answers to questions they cannot answer. However, they should not become expert on all technical aspects of the products they sell.

The sales trainees should acquire a thorough knowledge of the products they sell—but not at the expense of sales skills. Their technical knowledge need not be at the expert level to sell their products effectively. A problem can develop for a salesperson who gains too much technical knowledge on the firm's products. When calling on customers he or she may begin to spend too much time on unimportant technical points, while not spending enough time selling the product.

In order to assist a trainee to learn to answer customer questions, sales management should draw up lists of the most common customer questions, along with their answers. Companies know the type of questions their salespeople are asked. For example, in the specialty chemical business, a frequently asked question is, "What is the purity of a particular chemical?" In the life insurance business, the question might be: "What is the difference between whole life and term insurance?" The company should train the sales recruits to answer these most common questions. It should also school them in how to obtain answers to customer questions that they can't answer when the customer first asks them.

Competition in a Sales Territory

For a salesperson to sell aggressively and intelligently in a sales territory, he or she should know the strengths and weaknesses of the competition. These strengths and weaknesses are those that are related to specific accounts, and what competitor is strong or weak at a given account. The salesperson should also be taught the strengths and weaknesses of a competitor's product line. He or she should know the good and bad points of the competition's products.

Companies have competition that varies from one geographic location to another. A competitor may be strong at a specific account, in a small or large area, or in a region of the country. Another competitor may be strong at different accounts, in different areas and regions.

A competitor is strong in a given area because of some value added to its product. It may have a product that is in strong demand in a particular industry. It may have a good distribution system in an area. It may have a hard-working, well-liked salesperson covering an area. In any case, the sales trainee should be taught why a certain competitor is strong in particular accounts and areas.

While the new recruit is in the early stages of training, he or she should construct a competitive listing of the competition's strengths and weaknesses at every important account in the territory. This information will later become part of the individual customer profiles the salesperson will create for every account in the territory. He or she should be able to discuss this listing with senior salespeople in the company to develop an intelligent and aggressive approach to selling against the major competitors.

The senior sales management of a company knows what image it wants to project to customers. During the sales training process, management must help its salespeople learn how to project that image. A company's sales management should not be afraid to teach new salespeople about the competition. In fact, this topic should be stressed in the training process. This will allow the salesperson to sell aggressively and intelligently.

MANAGING THE SALES FORCE

The main factor that controls the management of the sales force is its organizational structure. This controls the reporting relationships and responsibilities within the sales force and its relationship to the rest of the company. The form of the sales organization structure must maximize the sales force's performance of the main functions management has decided it is to accomplish.

Many individual management or organizational structures can be described. However, it would be impossible to develop one management or organizational structure for a sales department that would accommodate all companies. This section of the chapter describes general organizational principles and structures that can be utilized in the management of almost any company's sales force.

Two organizational structures for the management of the field sales force are developed. The difference between them will be the amount of staff (service) functions they contain. One organizational structure will be developed along an operations line-type management form. This organizational structure would be appropriate for companies whose sales force is managed directly with an uncomplicated chain of command. It would probably be best for small to mid-sized companies whose total sales/marketing force is less than 50 people.

The other organizational structure contains more staff or service functions, or both. In this case, the sales/marketing organizational chart will show those service functions that are intended to support the field sales force. Within this structure there will also exist straight-line reporting relationships. This type of management structure would probably be best for larger companies whose total sales force plus support personnel is much greater than 50. Also in this case, the company's marketing department's advertising and market research budgets would be quite large.

The two generalized organizational charts contain elements of marketing and administrative staff functions. They show how the marketing and administrative departments relate to the sales function.

Operating-Line Organizational Structure for the Management of the Sales/Marketing Department

This structure is most appropriate for small to mid-sized companies that have fewer than about 50 people in the sales/marketing department. In this case, the advertising/sales promotion budget is smaller than the direct sales force's budget. It is called a "straight-line" organizational structure, because the sales force reports directly to the sales manager, who reports directly to the director of sales, who reports to the vice president of sales/marketing. There are no marketing management responsibilities below the vice president level within the chain of command of the sales force. It is called "operating" in the classical sense of the term; that is, a business function concerned with the day-to-day existence of a company.

Within the operating sales force structure of any organization, there should be an uninterrupted line of authority from the first level of sales management to the field salesperson. This is true whether the selling is done in person, over the phone, or in some other mode of contact. This increases the sales efficiency of the field salesperson, because it minimizes any confusion in reporting relationships within a company. Also, it improves the flow of information from the customer to management.

Figure 13–3 shows the hypothetical organizational structure within the sales/marketing department of a company where this type of reporting relationship exists. In Figure 13–3, the sales (line) functions are separate from the staff (service) functions and administration and marketing. In this example, the sales force is structured along geographic lines. An exception to this is the key account sales responsibility.

Under this type of organizational structure, the VP of sales/marketing basically holds a span of control over three areas: director of sales, director of marketing, and administrative manager. These three areas could contain as many as 50 to 60 people. The vice president in this case might also have a small private staff taking care of routine day-to-day tasks.

In Figure 13–3, the administrative manager reports directly to the VP of sales/marketing. This function is generally responsible for three areas: advertising/sales promotion, sales forecasting, and sales training.

The functions of sales forecasting and advertising are becoming heavily dependent on data processing skills. With computers, it is now possible to develop highly complex spread sheets on the sales of small portions of product lines. These data processing skills can bring better accuracy to the sales forecasting area. They can help make advertising more effective. The problem is that the necessary data processing skills are almost never found in the sales/marketing chains of command. For this reason, they have been evolving in the administrative sales area, at the headquarters level in the sales/marketing department. They are a purely service function, reporting to the VP of sales/marketing, but outside the chain of command of the marketing or sales directors.

Similar technological advances have affected the organizational location of the sales training function. Sales training involves a great deal of knowledge of advanced audiovisual equipment. Computer models are being introduced into sales training. Unfortunately, the skills needed to operate this complex equipment are not generally available in the sales chain of command. Also, this equipment is very expensive and cannot be duplicated at many locations. Usually, the skills and equipment reside at headquarters. For these reasons, sales training is becoming a headquarters function under the responsibility of

FIGURE 13–3
Typical Operations—Line Organizational Structure

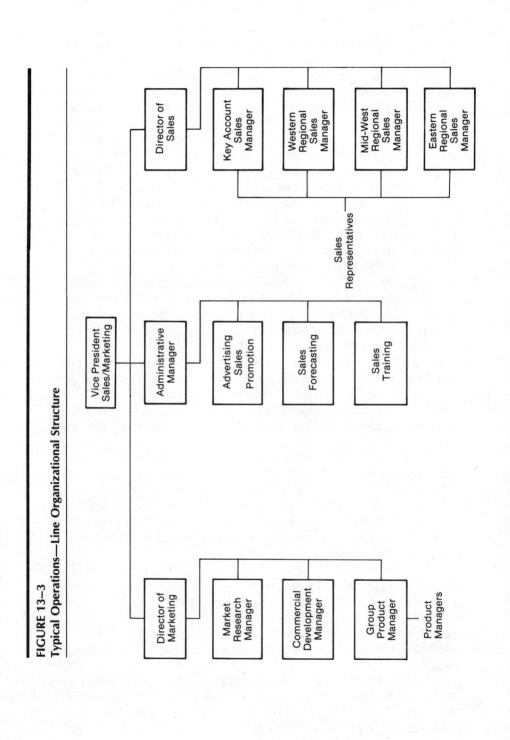

the VP of sales/marketing and supervised by an administrative manager.

The organizational structure represented by Figure 13–3 shows the director of marketing reporting to the VP of sales/marketing. The functions performed by the marketing department in this case are almost purely staff (service) in nature. There will be some overlap in communications with the direct-line sales functions through the market research, commercial development, and the product management group.

The commercial development manager reports to the director of marketing in this structure. This is an advantage for this type of organization. It is costly for the national sales department to handle a product. A new product often does not have the sales volume necessary to justify it being handled by national sales. In addition, the many problems and needs associated with a new product necessitate its sales being handled differently than mature products.

In Figure 13–3, the commercial development function is the only discipline in the marketing line (chain) of command that has operating responsibility. The commercial development people are responsible to shepherd a new product along until its potential can be completely actualized under the aegis of national sales.

Sales forecasting reports to the VP of sales/marketing. They forecast sales by product line and region. They determine when a new product is turned over to sales. They examine a new product's current sales, they forecast its future sales, and set the sales figure that determines when a new product becomes the responsibility of the sales department.

The group product manager is responsible for all product managers and reports to the director of marketing. A company could have a large or small number of products. These products might be sold to a few or many different industries. The product manager is responsible for the marketing aspects associated with the movement of the product to the consumer. He or she has no direct sales responsibility but is responsible for supporting sales.

The last function in the marketing chain is market research. The person in charge of this function by necessity will communicate with field salespeople and customers. He or she will have no authority over sales. Also, this person's contacts with customers must be circumspect so as not to hinder the company's sales efforts. The efforts of market research should also be orchestrated with the commercial development function.

A company using the organizational structure shown in Figure 13–3 will emphasize its field sales effort. The director of sales reports directly to the VP of sales/marketing. All of the line sales functions for this company report to the director of sales. The sales department's efforts can be quickly directed and focused by headquarters. This is an important advantage for this type of organizational structure. It is not encumbered by a lot of service functions and can quickly react to the companies and market needs.

If other direct sales functions must be added to the chain of command of the sales department, they can be added directly under the director of sales. Thus, if a distributor sales manager, or South Central regional sales manager function is to be added into the sales chain of command, it can be set up to report to the director of sales.

The regional sales manager's goal and the goal of the key accounts manager is to maximize the company's sales revenue at the accounts for which they are responsible. Their main function is to manage the salespeople reporting to them so their sales revenues are maximized. In this type of organization the reporting relationships are very clear: the salespeople report to managers, who report to a sales director, who in turn reports to the VP of sales/marketing.

The most important attribute of this type of organizational structure is its simplicity. It allows the company to focus quickly its sales efforts. It will assist the company in being the sales leader in the industry insofar as the company's sales efforts can be brought to bear on specific products, areas, or industries.

Staff-Line Organizational Structure for the Management of the Sales/Marketing Department

The structure of the sales/marketing department that will be described in this portion of the chapter is most suitable for companies that have many more than 50 people in the sales/marketing department. The total expense budget for this department might be many millions of dollars. In this case, the advertising/sales promotion budget will be large in comparison to the other expenses for the department.

Figure 13–4 is a typical organizational chart for a staff-oriented organizational structure. It is still a line organizational structure in that there are straight-line reporting relationships in each area. Reporting relationships in this structure will show some overlap; there will be contact between direct field sales and marketing through the market research function.

The type of company that utilizes the organizational structure shown in Figure 13–4 would be a large industrial or consumer products company. It would be using multiple channels of distribution to sell its products. In this case, the director of marketing has the various marketing functions reporting him or her, and the reports to the VP of sales/marketing. One of these functions, market research manager, has a dual reporting relationship. This person has a dotted-line responsibil-

FIGURE 13–4
Typical Staff-Line Organizational Structure

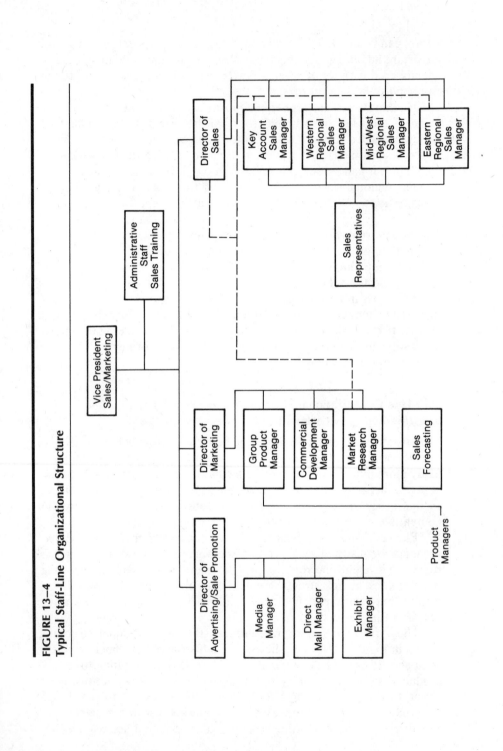

ity to the director of sales as well as a direct reporting relationship to the director of marketing. The market research manager has the sales forecasting function reporting to him or her. That is why there is the dotted-line responsibility to sales. The market research manager's primary reporting responsibility will be to the director of marketing.

There will be a closed loop between sales and marketing through the market research function. The regional sales and key account sales managers will have a dotted-line reporting relationship to market research. The primary reporting responsibility of these field sales managers will be to the director of sales. However, they will have a well-defined communications relationship to the market research manager. This will insure direct field sales communications into marketing.

The regional and key accounts sales managers will not have job ratings (standings in the organization) below the market research manager. In fact, their function can be rated higher. However, they will have a formal reporting requirement to the market research manager. This is needed to give rapid feedback on marketing programs, competition, sales forecasting, and the like to the marketing group.

This form of reporting relationship—field sales to market research to director of sales on a dotted-line basis—will allow for greater contact and communications between sales and marketing below the director level. It will free the director of sales and marketing from the requirement of communicating information into the lower echelons of each other's chain of command. *Also, and most importantly, it will allow both the marketing and sales functions to participate in sales forecasting.*

Figure 13–4 shows that the director of marketing also has the group product managers and the commercial development manager reporting into him or her. In this case, as in the examples given with Figure 13–3, these managers perform a staff service function. However, in many large organizations, the product management position begins to take on some of the responsibilities normally associated with sales. This can cause some of the reporting relationships to become a little more involved. In some situations, the product manager possibly could have a dotted-line reporting relationship into the director of advertising/sales promotion. Figure 13–4 does not show these more complex types of reporting relationships.

In the example covered by Figure 13–4, the director of sales also has a dotted-line responsibility for the market research area. In this case, market research does sales forecasting. This relationship is needed to insure that sales forecasts reflect the opinions of the sales department. The market research function is more of a staff responsibility, whereas sales is a line function. In this case, the traditional line function of director of sales begins to evolve into a staff-type function.

Another difference between the organization structure represented by Figure 13–3 and 13–4 is in the establishment of a formal advertising/sales promotion department. Depending on the size of the company, its advertising/sales promotion budget, and what its relationship is to advertising agencies, the functions residing in this department can become varied and complex. The figure shows a media manager. This person chooses in which media to advertise. There could be a large number of other functions taking care of advertising. This situation would be reflected on the organization chart.

Figure 13–4 also shows the functions of the direct mail and exhibit managers. Depending on what channels of distribution this company uses, these functions will be more or less important. If they only have a small trade exhibit effort, the function of exhibit manager could be shifted into the sales director's area. If the company has a large trade exhibit effort, exhibit manager might have some sales functions, and dotted-line relationships would connect this person into the sales area.

The line management responsibility of the administrative staff is less important in Figure 13–4 than it was in the organization structure shown in Figure 13–3. In this case, it is purely a support arm of the VP of sales.

In Figure 13–4 training again is shown in the administrative area. As a support function, sales training resides at the company's headquarters. Having the training function centralized is the most economical approach. It also allows the training of salespeople to be more uniform throughout the organization.

In the staff-line organization shown by Figure 13–4, the sales department has been described in geographic terms and the product management group in product terms. The description of these departments is controlled by the flow of goods analysis. This concept was explained in the Establishing the Sales Force part of the chapter. A company's flow of goods to the end user determines how the sales and marketing functions are organized. The channels of distribution for the company's products might require specialized distributor, wholesaler, or industry (chemical, cleaning, and so on) sales titles. The same thing might require market or some other description for product managers. The channel of distribution requirements for a company will not change its basic goals. However, the requirements will affect how these goals are achieved.

The typical organization structure described in Figure 13–4 is for a large company, with a substantial sales/marketing budget. This company utilizes multiple channels to penetrate the markets it is interested in. The multiple-channel requirement adds complexity to the organization. More and varied people are involved with the purchase of product. These people must be influenced. This requires a specialized sales, marketing and advertising/sales promotion effort. For these departments to have similar goals and work toward them in an organized way, there must be formal reporting relationships below the director's level.

Depending on the emphasis of effort in a large company, several departments may have dotted-line relationships. In an effectively organized company, the organization within departments should be straight-line from one level to the next. However, because of the complexity of the marketplace, several departments might have multiple dotted-line relationships. In Figure 13–4, one such relationship between market research and sales was shown.

The main reason for (and the advantage of) dotted-type cross-over reporting relationships is that it greatly improves communications at lower levels of a complex organization. This should make it more likely that everyone is working toward the same goals. The disadvantage of these dotted-line relationships is that they can confuse reporting relationships. Senior management must decide how much *possible* confusion can be tolerated as a trade-off for greatly improved communications. The answer is that, in a well-managed company, the trade-off should not be a requirement.

14

MANAGING THE SALE VERSUS MANAGING THE SALES FORCE

by
Jim Rapp

National Office Products Association

Because many sales forces operate on the principle of selling as much as possible, all other departments tend to operate in a supporting role. In this situation, there is little or no effort to "manage" the sale of a product or service—at least not from the standpoint of deciding in advance how much will be sold, in what areas, and at what prices.

Until such time as the corporation makes a decision to "manage the sale" completely through the distribution channels, the sales department or the individual salesperson will "call the shots" as far as what, when, and how much will be sold.

For certain products and certain selling arrangements, it may be perfectly all right to let salespeople sell as much as they can. For example, you may have a product which is more or less unlimited in supply. In this case, the more you sell, the more money you make. But even here, there are practical limits; and the *cost* of the sale should always be an important consideration.

Therefore, it seems that most organizations would be better off to manage the sale in harmony with "managing the sales force." In fact, to be successful over the long term, the two should be coordinated.

Managing the sales force, then, is only a part, albeit an important one, of managing the sale; and managing the sale is one part of the overall marketing plan. It might look something like this:

While an oversimplification, this points out that everything the sales force does should work toward accomplishing the overall sales and marketing goals of the organization. This, however, is easier said than done. Much of the work of most sales forces is maintenance—keeping existing products or services moving. Whenever the company wants to change direction or introduce a new product, it must "vie for the time" of the sales force.

The link, then, between the marketing goals and plans developed (mostly) at company headquarters and the day-to-day management of the sales force, which usually takes place in the field, is a good workable *sales plan*. A good sales plan must consider the needs of headquarters and the very practical needs of the salespeople on the firing line. There should be a "linking up" of the goals of these two distinct groups.

This link can best be accomplished by having the field people involved in the development of the overall marketing and sales plans, along with the product managers, research people, and advertising and promotion departments.

What should go into a sales plan? Here are the key ingredients:

1. Quantities to be sold.
2. Where they will be sold.
3. Time periods.
4. Pricing structure, special offers, and so on.
5. Sales promotion arrangements.
6. Customers or prospects to be contacted.
7. Systems for measurement.

ROLE OF THE SALES MANAGER

The sales manager is the key to making these things happen. He or she is the person who should be involved both in putting the plan together and into effect.

In many companies, the sales manager is the driving force. This is especially true where the face-to-face sales effort is critical to the company's success, such as in real estate or insurance. In small companies, the sales manager may also be the marketing manager. Because of the *power* of the sales manager and the sales force, most other functions of the organization, such as manufacturing, customer service, and the like, become sublimated to the sales organization. The sales department becomes all-powerful—not necessarily because it tries to be, but simply because its importance is recognized throughout the organization.

This can be a real danger. A sales manager or a salesperson more interested in dollar volume, for example, than profit, can soon ruin a company or a territory. It is incumbent upon the sales manager(s), then, to see that the power of the sales department is not misused. This will not be a concern if a good sales plan is developed—one which takes into consideration the key points noted above. *And,* of course, if it is carried out.

Managing the sales force, then, involves a great deal more than hiring and training salespeople—even more than achieving a sales quota. When the sales force is integrated into the overall organization and coordinated with all parts of the marketing operation, its value is enhanced significantly. Traditional responsibilities of the sales manager include:

— Recruiting and selection.
— Training.
— Sales administration.
— Compensation.
— Budget attainment.

When the sales management position is fully integrated into the marketing function, additional responsibilities will include:

— Analyzing sales territories.
— Recommending advertising and promotional programs.
— Involvement in price and service level determinations.
— Forecasting profits as well as sales.
— Assisting in the determination of marketing strategies.
— Having major responsibility for developing the overall selling plan.

In putting together the sales plan, the wise sales manager will involve the entire staff. Armed with the knowledge and wisdom of the entire sales team, the sales manager will certainly be successful.

POSITION (JOB) DESCRIPTIONS

If you do not now have written position (job) descriptions for every position in the sales organization, each should be developed. The position description should state the purpose of the position, the chain of command above and below, the duties and activities of the position, as well as how job performance will be measured. It is also helpful to include how the sales manager will work with each of the key headquarters staff people, especially those in the sales and marketing areas.

Let us now take a more detailed look at the position of sales manager. Although each organization will have its own unique characteristics, many common threads run through almost all sales management positions. Following is a brief description of each of the "general sales manager's" duties:

1. *Planning.* This area includes manpower planning, collecting and analyzing sales information from the field, forecasting sales and expenses, setting goals for and with salespeople, and establishing priorities and developing strategies and plans for the accomplishment of the goals. With this and other information from marketing and other departments, an annual sales plan can be developed.

2. *Recruiting and selection.* In most organizations, the sales manager has full responsibility for determining manpower needs, including the number of people in the department, where they will be located, their job specifications, and how and where they will be recruited.

3. *Training.* The sales manager, in most situations, is responsible for training or seeing that all of his or her people receive the necessary training. This applies to experienced as well as to new people. In some cases, training is provided by headquarters staff, at least for basic training of new reps. However, it is almost always the responsibility of the sales manager to see that his or her people follow through and put what they've learned into practice.

4. *Compensation.* Most organizations have compensation programs developed and administered by the personnel department, in conjunction with line managers. Because many salespeople are paid on the basis of sales performance, sales managers have a greater interest and involvement in the compensation program than do most other managers. In some cases, the sales manager actually sets the commission rate, in addition to authorizing salary increases.

5. *Establishing sales quotas.* This can be a part of item 1 (planning) but is so important that it is actually listed separately. The sales manager usually is involved in setting sales quotas by product, geographic area, salesperson, or account.

6. *Price and service levels.* In most organizations, the sales manager has a strong voice in decisions related to selling prices, terms, methods of shipment, and the type and frequency of service, including personal sales calls.

7. *Advertising and promotion.* In some organizations, the sales manager is involved in determining how products or services, or both, will be advertised. It is more likely, however, that he or she will be involved in field promotion. Promotion consists of special offers to customers, such as displays, cooperative advertising, free goods, and the like.

8. *Administration.* More and more sales managers are responsible for administering a wide variety of activities, including accurate and prompt reporting of sales, expenses, and competitive activities. Some have responsibility for sales service, including order processing, billing, and collection.

9. *Motivation.* While it is important to any manager, to a sales manager the term *motivation* has special significance. The professional sales manager must work constantly to keep his or her people motivated to do an outstanding job.

10. *Customer contact.* Most sales managers have some direct responsibility for customer performance, particularly with the headquarters officers of major accounts. Here the importance of the position carries considerable weight at all levels of customer organizations.

SUMMARY

In the past, managing the sales force was thought of as little more than being a super salesperson who cheered subordinates on to greater achievement.

Times have changed. The successful sales manager of today operates as if he or she owned the business. The "bottom line" is important. Every planned action must take into account profitability.

The successful sales manager of today must understand marketing. He or she must also help each person in the sales force realize their full potential by providing the necessary experience, education, and opportunities for growth.

To be truly successful, today's sales manager must give up the narrow objective of sales at any cost and broaden the perspective to include such goals as developing market share, opening new channels of distribution, and making the best use of information systems. The rapid changes taking place in the work world must be acknowledged, because they dictate changes in how people are treated and in the entire reward system of organizations.

15

HOW TO MANAGE A BRANCH/DISTRICT SALES OFFICE

by
Arnold L. Schwartz

Achievement Concepts, Inc.

Every company defines its branch and district managers' responsibilities differently. A branch or district office may be a large multilevel operation with sales supervisors or managers reporting to a branch manager. In some instances, the branch manager may have other departments, such as marketing, service, and technical support, reporting to him or her, with levels of management in between.

In smaller operations, the branch or district manager may directly supervise a group of salespeople with responsibilities limited to that function. The manager may even have personal account responsibility. Some firms provide office space for their managers. In larger cities, salespeople may work out of these offices where there is a physical branch presence. In other situations, there is no actual branch office—everyone works out of his home. In other cases there may be a combination of the above.

This chapter will focus on the situation where the branch manager's primary responsibility is for managing a team of salespeople, regardless of whether there is an actual office.

A good way to read this chapter is to imagine yourself recently promoted to manager of a branch, with responsibility for eight salespeople, all of whom work out of the same branch office. Several of these salespeople have outlying areas and do not physically report in everyday. As you mull over your new responsibility, you think about the steps you should take in establishing yourself as the branch manager—and perhaps more importantly, as a leader.

We are going to highlight some key areas of managing a branch operation. These are:

    I. Establishing leadership values.
    II. Goals and expectations.
    III. Recruiting and selection.
    IV. Training and development.
    V. Motivation.
    VI. Field coaching.
    VII. Appraisal and evaluation.
    VIII. The branch manager as a business person.
    IX. Personal development.

I. ESTABLISH A PERSONAL SET OF LEADERSHIP VALUES

The first three letters of the word manager spell "man" as in man or woman. You can't separate the person from the job—each individual's habits, personality traits, physical abilities and limitations, beliefs about morality, and so on come along with him or her to the position.

All of us have certain strong, fundamental beliefs about how we prefer to conduct our lives—what's really important to us. Examples might be:

— Family loyalties.
— Physical fitness.
— Intellectual development.
— Making money.
— Gaining power.
— Leader in the community.
— Service to others.

We tend to prioritize our time and activities toward enhancing and validating those values important to us. By identifying and clarifying your leadership values, many of which will be based on your personal values, you will formulate a framework for problem solving and decision making and develop a more consistent leadership style. Salespeople, as all subordinates, prefer to work for a person whose behavior tends to be consistent and predictable, because it adds stability and dependability to the manager/subordinate relationship and makes for a more secure work environment.

In defining your leadership values, you need to consider your company's values, traditions, and customary mode of conducting business.

There needs to be congruence between your values and the company "culture." If there is a real conflict between your beliefs and ideals and the company's, or those of your boss, they must be reconciled early or you will have problems in effectively implementing company policy.

Some areas for clarifying your leadership values are: meeting goals, dress code, promptness, integrity, how people are treated, fairness, loyalty, being liked by subordinates, customer service, how people get promoted, and the like.

You will assign different strengths to these values. The test of your value system comes when there is a conflict. A not uncommon example is the good producer who is habitually late for meetings and disdains call reports and other administrative responsibilities. Is it so important to get this much needed sales production to meet your goals that you overlook these deficiencies, or will you insist that everyone meet the same obligations, without exception? The point is that thinking about these situations in advance in the larger context of your overall beliefs and values will enable you to deal with these situations more fairly, consistently, and comfortably. In formulating a value system, you may want to consider someone you regard as an outstanding manager. What characteristics does this individual possess that makes him or her a fine leader? The following exercise will help you to formulate your leadership values:

1. What do you consider to be your most important values as a manager—those principles that form the foundation of your approach to leading others? These are values you will strongly defend—values which you will seldom, if ever, deviate from.

2. What qualities do you want to be admired for?

3. What character impressions will you try to avoid giving others?

4. Write out a general statement of your sales management philosophy in a few brief paragraphs. This will be the basis of how you will conduct yourself in your role as a manager of salespeople.

5. What are your attitudes toward subordinates, peers, and superiors in the following areas? Indicate whether your concern is likely to be very high, high, moderate, or little in each area:

— Promptness.
— Adherence to company rules, policies, procedures, and so on.
— Appearance.
— Women in sales.
— Administrative and reports.
— Performance versus quota.
— Absenteeism without due cause.
— Moonlighting.

— Subordinates going over your head without your knowledge.
— Office romances.
— Cheating on expenses.
— Knowingly exaggerating company capabilities to prospects/customers.
— Knocking competition.
— Heavy socializing among salespeople.
— Superiors contacting your people without your prior knowledge.
— A subordinate not respecting you or your position, or both.

While all behavior is situationally determined to some degree, understanding yourself and your core beliefs will make it easier for you to act in a way that is consistent with the kind of leadership you wish to exemplify.

II. GOALS AND EXPECTATIONS

One of the first steps to take in your new role of branch manager is to determine what is expected of you by your superiors, as well as what you expect from your subordinates.

As a manager of a part of the company operations, you have responsibility for maximizing the return on the resources allocated to you.

The productivity goals or "quotas" for your operation will be assigned to you. These quotas may be expressed in terms of sales volume, new accounts, percentage of increase over a previous period, units, profitability, and the like. You will need to clearly understand these specific objectives and how they relate to the overall organizational goals. Understanding the "big picture" fosters a team concept and gives more meaning and universality to individual effort.

You will need to know what your immediate superior expects of you—how your performance will be measured. What behaviors does your boss value? Are they consistent with yours? It may surprise you to learn that your superior's expectations and how he or she prefers you to manage may be at some variance with the stated goals of the organization. Spending time with your boss to insure that you are both clear about your mutual expectations for the relationship is critical. An updated job description written by you and approved by your supervisor, including a prioritization of your key duties, will be very valuable in putting your agreement in writing and avoiding misunderstandings.

This process of identifying and agreeing on mutual expectations is referred to as an "up-front contract" and can be used effectively with your subordinates as well as your boss. Up-front contracts eliminate "mutual mystification," which occurs when two individuals expect commitment and actions of each other to which the other person is unaware or has no intention of fulfilling. The result is that both parties end up disappointed. Up-front contracts should be specific, in writing, and should include rewards and penalties for not meeting the conditions of the contract—as with any other contract. It should include personal items, such as the way people will treat each other, communicate, and show respect.

We read about examples of mutual mystification in the newspapers when both parties to a dispute talk *at* each other with ambiguous statements to the press and TV instead of communicating *with* each directly over the real issues. Managers and salespeople operate in this realm when the manager complains that the salespeople have bad attitudes, instead of pinpointing a specific behavior that needs correcting, or holds sales meetings instead of working with individual salespeople on specific situations.

Salespeople practice mutual mystification when they sit in the office complaining about their boss, territory, state of the economy, and so on, instead of working. This generally occurs when the task is not clear or specific.

The branch manager should periodically set aside a chunk of time with each of his or her people to review goals, expectations, and strategies. Asking each sales representative to prepare a job description as he or she sees the job and reviewing it together is an excellent way of getting this process started.

The end result of this step, goals and expectations, is that the branch manager knows exactly what is expected, how the branch operation fits into the big picture, how job performance will be measured, what can be expected from the boss in terms of support, communication, and what his or her job description is. In short, everyone knows how they will be measured, what is expected of them, and when they have won or lost. When this is achieved, and people truly know what their job is and how they will be evaluated, motivation and productivity improve.

III. RECRUITING AND SELECTION

Without the right people, a manager's chances of being successful are slim.

Don't be deluded into accepting mediocre performers because of your prowess as a trainer, super-salesperson, or motivator. Why not use your talents where they can produce the best results, with people who have the potential and attitude to be successful?

Recruiting and selection is an on-going process for the manager because there will always be turnover in a growing, dynamic organization. You can improve your "hit" ratio by thoroughly knowing the job requirements, developing a profile of the type of person who would ideally fit the job, and then actively seeking that kind of person. You may never find Mr. or Ms. Ideal, but you will get close if you know what you're looking for. Write out in narrative form, in detail, everything about the individual that would best fit the job.

Even when there are no immediate openings, the wise branch manager will be interviewing—building a candidate pool. Just as a good salesperson is always prospecting for new accounts, new applications, and new leads, a good manager is building his or her "prospect" base!

A talent for recruiting good people into your organization will overcome deficiencies in other areas of branch management. This is one area where you don't want to shortchange yourself. The more people you interview for a job, the better chance you have of coming up with a good hire. It is a time-consuming process, but a necessary one.

Recruiting and Interviewing Tips

- Interview carefully and in-depth.
- Don't make a decision based on a single interview.
- Testing may be of value in getting beneath a carefully structured facade.
- Always check references.
- Don't settle for a mediocre selection.
- Mr. or Ms. Right will far outperform their so-so counterparts.
- Match the candidate's talents, abilities, and personality traits to the job at hand.

For a more in-depth treatment of this subject, you are referred to my chapter, "Recruiting and Selection," in *Sales Manager's Handbook,* ed. Edwin E. Bobrow and Larry Wizenberg (Homewood, Ill.: Dow Jones-Irwin, 1983).

IV. TRAINING AND DEVELOPMENT

An examination of the successful managers in most sales organizations will reveal that the majority of them excel in training their people. They do not hold the view that training is strictly the responsibility of the home office or that "we hire only experienced salespeople." Most of the so-called experienced salespeople have had little or no formal professional training, and, if they had it, they probably have forgotten most of what they learned. For many salespeople, their experience consists of having been "thrown" into the field to develop whatever habits came naturally.

Training is a lifelong process. In the absence of training, the alternative is ignorance. Even if your company has formalized training, it is your responsibility to augment and reinforce it at a local level. You can do this in a number of ways, perhaps coordinating your efforts with a centralized training staff, if your organization has one.

1. New Salesperson Branch Indoctrination and Orientation Program

The first few weeks of a new person's experience are crucial to the long-lasting attitudes he or she forms of you and the company. Make sure there is a set of planned activities prepared for the new individual—preferrably in writing, with his or her name on top—and monitored by you personally. Have ready all the necessary forms, materials, office space, car, and so on that the individual will need. You probably spent considerable time recruiting this person, so why not show that you're glad he or she is aboard.

Be prepared to give the new salesperson a generous amount of your time and attention those first few days and weeks. Appreciate that this is a time of uncertainty and confusion for a new person, so try to do everything possible to make him or her feel at home. Make it a point to introduce him or her to each member of your staff.

2. New Salesperson Branch Training Program

If the new person will be in the branch for an extended period before going to the home office for training, the branch manager should design a program which combines self-study, working with other salespeople, and learning how to demonstrate or present the product that will enable him or her to experience a sense of purpose and accomplishment—learning the business and progressing in a structured, productive way. This is not the same as simply assigning the new person to a senior salesperson.

3. Continually Conduct Product and Sales Skills Training Classes

The number of classes you conduct will be determined by geographic and economic constraints, but the importance of doing this on a regular basis cannot be overstated. Skills and knowledge must be continually re-honed, and your investment in this activity will pay rich dividends.

Plan meetings carefully, always have an agenda, use your own people as presenters and instructors, utilize visitors from corporate, ask for help from your training staff, purchase or rent materials from training vendors, or hire an outside professional to conduct certain portions of the program. A knowledgeable well-trained staff is a *must* if you are to win the battle against domestic as well as increased foreign competition.

4. Do Field Coaching and Training

There is only one place to determine a person's sales ability—on actual sales calls. When you work with a salesperson in "live" selling situations, his or her strengths and weaknesses are on vivid display and you can give specific and immediate feedback. This is the most effective method of training and establishing your credentials as a concerned leader who is confident in demonstrating ability under fire.

Plan your "field day" in advance. Review the accounts/contacts you both plan to visit, discuss account strategy, the objective you both expect to achieve. Appointments should be confirmed in advance to avoid delays and loss of valuable selling time.

By maintaining a continuous program of training, you will not only keep yourself current in state-of-the-art technology, but your people will be more confident and motivated.

V. MOTIVATION

Motivation is a subject that has been and is currently the subject of a myriad of books, articles, seminars, speakers, psychologists, psychiatrists, cassette programs, and so on. An in-depth probe into this subject certainly cannot be attempted here; but since it is prime responsibility of the branch manager, we should examine some techniques or approaches that have proved successful for other managers of salespeople.

The key to motivation is that it must be done one at a time and continuously. Every individual is unique and, thus, responds to a different set of stimuli and motivators. While it is beneficial to be informed about broad motivational constructs, such as the hierarcy of needs (Maslow), "hygiene factors" versus "motivators" (Herzberg), Theory X versus Theory Y (McGreggor), the various grid theories, situational management, and the like, no individual's motivational needs fits so neatly into these concepts that they can be applied literally.

Another important consideration is that you should not project your personal motivations onto your salespeople and expect them to react as you do. While one person may be "turned on" by contests and quota clubs, another may find motivation in customer relationships and being knowledgeable in the product.

You must get to know what makes each person tick, what his or her potential is, and then apply the techniques and strategies that you feel will work best for each individual. To make the job more difficult, what works today might not work tomorrow, and it is a never-ending job of experimenting, of trial and error.

The following suggestions are designed to provide you with some basic truths that apply to virtually every one of your people.

Principles for Motivating Salespeople

1. People like to do what they do well, so make your salespeople better by continuous training and development. As they grow in ability, their self-esteem will grow and they will enjoy working at a job which gives them professional respect and personal satisfaction.

2. People need appropriate and constant feedback on performance—positive and negative. Be sure to provide a generous dose of the former and present the down-side in a positive manner. All of us need to know how we're doing against specific standards. Only then can we measure our performance.

3. People need specific goals that they have accepted as realistic and attainable and that they will be measured against. Goals act as a magnet, pulling individuals toward their achievement. Definite goals usually get definite results—indefinite goals generally get no results. Personal goals that are integrated with business goals enable people to view their jobs as having intrinsic as well as extrinsic value.

4. A good incentive program that appropriately rewards above average performance is an important part of a motivational program.

5. Communicating with your people, keeping them informed of events at a regional or national level, and explaining company philosophy are important. Many salespeople feel they don't know what's going on in their companies and cannot relate branch policies with an overall company plan. Likewise, reporting your salespeople's suggestions, market information, and gripes to a higher authority, acting as their attorney, so to speak, is another aspect of communication.

6. Recognition and a sense of belonging are two needs that most people have. Fortunately, these are two forms of nonfinancial compensation that are available to branch managers. They need only use their imagination and creativity to find ways of providing recognition and team membership to each of their people.

7. Maintaining high expectations and belief in your people will foster those feelings in each individual. We tend to live up to a significant other's expectations of us—good or bad.

8. Spaced repetition—the constant application of the seven points listed above—will eventually turn these ideas from intellectual understanding to habit and action. View your salespeople *as your customers* and work at selling these customers on themselves, on their company, and on their manager.

VI. FIELD COACHING

This aspect of sales management is crucial for building a successful sales team. It affords the branch manager the best platform on which to display leadership and motivational ability.

It is in the field, working one on one, performing the very essence of the sales job, selling to the customer face to face, that you can accomplish the greatest good in developing the salesperson to his or her full potential.

Your role in field coaching is principally as an observer—carefully analysing your sales staff's strengths and weaknesses. In seeing first-hand how they prepare for their calls, their record-keeping system, their dress, how they handle themselves with receptionists and secretaries, if they are calling on decision makers, their rapport and relationships with customers, how they plan their day, their presentation skills, handling objections, closing, product knowledge, vocabulary, and follow-up, you gain understanding and insights that are impossible to get from behind your desk or from reports.

Coaching in the field allows you to give immediate and specific feedback and to share perceptions of events and happenings that you have experienced together. Unfortunately, many managers permit the administrative burden of their jobs to curtail the time they spend in the field with their people.

Some Key Tips for Field Coaching

1. Give positive as well as negative feedback. Use the "sandwich" technique—a slice of criticism between two slices of praise.

2. Focus criticism on specific skills and tasks, not on the individual as a person.

3. Allow the salesperson to express his or her views on performance—expect some disagreement. Be open to changing your opinion.

4. Don't place your emphasis on the process (i.e., how the task is handled, rather than the results). Everyone has their own approach.

5. If you don't work with an individual very often, spend at least one day (two is better) in making calls so you get a perspective based on multiple sales calls—not just one.

6. Always leave time at the end of the coaching session for a period of summary and critique, in which specific recommendations and action plans for improvement are presented, discussed, and implemented.

7. Do not take an active role in the coaching call unless absolutely necessary; your role is chiefly as an observer.

8. Be realistic about what skills or deficiencies the salesperson can correct or improve upon in the near term. Strive for one or two goals that the individual can achieve within 30 to 90 days, rather than for some "ideal" solution which can never be realized.

9. And finally, view coaching as one of your high-priority jobs as a branch manager. Make the time to do it on a regular basis.

Working in the field with your salespeople will enable you to assess accurately their sales techniques, attitude, and product knowledge. It will enable you to get to know them as people, will demonstrate your concern for their success, and will keep you attuned to what is happening in the "real" world.

VII. APPRAISAL AND EVALUATION

We have already established that salespeople need frequent feedback and evaluation on their performance. While coaching provides an opportunity for the manager to accomplish this on a somewhat informal and short-term basis, there is a need for a more formal process—where the salesperson's performance is evaluated in depth and for a longer time, six months to a year, against predetermined goals and standards. This enables the manager and salesperson to sit down together and evaluate the salesperson's skills, attitudes, and habits, and sales performance—the results achieved—and jointly arrive at a development program designed to improve sales performance.

Many companies require an annual performance appraisal—some even semiannually. Some performance appraisals are tied into salary review. A performance appraisal ideally should be done apart from salary considerations, since the salesperson's attention and interest is likely to be focused on the size of pay increase, rather than on a development program.

Even if your company does not have a policy on appraisal and evaluation, it is recommended that you set up your own, designing a form to measure those areas that are relevant to your selling environment. The salesperson's attitude, personal habits, effort, and potential abilities should be examined, in addition to the more quantifiable aspects of his or her performance.

In conducting a performance evaluation, the manager must do thorough homework. The manager should review the salesperson's file, call reports, coaching records, and correspondence. Also to be considered are influencing factors, such as the economy, business conditions in the salesperson's territory, competition, acceptance of the product in the market place, in evaluating the total performance of the salesperson.

The manager should examine any personal feelings toward the individual and not let these cloud his or her objectivity. The manager's evaluation must be straightforward and honest. Avoiding discussion of the negative aspects of the salesperson's job, to prevent unpleasantness in the interview, will negate the effectiveness of the appraisal.

It is recommended that the rating forms be given to the salespeople prior to the meeting so they can rate themselves. Then the ratings can be compared. The appraisal interview should be a dialogue, in which the views of both parties are expressed.

The desired result of the appraisal interview is the salesperson's awareness of the areas he or she needs to be working on to improve performance. But more than this, the manager and salesperson will construct an extended development program to correct the weaknesses. Specific objectives are established, the activities that the salesperson will be engaged in are identified, deadlines for accomplishments for each stage of the program are set, and the procedures for monitoring progress are put in place.

VIII. THE BRANCH MANAGER AS A BUSINESS PERSON

The branch manager must not only manage salespeople but must also manage the "business." It is not enough to produce sales; the real accomplishment is in generating *profitable* sales. Directing sales efforts toward the most profitable product lines, maintaining price levels, avoiding nonstandard or "special" applications, which cost the company more in time and effort, making too-generous concessions to tough customers, being overly lavish in entertaining prospects and customers, targeting your reps' selling efforts toward the prospects with the most potential—these are all legitimate areas of concern for the profit-minded branch manager.

Profitability can deteriorate through inadequate expense control. Sales expenses need to be monitored, accounts receivable kept within desired limits, salespeople trained to collect monies owed (if that is their responsibility), proper records maintained, and the physical plant maintained in good working order, with adequate insurance to cover emergencies. Office personnel need to be trained and motivated to be an extension of the sales force.

Many new managers are not trained or experienced in the administrative side of their jobs, and while it may not be the most important aspect of managing a branch sales office, it still requires skill and attention. Part of being a good administrator is maintaining good relations with other departments of the company. Departments, such as advertising, sales promotion, training, product management, engineering, manufacturing, credit, and customer service, can affect the success of the sales force, and these departments often have to be "sold" on cooperating with the manager and the manager's staff.

Control systems need to be designed to signal the manager when one of the "components" of the system is not functioning properly. An example of this might be a salesperson whose sales call rate suddenly takes a big dip. How can the manager know this before it critically affects productivity? If a call report system is in place, the individual's daily call reports might indicate a low number of calls or an inordinate number of calls to the same accounts. Call reports should have a legend on them clearly indicating the type of accounts they are visiting and trying to sell. Maintaining large customers is important, but expanding your customer base should be a high priority.

The manager must determine what constitutes the key indicators of danger. Is it sales calls, proposals, new account calls, demonstrations, phone appointments? Waiting until you find that the salesperson is not bringing in business may be too late. Identify the key indicators and set up a simple system for controlling them.

IX. PERSONAL DEVELOPMENT

Much of this chapter has been devoted to how the manager should develop others. Successful managers are typically committed to the task of continuing self-development and meaningful change. Your strengths as a salesperson or a sales supervisor, or both, probably earned you the promotion to branch manager. If you do not consciously engage in a development program, you may trigger the Peter Principle in motion—that is, you will have been promoted to your level of incompetence. The Peter Principle need not apply to any individual who is open to growth and change.

Work on your areas of "lesser strengths." Your company may provide management development courses—view them as opportunities for growth. Many universities and educational organizations offer courses in specific areas of management, such as strategic planning, financial management for the nonfinancial manager, and data communications. A good method is to take a 12-month calendar and plan a new service, product, or skill you intend to learn thoroughly each month. This will serve to reinforce your ability to deal with change.

Join organizations where you can meet other achievers who are in your industry or level of work. The Sales Executives Club of New York is an example of an organization where members can attend luncheon and evening seminars conducted by a variety of outstanding experts. Toastmasters is an excellent organization for improving speaking and presentation skills.

Broaden your mental horizons by reading books, newspapers, and magazines that will keep you current on events, not only in your own industry, but in the business world at large. *The Wall Street Journal,* the *New York Times,* and *Business Week* magazine are examples of the type of reading which will keep you on top of things.

Most of us need to work on our time management, communication, and human relations skills. They become more critical to a manager because he or she needs to get the job done through others—not only salespeople but others in the organization. We must constantly refocus our energies on our goals, continuously redefining our priorities so we spend our time where it has the biggest payoff.

CONCLUSION

The job of a Branch Sales Manager is diverse and difficult. You must have a strong self identity and be a combination of good salesperson, marketeer, product technician, planner, motivator, people developer, communicator, organizer, trainer, administrator and smart business-person. And you must blend these "people" and "task" skills in a way that accomplishes the results assigned by the company.

In addition, you must continually be working on improving these skills and keeping up with new trends in your industry and product technology.

In short, you need to be:

Faster than a speeding bullet, more powerful than a locomotive and able to leap tall buildings at a single bound.

With perserverence, enthusiasm, and planning—you can do it!
Good Luck.

16

ALTERNATIVE CHANNELS OF DISTRIBUTION

by
Robert La Rue

La Rue Marketing Consultants, Inc.

As market segmentation has become a way of life, it has become apparent that conventional approaches to distribution channels have not always proven to be the most productive. As a consequence of both need and opportunity, marketers of all sizes have detoured off the beaten path in search of solutions.

Several factors have contributed to diversity of distribution channels. The increase in working women, for example, has had its impact on time priorities. Studies show that shopping activity rates very low as a desired leisure activity. A severe recession has provoked price consciousness to the extent that the no-frills shopping environment is tolerated, if not actually sought. As the trend in off-price merchandising has accelerated, shopping has become an adventure for some consumers. For others it has simply become chic to save. With segmentation has come fragmentation. Almost as if it were a backlash to mass marketing, America has become dotted with specialty outlets catering to very narrow tastes and interests.

There are still other conditions in the marketplace that affect decisions on how best to "go to market." Several of the more significant are:

- *A reduced amount of selling space* among certain classes of retailers. An example is the reduction in floor space in conventional department stores—as they have moved from downtown locations to the suburbs.
- *"Edited" assortments by retailers,* in order to be represented in a fairly wide variety of categories.

- *An increase in self-service,* combined with decline in sales personnel effectiveness.
- *The advent of consumerism.*
- *Consumers' expectations*—they have become better defined.
- *Increased attention to the selection of products and services* by the publishing world—through books and periodicals.

It is important to consider not just the channels of distribution when evaluating the route to the marketplace. There is a need to consider business formats as well. Each format has its own peculiar set of opportunities and restrictions. With this much introduction to the subject of alternative approaches to distribution, it is now probably most helpful to take a look at some actual case histories, to analyze the opportunities and needs and then examine how the marketer evaluated the alternatives.

CASE HISTORY 1

As many marketers know, the traditional full-line consumer goods wholesaler is not usually effective in pioneering new products. He or she often carries dozens of lines and hundreds, if not thousands, of products. The sales, whether they be in the field or on the phone, are usually more oriented to order taking than to introducing a customer to a new line. This is particularly true when a new concept is involved, whether it be a product design concept or a merchandising concept.

Consider the case of a maker of garden sprayers, a product without significant design innovation for dozens of years. The company developed an improved product that featured lightweight containers. The burden of carrying it—as the consumer sprays shrubs, trees, lawns, and gardens—is greatly reduced. (Other marketers of sprayers were certain to have similar product innovations at about the same time.)

How to "go to market?" For this established marketer, the alternatives did not include giving serious consideration to changing the historic channels of distribution. While it is appropriate to weigh alternatives, once the decision has been made to follow established routes the challenge becomes how to be effective.

Here the task became one of determining which of the "channel partners" was to be given the greatest emphasis in the marketing communications activities. It was determined that a high degree of response could be generated with the retailer so the retailer would aggressively reach out for the line by contacting the marketers' wholesalers or field sales personnel. So the sprayer maker went directly to the retailer, through trade shows and trade magazine advertising. Target accounts were reached through direct mail. These elements in the communication mix were ideal for presenting the new concepts, and program components appeared to have meaningful initial impact on the retailers.

It was essential that the marketer be as innovative in its communications as in its product development. This called for a new name for the line of products, a new logo, a new "selling line," and introduction of a trade character. It was all tied together with a fresh approach to graphics, carried through in packaging and point-of-purchase materials. At the kickoff trade shows, "live marketing" in the form of fresh skitlike presentations clogged the aisles with curious and responsive retailers, backed up by a portfolio of program components for use by field sales personnel in presentations to their buying headquarters' personnel.

In this case history, the challenge was to make the best of the old way of going to market. It was appropriate to examine alternative routes to identify the problems in going to market and to mount a program that would most effectively utilize the strongest links in the distribution system. In arriving at such decisions, it should be obvious that the burdens placed upon the marketing communications elements must be understood and dealt with. One thing to be learned from this case is that existing channels can be more productive under certain sets of conditions and should be given that opportunity to continue as the primary approach to going to market. Once success is achieved through existing channels, it is then appropriate to examine alternatives in order to gain a still greater share of market.

CASE HISTORY 2

What do you do when a client asks you to provide counsel on what lines to add in order to get additional volume from an existing network of automotive jobbers?

The marketer was prepared to go the acquisition route in order to obtain additional aftermarket lines and was also prepared to consider supplementary approaches to distribution.

Initially, it was appropriate to ask some rather basic questions about the existing wholesalers' commitments to the present seven product lines. Analysis found that, on the average, wholesalers were distributing only 2.5 lines of the 7.0 available to them. Study of the situation showed that, if the wholesalers were to add only one line, it would increase the marketer's total volume by more than 25 percent.

It was learned that field sales personnel, charged with the responsibility to add lines, seldom had the opportunity to have meaningful one-on-one discussions with the decision maker. Their sales calls were heavily oriented to servicing the account, and, as a consequence, they seldom had an audience with key management. Part of the challenge in expanding volume through existing distribution channels was that of obtaining an audience with the primary decision maker.

Now the consultant's assignment shifted from one of line extension or distribution alternatives to the development of sales techniques. Because the salespeople were still required for account maintenance work, they had to have a program that could be implemented with minimal time demands. For them to embrace the program, a high percentage of closes, specifically first-call closes, was essential. It was not likely that they would get a key management audience more than once.

That the program was successful makes the point that, before considering alternatives or supplementary approaches to distribution, one should first examine opportunities within the existing channel partner relationships. To underscore the point that a program need not be complex, expensive, or time-intensive to be productive, let's examine the simplicity of this program.

The program theme got right to the point. It was the "sweet add-a-line" program. Headquarters sent postcards to preselected wholesalers. The message indicated that the field salesperson would be visiting the account during an indicated week. The key buying influence was told that the salesperson would come bearing a gift and that she would like to present it personally, since the gift was related to the long-standing business relationship the two firms enjoyed.

The salesperson was able to gain entry to the inner office by announcing that she was expected and had something for the executive. What she had was a phonograph record. A long-playing album of Mitch Miller favorites that included, you guessed it, a rendition of "Sweet Adeline." The Columbia Records album was inserted in a special printed sleeve. The back cover was not unlike a summary page commonly found in a flipchart presentation. The key points of the "add-a-line" program, along with the appropriate profit promises, were presented in boldface type and with appropriate graphics. The salesperson, still holding the gift in her hands, would refer to the key points on the cover before giving it to the decision maker.

This device worked—it got the salesperson in, it got the prospect's attention, it got the key points across. It demanded a reaction—far more often than not, a favorable reaction.

CASE HISTORY 3

A manufacturer of custom kitchen cabinets, historically distributed through dealers who plan layouts, prepare quotations, and install the units, finds it difficult to increase its number of highly productive outlets.

For an upscale line of quality cabinetry there seemed to be some basis for considering going into business with franchised "partners." However, the company was open-minded and was prepared to examine other alternatives. After an evaluation of the components of success, it became apparent that franchising was not the answer, partly because production facilities could not assure adequate inventories. Further, many of the outlets quite properly approached the marketplace with good/better/best product lines. This particular marketer was not oriented to the production of anything but "best."

Through the years, the relationship with existing dealers was a rather loose one. The marketer found itself forever engaged in keeping the dealer sold on the line and getting the dealer to "spec" the line. The challenge became to increase sales per dealer through closer dealer ties, and, when establishing new dealers, to appoint only those with whom there could be this closer tie. What evolved was what might best be called a "factory-associated dealer" relationship. Early on it was determined that what dealers most wanted in their relationships was an integrated and coordinated marketing communications program.

A study of dealer-created advertising, designed to position themselves in their market areas, showed this "homemade" advertising to be far less professional than the services and products they provided. Therefore, this marketer sought and developed a program that dealers used because it enhanced their image. Equally important, the dealers would utilize their own funds in the placement of advertising and the distribution of mailing pieces.

Borrowing from some of the basic principles of franchising, the marketer developed a selling system, including the accompanying materials, that made it easy for the dealer to manage each step of the sale in quoting and in inquiry conversion.

A Look at the Case Histories

Recapping these three cases, the outcome of the studies were:

1. *Stay* with existing channel partners, *after* identifying which one is given most "responsibility" for success.
2. *Stay* with existing channel partners, *adding* another line to wholesalers.
3. *Change* the relationship to one that is more structured. In the process, both the marketer and his primary channel partner become more important to each other.

An appropriate question is: What needs to be asked to determine how right existing partners are? A corollary question becomes: Do we want to change any parts of our plans, programs, policies, and procedures, to fit the needs of the channel partner?

These kinds of questions should surface particularly when a new product is being developed.

In the case of a manufacturer of do-it-yourself (d.i.y.) home improvement products, here are 15 points requiring review prior to proceeding. As you review them, consider the impact of the answers on the marketing communications mix.

1. *Are the performance characteristics needed and wanted by the d.i.y. consumer?*

It is critical to know the characteristics of the consumer segments to which any product is directed. Consumers have varying degrees of expectations. In fast-food, limited-menu restaurants, they expect predictable food quality, predictable preparation characteristics, and predictable levels of service and price/value relationship. So it is in practically all other categories of products and services. In the case of d.i.y. products: How simple, complete, and easy to understand are the instructions? How easy is the installation or application of the product? What amount of time is required? Is there an ongoing requirement for service or maintenance? How long should the product or repair job or installation last? What tools will be needed?

All these questions are in the minds of the consumer as he or she contemplates a project. Marketers must remember that often the consumer visits a store for the purpose of determining the simplicity or complexity of a project. Some of the questions cited above do not surface until he or she is confronted with the realities of the contemplated project.

2. *How right is the product for the d.i.y. user? Evaluation of the degree of skill or understanding required to make a purchasing decision . . . to use the product right*

It is vital that the consumer determine that he or she can attack the project with confidence—that it can be completed without too much trouble and with minimal embarrassment.

3. *Market research? Needed on price points? Perceived value? Motives in purchasing? Who makes the decision? Where do they expect to buy it? Would they prefer it in green? Do they think it's overpackaged?*

On the assumption that the product is, in fact, right for the d.i.y. market, other key questions are to be dealt with. If the answers are not known, then it is appropriate to undertake market research well in advance of market entry. The answers to each question can have significant impact upon decisions related to marketing communications: messages, media, merchandising.

4. *Full knowledge of competitive activities. Really?*

Often marketers know less than necessary about competitors' present and contemplated marketing activities. Sometimes the ignorance results from assuming that certain critical information is not available. Often that assumption is unfounded. Many marketers are not particularly resourceful or dedicated in their quest for competitive intelligence, or they are quite ignorant of the legitimate techniques that can be used to secure really useful information.

5. *Retailer categories. Which types of outlets are right: home centers? hardware stores? department stores? garden centers? catalog showrooms? others?*

Obviously the distribution channels to be utilized have a significant effect upon marketing communications strategies and selection of appropriate components of the marketing communications mix. For example, certain categories of retailers will not use manufacturers' posters. Others welcome them. Certain categories are set up to distribute manufacturers' literature. Others are not. Some categories are primarily self-service. Still others provide varying degrees of customer assistance.

6. *Account classification. Target account selection. What is required?* Within any given category, there are positive differences from one retailer to another. It is, therefore, highly desirable to categorize the accounts on a territory-by-territory basis. Once that has been accomplished, the marketer needs to select the accounts to be sold. In making up a checklist of desired characteristics for target accounts, many variables come into play. It is during this exercise that the marketer must face up to the realities of the marketplace and make an assessment about how well the intended programs square with the interest of target accounts.

7. *Do we have a program . . . or just product and price? What program is on-target for each distribution channel partner?*

It is almost too obvious to repeat that retailers don't buy products—they buy programs. However, even professional marketers have been known to forget or ignore that platitude as they rush to market with a new product. Further, it is one thing to acknowledge that the retailer wants a program, and it is still another to mount a program matching the retailer's needs and interests. The enlightened retailer looks to the manufacturer to be a "partner in profits." The two should approach each other in a cooperative manner, dealing openly and realistically with such matters as marketing functions. Who is to do what?

If the manufacturer approaches the retailer as an adversary, there is little hope for the kind of productive relationship that is possible in today's sophisticated marketing atmosphere.

8. *Pricing, discounts, margins . . . just right? Assortments, "deals" . . . what the distribution factors want, will take . . . are turned on by? Terms, conditions of sale . . . OK? Co-op ad/promotion allowances? What do do?*

As a marketer constructs tailored programs to fit the needs of target accounts, all these elements must be examined.

9. *How right is the sales organization for this effort?*

At introduction time, soul-searching is in order to determine how well the new product relates to the existing sales organization, particularly if there are significant departures from the norm, such as new channels of distribution or different services to be performed for, or with, channel partners.

10. *If not right, can it be made right through training?*

Usually a marketer hopes that any significant changes in sales organization roles and responsibilities can be accomplished through training. Certainly that should be the first approach. Sometimes the changes are so far-reaching that training will not correct the situation. In that case, the marketer faces alternatives that may include supplementing the existing staff or replacing some or all of it.

11. *Manufacturers' reps. All? Some? None? What kind? How to find? How to equip? To motivate? To compensate?*

Often a manufacturer's rep organization enjoys a higher level of acceptance and credibility with a target account than a "factory man." The rep may better understand the retailer's business, certainly on a more current basis, than the factory man with less-frequent contacts at the buying office. The rep has a history of counseling the buyer on a variety of programs. If the rep has given good advice and fulfilled promises, the buyer is likely to be receptive to anything brought in for consideration. If a marketer is not experienced in setting up a rep organization, it is wise to seek sound counsel. There are many opportunities for false starts and shaky relationships from which it is difficult to recover.

12. *How can this product be made important to everybody in every channel of distribution?*

This question is not asked often enough by manufacturers. It is a false assumption that a new product will command the attention of all channel partners. Quite probably not all are waiting with open arms for "just another product." This is indeed a challenge, and there is no single answer to fit all situations. This is a time for resourcefulness and creativity.

13. *Can claims for turnover and profits be presented with freshness and believability?*

All channel partners want turnover and profits. Too often a marketer promises both of these desired benefits but does it in a tired or hackneyed manner. Here is one of the real challenges for effective communications.

14. *Is there a chance to position ourselves in a desirable niche?*

Marketers have very limited opportunities to separate themselves from their competitors. If they are fortunate, a new product will have inherent characteristics that give the marketer an opportunity for exclusive positioning. Obviously, the marketer must first determine what position is best, then whether the product is capable. Then it becomes a challenge to communicators for programs that attain the desired ends. A word of caution: The position should be quite specific. If it is nebulous, such as "we are the widget people," or "the industry's standard of value," or "this is what widgets are all about," the marketer can expect very little recall, recognition, or believability.

15. *Do we know enough about "special" markets: premiums . . . incentives . . . government . . . export . . . catalog showroom?*

Before a marketer settles in with more conventional and comfortable channels of distribution, it is well to look at other opportunities, even though they may require the talent of specialists in these areas. To take one example: If the product being introduced can serve as a premium for a widely advertised product, it is conceivable that a significant amount of the initial awareness job can be accomplished through another marketer's advertising and promotion programs.

Many times a study will expose the need for considering alternative channels of distribution. A very long list of options could be created. Such a list most certainly should include:

1. Nonstore marketing.
2. Franchising.
3. Premium and incentive marketing.

Each of these deserves a fair amount of examination by marketers considering alternatives.

The following list for a retail concept is typical of the critical considerations when determining franchising feasibility:

1. Improvements in the economy.
2. Increase in working women.
3. The aging of America.
4. Increased segmentation of consumer markets, including accelerated development of luxury segments.

5. Increase in shopping as an activity for tourists.
6. Continuing consumer preferences related to leisure activity (time budgeting).
7. Increase in specialty outlets—boutiques and highly specialized catalogs.
8. Continued increase in off-price merchandising.
9. "It's fun again to shop"—as in factory outlet stores (adventure, challenge, surprise, discovery).
10. Continuing good track record for franchised operations.

The would-be franchisor must have a clear understanding of why his or her concept is franchisable or under what set of conditions it is franchisable, or both. Here a study concluded that a would-be franchisor's retail concept would be franchisable for 18 reasons. These are the most significant:

1. A variety of retail concepts have been franchised successfully.
2. The franchise agreements of somewhat similar offerings (in terms of product categories) indicate that, under present franchise law, it is possible to establish and maintain integrity of concept.
3. A regional marketer with a similar concept had been franchised successfully several years ago.
4. There are sufficient margins for the franchisee to permit profitability after payment of appropriate ongoing fees to the franchisor.
5. With a realistic initial franchise fee and opening inventory levels, sales of franchises should not be particularly difficult, time-consuming, or costly.
6. There are enough potentially good sites to make the structuring and operation of a franchised activity rewarding.
7. Entry into franchising can be accomplished without the addition of supplementary permanent personnel until the activity has been well started.
8. Present operations already in place can serve as prototypes for franchised units.
9. The "pilot" units prove that the concept is adaptable to a wide variety of environments.
10. The "pilot" units also prove that the concept is adaptable to a wide variety of available space sizes and configurations.
11. The concept is sufficiently adaptable that franchised units could be incorporated into existing retail formats (not unlike a leased department).
12. The "franchise division" will require certain specialized talents not now present in the company's management group.

Those talents can be added as needed in the form of full-time permanent personnel or purchased as needed outside the company, or both.

13. Relatively speaking, the cost to enter franchising is low.

14. Lead time for market entry is relatively low, probably six to nine months.

For many marketers considering franchising, the study of feasibility is not as simple as those used for these examples. If the concept has not been fully developed, if there are no prototype or pilot operations, if an identity system has not been created, if promotion programs have not been developed and tested, then the marketer must look at a test marketing period that may range from a few months (in the most ideal situation) to a few years, if there are many variables to be assessed.

When considering franchising, it is essential that there be an awareness of the realities of this alternative. It is almost certain that the go-to-market systems will have to be more structured than in conventional distribution. In effect, you are developing a new market entry. There must be testing before entry and certainly before roll-out.

Even though the overall record of business failures among new franchises is significantly lower than other new business start-ups, many of these—as well as franchisor failures—could have been avoided if those responsible for taking the concept to market had undertaken feasibility studies. A marketer who has not been in franchising is not likely to know what is required in a franchise feasibility study. Most marketing consultants do not know, because franchising is such a specialized field. Many so-called franchise consultants are not oriented to analysis as much as they are to getting the franchise offering into the marketplace.

SUMMARY

In summary, these points should stand out:

- The whole subject of channel management is critical to marketing success.
- Understand the needs of existing and prospective channel partners.
- Evaluate the opportunities to make those channel partners fully productive.
- Consider supplementing existing channels with others that better match new or peculiar situations.
- Determine if, when, and how significant departures—franchising, nonstore marketing, premiums, and the like—fit your changing needs.

17

AFTER-SALE STRATEGIES: A PERSPECTIVE ON PRODUCT SUPPORT

by
Dick Berry*

University of Wisconsin

Why should Xerox Corporation create the brand name (Americare) for a dealer-administered servicing program? The program to encompass maintenance, parts, and emergency service support for a variety of personal computer products? Why should Xerox promote this program with a media blitz employing a 10-page, four-color advertisement in a variety of trade press publications?

Why should Brandt, Inc., manufacturer of money-handling equipment, create a new service division with four regional managers, 15 district offices, and 160 service technicians throughout the United States? Why should it enhance this division with a new central computer system, distributed processing to the regional offices, and an independent parts-support warehousing and distribution system?

These two approaches illustrate extremes in the strategic warfare being waged to gain new business opportunities, on the one hand, and to gain customer acceptance, good will, and competitive advantage, on the other. The strategy in both examples is to provide customers with after-sale product support.

Manufacturers, in the first situation, lack after-sale support capability for their products. Additionally, the distribution system is unable to grow and develop adequately to suit evolving customer maintenance

---

* Copyright © Dick Berry, Madison, Wis., 1984

232

and servicing requirements for the new breed of desk-top computers being adopted by business and home users.

The manufacturer, in the second situation, has carefully analyzed the market opportunity and designed a product-support system to suit customer needs for installation, demonstration and training, maintenance, repair services, and parts support. An integrated product-support program has been carefully planned and implemented to suit the company's future marketing plans.

PRODUCT SUPPORT AND AFTER-SALE STRATEGY

The idea of product support and after-sale strategy is not new—it's just that the emphasis has changed. Customers have always expected manufacturers to stand behind their products, to offer warranties, and to provide repair services. Manufacturers around the world have recognized this need and have provided a modicum of support. But products have become more sophisticated and product systems have evolved— requiring high levels of after-sale support. And, most important, established businesses are seeing erosion of their market position as competitors make advances using after-sale and product-support strategies.

The office typewriter has become a word processing system, with terminals, monitors, and central processors, and utilizing daisy-wheel, dot-matrix, and ink-jet printers. Today's secretary functions as an information specialist, interfacing to local-area communication networks and online databases—linked to the world through long-lines and satelite communications.

The home heating system of yesterday is no longer available. Now, new homes are environmentally controlled, with high-efficiency furnaces, heat pumps, and electronic air filtration. All these components are configured in a system with microprocessor control of the environment in all areas of the home.

Manufacturing assembly lines now operate without people attending the assembly process, except to supervise automated machinery and a robotic "work force." Machine operations that make the components are ultimately flexible, set up and supervised by a computer, with the ability to rapidly change operations and tooling to suit the changing configuration of parts needed in the assembly process.

Yesterday's clerical worker, homeowner, and factory worker still have the need to be satisfied. And they are with the new products and systems. But they don't have a ghost of a chance of being able to maintain and repair the new products and systems themselves. They don't have the know-how and skills. They don't have the necessary instrumentation and servicing documentation. They must have service support.

Meanwhile, with the proliferation of this technology, many manufacturers have been oblivious to the idea of product support. Others have made some effort to adapt but have kept the service manager back under the stairway in his tiny office, replete with card files and three-ring binders of parts and service documentation. Little do they know that two of the products obsoleted in the late 1970s were the card file and three-ring binder.

The idea of after-sale strategy is evolving from this milieu—not clearly defined, but the result of experimentation, trial, and error. Manufacturers, distributors, dealers, and independent service companies are the actors in this drama. Still to be resolved is the concept of the "applications-support function," to assist the users with the complications of adaptation and use. The companies adopting word processing and microcomputer systems well know the dilemma.

THE SEARCH FOR CUSTOMER SATISFACTION

Customers, whether commercial, industrial, agricultural, or consumer, quickly set aside the good feelings arising from new product ownership and start looking for satisfactions from its use. They begin to ask cold, hard questions: "How is it doing?" "Is it working all right?" "Is the productivity still up?" Customers lose interest in the product or process and want the results. Customers don't like traumatic situations or to be hassled. They quickly succumb to the euphoric feelings that come from trouble-free operation. For this reason, customers are willing to invest in maintenance contracts to keep things running smoothly. Our insurance industry attests to the fact that we are a people who live in fear of breakdown, failure, or loss.

Quite like the "marketing mix," so useful in marketing-strategy evaluation and planning, is the idea of an "after-service mix," with the principle elements as follows:

- Warranty.
- Extended warranty.
- Maintenance agreement.
- Repair service.
- Emergency service.
- Inspection and calibration.
- Demonstration and customer training.

Each of these service offerings has a different value perception to customers. Warranty and maintenance agreements are the basic "insurance coverage" afforded to persons with ownership. The services of inspection and calibration are particularly important to owners of instrumentation and functioning products with high performance expectations. Emergency and repair services are the usual support that customers take for granted, as after-sale provisions. These are the services that are typically provided by manufacturers through their dealer organization, by arrangement with independent servicers, or by a field service force—the traditional service offerings. Demonstration and customer training are becoming increasingly important as products and systems become more sophisticated. These services, in many cases, serve to develop a long-lasting bond between a supplier and customers.

THE INSURANCE PERSPECTIVE OF SERVICE

The insurance dimension of after-sale service support is illustrated in Table 17–1. The table is an attempt to portray the perceived value and importance of different service elements to a company's customers.

The desire for uninterrupted satisfaction is the motivation for customers to purchase maintenance contracts, emergency service, or repairs. This desire equates with the opportunity to provide a variety of after-services, meanwhile cementing relationships, thus to assure repeat purchase of consumables, additional or replacement products, and systems.

It doesn't take a great deal of imagination to realize that IBM and Caterpillar, for example, achieved their positions of industry leadership and dominance because of customer support. Big Yellow goes so far as to guarantee 24-hour parts delivery, anywhere in the world—usually backed up with a well-trained mechanic and multilanguage documentation. Big Blue has pioneered remote diagnostics and has an online database of previously diagnosed problems and their solutions. An IBM customer can access support facilities in Chicago, Tampa, or Boulder to solve software problems. Dual levels of support are routinely available, on a 24-hour, 365-days-a-year basis. This is reported to lead to resolution of 85 percent of all software problems by phone—most within 30 minutes. The remaining 15 percent of problems receive the immediate attention of a local field engineer, dispatched to the customer. Imagine an invading army—a competitor—being able to penetrate these defenses and to take market share.

WHAT IS THE OPPORTUNITY?

IBM's field service divisions generate $6.4 billion each year, with an annual growth rate of 20 percent (1982). A portion of the "mother lode" is derived from installation and customer training, but a hand-

TABLE 17–1
Value of Service Support Programs to Customers

Value to Customer	Warranty	Extended Warranty	Maintenance Agreement	Repair Service	Emergency Service	Inspection Calibration	Demonstration
1. To insure against product failure.	(X)	(X)	X			X	(X)
2. To insure against high cost of repair or replacement.	X	X	X			(X)	(X)
3. To predict and control cost of investment and use.	X	X	X				
4. To restore failed product system.	(X)	(X)	(X)	X	X		
5. To prevent product or system deterioration.			X	(X)		X	X
6. To insure against large repair bills.	X	X	X				
7. To insure continued performance of an aging product.			X	(X)	(X)	X	(X)
8. To minimize or prevent system downtime.		(X)	X	(X)	(X)	X	
9. To assure proper use and application of product.			(X)			(X)	x
10. To assure availability of qualified repair maintenance services.	(X)	(X)	X			(X)	(X)

Legend: X denotes usual value perception.
(X) denotes additional protective value.

Source: Reprinted with permission from *Managing Service for Results* by Dick Berry. Copyright © Instrument Society of America, 1983.

some portion derives from after-sale support services. IBM's service revenue is approximately 20 cents of every dollar earned. This is a useful ratio to estimate the opportunity for durable goods industries.

To highlight the potential for a single product group, take desk-top computers—with 5 million units estimated to be in place in U.S. business establishments in the mid-1980s. Conservatively, this equates to annual service revenue of approximately $500 million dollars, with a gross margin of 50 percent at the manufacturer's level. It will require approximately 5,000 technicians to support this volume of product with contract maintenance and repair services. These numbers suggest the rationale for Xerox's Americare program and justify the heavy media expense for its trade advertising. Other major independent service organizations, such as Bell & Howell, Sorbus, TRW, Western Union, General Electric, and RCA are also pursuing this opportunity. Why? Because the desk-top computer manufacturers do not have adequate after-sale support to provide need-satisfying services to their customers.

SERVICE SUPPORT LEVEL

The manufacturer or distributor of a product or product system must make a decision about the service support level to be provided its customers. The planning for this support must anticipate both presale and postsale services, encompassing the requirements for technical information, repair and emergency services, installation, demonstration, and customer training to use the new apparatus, warranty provisions, use of consumables, maintenance services, and replacement parts support.

At the heart of this decision process for a manufacturer is the customer expectation for service support, serviceability of the product or system, quality level in the manufacturing process, expected level of product performance, and the technical complexity of the application. In the latter consideration, it must be determined if the "average customer" will be able to comprehend and use a complex system.

To illustrate the latter, the first introductions of medical patient-monitoring systems in this country, by Ohio Medical Products (then Ohio Chemical & Surgical Equipment Company), failed because health care professionals were unable to deal with the complexities of the new products and were not supported in their application, maintenance, and repair. The Technicon Company, a present-generation medical equipment company and provider of advanced multifunction blood analysis apparatus, plans its product development thrust, anticipating the level of technological capability of its customers. The company couples this with its ability to provide user applications support through its service engineering staff and Technicenter support capability. Technicon anticipates being part of each customer applications team, to support after-sale user requirements. This stance allows Technicon to use advanced technology and sophistication that otherwise would not be allowable.

STRATEGIC PERSPECTIVE FOR SERVICE SUPPORT

As a customer progresses through the various stages of acquisition and use, the different service elements assume greater or lesser value. Each company has a different perspective of their customers, as compared to competitors. It is this difference and the ability of each company to provide varying degrees of after-sale support that makes one company more successful than another. Each company, to be competitively strong, must carefully plan and implement its service strategy.

FIGURE 17–1
Objective-Setting and Strategy-Formulation Process for Service

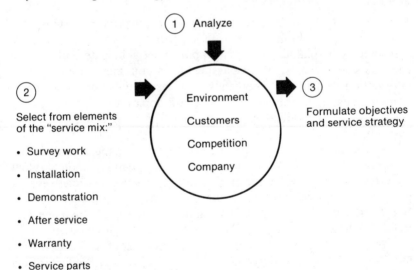

Source: Reprinted with permission from *Managing Service for Results* by Dick Berry. Copyright © Instrument Society of America, 1983.

Figure 17–1 depicts the strategic process to select the most important program offerings for its customers. Companies that use this strategy-planning approach in their management of new programs are assured opportunity to satisfy customers and offset competition.

INTEGRATED MARKETING STRATEGY

Evolving technologies are characterized by entrepreneurship, with lack of capitalization and poor cash flow. Consequently, technologically new products and systems offer promise of failure for many participants, simply because product support cannot be provided. The graveyards of automobile, appliance, and computer manufacturers attest to this supposition. Thus, evolving technologies offer promise for independent service organizations to grow and flourish.

The traditional mature industries are characterized by fragmented but abundant service support. The pre-oil embargo scenario of the automobile industry was a picture of a parts house in the middle of every downtown city block, with four service stations on every corner. All were willing to provide smiling, friendly maintenance and repair services, supported with free transportation while your automobile was confined. This happened because adequate after-sales support was not packaged and available with new automobiles. With demise of the "service station concept," starting in 1973, independent maintenance and repair service networks for automobile owners is a distinct opportunity waiting to be exploited, either by the automobile manufacturers, oil companies, or independents.

SERVICE-REQUIREMENTS PLANNING

Service-requirements planning should be carried out early in the design stage of a new product. This is the time when you begin designing an integrated marketing strategy for your company. The decision elements in this process are depicted in Table 17–2.

The objective-setting and strategy-formulation process, illustrated in Figure 17–1, suggests the importance of viewing your strategy in

---

TABLE 17–2
Decision Elements in an Integrated Marketing Program

Marketing strategy planning must anticipate customer requirements, competition, and the need to implement strategy elements "down the channel."

Product	Distribution	Service	Pricing	Promotion
Features	Channel	Parts	Amount	Publicity
Quality	selection	support	Terms	Advertising
Reliability	Facilities	Presale	Offers	Sales
	Locations	services		support
Serviceability		Postsale		
		services		

light of the total marketing environment. You must consider your company's business purpose and mission as the first step in the planning process. Your company's planned technological thrust and avenues of market expansion and development are the foundation for service-strategy planning. Service operations are supportive to these broader strategies and implementation.

After-sale service is but one element in a company's marketing-strategy package. Each element interlaces with the others—products, distribution, pricing, promotion, and service support—hopefully yielding the desired combination to satisfy customers and to offset competition. Service support must span the periods of customer investigation, trial, acquisition, and use. After-sale product support is but one phase of the customer satisfaction process.

A company's anticipated product population and locations are the basis for service requirements planning. This, coupled with maintenance and repair requirements, provides the quantification to plan service support.

If, on an annual basis, each product requires A hours of technician time for maintenance and B hours for repairs, then the annual requirement for technician support, designated Tt, is estimated by multiplying the time requirement by the number of products. Similarly, the requirements for parts and supplies, designed Mt, is the product of the materials needed, times the number of products.

FORMULAS FOR ESTIMATING SERVICE REQUIREMENTS

The technician and materials requirements for a service operation can be estimated using the following formulas:

Annual technician time requirement:

$$Tt = Np \times (Hm + Hr) = \text{Annual hours}$$

Annual materials requirement:

$$Mt = Np \times (P + S) = \text{Annual cost}$$

where: Tt is the total annual technician time requirement
Np is the number of products placed
Hm is the annual maintenance hours, per product
Hr is the annual repair hours, per product
Mt is the total annual materials for maintenance supplies and repairs
P is the annual parts cost for repair and maintenance, per unit

S is the annual supplies cost for repair and maintenance, per unit

Were we to estimate the potential for independent and dealer servicing in the microcomputer business applications market, previously discussed, these estimating equations would yield the following:

Estimate of service opportunity:

Units in place (1985): 5 million; assume 40 percent on maintenance contracts and requiring repair services
Maintenance labor requirement, annual, per unit: 2 hours
Repair service labor requirement, annual, per unit: 1 hour
Maintenance supply requirement, annual cost, per unit: $8.00
Repair parts requirement, annual, per unit: $95.00

$$Tt = 0.4(5,000,000)(2 + 1) = 6,000,000 \text{ hours}$$
$$= 9,230,770 \text{ hours at } 65\%$$
$$\text{efficiency}$$
$$= 1,153,864 \text{ technician days}$$
$$= 5,245 \text{ technician years}$$

$$Mt = 0.4(5,000,000)(8.00 + 95.00) = \$206,000,000$$

A dealer in a metropolitan area, or an independent servicing company, with a product potential of fewer units, need only to revise the magnitude of calculations to suit their specific requirements. In the previous example, were the population to be 5,000 units, the requirement would be for 5 technicians, involving parts and supplies of $200,000 each year.

ALTERNATIVE APPROACHES TO PRODUCT SUPPORT

Since 1970, IBM has had remote diagnostic capability engineered into its computer systems. IBM also has a so-called Maintenance Device, a hand-held maintenance processor that diagnoses product problems by interrogating the field engineer on a logic path that leads to identification of a failed component. Similar capability was available through hardcopy procedures "in the early years," now replaced by diagnostic software on floppy disks. These methods fall within the class of automatic test equipment (ATE), now being utilized extensively in high-technology products. Use of ATE allows a company to dramatically improve productivity of its service force, reduce requirements for service part inventories, and more importantly, adopt after-sale support practices that will enhance customer satisfaction and minimize downtime.

One variation of ATE is provided by the Teradyne Company. Its business is to conduct off-hours testing of telephone subscriber equipment. While customers sleep at night, a computer in a central exchange checks out user phone equipment to determine if it is working properly.

These sophisticated approaches allow a company to service its customers effectively, while maximizing service force effectiveness and productivity.

One company that is well tuned to the opportunity offered by after-sale product support is Federal Mogul Corporation. Federal Mogul has emphasized its after-sale business to vehicular, construction, general industrial, and aerospace customers. Among new programs is a hot line for technical services that generates about 150 customer calls a day. Promotion of this service increased the daily inbound call frequency from 20 calls a day to its current rate. The calls are fielded by a technical services manager and staff, providing information on parts and technical service. F-M also emphasizes its "Five Star Fleet" program, launched to provide after-sale support to its heavy-duty on-highway customers. The program promotes specific benefits of (1) nationwide parts availability, (2) a quality package of heavy-duty bearings and seals, (3) parts obsolescence protection, (4) single-source parts selections for distributors, and (5) product updates. To assure their ability to deliver on product support, F-M has designated one sixth of the space in its recent 17-million-foot plant expansion for an employee training center, dedicated to keep employees up to date on product application information.

KEYS TO GROWTH IN AFTER-SALE SERVICE

The General Electric Company, at its Bridgeport office in Connecticut, recently explored the importance of service support elements to the gain or loss of out-of-warranty service business. The program accomplished controlled testing to determine the relative importance of "readiness to serve," "performance quality of after-service," and use of promotional methods for service. The study resulted in a downplaying of promotion, with emphasis on balancing of service level and quality of service performance.

One interesting finding in the study was that adequate incoming phone lines and call-taker capacity were essential requirements to build a share of contract maintenance and repair business. Simply stated, customers are easily dissuaded from trying to seek out a provider if they have trouble gaining phone contact. Additionally, customers quickly changed service providers if the quality of service performance was low. These are two important but easily overlooked aspects in a company's efforts to optimize after-sale strategies.

SUMMARY

After-sale strategy is an often overlooked component in a company's customer service package. As products and systems become more technically complex, customers demand higher levels of maintenance and repair support to assure trouble-free operation.

Companies should carefully balance their mix of warranty coverage, maintenance programs, repair and emergency services, inspection and calibration services, demonstration, and customer training. Each of these offerings has a different value perspective to customers, contributing differently to a customers decision to continue relationships with a supplier.

After-sale services, in addition to supporting long-term customer relationships, also offer manufacturers and their distribution and independent servicers a lucrative opportunity for profitable business. Suggestions are given to formulate after-sale strategies to avail a company of this opportunity for profitable business.

The importance of providing adequate "readiness to serve" and "performance quality" of after-sale service is stressed.

READINGS AND REFERENCE

Berry, Dick, and Carol Superenant. *An Overview of Product Service.* Chicago: National Association of Service Managers, Service Executives Digest Series, 1979.

Berry, Dick. *Managing Service For Results.* Research Triangle Park, N.C.: Instrument Society of America, 1983.

Bluel, William H., and Joseph D. Patton, Jr. *Service Management Principles and Practices.* Research Triangle Park, N.C.: Instrument Society of America, 1978.

Hauk, James G. *Technical Service in the American Economy.* Ann Arbor: Michigan Business Studies, vol. 16, no. 1. University of Michigan, 1962.

"Editorial: An Overlooked Opportunity," "Miller on Service," "ATE & Productivity," "Attacking the Personal Computer Market," "IBM." *Computer/Electronic Service News,* September–October 1983, pp. 6, 20–24, 26–30, 36–40, 48–52.

"GE Generates Service Business by Shifting Dollars from Advertising to Order-Capturing." *Marketing News,* June 24, 1983, p. 12.

"Federal Mogul Tries Service Marketing Strategy." *Business Marketing,* April 1983, p. 22.

18

ESTABLISHING AND MANAGING TELEMARKETING

by
Stephen D. Boudreau, Jr.

St. Regis Corporation

Even a cursory and inexact study of communications costs establishes categories. This examination is the first and absolutely essential requirement in employing telemarketing in a strategy of communication (see Table 18–1).

A STRATEGY OF COMMUNICATIONS

The "mix" of these methods, the choice of one medium versus another for each customer classification depends upon the particular goals of the business. How we use each of them determines the cost effectiveness of our selling system. One medium may well support the other— personal selling backed up by the telephone will work with some customers. Telephone selling backed up by direct mail may increase the effectiveness of each, and advertising may be combined with each of them.

THE "ABOMINABLE NO-MAN SYNDROME"

The telephone as a marketing communications medium: whoever heard of such a thing? But to some: what an interesting idea? Why interesting? Because it *is* personal, and it is the only other means of *two-way* communications beside face-to-face contact.

But it won't work! You cannot sell industrial products on the telephone. Whoever heard of buying fasteners, strapping materials, pack-

TABLE 18–1
Comparison of Customer Contact Costs

Category	Estimated Cost
Personal selling, face-to-face	$100–$178
Telemarketing calls, personal contact	$2–$10
Direct-mail contact	$0.40 to $x
Magazine advertising (depends on publication)	$0.30 to $0.40
Exhibits and displays	$5 to $100
Bulletins and brochures	$0.40 to $x

aging, chemicals, paint, tools, ink, or rollers on the telephone? An industrial buyer must have samples, be able to see, feel, test.

The tired litany of the "abominable no-man" goes on and on. It is the same narrow view that held, "You can't sell groceries without a clerk—well, maybe groceries but not meat." And, "OK, you sold meat and groceries but not health and beauty aids—surely not clothing and shoes."

The unassailable fact is that telephone selling, becoming ever more sophisticated, *will* work, will become part of a strategy of communications for most companies because it is *cost effective!*

It is not an untried, untested concept. The "interesting gadget" of Mr. Bell's, the voice teacher, which was relegated to a parlor-game toy by the pundits of the late 1800s, now numbers over 250 million units in the United States alone. Estimates are mindboggling, ranging to 500 million calls a day, 70 million for business. Experts calculate that close to 70 percent—$2 billion—of Sears' $3 billion annual catalog sales are made through the telephone. With industrial corporations beginning to make 10 percent or more of annual sales through telemarketing, the savings can be very significant. A careful analysis must be made, however, before launching a telemarketing program.

SETTING UP A TELEMARKETING SYSTEM

There are seven basic steps to follow in evaluating and setting up a telemarketing system.

1. Customer/prospect cost analysis.
2. Classifying accounts/analysis of value.
3. Designating "T" (telemarketing) accounts (full and support).

4. Organizing the telemarketing department.
5. Selecting personnel and training.
6. Monitoring methods, control, and record-keeping.
7. Maintaining and developing relationships with other disciplines.

Cost Is the Key . . .

The average cost of an industrial sales call, reported by McGraw-Hill's Laboratory of Advertising Performance to be $178, may not be accurate in your operation. For example, a medium-sized manufacturer or a plant region of a large corporation may have a sales force that serves a very compact market. Overnight travel, airplanes, and trains are rarely used, and there may be minimal entertainment required. Such costs as meals and services may also be lower outside of major metropolitan markets. Sales call costs in such situations may easily be under $100.

Customer Classification

Obviously, certain customers are more valuable to a supplier than are others. More than sales volume alone must be considered, although that is the place to begin.

Numbers of people have identified the ratio of sales volume to key accounts, and studies have confirmed that the segments are generally accurate:

A. 15 percent of accounts equal 65 percent of sales volume.
B. 20 percent of accounts equal 20 percent of sales.
C. 65 percent of accounts equal 15 percent of sales volume.

Note that these classifications are based on sales volume alone. Clearly there are many other factors to consider. Some accounts presently identified as C accounts (based on volume) may have potential which qualifies them to be called on with A account frequency. Likewise, some A accounts, particularly those on contract, may be called on with a C account frequency.

Among other issues that affect customer value are: the adaptability to equipment, plant location, special handling, shipping and services, order size, and inventory. Each of these may be weighted according to its value to your organization. As an example, a weighting of 50 might be given to volume, 25 to margin, 5 to 10 to equipment, 5 to good order cycles, 5 to plant location. Services which cost money may have a negative value—the exact weighting will depend on the particular situation of markets and business . . . special handling might be rated at minus 10, for example.

In the earlier review of cost effectiveness, it was evident that a single sales call could cost from $100 to $178, and further, that an average of five calls was required to secure an order. Thus, an investment of $500 to $890 is made just to gain the order. If a 10 percent return on sales is sought, a $5,000 sale is required, or $8,900 in the second situation. If 5 percent return on sales is the goal, $10,000 to $17,800 is required just to break even.

Whether these numbers are identical to a particular situation is not the point; *a return on the time invested in an account is basic to a successful business.*

It is self-evident that there will be smaller accounts where it may be difficult to recapture this investment. Yet, if we add the sales volume of these accounts, we will find they equal a substantial total sales volume. If we do not want to give up this volume, we must find a less-costly way to generate orders.

Designation of Telemarketing Accounts

The smaller marginally profitable accounts referred to are generally the first goals of a telemarketing system. There are pitfalls, however, and one in particular provides a trap for the unwary. When the decision is made to transfer marginal or small accounts from a C classification to a T status, salespeople must transfer those accounts to a telemarketing responsibility. Experience has shown that the judgment for that transfer must not be left to the salesperson. The *sales manager* must direct the transfer, according to definite agreed-upon criteria. Without these agreed-upon criteria, there is a danger that sales may transfer old inactive accounts—which perhaps cannot be sold anything, anyway.

These accounts are essentially full telemarketing accounts, since not enough profits are likely to be generated by field sales calls. However, judgment also must be used; very occasionally a salesperson will be required to call, regarding a sample or a particular specification.

In practice it has been found that sales managers are not likely to identify clearly with their responsibility for telemarketing. This responsibility must be made clear and unequivocal: Telemarketing is as much a part of the customer/prospect call and contact as is field sales.

Support *or* Supplementary Accounts. Certain accounts, which traditionally were thought to require constant scheduled calls, may in fact be more than happy to reduce the number of personal face-to-face calls. If the account is well known, the simplest way is to ask. Another approach is to carefully use the telephone to supplement in-person calls, reducing the in-person calls over a time period. With a combination of face-to-face calls, supported by telemarketing, a high level of sales contact can be maintained while reducing total sales costs. If, for example, we could reduce the number of sales calls on an account from 12 to 8, filling in with four telephone calls, we would have greatly reduced our costs (33 percent). Perhaps as important, we would also free salespeople to contact other accounts.

New Accounts and Prospecting with Telemarketing. Although not always thought of as applying in a business-to-business situation, carefully prepared programs and well-trained people can be very successful in securing new business. Success depends on the selection of prospects to call, coupled with carefully prepared scripts and questionnaires (see Figure 18–1).

Lists can be developed in a number of ways. One is a review of all inactive accounts, and another is through various research services. Some of these provide data by four-digit SIC—including name, address, telephone number, number of employees, and dollar sales volume of business.

Other services provide all these data plus an estimated annual usage of *your* product. This estimate is based upon a "quantification factor," developed from the relationship between the total reported sales and the amount of your product normally required (an accuracy of 85 percent to 90 percent is claimed by the service).

Telemarketing Qualification Program (TQP). Inquiries generated by other communications pose a serious problem for most advertisers. On the one hand, they justify the investment in that particular medium, but they deserve a fast response. Sending such unqualified leads to the sales organization to follow up is ineffective at best. To send them to a distributor is a disaster. The reason, of course, is that a great many of the inquiries can be from people with only an idle interest. Any salesperson who has spent an hour driving to a remote spot only to find the company out of business or the individual interested in a single unit worth $10 has a very short fuse in terms of inquiries. The distributor

---

FIGURE 18–1
Script (*Telemarketing Initial Call—Qualification*)

Prospect: Good morning/afternoon.

                   This is ABC Company calling. My name is _____ . I'm calling about your widget product program.

[If the product ⌐ [Thank prospect and terminate (enter name on call record).]
is not used]

                   Are you the person responsible for buying widgets for your company?

FIGURE 18–1 *(concluded)*   **249**

[If yes]   We have developed a unique new widget—stronger, lighter in
                          weight, with much higher tear and bursting resistance than
                          other widgets now available. And since it is lighter in weight, it
                          will save you postage costs.

[If no, ask to   [Thank prospect.]
be trans-
ferred]

[If yes, con-   And what is your name, please?
tinue]
                          _____

                          And your title is?

                          _____

                          Thank you very much. Are there also other people who have an
                          interest in widgets. I'm thinking particularly of marketing/mer-
                          chandising people.

                          Record—if any _____ .

                          Well, Mr./Mrs./Ms. _____ :

                          Our new widgets can have a very significant impact on the cost
                          of your widget program.

                          They are made from a totally new kind of metal unique to our
                          company. They are manufactured differently than other widgets
                          and will give you much better service at lower cost. As you may
                          know, new ways to manufacture widgets are very rare and a
                          major investment is required.

                          Our super widgets upgrades widget programs—even the color
                          is different—a clear even color of light blue . . . it *looks* new
                          and modern—it feels like quality and it will protect your mail-
                          ings better.

                          And Mr./Mrs./Ms._____we will analyze the cost of
                          your present system through our computer-generated Value
                          Analysis Program at no cost or obligation on your part.

                          (1) How many widgets might you use annually?_____

                          (2) And how large might your average order be?_____

                          (3) And what style and size are they?_____

                          Giving me the information on the phone will speed up the
                          analysis—or I can send you a request card?

[If return   Thank you. We will respond as quickly as we receive your card.
card]
                          _____
[If data sheet
requested,   _____
follow in-
structions   _____
about size of
account]   Thank you. We will have our salesperson call you for an ap-
[If important   pointment to complete your Super Widget Value Analysis.
volume]

salesperson, who usually is on commission, will *not* invest his or her time in such lost causes. Telemarketing people can quickly qualify such accounts and determine whether the inquirer is really interested, what business he or she is in, and whether they really use your product and in what quantities. See Figure 18–1 (qualification script). Management should keep in mind that expert opinion fixes such telephone calls at the $2 to $3 range.

Costs. While no fixed and certain estimates of telemarketing costs exist, it is generally considered to be in the $6 to $8 per call range. These costs would include those for personnel, salaries and benefits, overhead, equipment charges, and the cost of the call itself. Note that these estimates are for industrial telemarketing, where calls lasting 15 to 20 minutes are often required.

When one considers $6 to $8 invested, sometimes less, it is clearly a more practical approach to handling inquiries than an investment of $100 or more in a personal sales call.

Careful records must be kept of such inquiries to determine their

---

FIGURE 18–2
Direct Mail Announcement

Dear Current Customer:

I would like to advise you of a new computer-based program which we have developed to serve your account even better than it has been in the past.

The program will benefit you immediately in several ways:

— It will save you time in placing orders.
— It will reduce your purchasing costs.
— It will help you maintain better inventory control.
— It will reduce or eliminate the need for emergency shipments.

Our new telemarketing program is based upon computer record of your order cycles and purchases. The system will allow you to obtain the same quality of service as the very largest account we have and makes order placement as simple and quick as picking up the telephone on your desk.

My name is _____ , your personal telemarketing sales representative.

I'll be calling you in a few days to answer any questions you may have and further explain the benefits of this program to you.

Sincerely,

value. If it is found from the qualification call that the account or person has general or future interest only, then literature can be provided *without* a personal call. And the uninitiated must not assume that such information is difficult to secure. People will provide an amazing amount of information over the telephone to a skilled professional. The sequence of questioning and the manner in which it is done is the key to success. Various scripts should be developed and tested (see Figures 18–1, 18–2, and 18–3).

FIGURE 18–3
Follow-up Script Direct Mail

Prospect:	(1) Good Morning/afternoon—this is ABC Widget Company calling. I'm *[your name]* _____ .
	(2) I'm calling to find out if you had received a mailing from us on our new Super Widget.
[If no]	(3) [Make record—and continue at (5).]
[If yes]	(4) That's fine—as we explained in that material, our new Super Widget will give you the protection and security of stronger widgets and at less total cost. It's even better looking—more modern—with a great printing surface.
	(5) Not only can you use a unit at least 20 percent lighter—it's less bulky and there's no loss in performance. You'll save on freight, reduce your warehouse and inventory space, save on postage charges, and material costs. Savings up to 30 percent or more depending on your usage.
[Note: make record]	About what is your annual usage of the old regular widgets? We believe we can prove it to you, Mr./Mrs./Ms. _____ in cold facts. As we said in the mailing, at absolutely no obligation on your part, we will do a computer-generated Value Analysis of your specific widget program—demonstrating your specific savings using our Super Widgets.
[If major account XXX or more]	When would it be convenient to call to start your personal Value Analysis? _____ Is the morning or afternoon best?
[If had not received mailing]	Mr./Mrs./Ms. _____ I'm going to put your copy of these materials in the mail today. Please review them and mail back the card for your personal computerized Value Analysis for your widget program. We'll look forward to receiving it. Thanks [end interview]. [Record follow up in tickler file.] [Set up prospect profile and call record.]

Organizing the Telemarketing Department

Since telemarketing is new, there are few rules to follow—logic reigns and practicality is the answer.

Considerable success has been attained by building on a competent, experienced customer service organization. In industrial marketing and selling, customer service representatives are often more in touch with customers than are the salespeople. Where the order entry process is even slightly complex, the salesperson may tend to leave the real job to the customer service representative. While sometimes the sale is made by the field sales person, the actual purchase order is mailed by the customer to the supplier. Reorders by telephone direct to customer service are not unusual.

However it comes about, customer service people readily develop a rapport with customers. They often correct errors, follow up details, assure delivery, and become quite valuable to the customer. Each time they are in contact, they have an opportunity to enrich an order, call attention to a better-quantity order or discount, reduce costs of shipping, and so on. Such people develop a very real skill on the telephone and can easily handle this assignment.

Experience in industrial telemarketing, however, has shown that some incentive seems to be in order. Unless customer service people are assigned to specific accounts, and unless a goal of numbers of calls to be made by each customer service representative is agreed upon and some form of incentive provided, early success appears to dwindle.

These same issues confront the management of field sales—the issues should not be taken as negatives in respect to telemarketing. It is always interesting to note how often managers, who recognize that a number of field sales calls are usually required to close an order, seem to be convinced that other forms of communication should be more effective. The reverse is always true—the personal, face-to-face call is most effective—and, on average, it takes five calls to get the order.

While no specific data on rate of closings are presently available for telemarketing, a ratio of 8 to 10 calls per order is considered by many industrial marketing managers to be fairly accurate. The same ingredients apply: persistence, plus a professional, disciplined approach with adequate records. The cardinal error is to "wing it." Memory cannot be depended on, and those who make up their phone conversation as they go along will nearly always fail.

Customer Service—Who's Got the Time? While this can be a legitimate complaint, a careful analysis of the job objectives of customer service people most often will disclose that a better-trained, better-organized customer service operation will free enough time—in an industrial operation.

Consumer telemarketing experts talk blithely in terms of 10,000 calls per person per year. But such a figure does not begin to apply to industrial applications. The experts also speak in terms of 20 telephone calls per hour. Most industrial applications think in terms of only hundreds of calls per person per year. This would apply particularly in multiplant operations with customer service personnel at each plant (see Figure 18–4).

There is a trend, as telephone equipment becomes more sophisticated and computer scheduling of manufacturing becomes more widespread, to centralize customer service operations. In such situations, the telemarketing program may be more effective by having specialists assigned solely to telemarketing.

It may also apply to telemarketing assigned to the "dispersed" customer service operations. It may be found that, in spite of a well-organized program, some people, although competent in customer service, simply lack the temperment and ability to do an effective telemarketing job.

Nowhere is it written, however, that adjustments cannot be made,—for example, assigning the telemarketing mission to a few selected, capable people while rewarding them for the effort and success.

Selection of Telemarketing Personnel and Training

The one obvious talent telemarketing sales representatives must have is the ability to communicate on the telephone. Therefore, no matter what the search procedure, whether in-company transfer or from the outside, the first interview must be by telephone. If responding to an advertisement, the respondent must demonstrate an understanding of what was outlined and an ability to respond to need.

It matters little whether the respondents voice is low or high, male or female, or has a northern or southern accent: Voice *quality* is important. Does the person sound interested, concerned? Is there good inflection? Is the speech clear, understandable? Is the speech well-paced, not too rapid? Does the person respond well to a rapid switch of subjects? Is the person easily distracted?

Another quality to consider is written communication skills. The only way to evaluate the outcome of a phone interview is through a written report. Writing skills, therefore, should be evaluated.

Call Planning—Selling Techniques. The same care and attention to detail must be observed in planning a telemarketing call as for a face-to-face sales call. Remember that a telemarketing call is just as personal. In some respects it is even more so. Your call comes unbidden and uninvited into the person's office, with direct dialing often right to the

FIGURE 18–4

Date:_____

Direct Mail/Telemarketing Report

Account Name _____   Telemarketing

Address: _____   Representative_____

                _____   Territory_____

Telephone   SIC Category_____

No.:   _____   Account

Type of   Classification_____

Business   _____

Account Contact(s) _____

(Name and Title) _____

(Indicate as   _____

1,2,3 etc.)   _____

                    _____

Direct Mail   _____

Description

and date out _____   _____

                _____   _____

First Call

Telemarketing   Date_____   Time_____

                Contact_____   _____

                        (Name)   (Title)

Comments

Type,   _____

Volume,   _____

etc.   _____

             _____

Action   To Sales   ☐   Quote requested   ☐

             Telemarketing follow-up ☐   Value Analysis Request ☐

             Mail follow-up   ☐   Order   ☐

person. It may come in the middle of a conversation, or another task, or even when someone else may be sitting at the desk.

There are many factors that are identical to the field sales call. Among these are the need for a sales-call planner to prepare for the first call, the necessity of having a customer profile and action plan, a report of results, and a follow-up system. The same sets of product needs exist, and the salesperson must satisfy the same kind of psychological human needs as well.

But from the very first words of the sales-call interview, we must recognize that there are differences in technique. There is no visual body language at play—it is not possible to *see* either impatience or dawning acceptance on the face of the prospect. It is not possible to generalize in telemarketing. The field salesperson, although trained to open an interview by getting directly into the subject, often relieves his or her own anxieties by talking about the weather, the ball game, and the like.

All field sales people should be *required* without exception to begin every sales-call interview with the words, "The reason for my call today is. . . ." The discipline involved in being forced not only to come up with a reason but to document that reason would significantly increase sales effectiveness.

There is no choice, no alternative on the telemarketing call. One cannot say, "I just happened to be passing a phone booth and. . . ." The only possible opening after saying "hello" is to say, "The reason for my call today is. . . ."

And the reasons for calling cannot be dreamed up from the imagination. They must be specific and objective. For example:

- To introduce XYZ Company's telemarketing service.
- To present a specific product/service offer.
- To follow up an order, a bid, a quotation, and the like.
- To follow up a salesperson's call.
- To qualify accounts.
- To provide shipping information.
- To provide data on customer's inventory and order requirements, and so on.

The Call Planner (see Figure 18–5) is the basis for early orientation of the telemarketing representative. It should cover all the facts and data that can be discovered about the account *before* the first call.

Ready Answers—Exhibit Knowledge. In field sales-call interviews, it is often possible, even desirable, to respond to some queries by acknowledging that, while you do not have an immediate answer, you will find out and advise the customer. Certainly the field sales representative should voyage forth well prepared, but better the honest answer, "I'm not sure," than an incorrect one.

There is apparently a psychological change which takes place in telephone communications. The customer or prospect appears to endow the calling telemarketing sales representative with more than a

FIGURE 18–5
The Call Planner

Date:_____

Telemarketing Call Planner

Account name   TQP classification

_____   _____

Address _____   Phone _____

_____

Contact _____ Title _____ Extension _____

Account history/background_____
  (if any)

Last purchase _____ New prospect _____

Frequency of purchase _____ Average order size _____

Opening statement/reason for call _____

_____

Customer business information _____

_____

Call objective—specifically _____

_____

Features and benefits _____

_____

_____

Information required from prospect
  Product use—Weight of widgets—Waste or damage data—Postal
  costs—Other applications—Importance of merchandising—etcetera

Possible objection   Planned response

_____   _____

_____   _____

_____   _____

Closing statement _____

_____

Other contacts/titles _____

_____

Plant locations _____

_____

Best time to call _____

_____

Product end use _____

_____

dash of omnipotence. There is an expectation that the caller has all the answers.

The professional and effective telemarketing sales representative, therefore, operates from a "command module," with everything at his or her fingertips: records, answers to specific questions, directories, catalogs, schedules, prices, shipping data, sample information. There must be truly effective records instantly accessible—microfiche, small programmed computer analysis, literature. This also means a properly organized, well-lighted, quiet work environment with comfortable chairs and efficient working space.

The Call Planner. (Figure 18–5). By whatever name, or in whatever form, a call planner disciplines the preparation for the call. The call planner establishes a goal—possible objections and resistance, the planned answers, questions, and order request. We refer to the customer profile as a resource. What specifically must we accomplish on this call? If it is to secure a second order, how long has it been since the last one? What was the quantity? Do we have a better quantity offer? What were the objections (resistance) last time? What kind of person are we dealing with? Preparation on all these points will increase our chances for getting that second order.

Customer Profile and Action Plan. The *customer profile and action plan* (see Figure 18–6) should be consulted in order to establish the present situation—the results of efforts to date, the anticipated objections, the logical goal of the plan, the state of the account's inventory, times to reorder. Without this critical record, the telemarketing sales representative (as the field sales representative) is forced to depend on memory (totally unreliable) or on bits and pieces of notes in a file.

In addition to the totally factual information contained in the customer profile, there must also be information regarding the personal human needs of the account contact. Otherwise, each call would be started uncertain of how to mold and define the product benefit for that specific customer.

Questioning and Listening. These two skills, essential to field sales call interviews, must be tailored to the telephone. In face-to-face interviews a question can be asked and a long pause, the magic of silence, employed to elicit an answer, providing the question is phrased in terms of why, when, who, how much, rather than, do, will, or does (which mean "yes" or "no" answers).

This is less-easily employed on the telephone, because too long a pause while waiting for an answer may turn off the customer. Explanatory comment on the question may bridge this point.

FIGURE 18–6
Customer Profile and Action Plan

TELEMARKETING
Customer Profile

Customer name _____   Date _____

Address _____   Location _____

_____

Telephone number _____   SIC# _____

Credit approval and limit _____   Date _____

Type of business _____   Account classification _____

Overall size—$ _____   Volume units _____

Product line	$ vol. potential	Unit vol. potential	% share

Key contacts:
  Name _____   Title _____

  _____   _____

  _____   _____

Annual use by product

	Year 1	Year 2	Year 3	Percent
Our sales	$ _____	$ _____	$ _____	_____ %
Competition	_____	_____	_____	_____
Competition	_____	_____	_____	_____
Competition	_____	_____	_____	_____

Pricing history   Year 1 _____

    Year 2 _____

    Year 3 _____

Targets/goals _____

  ☐ Increased volume   ☐ Reduce costs
  ☐ Increased profit   ☐ Enrich orders
  ☐ Increase price

FIGURE 18–6 *(concluded)*

Call schedule and record of contact

Strategy for selling (use of resources) _____

Alternate strategy _____

Special requirements

_____   _____

_____   _____

Shipping instructions _____

Marketing/sales information
Direct-mail sort—letter, brochure, sample, etc.

Name Date	Name Date	Name Date

Psychological (human needs)
Personalities _____
Likes/dislikes, etc. _____

Name/comment _____
Name/comment _____
Name/comment _____

Signed _____

Listening must be active, summarizing often to be certain of accuracy, feeding back details for confirmation. And in doing so we must recognize that some distortion of voices may occur through the telephone. Although we may try to articulate carefully, "No. 6606" may be heard as "606" or "6060." Names may be misunderstood, confusing orders and irritating customers.

Verify by Respelling. Using a word-code alphabet similar to that used by the armed services will help and should be required of all telemarketing sales representatives. While it ought not to be overdone, it should be employed for all important facts: company name, address, person's name, order quantities, order number, and so on. The customer may say, "My address is sixteen sixty Dobe Drive." The telemarketing representative repeats the numbers. "May I confirm, please? Is that one six, six zero Dobe Drive (d as in dog)?"

Voice Communication. In person, a change of pace, even rapid speech, on a point of enthusiasm adds spice and interest to a sales interview. The same rules apply to telephone speech, with some modifications. Without the body signals to read and to which we almost automatically respond, there is a danger of flat, monotonous speech, often too rapid and sometimes forsaking clarity. Volume control is critical, because those with very soft pleasant voices may not be intelligible on the phone. Some men with deep, resonant voices sound loud and overpowering. The only answer is to practice until one can effectively control the voice and use it as an effective instrument for communication. This can be done with tape recorders or with special telephone equipment.

Tone and voice quality can also be developed and improved. Watch how some people smile, frown, and laugh as they talk into the telephone. Note how their voice changes with their animation. Some training specialists recommend that callers always have a mirror before themselves to encourage this animation, and indeed it works. Others have suggested that in difficult call situations the telemarketing sales representative stand. This seems to give the caller a psychological sense of command.

In each of these illustrations care must be observed to avoid the theatrical. Obvious false enthusiasm, deliberate pressure, or phony sincerity will communicate itself to the customer. It is far better that the language be less polished but sincere.

Speaking at a professional rate of about 150 words per minute is desirable. This, too, should be practiced. Reading the following paragraph with an automatic timer or the help of another person will help. At the end of one minute, the number at the end of the line will indicate the rate.

The telephone may, in some cases, distort your normal voice	10
so that you don't sound the same as you do in person.	22
If you speak rapidly, in person, other people may feel	32
rushed and pressured. On the other hand,	39
speaking too slowly may give the impression of being	48

bored or uninterested. Because how you sound is as	57
important as what you say, each of us must become	68
aware of our own voice qualities, including knowing how	77
fast we speak, what our volume is, and how friendly	87
we sound to our telephone contacts. When we can	96
identify our weaknesses, practice and review will	103
help develop voice qualities which will enrich a	113
telephone image. Work with an associate to	120
listen in to your calls and to evaluate your voice	130
qualities. The only way to improve, whether it be a golf swing,	139
tennis stroke, or business skill is to be able to	149
identify and correct one's weakness. Then, persistent	156
and unremitting attention to technique will assure	163
the individual of improvement. Remember also that	170
no skill remains honed and sharp without this	179
constant effort. There will be a continuing reward	187
in personal relationships and in more effective	194
business performance.	196

Courtesy and Empathy. Listening attentively and actively is essential for good telephone technique, and courtesy is equally important. No one, particularly an account we are trying to impress, appreciates pushy or rude sales calls. Although most people won't literally hang up, the turn-off will be complete. Courtesy is far more than merely saying "please" and "thank you." It means being sincerely empathetic—understanding your customer's needs and feelings as though they were your own.

Part of this understanding is to avoid negatives. Don't emphasize what you cannot do. Don't use jargon (it may impress you, but it is likely to confuse or even anger the listener). Be certain to keep in mind that *communicating is not what I say . . . it is only what you hear.*

Penetrating the Screen. Since the ring of the telephone is compelling, it is always answered. Busy people, therefore, may have their calls screened. This may be good for the manager but bad for the telemarketing sales representative. However, there are ways to get around it.

- Off-hour calls—call before or after regular business hours. Many business executives come to the office early and stay late.
- Mail referral—refer to the mailing you sent: "I'm calling to discuss a letter I sent to Mr. Jones."
- Long distance—if you are making a long-distance call, identify the city you are calling from: "This is Stan Able calling from Buffalo. I'd like to speak with Mr. Jones."

- Call-back appointment—if contact is unavailable, set up a call-back date.

The most cardinal rule of all is persistence, persistence, persistence.

Results and Expectations. Research has shown that an average of five in-person calls are required to secure an order in industrial selling. Many companies, however, budget 10 telephone calls to secure an order. This includes calls which do not go through, or calls which cannot be completed, contact not present, and the like. We must keep in mind, though, the comparison of costs:

- In-person field calls 5 at $100 each = $500.
- Telemarketing calls 10 at $10 each = $100.

Order-call ratios should be carefully tracked so future plans can be more accurate. Costs will vary greatly, so each manager must develop his or her specific patterns. Costs must be viewed much the same as in field selling. If we secure an order on the 10th call, we have invested about $100 in the effort. If we relate this investment to the goal of return on sales (ROS) we find: assume 10 percent goal for return on sales, the B.E. (break even) = sales cost ÷ ROS, or $100 ÷ 0.10 = $1,000.

Combining Direct Mail and Telephone Calling. Many marketing managers have found a very specific pattern when combining direct mail and telephone communications. In fact, many managers now consider that telemarketing should really be defined as a combination of the two.

While precise data may not exist, patterns do. If one generally looks at a return of *2 to 3 percent* from business-to-business direct mail, a four-to-seven-times increase can be attained by combining it with telephone follow-up. No matter what combination is used, always follow the mail with a telephone follow-up, whether you use call-mail-call or mail-call. Clearly, the opportunity to say, "I'm calling about the letter (or brochure) I sent to Mr. Jackson," helps get through.

Timing is very important . . . a follow-up call made too soon may startle the customer and, in some situations, even precede receipt of the direct mail. Clearly a follow-up call made a month or more after a mailing is nearly useless. The ideal timing for telephone follow-up appears to be about 10 days to two weeks.

Record-Keeping and Monitoring Results

Telemarketing is a relatively new procedure in a communications strategy. It has precisely the same requirement for keeping track of activities and accomplishments as do other media. From planning the first call, to recording of orders received, to the scheduling of calls to be made, the following forms and reports have been well tested and will provide control required for a cost-effective operation.

Many of these records can easily be translated into computer programs. Customer profiles might be segmented by end-use market or by scheduled call-back dates. Whether we exercise manual or computer control, ordering/reordering is a most important element in telemarketing. Certainly, if we can accurately identify a customer's rate of use (ordering cycles), we can anticipate each cycle and contact the customer—thereby providing the small account an inventory control assist, offering information on pricing, increasing order size for quantity discounts, and so on. In fact, this process may then serve the customer *better* than the infrequent calls by a field sales representative.

The following forms will be useful in operating a telemarketing program. They should be altered as experience dictates and be designed for a particular business:

- Telemarketing Call Planner (Figure 18–5).
- Telemarketing Customer Profile (Figure 18–6).
- Direct Mail/Telemarketing Report (Figure 18–4).
- Direct Mail Announcement (Figure 18–2).
- Telemarketing Initial Call (Figure 18–1).
- Follow-up Script—Direct Mail (Figure 18–3).
- Letter to Customer after First Call (Figure 18–7).
- Phone Call Report: Follow-Up Date Form (Figure 18–8).
- The Tickler Card (Figure 18–9).

Telemarketing Limitations. These are:

- A loss of body-language signals and visual communication.
- More difficult to define a customer's human (psychological) needs.
- A new method for selling small accounts, but some accounts may still require some personal face-to-face contact.
- May be somewhat more difficult to handle specific product/service questions.
- Requires special skills in voice quality, questioning capability, and selling techniques, because visual language is missing.

Telemarketing Advantages.

- Provides dependable schedule contact and two-way communications.
- Offers a convenience second only to a personal visit.
- Lowers cost for contacting and selling.

FIGURE 18–7
Sample of Letter Sent to Customer after First Call

Date _____

_____
_____
_____
_____

Dear _____ :

Thank you very much for your time the other day. I enjoyed our phone conversation very much. I am very anxious to provide you and your company with ABC Company's fine service and quality.

I will be available most of the time in the Buffalo office. In my absence, _____ , our Customer Service Supervisor, and _____ , _____ , _____ , our Sales Service Specialists will be available to assist you.

I have enclosed my calling card and look forward to talking with you in the future.

Very truly yours,

_____
Sales Representative

Enclosure

- Provides either a high-impact replacement of direct mail or advertising or a supplement to them for selected accounts.
- Provides a new means for profitably selling small accounts.
- Provides on demand, current product and price information—new product information.
- Provides information on order cycles, requirements, and opportunities for better control of inventory.
- Offers a new element and opportunity in communications mix.
- Can reduce rush-order frequency.

FIGURE 18–8
Phone Call Report: Follow-Up Date Form

Customer service representative	Date of call Time
Customer	Call back date
Address	Phone no.
Person contacted	Title

☐ Follow-up required _____
☐ Quote requested _____
☐ Order_____
   Buying
☐ Potential _____
   Current
☐ Suppliers _____ ☐ _____ ☐ _____ ☐ _____ ☐ _____
Comments: _____
   Subject covered

_____

_____

_____

_____

_____

_____

_____

Results _____

_____

_____

Action _____

_____

_____

_____

FIGURE 18–9
The Tickler Card

To complete the Tickler Card, simply fill in the account
name, circle the month, and write in the day on which
Follow-Up is required. File this card in your index file behind
the appropriate month. At the beginning of each month, sort
cards for each working day.

ACCOUNT NAME: _____

FOLLOW-UP DATES

J	F	M	A	M	J	J	A	S	O	N	D

INSTRUCTIONS: In the column under the appropriate month, write in the specific date for a follow-up call. Place card in the Tickler File, in order, by month
and day.

Equipment Considerations. Telephone and telecommunications
equipment and technology is changing so rapidly that management
should check with suppliers before committing to a particular system.

The following checklist may help to avoid problems and save costs
by securing the information needed for decision.

- Are there enough lines to prevent "busies" on incoming lines
  while telemarketing sales representatives are placing outgoing
  calls?
- What geographic areas are involved?
- Will all calls be within your area code?
- What are the costs of service options available through your
  phone company?
- Are the following systems applicable?—800 WATS (Wide Area
  Telephone Service); FX—local call rate for distant points; remote call forwarding—an electronic means for setting up a local
  telephone in a different city.

SUMMARY OF TELEMARKETING

- Identify and segment markets and customers.
- Classify accounts—qualify by volume and value.
- Develop a strategy of communications (mix).
- All telemarketing ("T") accounts are assigned to specific telemarketing sales representatives.
- Job objectives and standards of performance are developed for all sales managers and telemarketing personnel.
- Call planners—customer profiles and call records established for each "T" account.
- Equipment, furniture, records and files, office layout developed for efficiency.
- Scripts, prepared for announcement, direct-mail follow-up, thank-you letter following call, phone call report.
- Tickler file—for scheduling next calls.

19

SALES MEASUREMENTS

by
Charles W. Stryker

Trinet, Inc.
A Control Data Subsidiary

BACKGROUND

A key problem facing marketing departments as we enter the mid-1980s is the inability to measure accurately and cost effectively the results of marketing programs. Upon reflecting for just a moment on the marketing function over the previous 10 years, several important observations are apparent. First, if one considers the nature of the marketing function in the mid-1970s, the basic process consisted of assigning a geographic territory to a marketing representative and equipping that representative with a sales presentation and promotional material that described the product or service. The representative was instructed to walk through as many doors as possible and display the sales materials.

As the early 1980s approached, marketing planners realized that it was important to *qualify* accounts. We could no longer afford the luxury of walking through every door, because the cost of a sales call became too high. So as the early 1980s passed, more and more marketing executives tested and applied new marketing techniques (e.g., telephone marketing, direct marketing, lead generation, computer analysis of lists, and so on) in an attempt to save wasted sales calls. However, the sales presentation and promotional material basically remained the same. That is, a product or service description was presented to the potential buyer.

As we enter the mid-1980s, more changes are rapidly affecting the historical methods of marketing. Not only must the account be qualified with ever-increasing accuracy, but the buying influences must also be qualified. In addition, the sales presentation and promotional material must be *customized* to meet an ever-expanding set of buyer needs and concerns. This effort is leading to a more complex and demanding marketing situation, with territories being developed along industrial or consumer segments, rather than along geographic lines, team selling concepts, and expanded consultive selling programs.

These changes over the past 10 years call for dramatic changes in the methods of marketing. A key ingredient in response to this change is a comprehensive measurement system. This system must have the capability to monitor and evaluate changes in the marketplace and in the distribution channel.

The problem in the past of developing adequate measurement systems has been the excessive cost. The following sections of this chapter will describe a measurement system that does the job and can be implemented at low cost.

It is impossible to describe a system directly appropriate for every case. However, the concepts presented here are useful to every marketing situation. This discussion should be viewed as a description of the basic concepts which can then be adapted to individual marketing situations.

To begin the discussion, it is important to recognize that measurement is composed of two basic activities. The first activity is *tracking* the marketing effort and the sales results. The second basic measurement process is *evaluation;* this is the ability to understand why marketing results are as good as they are and also to identify the barriers that limit the ability of the marketing activity to be more productive.

TRACKING METHODS—OVERVIEW

Tracking is the process of monitoring and controlling marketing activity and the related sales results. To describe the tracking process, consider the following example:

> A business marketing firm identifies several prospect lists containing 20,000 high-potential prospects. To further qualify the prospects on the lists, a direct-mail lead generation program is implemented. For the leads generated, lead cards are produced and distributed to the field sales organization for follow-up. There are four basic components to the tracking process appropriate for this example.

1. Tracking response rates. The first component of the process tracks *response rate*. For the lead generation program, 20,000 prospects were identified and responses were generated from a direct mail program. These responses were coded and identified as part of the tracking process. Periodically (e.g., weekly), as the sales program proceeds, tracking reports are produced that display response rate by week, territory, list source, executive title. The objective of this analysis is to understand the nature of the response and identify the key variables that relate to a high response rate. In addition to these reports, information is displayed that compares actual response rate to anticipated response rate.

2. *Tracking lead conversions.* The second tracking capability of the system is to track *lead conversions*. As leads are distributed to the field sales organization, lead conversion statistics must be tabulated. The method of collecting lead conversion statistics is typically via a call-reporting instrument. As leads are followed up by field sales representatives, they are asked to complete call reports. The call reports are then returned for tabulation. The lead conversion statistics are then tabulated by week, territory, list source, executive title. Note that the lead conversion statistics by territory are a valuable input to the sales management process since weak territories can be identified (i.e., sales representatives who cannot effectively close leads can be identified). Another result of the lead conversion analysis is the production of aging reports. A periodic monitoring of how well leads are being followed up is necessary. This tabulation can again be used by sales managers as a tool to ensure that leads receive appropriate attention.

3. *Tracking customer sales.* Once a prospect becomes a customer, it is typical for future sales activity to take place. The source of sales information is usually the billing or order-entry system. It is important to capture customer sales information in the marketing tracking system to allow marketing and sales planners to obtain a clear picture of the value of the sale in terms of future revenues. Also, marketing and sales planners can begin to observe important sequence patterns in the buying behavior. For example, it may prove easy to sell product 2 only after product 1 has been installed for at least three months. In addition, this analysis may indicate that certain types of customers may increase their sales activity over time, while other types of accounts do not order products after the initial sale. This information may identify for marketing planners those markets that will prove to be very profitable over the long term but, at first glance, do not appear profitable.

4. *Tracking attrition.* By the time a decision maker with a firm decides to choose your product or service, you have invested significant dollars in the sales situation. It is a great loss when your firm finally acquires a good customer only to have the customer cancel your product or service. The method of collecting information on cancellations varies from company to company. The most typical method is to classify a buyer as cancelled if future billing or order-entry information does not occur on the account for a specified time period (e.g., six months). The second method is to require either the customer or the sales executive to complete a cancellation request form. The latter tends to be the most accurate and timely form for the collection of cancellation information. This attrition information is typically collected, organized, and reported on a periodic basis (e.g., each week, month, or quarter) and reported by time period, territory, type of account, and the like.

For the above four components of the tracking system, the reporting of information is performed periodically—each week, month, quarter. It is also valuable to report on key trends that occur during these time periods. For example, if cancellations are increasing within the larger customer segment, this fact is critical to marketing and sales planners.

To summarize the tracking process requirements for this example, the inputs to the tracking process are the *prospect list, the identification of responses, call reports, billing/order entry data,* and *cancellation requests.* The system produces tabulations of responses, conversions, customer history, and attrition, broken down in a variety of ways (week, territory, list source, trends).

TRACKING PROCESS—IMPLEMENTATION DETAILS

When the number of prospects in the target market is large, it becomes very difficult to track results accurately using manual methods. Not only do manual methods cause a lack of accuracy but they also limit timeliness and flexibility of tracking results. When a target market list exceeds 10,000 names, computer tracking tools are necessary. To illustrate the tracking methods involved, consider the example of the industrial marketer as one appropriate for computer analysis. Note that if your prospect universe is less than 10,000 names, manual methods may prove adequate through the use of ledger techniques.

In the illustrative example, there are five basic files required for computerized tracking. These are:

- Prospect file.
- Response file.
- Call report file.
- Customer file.
- Attrition file.

Prospect File

When the prospect files are received from the list owners, they must be processed and formatted for mailing and tracking. The first task in preparing the prospect files is to put all list sources into a common format. For example, if a five-line mailing label is required, the executive's name, title, company name, street address, city, state, and zip code would be placed in appropriate data fields. Once the list sources are standardized, the list is processed to remove all duplicates, as well as other suppressions, such as current customers, terminated customers, competitors.

Once the file is standardized and selected records deleted, a set of computerized edits and tests should be performed on each record. The personal name should be checked to ensure that it is a valid name and that the first and last names are in their proper sequence. Also at this point in the processing, the name can be gendered (Ms., Miss, Mrs., Mr.) if necessary.

The next set of edit checks is performed on the title to ensure that it is valid, as well as to change unacceptable title abbreviations to expanded full titles. Then a set of tests is performed on the company name to ensure that the name is composed of reasonable characters (no special characters, numbers, and so on).

The final checks are performed on the street address, city, state, and zip code to ensure that these fields are valid. Following these processing steps, the file is in an acceptable format for mailing purposes. The only additional fields that should be added to each record for tracking purposes are the tracking code, prospect identification number, and the date of the mailing.

The purpose of the tracking code is to allow each response to be identified quickly in an appropriate category. For example, the following tracking code system may prove appropriate:

- Column 1—Sales Territory Code.
- Column 2—List Source.
- Column 3—Executive Title Code.
- Column 4—Creative Material ID.

If a precoded response was returned with a tracking code 3412, it would indicate this response is for Sales Territory (3), from List Source (4), and that the Chief Executive Officer (1) responded to Creative Package (2).

A second coding feature that assists in the tracking system is to precode each response piece with a unique prospect identification number. This allows for simple computer matching between the prospect file and the response file.

Of course, not all responses enter the tracking process in a precoded format (e.g., telephone replies). To facilitate the coding of these responses, a directory of the prospects contained in the prospect file should be produced. This list should be alphabetized by business name. In addition to displaying the mailing label information (business name, address, and so on), the prospect identification number and the tracking code should be presented. As responses enter the system, if they do not have a preprinted prospect identification number and a tracking code, these two fields must be added via clerical methods.

When mail is sent, a mail drop date should be attached to each record in the prospect list. Since most mail plans drop in zip code sequence, this function can most easily be performed by recording the proper date each zip code was mailed.

Response File

The response file should contain the same information for responses as the prospect file contains for prospects, including the prospect identification number. Of course, the business name, executive name, and so on may be modified, based on the information contained in the response. In addition to this information, the date the response was received should be kept with each response.

Call Report File

For the illustrative example presented earlier, as responses enter the system, sales lead cards will be distributed to the appropriate salesperson. The typical sales lead card should contain the following information:

— Business name.
— Address.
— City, state, zip code.
— Executive name, title.
— Telephone number.
— Type of business.
— Current customer (yes/no).
— Type of lead (list source, creative package, and so on).
— Date of response.
— Salesperson assigned.
— Lead identification number.

Attached to the sales lead card should be a call report. Typically, the first call report should be completed by the salesperson when the first sales call is made. This call report indicates the salesperson's view of potential within the account and indicates whether or not future sales-call follow-up is needed. A typical call report should collect the following information:

— Lead identification number.
— Contact date.
— Sold.
— Quantity.
— Dollar value.
— Pending.
— Excellent lead.

— Good lead.
— Poor lead.
— Future call scheduled.
— Dead.

The information on the call report, including the prospect identification number, is entered into the tracking system for analysis. In addition, if the salesperson indicates that future sales-call activity is planned, additional call-report forms are sent to the appropriate salesperson to report status information on the progress of the sales-call activity. These follow-up call reports are typically sent on a monthly basis.

Customer File

The customer file is the easiest one to define conceptually but often the most difficult to organize and maintain. The customer file should contain the identity of current customers (name, address, city, state, zip code, telephone number) as well as information that describes the value of each customer to your firm (e.g., value of orders to date). The problem, as with most things that sound simple, is that in practice the development of the customer file becomes difficult.

The first point of difficulty is in defining specifically what a customer is. Is a customer a corporation, a location of a corporation, a department of a corporation, a person within a corporation, a person at home? For example, if you were selling word processing systems, you could consider the secretary your customer; or the manager of the secretary your customer; or the head of the department as the customer; or the head of purchasing for that business location as the customer; or the head of purchasing for the headquarters of the corporation as the customer? The answer on how to define the customer rests on the level of authority that is "typically" required to purchase your product. For our example, let's say you identify the head of purchasing for the specific business location as the customer. If you can make your definition that specific, you have not only made the implementation of the tracking system possible but you have also made marketing planning possible, because now you can evaluate market share, penetration rates, and the like.

Having defined the customer, you may find that the manner in which the accounting or order-entry department chooses to organize its information does not relate exactly to how you need the information from a marketing viewpoint. For example, the billing department may have organized its information to correspond to the requirements of the customer's accounts payable department. In our example, the bill would typically go to the manager of the department, not to the head of purchasing. So your task, as the designer of the marketing measurement system, is to reorganize the billing/order entry records to correspond to the requirements of marketing. In our example, the task would be to group together those billing records that correspond to a specific business location. Of course, if you have hundreds of thousands of billing records, this could be an arduous task, and again, computer methods would be required. However, for the typical firm, clerical methods can effectively be used to reorganize the accounting/order entry information into a useful format for marketing measurement.

Once you have gone through the process of defining the customer from the marketing viewpoint and reorganizing your firm's billing/order entry records to support marketing, you have accomplished two thirds of the work. The last task is to associate with each customer record an estimate of the value of each customer to your firm. The value of any customer is typically represented in financial terms. The ideal measure would be to calculate each customer's contribution to bottom line profit, both now and in the future. For most products, this task simply proves to be too difficult. The practical compromise is to evaluate each customer's contribution to revenue both now and in the future. This estimation process, for most firms, proves to be adequate. In effect, you calculate a net present value of revenues generated by the account from the present time through a planning horizon. Again, this process could be as simple as having your salesperson estimate future revenues for a three-year period and discounting future revenues by an appropriate factor. More complicated systems may be required that rely on financial models of typical customer performance to project future revenues.

When you have completed these three tasks—defining the customer, reorganizing billing/order entry data, and determining the value for each customer—you will have built a customer file of information suitable for marketing measurement. Be certain that you perform these tasks in a manner that allows for convenient updating.

Attrition File

The attrition file is maintained to identify all customers who have cancelled your product or service. Depending on the nature of your product or service, attrition can be identified in one of two ways.

The first method of identification applies when your product or service is consumed on a periodic basis. For example, in the office supplies field, it is typical for customers to restock supplies on a monthly basis. If a customer did not order any supplies for three months, by definition you could classify the customer as cancelled. In this case, the mere absence of billing or order-entry information is the indication of attrition.

The second method of identifying attrition applies when your product or service is not consumed. In this case, either the customer or the salesperson must initiate a cancellation request. For example, if you sold word processing equipment and the customer wanted to return the equipment, the customer must initiate a cancellation request.

In both forms of cancellation, the attrition file contains the same information. Typically, the information includes company name, address, city, state, zip code, telephone number, date of cancellation, and reason for cancellation.

TRACKING RESULTS

Once the above five files are assembled on a periodic basis, these files are processed and tracking reports are produced for management. The system should have the capability to produce tracking reports by the following selections:

- Salesperson territory.
- List source.
- Age of leads.
- Date of response.
- Executive title.
- Creative material.
- Value of sale.

For example, a report could be produced from the tracking system that would display the number of leads distributed to each salesperson from list source 1, that used creative material 3. In addition, the system could break down this report by the status of the leads (sold, pending, cancelled, dead).

The following, Table 19–1, is a tabular tracking report of list performance statistics:

TABLE 19–1
List Performance Report

List ID	Number Mailed	Number of Responses	Response Rate (%)	Number Sold	Sale Rate (%)	Overall Sale Rate (%)
1	10,000	400	4%	120	30%	1.2%
2	3,000	270	9	108	40	3.6
3	2,500	50	2	5	10	0.2
4	2,500	300	12	150	50	6.0
5	2,000	100	5	40	40	2.0
Total	20,000	1,120	5.6	423	37.8	2.1

As seen from this report, list four (4) has the best overall performance (6 percent). This reflects sales versus number of pieces mailed. Note that this performance is due both to a high response rate (12 percent) and a high sale rate (50 percent).

Note that list three (3) has very bad performance both in terms of response rate and sale rate. List five (5) is interesting in that the leads generated are of above average quality (sale rate of 40 percent); however, the response rate to that list is below average. This type of result would indicate that the list should be used, possibly testing a new creative approach to increase the response rate.

This example is one of many possible reports that display marketing performance.

EVALUATION SYSTEM REQUIREMENTS

The second key component of a measurement program is the evaluation process. *The purpose of the evaluation process is to understand the prospect decision-making process*. The primary question to be answered is:

WHY AREN'T ALL HIGH POTENTIAL PROSPECTS CONVERTED TO ORDERS?

The approach found to be most successful in performing the evaluation process is based on *direct telephone contact* with decision makers who were exposed to the sales strategy. Questions are asked of the decision-making executive to understand their resultant buying behavior.

The process begins by identifying the segments to be analyzed. For the illustrative example presented previously, there are four basic segments. The first segment contains those executives targeted with the direct-mail program who did not indicate any interest (i.e., the lead generation program failed). The second segment contains those executives targeted with the direct-mail program who did indicate interest, but sales representatives assessed the sales potential to be low (i.e., the closing strategy failed). The third segment contains those executives targeted with the direct-mail program who responded with interest to the lead generation program, and the sales representatives assessed the sales potential to be high (i.e., the closing strategy was predicted to be effective). Figure 19–1 summarizes this segmentation for the first three segments of interest:

The fourth segment of interest is the cancellations. This segment represents those businesses that were customers and decided to cancel the product or service. It is critical to understand the decision-making influences that caused a good customer to cancel.

FIGURE 19–1

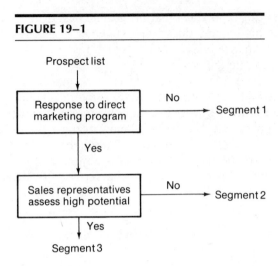

The above four segments represent those points where decision makers complete a transition in their thinking. The objective of the evaluation process is to understand accurately why decision-making executives act as they do and to identify the decision-making influences.

Segment 1: Nonrespondents to Direct Marketing Program

These executives are in decision-making positions within companies that have been assessed to have potential for a sale. The selected executive has been targeted via a direct-mail lead generation program. The executive in the segment declines to respond. The objective of this telephone interview is to understand accurately why this lack of interest exists. Of course, the interview need not be conducted with all executives who fall into this segment. A representative sample of these executives is appropriate. The questions to be asked, as part of this interview, address the following interest barriers:

- Does the account truly have sales potential?
- Was the correct executive targeted?
- Was the creative content of the direct-mail program effective?
- Are the perceptions that the executive has about the seller a barrier to interest?
- Are the perceptions that the executive has about the product a barrier to interest?
- Is the executive committed to a competitive product?

If the above evaluation indicates, for example, that the major barrier to interest is that targeted executives feel the product is too expensive, then the marketing strategy should be modified to address the cost effectiveness of the product. If, however, the research indicates a commitment to a particular competitor, the marketing strategy should be modified to highlight the advantages of your product over the competition.

Not only does the above research effort identify key barriers, this approach also provides a method to monitor continually the effects of competition.

Segment 2: Respondents/Nonbuyers

These executives are in decision-making positions within companies that have been assessed to have potential. When probed for interest via direct-mail methods, this segment of executives responds with interest. When sales representatives are directed to follow up with these interested executives, the sales representatives indicate that the account has low sales potential.

The objective of the telephone interview process with this segment is to understand accurately why executives who apparently have potential and have indicated their interest in your product are designated by the sales representatives as having low potential. Again, the interview need not be conducted with all executives who fall into this segment. A representative sample of these executives is appropriate. The questions to be asked as part of this interview should cover the same barriers as in Segment 1 (level of potential, correct executive target, quality of creative content, and so on). However, additional questions may be asked to determine the effectiveness of the sales call. These questions should include:

- Did the sales representative follow up?
- Did the sales representative have adequate product knowledge?
- Did the sales representative have adequate application knowledge?
- Did the sales representative have adequate sales skill?

If the above evaluation indicates, for example, that the major barrier to closing sales was lack of product knowledge by sales representatives, then a sales training course may be called for.

Again, not only does the above research effort identify key barriers, this approach also provides a method of evaluating the effect of sales training programs.

Segment 3: Buyers

The third group of executives to be interviewed are those who were indicated to be of high potential via the sales representative call report.

This segment forms the class of executives where the total sales strategy worked. The objective of this telephone interview is to understand accurately the decision-making process of buyers so this behavior can be amplified within the nonbuyer segments. Again, the interviews need only be given to a sample of executives who fall into this segment. The questions to be asked as part of this interview process include the following:

- What is the application for the product?
- What was the appeal of the creative material?
- What perceptions does the executive have about the company?
- What perceptions does the executive have about the product?
- What competitors were examined?

Segment 4: Cancels

The fourth group of executives to be interviewed are those who cancelled the product or service. Here it is very important that you clearly understand the decision-making process. This segment also tends to be one of the easiest and most fruitful segments to interview to understand weaknesses in your product or marketing program, or both. Again, the interviews only need to be conducted on a sample of executives who fall into this segment. The questions to be asked as part of this interview process include the following:

- What was the application for the product?
- What was the actual use of the product?
- What was the anticipated use of the product?
- What perceptions does the executive have about your company?
- What perceptions does the executive have about your product?
- What product performance factors affected the cancellation decision?
- What sales/support factors affected the cancellation decision?
- What competitive factors affected the cancellation decision?

To summarize the evaluation procedure, the objective is to gain an accurate understanding of the decision-making process. The most effective method of collecting the required information is through telephone interviews. The information is collected in such a manner that future sales programs can be modified to overcome identified sales barriers and capitalize on sales program strengths.

If the number of interviews to be analyzed exceeds 50, it may prove appropriate to code and load these results on a computer system to aid the analysis process. The programs required to cross-tabulate research results exist in the marketplace in numerous forms. Also, when the evaluation results are on computer, the identification of important trends becomes a practical process (e.g., a certain competitor is increasing his market penetration rate).

MEASUREMENT SYSTEM MANAGEMENT

As you consider the measurement system that has been described in this chapter, you will see that this concept is useful for corporate marketing and sales planning to answer questions that relate to performance of the product, performance of the marketing program, competitive activity, and the like. However, the concepts presented also play an important role in the control and management of local sales organizations. A field sales manager may implement these concepts for his office to aid in manpower planning, quota setting, territory planning, account planning, and territory review. The questions, therefore, are what capabilities should be implemented centrally, and what capabilities should be implemented through a decentralized program.

As a general rule, the centralized measurement program should be implemented first. This program has three basic objectives. The first is to establish a comprehensive tracking system to be used by both central staff and field organizations. There are obvious operational and cost advantages to having one tracking system, rather than a different system for each branch office. The second objective of the centralized program is to develop and refine the telephone research process to perform the evaluation aspects of measurement. This effort is required to establish workable procedures for interviews, as well as to refine the questionnaire and research techniques. The third objective of the centralized program is to gain insights into the buyer's decision-making process on those issues that affect the success of the marketing program at a global level (e.g., pricing, competition, target market).

Once the measurement system is implemented on a centralized basis, the technology can then be passed to regional and branch management for implementation on a local level.

SUMMARY

As marketing costs continue to rise, the need to measure and control the return on marketing expense is becoming increasingly important. It is critical that the measurement systems not only quantify results but also provide understanding about why sales programs work and why they do not. These measurement techniques must allow us to continue to learn in such a manner that our sales programs can be managed for maximum effectiveness, and future programs can be continually improved.

20

COMPUTERS IN MARKETING

by
Robert A. Moskowitz

Personal Productivity Center

Computers are without a doubt one of the most effective tools ever developed. From the smallest personal computers to the most powerful mainframe giants, they have extremely broad potential for applications in nearly every field. Even within specific fields, the opportunities that computers present are usually astounding.

This is no less true in the field of marketing than in any other area of human endeavor. The proof of this will be seen many years hence when innovative marketing experts are continuing to find new and exciting uses for tomorrow's more powerful computing systems.

Rather than discuss just one application of computers in marketing, this chapter will cover a variety of interesting applications and examine the possibilities for several others. Although cost is always a significant factor, the dominant rule of thinking where computers are concerned must be: If you can think of a job that would be useful to do, there is some way to have a computer do it. The problem is not to get the job done but to do it cost-effectively. With this in mind, let's explore what computers are doing today, and what they are very likely to begin doing tomorrow.

COMPUTERS HANDLING SALES LEADS

Calling on prospects is a fundamental aspect of selling, and managing the process of obtaining and investigating sales leads is an important part of the marketing function. Unfortunately, there is a lot of tedious, difficult work involved in doing this well. Computers are an ideal mechanism for taking this work away from the sales professional and leaving more time for face-to-face contact. Moreover, the computer usually does a better job of culling poor prospects and compiling relevant information to make a qualified sales lead even better.

The key element in making the computer system useful, of course, is to give it a large database of prospects to work with. (A database is simply a collection of information.) Because a computer is too expensive to operate on just a few sales leads, cost-justifying the use of a computer system generally requires the company to enter all sales inquiries into the computer system. The basic information required, at a minimum, is:

— Contact information, such as name, company name, and address.
— Date of inquiry.
— The main interests expressed in the prospect's first inquiry.
— Simple qualifying information, such as the size of the business, its geographic location, what items and how much it typically buys in a year, and whether the person named can make the buying decision.

Once the information is entered into the system, the salesperson literally can forget about the inquiry and leave all the details to the computer. The well-designed systems remember all the facts about the inquiry, prompt the salesperson to make call-backs and to follow up as appropriate, and give the sales manager or marketing director solid information on the effectiveness of various prospecting procedures and follow-up efforts. The same computer system can also update, search, and select from this database of information, usually from some centralized location, such as the home office. But this comes later.

The first step is to have the computer assign the lead to a specific sales professional. This assignment may be made on the basis of who generated the inquiry, territorial restrictions, product line specialization, or a simple rotation within the sales force so whoever is "up" gets the next inquiry. Whatever the basis, the computer delivers to that salesperson a complete "report," the organized set of information that provides a basis for starting the selling process. This first report is usually a little sparse because little is known about the prospect.

As time goes by, however, the company learns more and more about the prospect because all sales-call reports, purchase information, and general notes on the account are appended to the computer's database. The computer maintains complete records on all the names in its system and can be asked to provide any of this information as needed. In some of the more sophisticated lead-handling systems, each new lead is compared with a list of current and past customers. When the computer detects an inquiry from one of these groups, the lead is flagged for special attention by the sales force, and the computer automatically kicks out some background material on the account so the salesperson goes in fully prepared and ready to sell. When the customer is considered a "house account," the inquiry is shuffled off to the in-house sales staff, preventing a lot of confusion and providing higher-quality service for the company's best customers.

Many companies have the computers print on color-coded paper. Thus, call information printed on *red* paper might be "hot prospects" or proven customers who are considered due for a reorder, while similar information printed on *blue* stock would cover prospects who are less likely to buy, and *green* cards might provide information on new leads of unknown quality. Because the computer can track a lead from its source to its conclusion, including its current status at any moment, it makes possible singling out prospects from trade shows or coupons, for example, and giving them the quicker response they typically want.

When the marketing department continues to update its information on sales leads, the computer is able to print reports showing the prospecting efforts made by each member of the sales force in a given period. In addition, the computer can keep track of what further actions might be required, as well as the completion dates for each one, and can notify the salesperson—electronically or by mail—in good time to make sure the service is provided.

One advantage of an automated system is that, when the computer keeps track of prospects and customers, the salesperson does not have to. The computer system does it better, faster, cheaper, and in a more useful format than anyone can do with the usual shoebox full of dog-eared index cards! Relieved of this duty, the salesperson can simply tear the reports off the computer printer and rush out to make additional sales calls, armed with more complete, more up-to-the-minute information than he or she would most likely obtain from a manual information system.

In most companies that convert to a computerized lead-handling system, salespeople report that the leads they receive are fresher and more active than ever before. For example, a conventional system might cause a two-week delay between the date a prospect responds to an advertisement or calls the home office and the time a salesperson can respond. In some large companies, the delays stretch even longer. But well-planned and well-implemented computer systems are very fast, so the delay between the date of an inquiry and the scheduling of a sales call is often cut to just two or three days.

Another advantage is that the computer can be adjusted to print new reports and send them to the salespeople as the prospects "age." The interval can be varied systematically to experiment with various call-back schedules. Because the information is in a computerized database, it becomes very easy to run comparisons and see whether the volume of sales increases or decreases as the call-back intervals are varied.

Because of the computer's ability to sort and compare information in its memory, computerized sales information makes it easy to compare new leads to the patterns of proven customers. For example, a computer analysis of current customers might show that most are medium-sized, family-owned businesses, in large urban centers. No matter what characteristics are discovered, the computer can search new leads for these same characteristics. Leads that possess the characteristics can be printed on *red* paper and given top priority by the sales team. In one company, the marketing team has developed a series of classifications for inquiries that range from "hot prospect" through "consultant/advisor to decision makers" and all the way to "literature collector"—a person who will never make a purchase. They go after the first group, provide information and advice without expecting sales from the second group, and cull the people in the third group as soon as the computer identifies them.

This type of analysis dramatically increases the quality of the leads that ultimately reach the sales force. For example, one company that has converted to computerized lead handling normally receives about 20,000 inquiries each year. There is no way the sales force could make contact with all these people. Instead, the computer screens the inquiries and eliminates those least likely to buy. One screening method is to compare new inquiries with old inquiries that have never become customers. Any that match are from people who have inquired before but not made a purchase. The company considers these to be lower-quality leads than first-time "virgin" inquiries.

Another screening technique is to qualify inquiries on the basis of demographics. People who match the company's computer-developed profile of buyers are considered to be stronger leads than people who are outside the profile.

The advantage of the computer for handling sales leads does not end with the dispatch of information to the sales force. The call reports from the sales force can of course be used to update and maintain the database of prospects and customers. In addition, the information can be used to show the prospecting activity and success levels of each salesperson. One danger is that salespeople are fearful of being too closely monitored by computer systems. But smart sales managers overcome this fear by involving salespeople in the development of the new system, and continue to involve them in future modifications, improvements, and in the use of any reports which the system is set up to deliver.

A separate analysis can also help the company spot developing and dying markets. The patterns of information requested by those who make inquiries can be translated by computers into trendlines and projections of market size. As these patterns change, a company that uses its computer to handle inquiries and sales leads can sometimes stay in closer touch with the market than a company which flies by the seat of its pants.

Finally, a good system tracks leads from their initial development and records their source, such as coupons, advertisements, trade shows, or other promotional programs. The computer can easily compare the closing ratio that each group yields and provide breakdowns on the relative quality of each group of leads and on the cost-per-lead and cost-per-sale amounts for each promotional program.

Another aspect of the sales lead story is the use of computers to generate the leads. Computerized "calling" systems are becoming quite popular with companies that need vast numbers of moderately qualified leads. In such a system, a computer is used to store thousands of telephone numbers. It will dial each number in sequence and wait for the telephone to be answered. When someone picks up the receiver, the computer triggers a tape recorder that plays the desired sales message. In most cases, the message is a basic benefits pitch. The taped voice usually asks the person who has answered the phone to contact the company for more information, if interested. In more sophisticated calling systems, however, the taped message can ask one or more questions and another tape machine can record the replies. Obviously, there is a tremendous potential for poor-quality sales leads in such systems. Not surprisingly, some consumer groups are opposed to the proliferation of machines making sales pitches over the telephone. Yet, despite the problems, these machines can make thousands of calls a day to potential prospects and do it at a very low cost. More important, companies that rely on these leads report remarkable high rates of success with the leads these computers develop.

COMPUTERS AT THE POINT OF SALE

One of the most progressive uses of computers in marketing has been the move toward "electronic funds transfer" in high-volume supermarkets. This involves the installation of a computer terminal in the store and the instant transfer of money from the customer's account to the store's account at the time and place of the purchase.

The main incentive for such a sweeping change has been to reduce the "float" between the time a customer pays for an order with a check or charge card and the time the store's account actually gets credited with the money. As a side benefit, the bank usually eliminates the charge for each check deposited in the retailer's account. Customers appear willing to sacrifice this float in return for the added convenience of the money transfer system.

In their current form, the terminals are activated by a special plastic "credit card" that has been issued to the customer. The card's magnetic strip or imbedded microchip contains information on where the money can be drawn. The terminal, which is installed in a particular store, automatically adds information on where the money should be transferred.

To make it happen, the customer inserts the card into the terminal and punches in a personal identification code. Then the machine either reads the amount of the purchase directly from the cash register or accepts the dollar information punched into its own keyboard.

There are reportedly some 2,000 such machines installed in groceries across the nation and more are being installed every month. The leading chains in this appear to be in Iowa, possibly because that central state is seen as a barometer of consumers everywhere. The early evidence seems to show that consumers are accepting the new equipment without a murmur. In one store there were more than 26,000 electronic fund transfers in a single year—that's an average of one every three minutes!

The system has the potential to do even more. For example, such computerized transactions can tell the store's marketing manager both the amount and the patterns of purchases made by individual customers. From there, it is a short step to developing new "intelligent" merchandising campaigns that will prompt people to come in and stock up on their favorite items. Imagine a time when these campaigns are organized to "remind" people at the point of purchase about some additional items they normally buy.

In recent experiments, supermarkets and their suppliers are linking their computers to pass orders directly from retailer to manufacturer for rapid and low-cost fulfillment. What better way to market your products than to have your customer wired into your inventory and shipping control system? At a minimum, the system reduces the cost of doing business. But psychologically, customers who are linked to their suppliers electronically are less likely to look elsewhere for competitive prices or replacement products.

Industrial firms are already moving in this direction. For example, one of the largest suppliers of electrical equipment and supplies to electrical contractors, utilities, and commercial businesses has moved to a completely computerized ordering system. The computer in the company's home office monitors inventory levels in all of the company's 160 local warehouses, making it possible to keep stocks of every needed item without overstocking any low-volume items. Because of this capability, the company offers its customers a guarantee that the items they order will be in stock and available—a very powerful tool for salespeople seeking to land new customers. To obtain this guarantee, customers have to agree to purchase a specified quantity of an item during a given period. If they agree to this, the company agrees to have the item in stock and ready to ship at a moment's notice at a specified price.

But even more significant, customers can use their own terminals or computers to communicate with the company's order processing computer. This computer maintains a database "catalog" of all items stocked and sold by the company. In addition, it records the prenegotiated price for each of these items for each of the company's customers. Each customer can browse through this catalog or search it electronically to find the items needed for a particular purpose. Interestingly, each customer sees only his or her own pricing information, not any of the prices that apply to other customers.

Using the terminal or computer, the customer can then place an order directly with the company's computer. The computer identifies the customer, asks for billing and shipping addresses, and then accepts information on the items needed. The computer does all the order processing and prints out a purchase order, order acknowledgment, and shipping ticket. The information is routed to the nearest warehouse so the order is shipped to the customer without delay. If one warehouse is temporarily out of stock, the computer system can locate the needed items in the next nearest warehouse and have the items shipped to complete the order. All follow-up invoicing is also handled by computer. A few customers have sophisticated computers of their own, and these are linked directly to the company's computer so the needs of the customer organization are immediately transmitted to the company for shipping and invoicing.

Customers are happy with the system because the tight control of inventory guarantees the company will have what they need in stock when and where they need it. They save money because the customers can carry smaller inventories, confident they can resupply from the company with very little delay. The computerized ordering system streamlines the buying process for each of them, reducing clerical and paperwork costs by 75 percent or more for each transaction. Because of the guaranteed availability, customers have no problems with out of stock situations, shipping delays, or keeping track of pending back orders. It's a time-saver, too, because buyers from the customer organizations can find what they want in the database catalog and see the prices in very little time. Buying from other suppliers, who do not provide this type of automated ordering system, takes longer, is more difficult, and consequently costs more. Moreover, the tight computer control of inventory and shipping means the company makes its deliveries on time, and is now rated by its customers as one of their best, most reliable suppliers.

As an added benefit, the company's computer system provides both the company and all of its customers with detailed reports on their transactions. All the reports are provided to the customers free of charge. One very useful report, for example, describes what the customer ordered from the company during the previous month and breaks out these orders according to the customer location where they originated. Contractors with many projects going at once appreciate such a report to help pinpoint their expenses. And the job-by-job breakout allows the contractor to compare each job's estimated usage of materials with actual usage. When there is a wide discrepancy, everyone is alerted to the situation and can look for the cause of the problem.

The same type of computer link between customer and supplier is being implemented in pharmacies. At least one drug company is offering thousands of pharmacies the opportunity to install an online terminal through which they can order drugs for next-day delivery. The system frees salespeople so they can concentrate on penetrating new markets and pushing new products. As one can certainly reason, it also eliminates human errors, a significant problem in an industry with complex drug names and with so many similar products on the market. At the same time, the computer automatically provides a total tracking system for all orders put through the system. This information is available for marketing analysis and planning, as well as for inventory control and other techniques of improving profitability.

A new wrinkle on standard directory and catalog publishing is the "on-line catalog," which is rapidly becoming popular. For example, one of the major publishing companies recently began computerizing its 39-volume directory of companies that manufacture building products. Rather than make the information available through an electronic network, the company decided to publish the directory in book form, with a companion floppy disk. The disk contains the entire contents of the catalog, stored electronically. Customers can insert the floppy disk in their own computer systems and have the electronic system search the catalog for the particular items or category of product that they want.

Another computerized marketing tool is the optical scanner, or some variation of it, such as the handheld "magic wand" that can read either special alphanumeric characters or a standard bar code. Whatever variant is employed, the main idea is to enter information directly into the computer without having to use a keyboard. When the computer "reads" information directly, there is less room for error, greater speed for entering the data, and less training required for the person operating the computer.

Although only a handful of retailers use some form of scanning equipment in the late 1970s, by the early 1980s the new equipment was installed in nearly 30 percent of department stores and in all new and newly refurbished supermarkets. Systems of this type were also on trial in a wide variety of chain stores selling everything from toys to recorded music.

From a marketing point of view, the systems are important and useful because they provide very accurate methods of monitoring inventory. Since the computer identifies every item sold, it keeps a running count of remaining stock. It can also be programmed so, when stock of an item is reduced to a certain level, the computer either alerts the purchasing department or—as we have seen in other advanced systems—reorders the item automatically and directly.

In retail clothing and specialty stores, where every item has its own tag that the computer can read, actual inventory counts become very easy. Portable computers fitted with the magic wand scanning devices allow people to scan every ticket without moving the merchandise. When the information in all the portable computers is communicated to the central computer, it can instantly print a report detailing the size, color, style, price, purchase date, and location of every item in inventory. And the cost for such detailed inventory information is relatively low.

COMPUTERS FOR MARKET ANALYSIS

The potential for computerizing market analysis is also quite large. Marketing directors have been quick to realize this. According to a 1983 survey of sales and marketing executives, more than half already own some form of desk-top computer, and another quarter of them have plans to acquire one soon. A second survey by the University of Wisconsin reported that only one out of five marketing executives was not interested in computerizing.

One of the fundamental uses of computers in this area is to analyze a new market to see if the company can attack it profitably. Computers can connect with databases produced by Standard & Poor's or similar companies, and obtain information on companies in various SICs. This makes it easy to identify all the companies in a particular industry or those doing a particular type of business. Other computerized databases provide information on businesses in specific geographic regions. Most of them provide information on the names of key officers, street addresses and telephone numbers, company size, and other pertinent details. By conducting a computerized search for companies of a given size in a certain region doing a particular type of business, the computer can easily compile lists of prospects and help marketing analysts estimate the size of a new market.

But more and more companies are creating and maintaining their own databases, in order to have immediate access to more pertinent information and to try to attain a competitive edge in their industries. One supplier of industrial gases has a computer system with market information for half a dozen years back. An analyst can sit down at the computer and in a few minutes obtain market information that would take days to extract from traditional printed sources. A typical session, for example, involves establishing trendline data on purchases, and organizing them by customer industry, by customer application, and by region or zip code.

One of the most versatile features of modern computers is their ability to display rows and columns of figures in a so-called electronic spreadsheet. Because of the computer's innate mathematical abilities, it can build such a spreadsheet quite rapidly on the basis of a few starting figures and formulas that describe how to manipulate those figures. For example, one can type into the computer a base figure of $100,000 annual sales and a formula of "sales + (10 percent of sales)." This would be all the computer needs to build a straight-line sales projection showing a 10 percent annual increase for each year in the future. But the real advantage of electronic spreadsheets is that the computer can modify all the figures in the wink of an eye, and so display the impact of a 9 percent or 11 percent annual increase by simply changing the pertinent figure.

Since electronic spreadsheets can support many more figures and much more complicated formulas than this simple example, they make it possible to use the computer for very sophisticated analysis of many interrelated sales and marketing performance factors.

To illustrate, a territorial analysis for all sales regions might compare actual sales to expected sales for each region and calculate a performance ratio for each regional sales manager. In this case, once the formula—perhaps something like actual sales divided by expected sales—was entered into the computer, it would be a simple matter to duplicate this calculation for as many regions as required. In addition, the expected sales could themselves be calculated automatically by the computer on the basis of the company's national sales projections, which could be prorated into each region according to some formula that describes how this should work. In the absence of such a calculation, simply typing the actual sales for each region into the appropriate spot of the electronic spreadsheet would cause the computer to perform all the indicated calculations and display the results.

Although the numbers alone would be valuable to a sales manager trying to compare performance from one region to another, some computer systems allow the data to be instantaneously displayed as full-color pie charts or bar graphs. Such graphs add a more visual dimension to the analysis, and have other purposes, as we shall see later.

Another important application of computers is for sales forecasting. For example, aftermarket firms now use computers to manipulate data on the number of units sold in the primary markets and project from this the expected size of the aftermarket. The three largest manufacturers in the automobile aftermarket consider carefully how many models of a particular car have been sold. Their computers can then project sales of a new aftermarket item for that car using computer-derived information on: the percentage of car owners who are likely to purchase the aftermarket item, the wholesale price and discounts under consideration for the new item, and the cost of sales as a function of sales volume. The computer makes it very easy to experiment with different formulas for these analyses and with different values within each of the formulas. Comparative and iterative analyses that once took days of tedious and repetitive calculations are suddenly transformed into less than an hour of challenging analytical work.

Other types of sales forecasts depend on other factors, such as economic growth and retail price, which in turn may depend on dozens of other factors, such as the cost of energy and the cost of raw materials. Marketers are now using computers to construct sales forecasting "models" that project sales and profits on the basis of various "input values"—or givens—which you simply type into the computer. The calculations and display of bottom line results takes place in a twinkling.

For example, a supplier of a basic industrial commodity uses a computer to do extensive and detailed profitability analyses before making a go/no-go decision on building a new plant. The computer is set up with basic information on "base loads," or fairly continuous production runs envisioned for the new plant. Then assumptions or even guesses about sporadic or cyclical demands are laid on top of this base-load data. Finally, such factors as energy prices, shipping, and labor prices are added to the computerized model of the new plant. With all this in place, market analysts can vary the different values to see how profitable the new plant might be under a variety of economic conditions and demands for its output. As a result, the company feels a lot more confident about its decisions regarding whether to build its own new plants or to buy from other suppliers in order to meet growing customer orders.

This same spreadsheet/calculation capability allows marketing experts to see the effect of various changes in the manufacturing/distribution/sales stream. For example, how will sales be affected if the cost of distribution doubles from Poughkeepsie to Pacoima? With a suitably constructed computer model, the answer is obvious, and the knowledge such a system makes possible helps marketing experts develop the most effective plans and consider possible contingencies, as well. Computer systems are also useful in bidding situations, where a great many factors can influence the price a company wants to offer. The computer can do complex calculations very quickly, and thereby allow the marketing team to play around with different variables, such as sales volume or different distribution channels, in order to find the best-possible price.

By taking the same sales data and using the computer to analyze it a different way, the sales manager can see the profit contribution of each product, each sales territory, and each product in each territory. The key here, of course, is to give the computer the sales information product by product and territory by territory. From here, the computer—with a suitably constructed internal model of the sales system—can attribute costs, allocate fixed expenses, and come up with a bottom line figure that shows who and where the "weak sisters" are.

But even where such detailed data is not available, the computer can start with aggregated sales data and break it down into product lines and territories in accordance with estimates or with past patterns of sales activity.

The toughest part of all this, naturally, is supplying the computer with the relevant sales data. At some point, someone has to sit down and type in all the names, dates, and figures. The work is called "data entry," "keyboarding," or "keying in data." If the person who keys in the data has to be the marketing specialist, or a secretary who is uncomfortable with computers or already overcommitted to other work, or both, chances are the advantages of computerized market and sales analysis will have to take a back seat to more immediate office demands.

This problem is all the more poignant because many companies already have their sales data in computerized form. Order processing systems, inventory control systems, and other computerized sales-related systems usually contain a good deal of the information needed for sales and market analysis. The difficulty is moving that data intact to a computer set up to do the analysis.

This long-sought-after capability is now available for a limited number of computers, and more manufacturers are developing the capability every month. Basically, these newer, more advanced computers are able to communicate with a company's main computer system—usually an IBM mainframe, but potentially any brand and size of computer. At this point, the marketing analyst's computer must have the knowledge, provided through programming, of how the main computer stores the data, and how to extract just the portion the marketing analyst needs. If it has this sophistication and the communications capability, it can literally "talk" to the company's main computer and receive the required sales data without disturbing the main computer's ongoing operations. The process of taking information from another computer in this way is called "downloading."

Downloading data creates a copy of the sales information in the marketing analyst's computer. This computer can then break the connection to the main computer and make the data available for analysis.

There are two main advantages to a communications/data retrieval capability. First, it eliminates any need for a secretary or a manager to type in the data. This automatically eliminates a lot of potential for human error, such as mistakes in copying figures, and reduces the problems of fatigue, demotivation, and frustration that often come with hours of tedious, repetitive work. Second, and more important, it makes up-to-the-minute data available for instant analysis. This means the marketing specialist can now do sales analyses as often as desired and know that the information is as current as possible. Similar sales and marketing analyses, done manually, are usually performed on last week's, last month's, or even last year's figures. Obviously, older figures provide information that is far less valuable for planning and decision making than more up-to-date figures.

COMPUTERS FOR SALES TRACKING AND CONTROL

Most organizations would like to have the problems of too-rapid sales growth. But these problems can become serious when paper-based control systems fail. One common result is that customers receive poor service, orders are filled improperly or not at all, inventory goes awry, and the company begins to lose its market share.

Computers offer marketing departments the opportunity to track every sale and thereby keep tight control on every aspect of company operations that is related to sales and sales volume.

The basic procedure is to enter every order into a computer as soon as possible. New and improved computer networks and computer communications systems allow these machines to exchange data at very high speeds, whether they are down the hall or across the country. This capability makes it feasible and advantageous to decentralize the people who give the computer its sales information. Ideally speaking, it is now perfectly possible to have many small-scale data entry centers, or even to have salespeople enter their own orders directly into the computer. Experience shows that the decentralized systems often reduce the number of "typos" (keyboarding errors) and almost always cut down on the delay between the time the customer places the order and the time it is entered into the company's computer system.

But automation has not taken over in all companies, quite yet. The most common approach to order entry is still for salespeople to "write up" the order on paper when they close it. Later, these written orders are physically mailed or carried to the company's offices where a data entry clerk can key the information into the computer system.

A more modern approach that is becoming popular is for salespeople to carry "portable" computers on which they can write up the order electronically. This computer can then "talk to" the company's larger computer system via telephone wires and send the details of the order directly into the system. If the salesperson uses the customer's telephone line for this linkage, the portable computer can also be used to verify price quotes, help determine which company products are most suitable to the customer's needs, check the availability of the products, and even to reserve the items ordered so the customer can be sure of immediate delivery. A compromise approach is to have the salesperson call and talk to a computer operator, who works on a terminal in the company's offices and serves as the link between the salesperson and the computer system.

One successful implementation of a fully computerized system is working in a large cosmetics company. The new equipment and the methods it makes possible have cut the average time to process and ship an order from 10 days to 2, and at the same time reduced order errors by nearly 60 percent. Not so incidentally, the company has also saved considerable money by cutting out most of the postage, phone calls, and sales force time that used to be spent processing orders. The central idea behind the system is to streamline the process and to leave salespeople in control of the orders they file, so they can be sure their customers are properly and promptly serviced. An unanticipated side benefit is to allow salespeople to make 30 percent more sales calls in a day.

The purpose of any and all of these systems is to make sure each order is ultimately entered into the company's computer system. Once that is accomplished, the information on all orders in the system is available to the marketing people as well as to others—such as production managers—whose responsibilities link them to sales.

One of the key departments which uses this sales information is accounts receivable. With this department online to the database of new orders, these people can routinely look at every transaction and verify that the customer has approved credit or has paid for the order. Once this verification is complete, they can earmark the order for shipment by the warehouse.

The warehouse/shipping unit has full access to sales information the moment it is approved by accounts receivable. This minimizes any delay between the date of an order and the date of shipment. If the items are in stock, they can be shipped immediately. If not, the shortage is recorded in the computer system, where it can come to the attention of manufacturing or purchasing people, or both, who will have to take steps to restock the warehouse with the needed items.

A soft-drink company has used its new sales tracking system for slightly different benefits. Daily orders for next-day delivery are processed and organized by the computer very quickly. It immediately prints out a loading manifest for each truck in the fleet. Work crews can load each truck with the exact amount of product to be sold on the next day's route, in all the required sizes, packages, and flavors. As a result, the loading goes faster and the trucks always come back empty at the end of the day. Although the system has increased sales for other reasons, the company is pleased that it has also helped to reduce labor costs for the loading crew and lower fleet costs for operating the trucks.

Meanwhile, the marketing department is also monitoring the pattern and volume of sales, item by item and territory by territory. To illustrate, in one retail company the computerized sales monitoring system makes it possible to see the daily, monthly, and year-to-date totals of each item in a product line of several hundred items. In this case, the computer constructs charts for each group of products that compares actual sales against projected volumes and minimums required for profitability. But whether the analysis is conducted by looking at graphs constructed automatically by the computer or at columns of figures it produces, such a system makes it easy to identify which items in the product line are the fastest and the slowest movers. As these patterns develop, they can be monitored daily—even hourly where appropriate. This gives management the best possible opportunity to revamp the product line, control inventory, and otherwise control the company for maximum profitability.

The same data provides a solid basis for projections of future sales. For example, one retail toy company routinely looks at several hundred new products and product ideas before settling on its line for the retailing season six months to a year in the future. To do this, the marketing vice president "classifies" each possible item as being similar to one or more products the company has tried previously. The computer, with its instant recall of past product lines, makes it easy to find previous products that have similarities to the item under consideration. In addition, the computer can provide the sales figures on any previous product, which helps to establish a factual basis for comparative sales projections.

But, of course, the computer does not make the decision to go or not to go with a particular item. No computer system can provide sophisticated retail management judgment on such factors as how similar is this product to others in its classification? how similar are market conditions to those prevailing when the other products sold? and what expectations would we have for this product on its own, regardless of similar products' sales histories?

COMPUTERS IN SALES CALLS

There are literally hundreds of companies using computers to help estimate sales potential, demonstrate benefits, and even close sales. Although there are quite a few different sales-related applications where computers can provide a lot of help, generally salespeople seem to prefer computers that provide detailed analysis of sales patterns. In addition, they like systems that help them follow up on inquiries and orders. Finally, salespeople are happy with computers that help with their paperwork, particularly with writing up orders, sales-call reports, and daily or weekly activity reports. What follows is a limited selection of ideas and possibilities. There is no doubt that what will develop in this area in years to come will far outstrip the wildest possibilities we can conceive of today. Nevertheless, the handwriting is on the wall, and it forecasts exciting opportunities.

To give an example, one of the nation's largest bottlers is moving to handheld computers for the company's advance sales team. These computers replace the handwritten call reports they formerly had to turn in. Now, the salespeople call on new customers, size up the potential of their purchases, and key all the data into a handheld computer. At the end of the day, they telephone the company's main computer and have their little handheld units send in their reports electronically. As a result, the company is continually building and updating a giant database of information on its customers and prospects. This makes it possible to have the computer help the company estimate the potential impact of virtually any marketing move it might contemplate making.

Another very interesting use of computers is to provide computations and technical information to the customer on a moment's notice, so the salesperson can use the information to help close the sale. One example of this procedure involves a large manufacturer of parts for construction vehicles. Suppose the salesperson is trying to sell the vehicle owner a set of automatic brake adjusters. Normally, it might be difficult to prove the benefits of such a product. But, with automation, the salesperson can use a portable computer to calculate the actual savings in downtime, replacement parts, and labor costs, once the new brake adjusters are installed. That kind of very specific, very factual information can have a powerful effect on a prospect. In fact the company using this computer system has seen sales increase since the salespeople began offering such calculations to their customers.

A similar system is being used by a company that provides direct marketing services to its clients. Each salesperson is equipped with a portable computer that can communicate with the company's central system at its home office. Direct-mail campaigns are complex, involving dozens of interrelated factors, including the number of pieces to be mailed, the design and layout charges of the printing job, weight of the complete package, cost of renting the mailing lists, costs of getting all the printed materials assembled and into the mail, and much more. A typical campaign goes through lots of changes before it is completed, and lots of other changes are considered and carefully weighed. The time and effort involved to recalculate the cost of the campaign often can be astronomical. The remedy has proven to be a computerized estimating system.

With their portable computers, salespeople can enter all the factors associated with a client's campaign and, within a few minutes, receive an itemized and highly accurate cost estimate. If a change is made, or the client wants to see the effect of a particular change, the computer can recalculate the itemized cost in a few seconds. The computerized system makes clients happier because they can quickly and easily discover the cost impact of any change they might want to make. The sales force likes the system because it helps them provide better service to their customers and generates the kind of concrete data that turns prospects into customers.

A third example of using computers to provide prospects with solid data can be found in an equipment leasing company that uses computers to examine and compare the impact of the vast web of tax laws on various financial arrangements. Salespeople first ask each prospect to complete a questionnaire on matters of finance and income. This information is fed into the company's computer, where it can be analyzed by a specially written program. Once the analysis is complete, the computer can project the cost of ownership versus the cost of leasing a particular piece of equipment for the prospect over as long as five years. The system has been so well received by customers that the sales force has more than doubled the closing ratio since the system was first installed.

A related use of computers is for sales presentations. Computers can quickly and easily translate columns of figures into colorful business graphics, such a pie charts, bar graphs, trendlines, and the like. Salespeople who rely on numbers to prove the benefits of their products are finding that computer graphics are making their sales presentations more effective. A typical system can accept information on the prospect's business situation, then spew out charts and graphs that demonstrate the value of buying the salesperson's product or service. Most of the time, these graphics are presented on paper. However, as portable computer systems evolve larger, better, and more colorful display screens, it will become possible to create the graphics right in the prospect's office, and even leave behind "hardcopies" of the graphics, on paper.

Another use of small computers is to allow salespeople to perform their own sales and territory planning. In one soap products company, the salespeople feed their computers basic information on customers from the company's central computer. They can then have their computers arrange their own customers into a convenient and timely list of sales calls. They can record the results of each call in the computer and recall it later for planning the best follow-up actions. Also, the database of sales information thus collected helps the sales manager monitor performance against sales goals.

In a related application, at least one consulting company has developed a sales planning system that allows the computer to help a salesperson determine how much time a given prospect is worth. The salesperson using this computer program rates each prospect from 1 to 10 on a variety of significant factors, such as size of business, likely size of next order, readiness to buy, and other subjective scales. The computer then does an instantaneous computation and "rates" the prospect. Although the system is no more accurate than the salesperson's own gut feelings, many salespeople find it a comfortable tool that takes some of the burden of managing their time and territories from their already overburdened shoulders.

One of the most basic ways in which the computer can lighten this burden is by helping salespeople write up orders. Many large companies are supplying their sales staff with portable or handheld computers specifically designed for this purpose. We've already touched on this capability very briefly above. The idea is to use the computer to record each item ordered by a particular customer. The computer makes this fast and simple by automatically adding the price, multiplying out for the price extension, and then applying any discounts or special offers which might apply. All the salesperson needs to do is enter the item by name or number and the quantity desired. When the sales call is over, the computer has a complete record of the transaction. The salesperson then calls the company's main computer either after each call or once at the end of the day and transmits the order information at high speed. The system reduces paperwork, saves time, and gives the salesperson more time and energy to make extra sales calls during the day. Salespeople tend to like these systems not only because they take some of the drudgery out of their work but because they eliminate most opportunities for errors in order processing. Most companies using such systems report dramatic increases in sales volume, without a comparable increase in the number of salespeople in the field.

In a computer manufacturing company, the sales force uses portable computers to retrieve information from the company's main computer before making every sales call. At the end of the call, the salesperson can type in the call report and transmit it electronically to the home office. In this way, salespeople can stay out in the field for days or weeks at a time without the sales manager losing touch and without sacrificing their access to the company's vast information banks.

Other companies are setting up full-scale communications systems to help their salespeople keep in touch with the home office. One very common method is to sign up with one of the many available electronic communications networks and assign each salesperson an "electronic mailbox." This is a unique code which can be used to identify computerized messages to or from the salesperson that are stored within the electronic network system. Using the computerized system, it is easy for the sales manager to send a "memo" to every salesperson or a special message to any one of them. In addition, each salesperson can connect with the system at any convenient time, retrieve all messages meant for him or her, and send messages back to the company. These messages can cover orders recently written, results of sales calls, special requests for information, or whatever else is important. The communication costs for such a system are usually far lower than for comparable telephone calls. And the networks make it very convenient to communicate across time zone differences and to keep in touch with people who are constantly on the move or have very busy schedules.

A very imaginative application of computer power is the development of prospects for newspaper and magazine advertising. To make this happen, the marketing analyst loads a computer with standard research data on purchasing patterns in the geographical areas of interest. For example, a newspaper publisher would want market information covering the newspaper's distribution area. The computer can be programmed to compare these buying patterns against national or regional averages. When it finds a particular product or service with unusually high sales levels or demand, the computer takes note of that industry. When all products and services have been scanned, the publisher has a list of industries that can profit from additional advertising in the newspaper's geographical area. If the same computer can retrieve information from databases of business names, such as the Yellow Pages or a Better Business Bureau listing, it can immediately generate a list of prospects—companies that provide the wanted products or services in the newspaper's geographical area.

In a slightly different application of the same principle, a retailing chain can scan income, sales, and demographic information for the entire nation. The computer can be set to find a region that provides enough population with enough income to support a new retailing outlet for the company. The computer can conduct either of these searches in much less time, at a much lower cost, than nonautomated methods of obtaining the same data.

Initially, most salespeople express some resistance to the installation of computerized sales assistance. This is quite natural. They usually fear the computer is threatening to replace them, to limit their freedom and independence, or to increase management's ability to monitor their every action. But if they are properly involved from the very beginning of the planning stages, salespeople are usually the ones who most appreciate the resulting computer system.

COMPUTERIZED CUSTOMER SUPPORT

Another area where computers can assist the marketing effort is customer support. In a variety of situations, marketing efforts are enhanced by providing customers and prospects with information, advice, service, suggestions, plans and variations, projections, and technical information. In all of these cases and more, computers can help provide this type of support at a very low cost. When information must be timely, the computer can create a customized individual report or document, thus totally circumventing the time-consuming process of typesetting, printing, and distributing information.

For example, a California software wholesaler is providing its dealers with detailed information on its products via one of the electronic networks that allow computers to communicate between two points virtually anywhere in the United States or in the world. Dealers use their own computers to connect with the network and then to call up the information placed there by the software company. This "information bank" eliminates any need for most of the telephone calls which dealers used to make to the company with specific questions about problems and capabilities of the company's products. Now those same questions can be answered at any time, 24 hours a day, seven days a week, with a call to the electronic network.

Even more important, the company can update and rewrite the information and instantly replace the older version in the network's databank with the newer version. This means customer-supported materials and technical data are never out of date or out of print the way they once had to be from time to time. Any dealer can look at the material at any time, even print a copy of it using his or her computer.

The company also appreciates reducing its printing and distributing costs. The new electronic distribution system costs less than $10 to send the complete package of information to the electronic network and less than $20 a month to maintain it there. Of course, dealers must pay a few cents each time they look at the material, but they are more than happy to do so because the information they get with this new system is so much more timely, accurate, and available than ever before.

Another company, this one a major chemical supplier, provides computerized information on typical customer problems and how to solve them. The information is available to salespeople and to customers via one of the major electronic network systems. When a question or problem comes up, any terminal can be used to access the information bank, search for the needed information, and display or print it, as required. A more sophisticated version of the same system helps customers decide which products they need for particular applications. If the customer wants to manufacture a plastic bottle or a part for a piece of equipment, the engineering staff can key into the company's computer all the technical specifications for the end product or item. The computer then uses a customized program to determine which of the company's chemical or plastic products can best meet the customer's requirements. Both parts of the system help the company by cutting down the cost of providing technical advice and expertise. The customers appreciate the added service and the convenience of being able to get the answers they want at a moment's notice.

Another application of the same system is in farming, where farmers require very specific chemicals for fertilizing their crops and treating them for diseases and pests. With one company's computer system, the farmer can tell the salesperson exactly how much acreage he plans to put into each crop this season. The information is punched into the computer and in a few minutes the farmer knows exactly what chemicals he will need, how much of each type, and when to apply them. If he confirms the order, the computer automatically records the transaction and arranges for each of the chemicals to be delivered when, where, and in the quantity the farmer needs.

COMPUTERS IN POLITICS

To some people, electoral politics is just another form of marketing, one in which the "product" is a person instead of a thing. To the extent this is true, computers are doing their bit to increase the "market share" and "sales" of our most powerful political leaders.

In the 1970s, for example, the Republican party was in poor financial shape, wracked by the scandal of Watergate and in severe danger of "going out of business." Then key leaders discovered the advantages of "marketing" through direct mail.

The first efforts relied on a list of some 25,100 proven party stalwarts. But the mailings worked and, by the early 1980s, the Republicans were marketing themselves to more than 2.5 million people and raising nearly $100 million annually! The Democrats have been a little slower, but are picking up momentum in their marketing programs. The major political parties are not the only ones to market themselves and their causes via direct mail. In the last four or five years, nearly a dozen or so major lobbying groups have come to the fore by virtue of their ability to reach out to voters and generate action through the judicious use of direct-mail programs.

Computers, of course, are the key to such direct-mail programs. In one recent example, a key vote in a state legislature was influenced by a single lobbying group. The group obtained the zip codes of the legislators whose votes were still undecided. Then its computer matched those zip codes with the organization's membership list and came up with the names and addresses of thousands of people who lived right in the legislators' home neighborhoods. It was relatively easy to draft a motivating message and have the computer transmit it through the post office's "electronic mail" facility for next-day delivery to all of those members. They responded by writing their own letters and making phone calls to the legislators' offices. The result: A good portion of the legislators swung their votes the way the lobbying organization wanted them. The whole process took just under a week!

As you can see, there are a great many uses of computers possible in marketing. This discussion has by no means been exhaustive. As computers become faster, lighter in weight, and cheaper to buy and operate, there is no doubt that they will find ever more interesting, exciting, and profitable uses in this all-important field of business.

List of Suppliers for Computer Applications in Marketing

Descriptive Codes:
BA = Budgeting & Accounting
D   = Distribution Software
F   = Forecasting
H   = Hardware manufacturer
I/O = Inquiries/Orders
M   = Mailing Lists
MG = Management
MP = Market Planning
R   = Market Research
T   = Telemarketing

Adelie
"CLOSE"—I/O
840 Memorial Drive
Cambridge, MA 02139
617-661-8400

AIM Computer Systems
"Sales Lead Information Processor"—I/O
30432 Euclid Avenue
Wickliffe, OH 44092
216-943-2900

Amcor Computer Corp.
"Amfacs"—R
1900 Plantside Drive
Louisville, KY 40299
502-491-9820

Burroughs Corp.—H
Burroughs Place
Detroit, MI 48232

Cambar Business Systems
"Control"—D, R
2864 Azalea Drive
P.O. Box 10067
Charleston, SC 29411
803-554-9550

Cambridge Computer Associates
"Crosstabs"—MP, R
222 Alewife Brook Parkway
Cambridge, MA 02138
617-868-1111

Control Data Corp.—H
8100 34th Avenue South
Minneapolis, MN 55440

Data General Corp.—H
Route 9
Westboro, MA 01581

Digital Equipment Corp.—H
146 Main Street
Maynard, MA 01754

Economic Sciences
"EMS"—F
2150 Shattuck Avenue
Suite 1130
Berkeley, CA 94704
415-841-6869

Executec Corp.
"The Software Bus"—"SeriesOnePlus"—BA, MG
12200 Park Central Drive
Dallas, TX 75251
214-239-8080

Geographic Systems
"Geofiles"—M, R, MG
"Geomap"—MG
100 Main Street
Reading, MA 01867
617-942-0051

IBM
Old Orchard Road
Armonk, NY 10504
914-765-1900

Impact Systems
"Comprehensive Marketing Support"—R, MG
57 Main Street
Concord, MA 01742
617-369-0270

JEB Systems
"Marketing Management System"—I/O, M, T
Main Street
P.O. Box 70
Franconia, NH 03580
603-823-7021

Lifeboat Associates
"Formula"—BA, M
"Sales Prospect Management"—I/O
1651 Third Avenue
New York, NY 10028
212-860-0300

Micro Associates
"Saleslog"—MG
Ridgelake Drive
Metaire, LA 70001
504-831-3560

NCR—H
1700 South Patterson Boulevard
Dayton, OH 45479

Peachtree Software
"PeachCalc"—BA, F
"Sales Tracker"—I/O, R, MG
"Mailing List Manager"—M
3445 Peachtree Road, N.E.
Atlanta, GA 30326
404-239-3000

Precision Visuals
"Grafmaster"—MG
6260 Lookout Road
Boulder, CO 80301
303-530-9000

Profimatics
"GRTMPS"—D
77 Rolling Oaks Drive
Thousand Oaks, CA 91361
805-496-6661

Rand Information Systems
"Comprehensive Industry Distribution System Package"—D, I/O
98 Battery Street
San Francisco, CA 94111
415-392-2500

Ross Systems
"Management Aid For Planning Strategies"—BA, MP, F
1900 Embarcadero Road
Palo Alto, CA 94303
415-856-1100

Software International
"Forecasting, Modeling & Reporting System"—BA, F
2 Elm Square
Andover, MA 01810
617-475-5040

Systems Management
"Business Control Programs"—BA, D, M, T
6300 N. River Road
Rosemont, IL 60018
312-698-4000

Vector Graphic
"Execumodeler"—F
500 N. Ventu Park Road
Thousand Oaks, CA 91320
805-499-5831

Visicorp
"VisiCalc"—BA
2895 Zanker Road
San Jose, CA 95134

WANG—H
One Industrial Avenue
Lowell, MA 01851

Waters Business Systems
"Sales & Marketing Information System"—I/O, R, MG
47 New York Avenue
Framingham, MA, 01701
617-879-2503

Whelan Associates
"Telephone Fulfillment System"—T
Gwynned Plaza
Spring House, PA 19477
215-643-7470

Xerox Computer Services
"Interactive Accounting System"—BA, I/O, MG
"Praxa"—I/O
5130 Beethoven Street
Los Angeles, CA 90066
213-306-4000

21

TRAITS OF A
GOOD MANAGER

by
Marvin Rafal

Marvin Rafal Associates, Inc.

OVERVIEW

Over the years, there has been much folklore about what traits make a successful marketing manager. The same is true for the product manager, the springboard that has propelled many people into marketing management.

One popular book on product management makes reference to "courage," a quality described as essential because marketing and product managers must go out on a limb in forecasting. Additionally, he or she is described as "dynamic," or at least responsive to the dynamics that take place in marketing management. Other traits frequently mentioned include "individualism" and "nonconformity." One characteristic purportedly owned by marketing managers—creativity—is mentioned so frequently it has become a cliché.

These stereotypes are of little use to a current marketing manager and of even less use to one who aspires to that position. To begin, the terms are clearly ambiguous. What do courage, nonconformity, individualism, and creativity mean, and in what situations are they supposed to be shown? How can they be measured? Is it possible for someone to be evaluated as having 5 units of creativity when it has been established that 10 are needed for success on the job? How can the marketing manager reader learn whether he or she is achieving the necessary quantity? And, even assuming measurement is possible, just how does one go about developing these traits or qualities?

Finally, who says so? Is there any research documentation that proves the need for these traits, or, more likely, are they merely someone's ad hoc empirical judgments, arrived at by thinking about the subject, and repeated by others?

It is in the reader's best interest to disregard such shibboleths, however frequently they may be encountered in print. And this is really good news. If those traits really did exist, it would be tantamount to saying that if you have them you're in good shape, and if you lack them, tough luck—forget about marketing management as a career. One would be better advised to take seriously those descriptions of traits that have some research documentation.

RESEARCH FINDINGS

Results of Study

The author conducted a number of nonpublished studies in 1980. Product and marketing managers of firms in the health care industry were asked in 1980 to participate in a number of unpublished studies on the traits of a good marketing manager. They were asked to complete three standardized psychological tests. Ninety-six managers agreed to participate, representing 19 companies.

One might gain from this study by comparing his or her self-insights and perceptions with the traits shown by presently employed product and marketing managers.

The Study of Values

This test, the "Study of Values,"[1] is described by the author as having as its aim the measuring of "the relative prominence of six interests or motives in personality: the theoretical, economic, aesthetic, social, political, and religious. It is based on work that suggests that the personalities of people are best known through a study of their values."

Here is the meaning of each of these values:[2]

1. The Theoretical.

The dominant interest of the theoretical person is the discovery of *truth*. In the pursuit of this goal, he/she characteristically takes a "cognitive" attitude—one that divests itself of judgments regarding the beauty or utility of objects, and seeks only to observe and to reason. Since the interests

---

[1] G. W. Allport, P. E. Vernon, and Gordon Lindzey, "Study of Values" (Iowa City: Houghton Mifflin, 1970).

[2] Allport et al., from the Manual to the "Study of Values," pp. 4–5.

of the theoretical person are rational, he/she is necessarily an intellectualist. His/her chief aim in life is to order and systematize his/her knowledge.

2. The Economic.

The economic person is characteristically interested in what is *useful*. This interest develops to embrace the practical affairs of the business world—the production, marketing, and consumption of goods, the elaboration of credit, and the accumulation of tangible wealth. This type is thoroughly "practical" and conforms well to the prevailing stereotype of the average American businessman.

3. The Aesthetic.

The aesthetic person sees his/her highest value in *form* and *harmony*. Each single experience is judged from the standpoint of grace, symmetry, or fitness. An individual who has aesthetic values finds his/her chief interest in the artistic episodes of life.

4. The Social.

The highest value for this type is *love* of people. The social person prizes other persons as ends, and is therefore him/herself kind, sympathetic, and unselfish. He/she is likely to find the theoretical, economic, and aesthetic attitudes cold and inhuman.

5. The Political.

The political person is interested primarily in *power*. Leaders in any field generally have high power value. Since competition and struggle play a large part in all life, many philosophers have seen power as the most universal and most fundamental of motives. There are, however, certain personalities in whom the desire for a direct expression of this motive is uppermost, who wish above all else for personal power, influence, and renown.

6. The Religious.

The highest value of the religious person may be called *unity*. Some people of this type find their religious experience in the affirmation of life and in active participation therein. With their zest and enthusiasm, they see something divine in every event.

On the other hand, others seek to unite themselves with a higher reality by withdrawing from life. They find the experience of unity through self-denial and meditation.

Mixtures.

A person may not necessarily belong exclusively to one or another of these types of values, but may represent mixtures.

These are the results achieved by the 96 health care industry product and marketing managers:

	Very High	High	Average	Low	Very Low
Theoretical	0	10	56	18	12
Economic	40	22	30	4	0
Aesthetic	10	28	46	8	4
Social	2	4	40	36	14
Political	24	32	34	4	2
Religious	2	8	40	24	22

How can this be interpreted?

Functioning product and marketing managers are:

About as interested in a search for truth "for its own sake" as the average person. In this regard, they are unlike scientists and researchers.

Of them, 62 (out of 96), close to 65 percent, are above the average in valuing the practical, the economic, the materialistic.

About half of them (46 of 96) are average in their aesthetic and artistic values, but more of them are above average (38) than below average (12) in this value.

There is a suggestion of some degree of concern with the artistic (of product packaging, advertising art, and so on).

Fifty percent of them are below average in their social value. Few marketing and product managers are social welfare minded.

Fifty-six are above average in their power drive. Power can be expressed in ways additional to line management. Persuasion—changing the behaviors and thinking of other people through persuasive techniques—can meet people's power needs.

Forty-six are below average in their religious values.

In short, the portrait that emerges is that product and marketing managers are every inch business persons—practical, materialistic, economically motivated, and ready to exert their influence over other people.

This does not sound like the individualistic, unconventional, nonconformist described by some.

The Interest Inventory

A classical instrument in the field of "people measurement" is the Strong/Campbell Interest Inventory.

This test does not measure abilities. Rather, it tells something about the pattern of interests. Although most of us know something of our own interests, we're not sure how we compare with people actively engaged in various occupations.[3]

Included below are data regarding how the product and marketing managers scored on "General Occupational Themes."

Following are brief descriptions of these, condensed from the authors' statements.[4]

Realistic theme

People scoring high here are usually rugged, robust, practical, physically strong: they usually have good physical skills, but sometimes have trouble expressing themselves or in communicating their feelings to others. They like to work outdoors and to work with tools, especially large, powerful machines. They prefer to deal with things rather than with ideas or people.

Investigative theme

This theme centers around science and scientific activities. Extremes of this type are not particularly interested in working around other people. They enjoy solving abstract problems, and they have a great need to understand the physical world. They prefer to think through problems rather than act them out. Such people enjoy ambiguous challenges and do not like highly structured situations with many rules. They frequently have unconventional values and attitudes and tend to be original and creative, especially in scientific areas.

Artistic theme

The extreme type here is artistically oriented, and likes to work in artistic settings that offer many opportunities for self-expression. They resemble I-Theme types in preferring to work alone, but have a greater need for individualistic expression, are usually less assertive about their own opinions and capabilities, and are more sensitive and emotional. They score higher on measures of originality than any of the other types do.

Social theme

The pure type here is sociable, responsible, humanistic, and concerned with the welfare of others. These people usually express themselves well and get along well with others; they have little interest in situations requiring physical exertion or working with machinery.

---

[3] Strong-Campbell Interest Inventory (Stanford, Calif.: Stanford University Press, 1974). Reproduced by special permission of the distributor, Consulting Psychologists Press, Inc., Palo Alto, Calif., acting for the publisher, Stanford University Press, from Manual for the Strong Campbell Interest Inventory Form T325 of the STRONG CAMPBELL INTEREST BLANK (3d ed.) by David Campbell & Jo-Ida Hansen, © 1981.

[4] Ibid.

Enterprising theme

The extreme type of this theme has a great facility with words, especially in selling, dominating, and leading; frequently these people are in sales work. They see themselves as energetic, enthusiastic, adventurous, self-confident, and dominant, and they prefer social tasks where they can assume leadership. They enjoy persuading others to their viewpoints. They like power, status, and material wealth.

Conventional theme

Extremes of this type prefer the highly ordered activities, both verbal and numerical, that characterize office work. People scoring high fit well into large organizations but do not seek leadership; they respond to power and are comfortable working in a well-established chain of command. They dislike ambiguous situations, preferring to know precisely what is expected of them. Such people describe themselves as conventional, stable, well-controlled, and dependable. They have little interest in problems requiring physical skills or intense relationships with others, and are most effective at well-defined tasks.

On the "occupational themes," these were the results by the 96 product and marketing managers:

	Very High	High	Moder- ately High	Average	Moder- ately Low	Low	Very Low
Enterprisal	14	26	24	26	4	2	0
Realistic	6	6	6	28	22	18	10
Investigative	8	8	14	46	6	14	0
Social	4	4	18	36	24	6	4
Conventional	0	6	12	48	16	6	8
Artistic	12	12	16	32	12	6	6

This is a different test, and it measures a different trait (interests) and not values.

And yet, the results reinforce the picture of people interested in business (enterprisal); whose interests are low in the realistic and "robust" occupations, who are not scientifically or theoretically minded (investigative), who have little concern with social welfare or in the "do-gooder" occupations (social), nor in accounting, office, nor bookkeeping types of positions (conventional), but who have a slight tilt toward the artistic and aesthetic.

This same test is based on the concept of "birds of a feather flock together." That is, if a person shows the same likes and dislikes toward people, activities, recreation, and so on, as people who are successful in advertising management, that person is likely to be interested in advertising.

Here are the interests of the 96 health care product and marketing managers, compared with those of people successful in certain selected occupations:

	Very Similar	Similar	Moderately Similar	Average	Moderately Dissimilar	Dissimilar	Very Dissimilar
Tangible sales	8	20	16	30	8	12	2
Intangible sales	6	32	18	28	8	2	2
Sales manager	12	26	10	26	2	2	2
Advertising exec.	24	32	12	20	2	4	2
Purchasing agent	20	28	16	16	14	2	0

It is pretty clear that the tested product and marketing managers share the same likes and dislikes of people engaged in the persuasive occupations.

The results of this study and its potential benefits to readers may be summarized:

Readers who are interested in comparing the insights and perceptions they have gained about themselves with the measured traits of people presently employed successfully as product and marketing managers should think of the comparison this way:

There is evidence that the traits of a good manager in marketing include an unmistakable interest in the persuasive occupations, such as tangible and intangible sales, sales manager, and advertising. They have an interest also in the other side of the desk— in purchasing.

Their general occupational theme is enterprisal—the business theme. They may or may not have some interest in other themes (realistic, investigative, social, conventional, artistic), but those other themes, with the minor exception of artistic, are not relevant to success in marketing and not characteristic of marketing managers.

A Competency-Based Approach

Another useful way to consider the traits of a good manager is by considering the particular competencies (skills, abilities) he or she must have to perform successfully.

Of these, there are three types:

Specific Job Competencies. These have to do with skills and abilities specific to the job. They are useful only in product and marketing manager jobs. They cannot be used in another kind of job.

Assuming a person is well suited for the job, it is important for that person to develop these competencies.

A study conducted by the author involved polling groups of product and marketing managers to discover the most important specific job competencies of their positions. The following list emerged, not necessarily in the order of importance.

Ability to:

— *Understand* the nature of assignments regarding economic potential of product based on minimal data and to carry out investigations.

— *Interact with,* collect information from, and secure cooperation from other people and entities in developing an investigation.

— *Draw conclusions* based on a large amount of subjective and objective data, and communicate conclusions effectively in written or oral form.

— *Establish* market and product forecasts.

— *Develop* positioning and promotional strategies along with budgets to accomplish forecasts.

— *Establish* a timetable to plan for the execution of necessary activities, and implement the timetable.

— *Hold meetings* and persuade people in those meetings.

— *Evaluate and discriminate* among strategies relevant to such functions as direct mail, news release, and packaging.

— *Interact* successfully with other people and be persuasive despite pressures and stress.

— *Utilize time* effectively by apportioning it among activities based on factors such as importance and immediacy.

Personal Competencies. These are the abilities people develop, or begin to develop, early in life. They are a frequent cause of job failure among all managers, including, certainly, product and marketing managers. Intellectual brilliance, experience, and good ideas rarely overcome or can compensate for serious deficiencies in personal competencies.

Most of these competencies have to do with how an individual has learned, since childhood, to deal with people, oneself, and with life.

The following personal competencies are especially important in such positions as product and marketing manager:

Openness, spontaneity, naturalness. These express the competency to deal with others and with the world in an open and natural way. In everyday conversation, it would be described as "what you see is who he is."

The opposite of this competency is role-playing, or pretending to be what one is not. Usually, others can see through the pose and, as a result, it undermines trust and credibility.

The personal competency involved here is the ability to know when one is role-playing and what there is in the situation or the perception of it that causes one to do so. Knowing this enables one to quit role-playing and to be open once again.

Ability to improve behaviors. Some people are receptive to and even solicit feedback from others on their mistakes. Thus, they are able to correct them. Others close their eyes to such information, deny the mistake, or act in other defensive ways.

Healthy relationship with the boss. Early in life one develops characteristic ways of dealing with authority figures, such as parents. Those patterns later carry over to relations with teachers and then bosses. Some people learn to be dependent, even subservient; others become rebellious; still others manage to have healthy, interdependent relationships.

Successful product or marketing managers have the competency to evaluate realistically their relationships with their bosses so they can modify their own behaviors and understand, in fact, the bosses' behavior toward them.

Ability to deal with conflict. Conflict is a part of life—inevitable, normal, and encountered in all settings. Some people deny this and flee from conflict. Others fight and try to "give better than they get." Still others look for someone to help them, an ally. These patterns are learned in childhood.

Product and marketing managers are not insulated from conflict. The competency they need is to recognize the proper way to respond to a particular conflict situation and have the repertoire to employ that response.

SELF-EVALUATION

Readers who seek to improve their performance, or who aspire to become product and marketing managers can use information on traits of a good manager this way:

Values and Interests. People who see their own values and interests as similar to those of people who are successful in product and marketing management can derive comfort and reinforcement from the fact that they seem to be placed in or aiming toward work appropriate to their interests and values.

People who find dissimilarities need to consider that they must use compensatory mechanisms—determination, hard work, exploitation of other abilities—to make up for inappropriateness in values and interests.

Specific Job Competencies. These basic skills and abilities can be acquired. One of the best approaches is to study the behaviors and actions of people who are especially effective in each of these competencies and try to model those behaviors and actions.

Personal Competencies. No person has developed and mastered all these competencies. There is no perfect product or marketing manager; there is no perfect person. The important and realistic viewpoint is to investigate and assess the extent to which one has these competencies, to learn more about oneself, to move toward slow but steady growth in the competencies where there are deficiencies—and thus toward becoming a more productive marketing manager and a more fulfilled person.

Part 2

NEW PRODUCT DEVELOPMENT AND MANAGEMENT

22

INTRODUCTION TO NEW PRODUCTS MANAGEMENT

by
Larry Wizenberg*

Yankelovich, Skelly, and White, Inc.

New products are now recognized as the lifeblood of just about every business—they are the basis for maintaining profitability and market share in highly competitive markets. Sooner or later most products are preempted by other products or else evolve into less-profitable products due to extremely competitive pricing and promotional pressures. The degree of per-unit profit contribution tends to diminish during the "late growth" and "maturity" stages of the product life cycle. Because the profit margin curve tends to start descending, while the sales curve continues to rise, additional new product profit is needed to sustain company growth.

An effective new products management program should focus on the development and launching of various types of new products responsive to the opportunities of the marketplace. Few companies can rely solely upon the limited notion of new products being those with unique patented features which every customer wants and no competitor has.

Viable strategies may range from a role as an originator of product concepts to a more passive role of replicating or modifying new offerings by others. These strategies can coexist in order to optimize the new products management program. As long as the problems and challenges in introducing the product have not previously been faced by

---

* Mr. Wizenberg is editor of Dow Jones–Irwin's New Products Handbook, to be published, fall 1985.

management, it should be treated as a new product. This includes new categories to a company, new brands, and repositioning existing products.

We should recognize gradations of newness and should design marketing programs related to their specific nature. On an overall basis, new products can be viewed as products, services, and processes that are marketed to gain widespread use. We often refer to the terms *invention* and *innovation* when defining new products. While sometimes used interchangeably, there is a fine distinction between the terms.

An *invention* is literally a creation, a new device, method, or idea.

An *innovation* is concerned with the introduction of a new device, method, or idea into general use. Innovation is the successful introduction of change by the widespread acceptance of an invention. An invention is not a new product until it is produced and available for purchase. Essentially, new products management is the planned process of turning inventions into innovations.

We can improve the probabilities of successful new products management by understanding the various facets of new as perceived by the company and its customers.

From the corporate perspective, it is helpful to relate the degree of newness to the risk involved. In this way appropriate performance measurement criteria can be established. To evaluate the risk, both technology and market dimensions should be considered.

- *Technology*—the relative newness of the reservoir of knowledge enabling the product to be produced.
- *Markets*—differences in the customer base and channels of distribution through which the product is to be sold.

As the similarity of existing products decreases in terms of technology or markets, or both, the risk involved increases.

From the customer perspective, new product offerings are evaluated in terms of the perceived impact on their consumption patterns. Consumers and industrial product end users tend to view new products according to the behavioral change or new learning required in order to use the product.

The highest gradation of newness involves the establishment of totally new consumption patterns. Breakthrough products, such as video tape recorders that enable users to "time shift" by taping programs for subsequent view, involve a relatively high degree of learning. On the other end of the continuum, fashion changes, new brands, and modifications in packaging involve the least disrupting influence on established consumption patterns.

As the amount of behavioral change required to use the new product increases, marketing strategies should focus on reducing complexity and anxiety involved with the purchase. Information, demonstrations, and warranties will facilitate trial. Probabilities for successful new product introduction can be enhanced by relating strategies both to the internal needs of the company and those of the target customer.

While any approach and sequence to new product development should be tailored to meet the unique characteristics and personality of the company, there are fundamental actions that need to be taken—or consciously avoided.

Part of the definition of new products management is encompassed by the process of developing product concepts and evaluating the prospects for successful commercialization. Before we focus on these stages of the new product development process, we should acknowledge the importance of the neonatal phase—the planning that sets the stage for the balance of the process.

The rational determination of where to go and how to get there should be identified and communicated to those involved as early as possible. This will minimize the waste of resources . . . both time and money.

Planning parameters should be established as guidelines for idea generation and the evaluation process. Each factor should be identified as either:

1. Critical—must have.
2. Nice to have.
3. Fringe benefit.

The following set of parameters can serve as a starting point to develop your own guidelines. They should be communicated to management as guidelines, not as a rigidly defined road map. Deviations should be considered if the trade-offs appear to be worthwhile.

— The primary focus should be consumer market-oriented.
— The product formulation should contain (ingredient).
— The use of (ingredient) should provide a real added value to the product performance.
— The degree of functional uniqueness should be significant, wherever possible.
— The product should be conducive to a premium pricing structure.
— A potential sales volume of $_____ million or more should be feasible, within _____ year(s).
— The product should have an expected life cycle of _____ years.

— Although the use of existing sales and distribution channels is preferred, opportunities requiring distribution modification should be considered.
— Product improvements and product line extensions should be considered.
— Products should be "push" in nature, requiring minimum national consumer advertising support.
— Products need not be fully manufactured by (_____); subcontracting would be permitted.

As the process of new product development involves a series of management decisions, it becomes more expensive to discard a product concept as we progress with each phase. The objective is to do a better job of eliminating concepts of limited potential before they reach the more expensive latter phases. The delicate balance involves not discarding concepts prematurely. Therefore, companies should clarify that the expressed goals and objectives are targets, parameters that are not to be rigidly followed but are to be used as a frame of reference.

The first phase of the new product development process is *idea generation* or *exploration*. This involves the search for product concepts to meet the company objectives. One of the challenges that we face is to instill creativity. Self-inflicted barriers to creativity should be broken in order to facilitate the search for a new order of meaning. Participants can be stimulated, asking them to view existing products in terms of potential substitutions, combinations, magnifications, miniaturizations, new uses, and new users. Also, they should be invited to reassess abandoned projects, analyze manufacturing process by-products, and probe company personnel, customers, converters, and raw material suppliers.

The next phase is *concept screening*. This is an internal analysis to determine which ideas are pertinent and merit more detailed study. Screening is the systematic process of qualitative selection of product concepts based upon management judgment. It is the process of collecting facts and opinions about the viability of each product concept. An estimate of potential profit, time, investment, and risk should be developed.

After the screening phase, an in-depth *business analysis* should be conducted. This involves a detailed appraisal of the product, potential competition, and overall marketing characteristics. Market and technical research, focus groups, and social trend data should be used to develop an understanding of the trends and characteristics of the market. This would serve as the basis for the eventual marketing program and product positioning.

The final phase prior to commercialization is *testing*. This involves laboratory and commercial experiments that verify or disaffirm previous business judgements. Tests might include user panels, laboratory test markets, perception research, and test marketing. These tools enable management to experiment with various elements of the marketing mix and can serve as a measure to forecast national sales.

When final plans for production and marketing are completed, we enter the *commercialization* phase. This is the actual launching of the product on a regional or national basis, monitoring acceptance and competitive reaction.

Increased sensitivity to these factors should enhance the new products management process.

23

FINDING AND LAUNCHING SUCCESSFUL NEW PRODUCTS

by
Stewart A. Washburn CMC

INTRODUCTION

Among marketing people, it is an article of faith that continued success in the marketplace requires a continuous flow of new products. The number of new products each year will vary from situation to situation, but the need for them is continuous. Established products eventually become obsolete, and markets shrivel and die. Even Big Macs have peaked and a McDonald's franchise is no longer the money-maker it once was.

These days, especially, new products take on an added significance. The income new products generate is found money. If the product is new and for an established market, its superior benefits will assure sales at the expense of existing products. And if the market itself is new, so, too, will be the income.

So important is the subject of new products that the literature is studded with articles concerning the life cycle of products and the life cycles of markets. Such articles tell us how much time we have left before a new product will be required or a new market must be found. Further, it is not difficult to find good articles about the techniques for launching a new product so that all the pieces come together properly. Nor is it difficult to turn up articles on the management of products in the marketplace. One can even find learned articles about the life cycles of industries and technologies. MIT's Systems Dynamics Group, for example, writes and talks about the 40- to 60-year Kondratieff waves that control the lives of basic industries.

It is important to know how to bring a new product to market, and how to manage it once it is there. It is also important to know where it is in its life cycle, although some products like Ivory soap and Campbell's Tomato Soup seem to go on forever. But first, and these are problems we all face, we ought to know what an acceptable new product is for us and, as important, we ought to know where to look for and how to recognize viable new product ideas.

To illustrate this point, consider the case of a mechanical engineer (and a good one). He has been out of school for about 10 years and has just started his third job. His first was with a manufacturer of electronic controls, where he worked with a new product group. In the six years he was there, he had a hand in developing and bringing to market five or six new products.

Three years ago, another electronics firm made him an offer he couldn't refuse. He accepted and was put in charge of new product development. He was given a secretary, a nice office, two phones, all the credit cards he could use, and a fine budget. And he was told to go—develop some new products.

He was very conscientious, and, after a year of traveling and talking with customers, he proposed five new product ideas. Three were turned down by management as being unsuitable. Two went to engineering for further study. Six months later, he proposed three more new product ideas. These, too, were turned down. At that point he said to management, "Look, you have turned down six new product ideas because they were unsuitable. What is an acceptable new product idea?" The answer he got was this, "You are the new product expert, you should know."

He quit, called his former employer, and now is back there in charge of new product development.

Clearly, any continued and successful effort to identify, evaluate, develop, and launch profitable new products ought to begin with an understanding of what constitutes acceptability.

A second story concerns the operating vice president of a machine tool firm, a firm with a reputation for innovation. In discussing new products one day, he said this, "We really don't know what we are doing. Half, maybe two thirds, of our new products die. We try to bury them before anyone notices. What it boils down to is this . . . We take a hard look at who is proposing the new product. If we trust him and think he is mature and aggressive enough, we let him go ahead. It is as simple as that."

This might be called the advocacy approach to new product selection and development. However, there may be no necessary relationship between the quality of a product and the quality of its champion. The danger here is institutionalizing the selection of a "Product Champion" and not institutionalizing the identification, evaluation, development, and launching of profitable new products.

These two situations may not be typical, but they are common enough. For most firms, developing new industrial products is a chancy business. There are few guidelines for an acceptable new product. We do not know where to look for new product ideas, although we are assured that they are all around us . . . somewhere. There are even a number of publications available which describe new products, new processes, and new patents. These not only describe the significant new products, patents, and processes which may be available for licensing, but they also serve as useful sources of new product ideas. (See Figure 23–1.)

FIGURE 23–1
Typical Publications Describing New Products, New Processes, and New Patents

---

New Product Development Newsletter
New Product Development
P.O. Box 1309
Point Pleasant, N.J. 08742

New From U.S.*
Prestwick Publications, Inc.
19 Airport Road
Scotia, N.Y. 12302

NASA Tech Briefs
National Aeronautics and Space Administration
400 Maryland Avenue SW
Washington, D.C. 20546

New Products and Processes
Newsweek, Inc.
444 Madison Avenue
New York, N.Y. 10022

Venture/Product News
General Electric Business Growth Services
120 Erie Boulevard
Schenectady, N.Y. 12305

The Official Gazette (Patents Section)
Superintendent of Documents
Government Printing Office
Washington, D.C. 20402

---

* Also available: *New from Japan* and *New from Europe*.

When we do eventually have an idea, our procedures for evaluating it and putting it into development are neither clear nor firmly established. And, finally, once we have the new product, we may not be able to get it off the ground as quickly as we would like.

In view of all this, what I propose is to explore the requisites for a successful system for identifying, evaluating, developing, and launching new industrial products. (There are five of these summarized in Figure 23–2.)

FIGURE 23–2
Requisites for Successful New Products

---

1. Strategic guidelines for identifying acceptable new product ideas.
2. An understanding of where and how to look for new product ideas.
3. Effective market research and audit procedures.
4. A final evaluation screen for selecting the product to be developed.
5. Effective launching tactics.

First, we need some broad strategic guidelines to show us the kinds of new products that are best for us and our firms.

Second, we need to know where and how to look for new product ideas. The possibilities here may be new to most. So, we'll explore this subject thoroughly.

The third requisite for an effective system for identifying, evaluating, developing, and launching new products is a simple way of auditing what's going on in the marketplace and conducting necessary market research.

Fourth, we need a final evaluation screen that will tell us which of several new product ideas should go into development. This important subject will be covered here.

Finally, we need an effective process for actually launching the new product, and, as we shall see, it is a much simpler process than one might think.

Most new products are not breakthroughs. They are rather unglamorous and ordinary, running from freeze-dried snow peas to a robotized assembly line. All they do is make or lose money. These are the ones we will be concerned with (preferably just the money-makers).

DEVELOPING STRATEGIC NEW PRODUCT GUIDELINES

As a starting point, let's take a close look at what we know about successful marketers. We'll examine a few characteristics which successful firms share and which are absent from the not-quite-so-successful firms. Success here does not mean anything extraordinary or hard to understand; rather, it refers to those firms that make more money than other firms in the same business, while serving a broader and happier customer base.

These firms are successful today because of the things they have done in the past. Firms that have met our definition of success do not achieve that position overnight. One of the things that has made them what they are is that over the years they have introduced a number of successful new products. Today's standard products were, after all, yesterday's successful new products.

We can identify a number of characteristics shared by successful marketers. We can relate those characteristics to the identification and development of new products. Thus, we have useful strategic guidelines to aid us in the selection of successful new products. If we follow these guidelines, over time we, too, will become increasingly successful.

Over the years, and in connection with the problems of strategic planning, a number of organizations have been looking at or looking into what makes one firm more successful than another.

Return on investment (ROI) is the criterion used to measure success. The ROIs of firms in the same businesses (i.e., serving the same markets) were compared with one another. The leaders in each group, regardless of the kind of businesses, shared 30 or so characteristics, each of which influenced ROI independently of the others. Among them are the 11 shown in Figure 23–3. These 11 characteristics seem to have the most use in establishing strategic guidelines for the selection of new products.

Throughout what follows, real products will be used to illustrate the points being made. Because there is a great diversity among indus-

---

FIGURE 23–3
Common Characteristics of Successful Industrial Marketers

1. High-quality products.
2. Broad product offerings.
3. Narrow market segments.
4. High market shares.
5. Healthy margins.
6. Marketing efforts which stress direct sales and minimize advertising.
7. Moderate new product activity.
8. Low-to-moderate investment intensity.
9. High value added per employee.
10. Vertically integrated.
11. Low-to-moderate R&D aimed at product and process improvement.

trial products, markets, and methods of distribution, those products tend not to be reliably illustrative.

However, since we are all consumers, shopping for the same kinds of things at supermarkets, auto dealerships, and drugstores, it is consumer products that will be used to illustrate relevant points.

High Product Quality

This may be the most important characteristic of successful firms.

Product quality is the basis of reputation and, of course, reputation or image is what makes it easy to sell existing products and to get new products accepted quickly. As simple as this notion is, some firms don't seem to grasp its significance, let alone implement it.

The domestic passenger car market provides a good example of the importance of quality. Here's the way things stand with the five principal suppliers to that market.

General Motors, plagued with charges of low gasoline mileage and innumerable model recalls, has seen its market share drop from over 50 percent 20 years ago to about 30 percent today.

The Ford Motor Company's TV commercials stress that, "At Ford quality is No. 1 and has been since 1982". Full-page newspaper ads deliver the same message. One wonders, if quality at Ford has been important for only these few years, with which model year does one begin to take the quality of its products seriously.

Chrysler appears to have taken a deep breath and offers to warrantee its cars for five years or 50,000 miles. GM and Ford go two and 20.

American Motors, with a long history of extended warranties, makes the same offer as Chrysler. Its volume, however, rarely permits it to reach breakeven.

Foreign, which is the easiest way to identify the fifth supplier, has seen its market share grow from 5 percent 20 years ago to nearly one third today. Its share continues to grow.

As one more commentary on the quality of passenger cars, consider this: Nearly one third of the new vehicles sold as passenger cars in the past few months are pickup trucks. Pickups—and it doesn't matter if they are domestic or foreign—are perceived by one third of the market to be of higher quality than the vehicles actually designed to carry passengers. Further, quality is such a chancy business that many states have seen fit to enact "lemon laws" to protect customers.

The implication here for new product development is clear: High quality is essential. Even though some aspects of quality are subjective, there should be little trouble in establishing what high quality is for the markets we serve.

Just so there is no misunderstanding, high quality does not necessarily mean high priced. There is, for example, no finer general-purpose writing instrument than the ten cent BIC Stick. A Cross or a Mont Blanc pen has other attributes which justify high price.

Broad Product Offerings and Markets Served

Another characteristic of successful marketers is the breadth of their product offerings and markets they serve. Eastman Kodak provides a fine example of this. If you need film for whatever purpose—medical X-ray, industrial X-ray, measuring radiation exposure, making offset printing plates—the list can go on and on—or just for the ordinary garden-variety of picture taking—Kodak has a high-quality film available.

To clarify, new products must really be new for the producer and not merely extensions of existing product lines. For example, if Campbell comes out with another kind of soup—Crispy Vegetable condensed or Chunky Style single-strength—that soup will still wind up on the soup shelves at the supermarket. A new product would wind up in a new section.

The new product should actually increase the number of markets served or broaden the offering to them. Merely offering a new size or color is not enough.

Serve Narrow Market Segments

Successful firms serve very narrow, well-defined market segments. But it must be remembered that neither markets nor market segments last forever. Once there was a sneaker or athletic shoe market. Keds was the big name. Then came Etonic, which carved out the golf shoe market. Then Topsiders carved out a sailor's or yachting market. Adidas took care of the tennis people, Nike the joggers, and Converse the basketballers. Five new markets—where once there was only one. Trying to find a simple pair of sneakers today is nearly as difficult as finding a bottle of Moxie.

The implication here for new products should also be clear: The new product should serve a narrow and well-defined market. If possible, the new product should help define or create the market which it will serve.

Secure a Healthy Market Share of Served Markets against Few Competitors

Successful firms enjoy a healthy share of the markets they serve and generally compete against only three or four others. The market shares of the successful firm tend to peak at between 30 and 40 percent. The ROIs tend to peak at about this share level, too.

Campbell, which serves at least six segments of the grocery market, provides a good illustration of this, one that is easy to see the next time you are in a supermarket.

So far as soups are concerned, Campbell dominates this segment of the grocery market. Its share is way above the 30 to 40 percent just mentioned. Heinz is there, plus a couple of gourmet brands and some generics, but they offer no serious competition. Campbell owns the canned soup market; its other products are more illustrative of the point we want to make.

Walk to the bread shelves, and, after setting aside the common white breads like Wards, Sunbeam, and Wonder, it's Campbell's Pepperidge Farm, Arnold's, and a few regional ethnics.

With baked beans, it's Campbell, B&M, Friends, and Van Camp, with maybe a house brand or a generic.

You'll find the same situation in the potted meats section. If you want chicken, it's Campbell's Swanson, Richardson & Robbins, Wm. Underwood, or Hormel.

If you want tomato or mixed vegetable juice, it is Campbell's tomato or V-8 against Stokley, S&W, DelMonte, Ocean Spray, and the house brands.

The implications are clear: Where possible, the new product should serve a market segment where there are few competitors and where a sizeable market share is possible.

Healthy Margins

This characteristic should come as no surprise. It is what would be expected from high-quality products enjoying strong positions against few competitors in the markets which they serve. Beyond this obvious benefit, there are others.

Because of the broad-based product offerings, should a single product come under price pressure and require that its margin be shaved to maintain share (a bad move, by the way), the impact on totals would be small. Additionally, high margins mean that finished goods inventories do not have to turn rapidly to sustain a high ROI. Because of this, the business can proceed in a much more controlled, deliberate, and orderly fashion.

The implication here for new products should also be clear: The successful new product should support a high margin, certainly no lower than the company average, and much higher if possible.

These five characteristics of successful marketers, and the new product guides we have extracted from them all, relate to the generation of income. But we must also be concerned with how the new product affects the ability to hang onto and convert that income into profits. The next characteristic of success serves as an interface between these two kinds of concerns.

Marketing Efforts Stress Direct Sales and Minimize Advertising

With successful marketers, the main thrust of the marketing activities is in direct sales and promotional activities, with advertising at a minimum. That this should be so follows from the first five considerations. If the markets served are narrow, customers and prospects should be easily identified. Therefore, advertising aimed at lead generation can be minimal. Further, because of the firm's reputation and market position, claims for new products should gain ready acceptance. Therefore, the need for advertising to educate and condition the market should also be minimal.

Japan, Inc., is in the enviable position of being able to introduce a new product and have it accepted immediately. The consistent superior quality of its cameras, cars, office equipment, electronic devices, and earth-moving equipment has conditioned us to accept new products almost on faith. Indeed, so strong is its reputation that some claim that the current governor of New Hampshire owes his election to the similarity of his name, Sununu, to that of a Japanese car, Subaru.

However, there will be occasional missionary activities in which heavy advertising plays a role. The firm, for example, may be unknown in the market it wishes to serve. The product itself may satisfy a need that is not well-recognized. Or, a technology may be involved that is neither understood or accepted. The Polaroid film pack and camera, for example, required massive missionary work to gain market acceptance. When IBM, Phillips, and Burroughs first introduced the small (for its time) self-contained business computer, there was enormous resistance from people who were accustomed to the NCR Bookkeeping Machine. And, of course, some of us even remember Mr. Reynolds demonstrating his new ball-point pen at the bottom of a swimming pool.

Therefore, our strategic goal in this area is to have a new product that requires minimum advertising support and which responds well to direct selling and promotional efforts. Properly selected launching tactics can help achieve this goal.

Now, let's take a look at five characteristics of successful marketers that relate to their ability to hang on to margins and convert them into net profits.

Moderate New Product Activity

Successful marketers have very little new product activity. And, in this context, by a new product we mean one that has been on the market for under three years. ROI is usually greatest when new product sales are between 3 and 10 percent of total sales.

Sometimes it is forgotten that new products have a way of tying up capital in raw materials, finished goods inventory, equipment, space, spare parts, sales literature, and the like. But more important, perhaps, each new product also ties up a considerably greater portion of management and sales time than do established products of proven profitability. It takes a while for the twin investments in time and money to begin to generate a return. Successful firms do not have too much at risk in this area.

The strategic goal here would be to limit new product introductions to some small number, four or five per year, or to limit them in such a way that demands on time and money are limited.

Low-to-Moderate Investment Intensity

This idea may come as somewhat of a surprise. But another characteristic of a successful industrial marketer is a lower ratio of invested capital to sales than less successful firms. This ratio seems to vary inversely with ROI: low investment intensity, high ROI; high investment intensity, low ROI.

We have all been led to believe that machine-made products will not only be somehow better but cheaper as well. In some ways this is true. But what is certain is that, as the ratio of investment to sales increases, firms change from aggressive marketers to defensive marketers. To emphasize shifts from finding profitable new marketing opportunities to keeping its expensive plant and equipment busy. If the whole industry is investment-intensive, then everyone's prices and margins continually erode.

Here is an example. A local firm worked two shifts to satisfy sales. Then it bought an enormous piece of equipment which could stamp out everything it needed on just one shift. The firm saved money and the machine paid for itself on this one-shift operation. However, the machine was idle for 16 hours every workday and for 48 hours on weekends. This thought horrified someone who could only calculate carrying charges. So a decision was made to put the machine to work for two shifts. This resulted in twice the production needed to satisfy the market. The only way to move all of this product was to cut prices—with a consequent reduction of margin, profitability, and ROI.

The implications here are easy: A new product should not require that a firm increase its investment intensity, but it should tend to decrease the ratio of invested capital to sales.

High Value Added by Each Employee

This characteristic of a successful marketer may be a corollary of the last. Among successful firms, the value added per employee is higher than with less-successful firms. This is, of course, another way of describing productivity and recognizing that highly productive, labor-intensive production is more profitable than investment intensive production. Increased labor costs are invariably handed on to customers with no necessary negative impact on profitability. However, when automated production is substituted for handwork, any savings tend to be handed on to customers through lower prices, with a necessarily negative impact on profits.

The implication here is also obvious: New products should increase the value added per employee without necessarily increasing the investment intensity.

Vertical Integration

Vertical integration seems to be characteristic of successful marketers. Conventional wisdom, however, says that when markets are unstable and product technology changes rapidly, it behooves a marketer to remain flexible—horizontal. This means buying and assembling, not making, items supplied by others, and letting the others take care of frequent design changes and retoolings.

Something like this has happened in the silicon-chip market. As the chip capacity increases—64, 128, 256—firms that used to grow their own, no longer do so. They buy excess production from fewer and fewer sources who enjoy fewer and fewer competitors in a narrowing and increasingly defined market.

Conventional wisdom also says that in stable markets with stable technologies and products, vertical integration is to be encouraged. However, who is to judge stability? It is ironic to note that the chip market, which appears so turbulent to some, is apparently quite stable, at least to the remaining manufacturers of chips, who, we assume, are doing quite well.

Moderate R&D Aimed at Product and Process Improvement

Finally, the successful marketer has a low-to-moderate R&D effort compared with others in its field. Further, those R&D efforts are aimed mostly at improving the quality of existing products, improving the processes by which they are made, or investigating new applications for existing products.

Basic research aimed at increasing understanding of the universe is a luxury few firms can afford. Often such research is funded with full recognition that the results will have little or no impact on earnings. Bell Labs appears to be in such a situation. Fibre optics and satellite communications technology, which are so important to phone communications today, were developed outside the Bell System. And most of the improvements in existing telephone equipment originated with Western Electric, the manufacturing arm.

Another much smaller firm quite consciously and courageously invested a large portion of its income in the development of a new technology. It did this knowing that it might be 10 or a dozen years before a market would develop for the new technology. Such firms are, however, unique.

Each industry has its own built-in level of research and development activities. Firms with the more moderate activities seem to make more money than the rest. The pharmaceutical industry is commonly thought of as being a high-level R&D industry. However, when looked at closely, that R&D is concerned with compliance and product liability; with the production and the prefabrication of larger and larger molecular building blocks; and with the further exploration of technical literature to see what of value remains in the public domain. Most new ideas for this industry come from external sources and are often the result of university research grants.

The computer, telecommunications, and medical instrumentation industries are others where high levels of R&D are expected. *Inc.* magazine has published figures from these industries showing that the fastest growers among them are also the ones who spend the most for R&D. (Growing firms commonly have very low ROIs.) Even here, the R&D expenditures are for product improvement, expanded applications, or improvement in the manufacturing processes.

Research and development at General Motors, the most profitable of the domestic car companies, concerns product and process in a very hard-nosed way. For them, it is cheaper to achieve improved fuel economy by reducing drag and wind resistance—that is, just changing body contours—than it would be by designing a more fuel-efficient engine or by fiddling with weight reduction. Even a firm like General Motors will let someone else do the basic developmental work, make the basic breakthroughs.

So far as new product development is concerned, two implications follow from this modest R&D characteristic of successful industrial marketers: (1) Ideas for new products come from the marketplace, not from the lab; and (2) each new product should contribute to holding down the R&D burden.

In this connection, it is interesting to note that the new federal tax statutes permit up to one quarter of any increase in R&D expenditures to be taken as a direct tax credit. Quality-control testing, which is part of normal production processes, may not be used to calculate the credit, nor can customer surveys and other market research of that nature. These regulations seem to favor industrial products, for, as we shall see later (Part III), the nature of industrial selling and new product development does not require the same kind of market research that consumer new product development seems to require.

Thus, these 11 characteristics of successful firms are readily converted into strategic goals for new products to achieve, or, put another way, converted into new product-selection guidelines (Figure 23–4).

FIGURE 23–4
New Product Selection Guidelines *(Strategic Goals for New Products)*

1. Provide higher quality than is customary in the market served.
2. Broaden the offering to the market served.
3. Help narrow and bring into high focus each market served.
4. Afford an increased share of the market served.
5. Provide above-average margin.
6. Respond to direct selling and promotional activities, require minimal advertising.
7. Limit annual new product introductions.
8. Require below-average investments.
9. Enhance productivity.
10. Encourage vertical integration.
11. Give priority to ideas generated by the marketplace.

None of them, by the way, aim specifically at cost reduction. Rather, the goal is improved quality.

These strategic considerations ought to become part of the way we think about and calculate new products before we invest heavily in their development. It is apparent, for example, that the management of young, successful, and growing firms evaluates new products in this way almost by instinct.

However, as firms grow, the number of markets served increase, and more people become involved in the selection and development of new products, that instinct becomes dull and blunted. In only a few of these areas are new product people selected because of their strengths or expertise. They know a market, for example, and understand its technologies and quality requirements. Rarely, however, will they understand either intellectually or by instinct all 11 of these goals and guidelines.

The organization itself must make up for these personal lacks. It can do this through training and indoctrination. It can, by the use of procedures and checklists, establish formal screening processes. And, it can, through example and attitude, build these considerations into the organization's value system and culture.

The larger the organization, the more likely it will be that all three elements (training, procedures, and examples) must be employed to assure that these considerations are not overlooked.

It is hard to tell exactly what accounts for the ability of firms like Hewlett-Packard, Eastman-Kodak, P&G, or John Deere to introduce a stream of high-quality new products year after year. It can be assumed that these 11 strategic considerations or their equivalent are inherent in the corporate culture. It is essential, then, that the entire organization, not just its new product people, understand all 11 of these strategic considerations. It is equally essential that each new product idea selected for consideration also satisfy each of them.

Obviously, if there is a business plan, these strategic new product guidelines must conform to it. They will, in fact, help to flesh it out. And if there is no business plan, these guidelines will be a start in formulating one.

FINDING NEW PRODUCT IDEAS

There are just five ways in which new products come into being for a firm (see Figure 23–5).

New industrial products are invented, they are acquired, they evolve from existing products or existing technologies, they are picked out of the wastebasket, or they are developed from the requests and suggestions of customers.

Invention

Most people are inclined to think that new products are invented. There is a flash of inspiration, a stroke of genius, and presto! a new product. This happens, but not very often. It is possible that the Phillips Head Screw and Screwdriver came about in this way. More likely, however, the invention starts with an idea of the finished product—an incandescent lamp or self-developing film—and the process of invention is a lengthy series of trials and errors until the product comes into being, together with an economic process for making it.

The development of xerography provides a good example of how a

FIGURE 23–5
Common Sources of New
Product Ideas

1. *Invention:*
   Strokes of genius.
   Concept and hard work.

2. *Acquisition:*
   Purchase.
   License.
   Theft.
   Copying.

3. *Evolution:*
   Fill-in.
   Extension.
   Repackaging.
   Combination and integration.
   Specialization.
   Adaptation.
   Pruning.

4. *Rejects and failures.*

5. *Customers' requests.*

breakthrough comes to market. The concept was of a dry nonphotographic process for making multiple copies. Chester Carlson filed his first patent application in 1937. Ten years later, he formed a partnership with the Haloid Company for the manufacturing development of the process. Ten years later, the English flour miller and motion picture producer, J. Arthur Rank, supplied capital for its commercial introduction. In 1959, the first Xerox machine was introduced.

The development of the Land Camera provides another illustration. The idea of self-developing film came to Edwin Land when his daughter asked why she had to wait to see the photograph he had just taken of her. Within an hour, Land had the whole process outlined—camera, film, and chemicals. That was in 1944. Four years later, after the design, manufacturing, and marketing problems had been solved, the Land Camera was introduced successfully. It was profitable from the start.

Breakthroughs are rare, very rare indeed. Developing new products in this way is not a field for the typical marketer to plow. We must look elsewhere for reliable sources of new product ideas and new products.

Acquisition

Acquisition of an idea or a product from a third party is a common source of new products. Sometimes the acquisition results from an outright purchase. Sometimes not. Either mode has examples of kosher and not so kosher practices. Parker Brother's *Monopoly,* Selchow & Righter's *Scrabble,* and Ideal Toy's *Rubik Cube* are all simple examples of new products acquired through purchase. In each of these situations, the company and the inventor have benefited enormously. Many firms routinely add to their product lines through purchases.

Johnson & Johnson, for example, has a long history of acquisition. It acquired its Reach toothbrush from Du Pont for a considerable sum, added it to its health and beauty aids products line, and seems to be doing reasonably well with it. Not all its acquisitions, however, are so successful. Johnson & Johnson recently acquired the firm of Stimtech, which owned a new pain-killing technology. But here the goal was not to broaden its product offerings but to suppress what was viewed as a threat to Tylenol, another acquisition. The courts have declared it to be an illegitimate acquisition.

Licensing is another common means of acquiring new products. In the fashion industries, many manufacturers are able to introduce new products through the simple expedient of licensing designers' names. Designer names are attached to everything from bed sheets to underwear. Coming closer to home, many of the newly formed manufacturers of telephone equipment owe their product lines to licensing arrangements with AT&T. Most video games are manufactured under license from Magnavox, a subsidiary of North American Phillips. The original patents are held by Sanders Associates, which has licensed them to Magnavox.

Acquisition through purchase or license is just one kind. There are acquisitions which do not involve any form of compensation. One such manner of acquisition is outright theft. Stealing new products and new product ideas occurs more often than we would like to think. Complex patents and ponderous court procedures occasionally make it hard to tell outright theft from situations in which great minds have come to think alike. However, the courts cough up guilty blue-chip firms often enough to suggest that acquisition through theft is not unusual. Johns-Manville, for example, was recently found guilty of stealing the design of a patented lighting fixture from the much-smaller Massachusetts firm that developed it. And even mighty Sears, Roebuck has been found guilty of short-changing the inventor of a patented socket wrench.

While thievery is a reprehensible means of acquiring new products and new product ideas, there is another quite legitimate means of acquiring them without paying for them. Some call it copying, and occasionally that is just what is it. "Knock-offs" are a way of life in the garment industry.

As soon as the first Hula-Hoop hit the market, anyone with spare garden hose and a knife was in the business. Copying is an honorable tradition, with large payoffs—so long as discernment and discrimination are used to select what to copy. The first Datsun, for example, which Nissan Motors introduced into this country, was an exact copy of the Crosley, even to the location of the impossible-to-reach block drains.

Copying is not, however, a technologically elegant term. Some prefer to call the process "reverse engineering," which comes closer to describing what actually happens. Perhaps the classic example of the technique was the conversion of the woven Chinese finger-trap toy into highly effective low-bulk industrial cable pullers.

A more current example is the Merrill Lynch "Cash Management Account." It was introduced in 1977 to a chorus of "who needs it" from competitive firms. Four years later, Merrill Lynch's CMA had nearly 600,000 customers and over $35 billion as assets. In the money management industry, copying Merrill Lynch became the thing to do.

A marketer's goal, after all, is not to have a completely original product line. Rather, it should be to have profitable products with long lives, products that conform to the 11 strategic goals discussed earlier. If someone else's product provides us with an idea which we can adapt and improve upon (improvement is the key word), and which will contribute to the health of our business, we would be foolish not to take advantage of it. The genius of Japan doesn't lie in its innovativeness or in its ability to buy IBM secrets from the FBI, but rather in meticulous attention to high quality and the consistent production which assures it. However, some may say that that in itself is an innovation.

Evolution

Invention and acquisition are not likely to become the major source of new products. Like it or not, we are going to have to develop by ourselves, the new products we require. That is a big challenge. An immediate response to it might be, "Yes, but I am not a scientist or an inventor. I'm a marketing person." Fortunately, and because we are marketing people, that challenge is not as difficult as it might seem.

Most products develop through an evolutionary process of change and adaptation in response to the needs and opportunities of the marketplace. It is our obligation, therefore, to know our markets, our customers, our products, and our manufacturing and technological capabilities and limitations. We must know them well enough to recognize both the market's needs and our opportunities when they manifest themselves.

Where many of us have problems is in failing to recognize those situations which may be signaling a need or an opportunity. New product development activities seem to be random, carried out on a hit-or-miss basis. However, if we can identify those sources from which the signals are most likely to come, we can focus our attention on them. There are seven such areas (see Figure 23–5) that we should explore periodically. Each could provide us with a viable new product idea.

Fill-ins. It is generally assumed that the products offered to a market form a price and quality continuum; that is, if they were laid out side by side in order of increasing quality and increasing price, there would be no gaps or discontinuities. Occasionally, this is so; more often it is not. Wherever the continuity is interrupted, there may be a new product opportunity. Periodically, it is important to lay out all the competitive offerings to a specific market segment to see if there are large holes or discontinuities in quality, price, or best of all, both. Where such a hole does appear, we need to find out if we can profitably plug it with a new product (see Figure 23–6).

FIGURE 23–6
Filling In Competitive Offerings

	Before		After	
Quality	Unit Cost	Percent Share	Unit Cost	Percent Share
Overkill	6¢	20%	6¢	10%
Superior	—	—	4	25
Adequate	2	50	2	45
Quick and dirty	1	30	1	20
Total		100		100

To illustrate:

Six firms filled the same market need with essentially the same three products at the same three price and quality levels: the quick and dirty models cost one cent each and had a 30 percent share of the total market; the model which was adequate cost two cents each and had a 50 percent share; finally, the quality overkill model cost six cents each and had a 20 percent share.

One of the six firms looked at this situation and saw a new product opportunity. It modified the performance characteristics of its two-cent model and nearly matched those of the expensive model. The result was a superior model at four cents each, with an extra margin of nearly two cents. Through a very adroit launching effort, it captured 25 percent of the total market before competition knew what had happened. This was calculation. Luck made the results even sweeter. Capacity was limited, and as the four-cent volume built, something had to give. The one-cent quick and dirty model, which had become a price football, was abandoned.

Extensions. The same technique of laying out the entire competitive offering to a market by price and quality may show that the opportunity is to extend the series, not to fill a hole in it. The new product may extend the series upwards from the high end, or it can be downward towards a lower price. However, being forever mindful of the strategic guidelines discussed above, there should be no diminution of either quality or margin should the new product fall below the low-priced end of the range.

Recently, we have seen an instance of this in the United States writing instrument market. BIC, for example, looked at the range of offerings and decided that it could be extended downward. It introduced its low-cost models. Koh-i-noor, on the other hand, looked at the same market and saw its opportunity at the high end. It began importing Mont Blanc fountain pens, which top out at over $7,000 each.

Repackaging. Often it is possible to create a new product simply by repackaging an existing product or changing the way it is brought to market. Repackaging takes many forms but is always aimed at easing the movement of the product into the market. Blister-packed nuts, bolts, and other small hardware items are simple examples of this kind of opportunity. Rental or lease-purchase plans, which make capital equipment available from operating funds, may be another example.

The reconstituted orange juice that Minute Maid offers in cartons is not merely just another way of making its frozen concentrate available; it has opened a new market. For, in addition to being a new product, it has a new buyer. Minute Maid now sells to the supermarket dairy buyer as well as to the frozen food buyer. The basic Polaroid camera, for another example, has been repackaged to produce drivers' licenses and employee identification cards with photos attached.

This kind of repackaging can be further illustrated by an example from the men's clothing business. A manufacturer of men's work clothing found that sales through normal retail channels were not as profitable as sales to an industrial laundry with a uniform rental program. The manufacturer bought the laundry and several others, thus making his clothing available in two ways. The outcome here was predictable.

Eventually, the manufacturing operation was sold. New uniforms for the laundries are now purchased from offshore contractors.

Integration and Combination. Frequently the market signals a situation in which new products can be developed through the combination or integration of existing products or processes. Prefabrication and preassembly are simple examples of this.

For a homey example of the combination of products, there are packaged cake and piecrust mixes. And for an example on the process side, there is the Cuisinart, which combines a blender, a slicer, and an old-fashioned electric mixer.

An industrial example of process integration is provided by the Sanborn coolant and cutting oil recovery system for the metalworking industry. Metalworking fluids become contaminated by solids, by bacteria and fungus, and by other fluids, all of which limit their lives. Conventionally, coolant life is extended somewhat by separate processes that screen out solids, add disinfectants, and skim off tramp fluids. The Sanborn process accomplishes all of this in a single system, which extends the life of these fluids indefinitely.

Market Segmentation. Often a market that appears to be monolithic turns out to be neither uniform nor continuous. Sometimes this occurs because the market itself grows and changes. Where once there was one market, there are now several. Earlier we discussed the men's footwear market and saw how the market for sneakers had become several separate markets. Here, growing affluence and sportsmindedness have led people to think about and afford more specialized footwear.

Market segmentation occurs in other ways as well. Frequently, the change comes about because we have acquired a greater mastery of our own technology and can satisfy narrower needs. Changes in the offset duplicator market illustrate this. The original offset duplicator was sold to a market made up of those who needed a sheet-fed press capable of turning out a moderate volume of fair-quality work at a modest cost. The equipment used photo-etched zinc plates, required a skilled operator, and needed constant monitoring. It found a ready market among small commercial printers and in-plant duplicating operations. As the technology improved, operations became more reliable and high-volume, high-quality paper plates were developed. Coincidentally, the quick printing market, exemplified by such firms as PIP or KWIK-KOPY, was being established.

One manufacturer of offset equipment, A.B. Dick, Inc., took advantage of the improved technology to develop a lightweight simple-to-operate high-speed press that delivered moderate quality and occupied very little floor space. This manufacturer now dominates the quick printing business, the fastest growing segment of the printing industry, and has a 50 percent share of the total market for offset duplicators.

Adaptation. Another evolutionary source of new products is the adaptation of an existing product to another use, or the adaptation of an existing product idea to another market. For example, Roger Tory Peterson's *Field Guide to the Birds* was first published by the Houghton Mifflin Company in 1934. The idea of this kind of guide was then adapted to other areas of interest. There are now 25 titles in a series that covers animals, flowers, trees, and so on.

And there are other examples. The miniaturization of commercial amonia refrigeration systems with freon has produced the home freezer and refrigerator. Miniaturization of industrial forced-air space heaters has produced the common blow-dryer. And, going in the other direction, beefing up the common desk stapler has provided packers and shippers as well as the construction industry with a most versatile tool. Further, the Ramset device is merely a special .22-calibre single-shot pistol with a spike or bolt in the place of the bullet. And for one more example—a child's toy and laboratory curiosity has become the gyroscopic stabilizer.

Pruning. Additionally, there is another drastic, but natural, means of encouraging the development of new products—pruning. When a tree or shrub stops producing or becomes rank, the gardener prunes it back drastically. Horticulturalists are used to this kind of surgery; marketers are not. Sometimes the only way to stimulate the development of profitable new products is through the ruthless cutting away of the dead, the dying, and the unproductive from existing offerings. With the deadwood removed, existing opportunities are more visible. Often the market responds with a new product suggestion or two of its own.

Davis-Standard, a division of Crompton and Knowles, makes extrusion equipment for the plastics industry. Over the years its product lines had so expanded downstream that each extruder sold was part of a specially engineered system. Davis-Standard shared a highly fragmented market with 160 known equipment manufacturers. No one was the clear leader in the manufacture of the basic extruder, Davis-Standard's original business. The firm saw its earnings evaporate as it sank further and further into this mess. It decided that it hadn't the resources for this game and withdrew. It slashed away all auxilliary equipment and focused again on making single-screw extrusion machines. Within four years it had become the market leader, manufacturers of auxilliary equipment adapted to the Davis-Standard extruder, and ROI increased by a factor of 10.

Catalogs require frequent pruning. A common practice involves setting an income or profit goal for product categories, part numbers, or even pages, and dropping anything that does not rise above that threshold. Often, as a result of this process, it is possible to combine several of the eliminated items and, from them, make a new and viable product. This leads to the next large source of new product ideas.

Rejects and Failures

Often, quite viable new product ideas can be found among our rejects and failures. This does not mean that we become bag-ladies or archeologists rooting around in the trash. What it does mean is that we should be aware that available materials change and markets change—and so do technologies.

The advent of a new material, Teflon, for example, made it possible to manufacture many high-performance parts of molded plastic. Thus were eliminated less-reliable and more costly parts of cast or machined metal, as well as the cheap molded plastic parts that guaranteed unreliable performance.

Many product ideas are rejected because existing technologies cannot produce the product at a reasonable cost or permit it to be sold at a reasonable price. And, many products fail because there isn't a market large enough to support them.

Light or low-calorie beers provide excellent examples. Twenty years ago, Gablinger's, a low-calorie beer produced by a complex Swiss process, was introduced. It failed miserably. Shortly thereafter, Piel Brothers introduced another low-calorie beer made by a more conventional brewing process. It, too, was a marketing disaster. Now, everyone seems to be conscious of physical fitness, nutrition, and calorie intake. Even respected vintners tout their low-calorie wine. In this market climate, low-calorie beers are a marketing success.

Customer Requests

Finally, of course, there are customer requests. These can be a powerful source of profitable new product ideas. However, because the ideas come from customers, they tend to be less-carefully screened than home-grown ideas. They can, therefore, become serious distractions and even profit drains.

Occasionally, the simple suggestion or request of a customer or prospect can result in an extremely profitable new product. Thus, a simple request to Henry Ford to replace the rumble seat on a Model-T coupe with a small cargo carrier resulted in the pickup truck.

More frequently, however, we find that what should have been a special order or a specially engineered device has in fact become a standard product, often merely a line extension. The catalogues of stationers, fastener houses, and the manufacturers of washers, gaskets, and electronic interconnection devices are replete with items which have no potential beyond the original order, or which differ from each other only in color or in an unimportant dimensional characteristic.

Padding catalogs in this way is a common device used by new firms to give themselves a greater presence than is actually warranted. The large numbers of essentially similar products may even suggest a special order to a customer. Mostly, however, this effort is self-deluding.

It is a general rule that when customers talk about problems or performance, listen; there is the possibility of a new product idea. But when customers talk color and dimensions, dig out your pencil; there may be a special order in the offing.

CONDUCTING MARKET AUDITS AND MARKET RESEARCH

From the discussion of the sources of new product ideas, and as a clear implication of the 11 new product guidelines discussed earlier, it is obvious that nearly all new product ideas will and should come from the marketplace. This, in turn, suggests not only a little formal market research but a periodic audit of our product lines, of the markets those products serve, and of the competitive offerings in those markets.

Market Audits

There are two points that are critical here. The first is simply that, in looking at a market or market segment, we should consider all the products offered to it, and those of our competitors, as well as our own. And, to the extent possible, this means looking at these offerings from the customers' point of view. It means, if an illustration is needed, that we should look at the BICs, the Papermates, the Parkers, the Schaeffers, the Crosses, as well as the Mont Blancs and all the no-names. Looking only at our own offerings and those of the competitors at our price points is to wear blinders.

The second critical point is how often we conduct the audit. Periodically to be sure; but how often is periodic? For most product lines in most markets, a once-a-year audit might be enough. But for more volatile markets, more-frequent audits would be required. And for some, perhaps the audit should be continuous.

The goal, of course, is to find clear opportunities for new products, or, at least clues and suggestions that a need may exist. The audit should answer questions like the following:

— Where can we extend or plug a hole in the offerings made to a market?
— How can we repackage an existing product or service to expand a market or create a new one?
— Where can we integrate or combine several products or processes (our own or competitors) to create a new product or a new market?
— What segments of an existing market are beginning to develop different needs and requirements? Do these changes create a new product opportunity?
— How can we adapt what's offered in one market to the needs of another?
— What products have outlived their usefulness to the market, and how do we replace them?
— What do customers and prospects say about their current problems and future needs that suggest new products?
— Which of our failures or rejections deserve another look?

In addition to developing answers to these questions, the audit should also include an analysis of competitive advertising, product literature, pricing, distribution, available share information, and the occasional testing of competitive offerings. As important, the audit should also include discussions with representative customers and prospects: buyers and buying committees of retailers, for example, and purchasing agents, engineers, and manufacturing people at industrial accounts.

In this process, we can rely on our sales force to provide some of the input we require. They can provide, for example, lost business reports, as well as some of the other information needed: competitive ads, literature, and prices. They can provide information on distribution and even product samples. They should be able to identify the buying influences and the decision makers at important accounts in their territories.

But there is one thing they cannot do for us. They cannot pick the brains we need to have picked. They cannot have the free-wheeling discussions of current problems and future needs that lead to the identification of new product opportunities.

It should be kept in mind, though, that salespeople have one job— selling current products. This imperative colors the way they react to customers and to prospects. More important, it affects the way customers and prospects react to them. The potential for a sale blinds the salesperson to all else, and it causes the customer to become guarded. There are exceptions, but they are rare. When they occur, consider yourself lucky. But for the most part, the kind of field research described here will have to be done by us. It cannot be delegated to our sales force.

No matter how unfamiliar we are with a market, after one or two conversations with a few key customers and prospects, a sense of that market will begin to grow. That sense, coupled with what we have learned from other parts of the audit, will eventually lead to one or two new product ideas. These ideas will be further refined and eventually will be either abandoned or tagged for serious investigation.

So far, so good. But here is where a potentially serious problem begins to arise. Unless we have been extremely lucky, can devote all our time to new products, or are concerned with only one market or market segment, we will have been able to talk with people at only six or eight firms. If these six or eight have sufficient buying power, their inputs may be enough to justify moving ahead on a new product idea.

Market Research

Usually, though, the people we are able to talk with are not representative enough of the marketplace. Their needs may suggest an idea, and a good one, but before it gets more serious attention we will need the reaction of a broader sample of the potential market. This means market research of a more formal kind.

Market research of the complex and sophisticated kind practiced by the manufacturers of consumer goods has received quite a bit of publicity of late. Only 35 percent of new consumer products ever survive market tests and go on to win consumer acceptance. Perhaps information like this has colored our understanding of what and how much market research is necessary and what we can expect from it.

One of the results of applying the 11 strategic guidelines should be a product which serves and helps define a very narrow market. This, in turn, should make our market research burden that much lighter.

A sample of 50 well-selected firms in a market is more than sufficient to qualify a new industrial product. Further, within each firm that makes up the sample, there are only three functions with which we need to be concerned: the specifier, the user, and the buyer. With most firms and for most products we need to e concerned with only engineering, manufacturing, and purchasing. Our 50-firm sample becomes at most 150 people. This brings the size of the market research project within reasonable means.

Further, each of these three functions will have a different and predictable interest in a new product or process. The specifier, the design engineer, is interested in the performance and reliability of the final product. The user, the manufacturing or production supervisor, is interested in what, for want of better words, can be called the handleability or workability of the product in the manufacturing processes. And finally, the buyer or purchasing agent is interested chiefly in the availability of the product when it is needed. All are interested to one degree or another in costs or cost effectiveness.

The small size and the predictable interests of those in the sample should begin reducing the market research task to a more manageable proportion. The task becomes even simpler when we take into account considerations like these:

- With samples of this size, the people to be included can be identified by name. If one person isn't available, an acceptable stand-in can be found.
- Unless the people providing the inputs are of so high a position as to require a personal visit for courtesy's sake, data are most conveniently gathered by phone. Mail surveys are not recommended; too much time is lost before the number and the quality of the inputs is known. With in-person or by-phone interviews, the desired kind of feedback is immediate.
- Elaborate or multipart questionnaires are to be avoided. They complicate the task of analysis, exhaust the patience of those being questioned, and seem to provide more useful information than they actually do.
- Only those questions should be asked which the respondent is competent to answer. Too many questions that must be answered "I don't know" discourage conversation and end the interview prematurely. In surveys of this type, it is often the volunteered information, not the answers to the questions asked, that provides the substantive inputs.

For most surveys of this type, only five or six questions are required to develop all the information needed. Interestingly enough, the same series of questions works equally well with specifiers, users, and buyers. (Figure 23–7 shows a typical questionnaire.)

The simplicity of the questionnaire and the directness of the questions may come as a surprise to many. But it should be remembered that this kind of research is conducted not so much to develop new information as to confirm hunches and near-certainties developed through other means. By the time this kind of research is required, competitive literature will have been analyzed, competitive products examined and tested, and specifiers, buyers, and users from key prospects will have been interviewed face to face. Under these circum-

FIGURE 23–7
New Product, New Market Evaluation Questionnaire

1. Do you specify, use, buy _____?
2. When you consider a new _____, what's most important to you?
3. How many _____ do you think you use?
4. In considering a new _____, what information is important to you?
5. Are you familiar with the following manufacturers of _____? If so, how would you characterize each?

stances, the handful of questions shown in Figure 23–7 are more than sufficient.

The first question must always be the qualifier. There is no point in running up the phone bill by interviewing the wrong person.

The second question begins to develop substantive information about the subject of the inquiry. Here, and in question four, it may be necessary to furnish the interviewer with a list of *for-instances* to be used as thought starters.

> Preliminary information may suggest that it would be desirable for the product to meet third party specs—a military specification, an Underwriters Laboratory test, or the Pennsylvania Department of Agriculture regulations. If so, it may be necessary to suggest this possibility to the person being interviewed.

> Perhaps packaging is important. If so, maybe a few packaging options should be suggested. The results of the first few phone interviews will tell if such thought starters should be furnished to the interviewer.

The third question asks for quantitative information that the respondent may or may not be competent to provide. Discrepancies among the numbers furnished by user, specifier, and buyer may be significant.

The fourth question gathers more of the kind of information asked for in question two. It is not uncommon to find contradictions between the answers to question two and question four. During a phone interview, these differences can be easily explored and resolved. Such problems are impossible to resolve in mail surveys.

The fifth question establishes the images—perceived qualifications—of everyone serving the market or market segment.

On occasion, it is necessary to offer a brief summary of survey results to get willing participation. If there is a sixth question, it would concern this: "May I have your title and mailing address?"

As a means of gathering important and useful information about the new product and its market, this process is straightforward and simple. All that's missing is the person to do the phone interviewing. In selecting someone for this purpose, there are a few simple but important requirements:

— Your anonymity must be preserved. As long as the interviewer remains a bland, nonthreatening third party, accurate and useful information will be forthcoming.
— The interviewer must have a plausible, nonthreatening reason for gathering the information. Consultants and researchers for banks and brokerage houses are acceptable interviewers.
— The person doing the work must be an experienced phone interviewer. Interviewing skills are more important than technical knowledge, although the more of each, the better.
— Finally, the results of the first few calls must be reviewed. Generally, after 8 or 10 calls, enough information will have been gathered to indicate the quality of ongoing responses. Usually, there are no problems, but occasionally you'll find that questions two and four need to be made a bit more directive to provoke useful information.

Most such information is gathered by a market research, or a sales or a marketing, consultant. They have the skill and experience, can easily preserve the anonymity of the sponsor, can complete such assignments swiftly, and can interpret the results accurately. However, with all due respect to the profession, the job can be done as well by an experienced secretary on maternity leave.

Eventually, through research like this and through the market audit which you have made, enough preliminary information will have been assembled on the new product area to indicate that a formal evaluation is in order.

SELECTING NEW PRODUCTS FOR DEVELOPMENT

Developing and launching a new product does require the investment of considerable time and money. The decision to proceed with a new product cannot be made lightly. It should only be made after a number of tough questions have been considered and answered. A list of such questions is shown in Figure 23–8. It is not a static list but changes a bit to fit each client organization. What's important is not the actual questions on the list but the attitude toward new products which the list reflects. Frequently, questions are combined.

FIGURE 23–8
Final New Product, Develop and Launch or Reject Decision Screen

1. What is it? What does it do? What are its performance specs? Its physical specs?
2. What are our qualifications to make it? Mastery of the technology? Ownership of the manufacturing processes? Knowledge of its market? Knowledge of the channels of distributions to the market?
3. Who can use it? Why should they be interested? (Specific customers and SICs.)
4. Are we currently serving these markets?
5. How does the market view our qualifications to make it? To serve it? To sell it?
6. How many can be used (by specific customer and by SICs) at various price levels? On introduction? In six months? In one year? Etc.?
7. What does competition have that comes close?
8. What would our competitive advantages be?
9. Is the technology available to build it? Do we have it? Do others?
10. What's required to build it? Tools? Machinery? Space? Personnel? Storage? Test equipment? Other requirements? What do we have? What do we need to acquire?
11. Are the materials needed to build it available? From current suppliers? Elsewhere?
12. What are the approval lead times and ordering cycles likely to be?
13. How will samples or test and approval models differ from production models?
14. How long will it take to have samples and test models available? Production models?
15. What will it cost to make at various levels of production? In various modes of production?
16. Are subcontractors available? For parts? For major components?
17. How will it be distributed and sold? Our own distribution and sales organization? A new distribution and sales organization?
18. What will its impact be on competitive products? On our own products?
19. What is the competitive response likely to be? Overall? By specific competitor?
20. What are the sales support requirements? Training? Literature? Service? Spare Parts? Other?
21. What should our pricing, sales, and marketing strategies be?
22. What are the advertising, lead-generation, market conditioning, and sales promotion requirements?
23. What product performance tests have been made? In-house? By customers? What were the results?
24. How will it be introduced? Customer by customer? Regional roll-out? Nationally? What are specific plans? Timetable?
25. What serious sales and manufacturing problems can we anticipate? How will we handle them?
26. What will it cost to bring the product to market? How long will it take to get our money back? Thereafter, what will be our rate of return?

FIGURE 23–8 (concluded)

27. If we do not make it, how will it affect our manufacturing capability, growth, market position, customer base, and profitability?
28. If we do make it, how will it affect our manufacturing capability, growth, market position, customer base, and profitability?
29. How does it satisfy each of the 11 strategic guidelines?
30. How does it compare with our other new product options?
31. What assumptions have we made (1 through 30 above)? Are they valid?
32. What is our decision? Do we make it? Or, do we set it aside and move on?

Providing answers to such questions requires serious efforts and careful inputs from marketing, sales, engineering, manufacturing, purchasing, finance, and, perhaps, even a few others—customer service, for example, or even field service. In organizations where the 11 strategic guidelines are part of the corporate culture and there is a long history of successful new product development, the list can be a short one. In other organizations, where this kind of new product effort is new, the list must necessarily be long and exhaustive.

In smaller growing firms, the necessary answers are provided by the managers of the input groups involved: sales, manufacturing, finance, and so on. However, as the size of the firm increases, other duties and responsibilities may prevent these department heads from sitting in on the new product evaluation process. A practice has evolved, therefore, of establishing a basic cadre of regulars to provide continuity for the effort and supplementing it with others to form an ad hoc evaluation group for each new product.

The group is variously known as a *new product evaluation team,* a *core sales group,* or a *new product task force.* Its job, of course, is to consider the answers to the questions asked on the new product evaluation screen, arrive at a recommendation for the new product, and, eventually, even supervise the successful launch of the new product.

The composition of such groups varies from firm to firm and from product to product. The most effective way of determining who should belong to the group is by using the list of questions. Whoever is in a position to supply the most authoritative answers to blocks of questions belongs on the task force. When carefully managed and supervised, such task forces can become important elements in a firm's motivation and reward program, and they can be a useful means of identifying promotable talent.

Such groups are, however, only as good as their management. The chairman must make certain that the tough but significant questions are seriously considered, and that realistic answers are found to them. Top management must support the group's efforts, provide the strategic guidelines discussed earlier, demand excellence, and abide by the group's recommendations. This may even mean an occasional failure. Second-guessing the group's efforts will only subvert a very essential process.

Several of the questions listed in Figure 23–8 have proven troublesome and should be discussed. Others are a bit more straightforward and obvious.

2. *What are our qualifications to make the new product?* There is room for large self-deception here. A simple example will illustrate the kind of pitfalls that await those who make emotional decisions, not decisions based upon a hard-nosed evaluation of qualifications. The management of a respected manufacturer of miniature electronic components coveted the hobby and prototype shop markets. Each bought in small quantities (blister-packs) and paid high unit prices. The firm reasoned that it could supply these market requirements from its regular production. It surveyed the hobby shop markets and distributor markets to see what was available in small-quantity prepacks. It then selected from its own catalog the items that would complement what was available. It designed packages, installed packaging equipment, and commenced to develop its line. It then discovered that it knew nothing about the hobby shop market, its economics, or how it was supplied. Further, it discovered that the distributors it had surveyed were phasing out the blister-pack lines because they did not move except through pilferage. The effort was a costly failure.

5. *How does the market view our qualifications to make it?* Action on a new product, even a good one, may have to be postponed until the firm has earned the right, in the eyes of the market, to make, sell, and service the product. In a classic example of this, not so long ago, Lionel Trains hired the army's chief of ordnance and tried to solicit defense business. Even with its very capable figurehead, the firm was never perceived as being capable of doing defense work and the effort failed. RCA and GE failed to crack the computer market, primarily because the market did not see them as being qualified to do so.

7 and **8.** *Competitive offerings and competitive advantages?* In this situation, the new management of an old established firm, which manufactured the most reliable liquid flow meters available, viewed with contempt the failure of a competitor to launch another type of meter. It reasoned that, because of its experience, it could succeed with the new but imperfect technology when the competitor could not. Its ego trip became an extremely costly failure.

13. *How will samples differ from production models?* A common source of new product failure is samples which differ significantly from production line models. Samples from a prototype shop typically are more carefully made than the items which will come from regular production. This situation is commonly encountered in the clothing business, where samples are made in a sample work room. Detailing of the garments and the amount of handwork give the sample garment a look of higher quality than will be available in production models. The result is that the retailer's expectations are seriously disappointed.

18. *Impact on competitive or our own products?* Failure to consider this question often leads to the introduction of a new product that competes head-on with another of the firm's products. Diet-Pepsi and Tab provide a good illustration of this. Tab, for example, created its own niche in the diet-drink market and achieved its sales goals without cutting into the sale of its sister product, Coca-Cola. Because of similar names, however, Diet-Pepsi and Pepsi competed head-on, forcing the customer to select one or the other. As a result, Pepsi sales declined a bit, and Diet-Pepsi never achieved the goals expected of it. More than one manufacturer of sterling silver has seen its market deteriorate because it duplicated its sterling patterns in plate. The Osborn computer created, developed, and dominated the portable computer market. After a number of years, the firm designed an improved model that would make its initial offering obsolete. However, it made the mistake of announcing and advertising the new model before it was in production and before units were available for sale. With the announcement of the new model, sales of the initial unit dried up. Without income, the firm could not bring the new model to market. It filed under Chapter Eleven.

19. *Competitive responses?* This question requires serious consideration. Davids should not inadvertently take on Goliaths. BIC, Gillette-Papermate and Scripto-Wilkinson are well-enough financed to support a grand fight for dominance of the disposable razor, lighter, and ball-point pen markets. Other firms may not be able to support such a struggle. To cite another example, over the past few years, a number of firms have made a nice living making "plug-compatible" peripherals for IBM equipment. When IBM changed the configuration and power of its equipment, that compatibility and market evaporated.

21. *What should our strategies be?* Other strategies are available besides a head-on confrontation with the competition. One firm, for example, succeeded in introducing a number of new products and breaking into a number of new markets by the simple expedient of becoming an approved second source. Being a second source not only permitted higher prices, but accommodated a limited productive capacity. Further, it allowed the firm to gain experience in those new markets and made it easier to introduce other new products to them. The introduction of the Volkswagen into North America provides another example. Its limited number of models were introduced with nearly complete disregard for competition. Detroit touted power, big-car roominess, and options. VW joked about its funny looks and offered reliable and fuel efficient and economical transportation—and created its own market. Eventually, Detroit figured out that there was a small-car market. By then VW, under new management, abandoned its successful strategy, began offering "different Volks for different folks," and went head-to-head with Detroit. It is now an also-ran.

23. *What tests have been made?* It is well known that if a child is left alone with a fistful of beans, more than a few will wind up in his ear or up his nose. People, experienced with children, keep the beans out of reach. In the area of product test, the sins of omission are legion. For example, a well-regarded manufacturer of control equipment introduced a line of microprocessors to replace old-fashioned but highly reliable relay controls. The performance of the microprocessors was exceptional in all tests, and the product moved like hot cakes. Unfortunately, the new controls had never been tested in the hostile environment in which they would be used. Serious malfunctions resulted, and the firm is now nearly bankrupt. Another firm developed a waterproofing compound for raincoats. It did not affect the appearance or the hang of the garment, and, more importantly, did not lose its effectiveness after repeated dry-cleanings. The new product apparently satisfied the needs of the textile care (dry-cleaning) industry. Unfortunately, no one had ever tested a raincoat treated with the new compound after exposure to several rain storms. Each exposure caused the coat to shed a little bit of the compound. After several exposures the garment became less waterproof than an untreated coat.

30. *How does it compare with our other new product options?* The decision to develop and launch a new product will be more correct and certainly more comfortable if that product is selected from among several possibilities. And this doesn't mean crowding the field with a bunch of second-raters just to provide a little action. It is in this area that the 11 strategic guidelines become extremely valuable. If all the contenders satisfy them, then the decision on which to develop and launch can be made on the basis of the tactical considerations reflected in these 32 questions.

31. *Are our assumptions valid?* The assumptions made about a new product, its markets, and its profitability require very careful exploration. All of us, for example, assume, as the basis for our daily lives, that our paychecks will be there next time around, and that our families will be waiting for us when we get home. Questioning such assumptions is very difficult even to contemplate. Yet, when it comes to new products, we make equally basic assumptions which tend to be overlooked, and which go unquestioned. We project volume on the assumption that certain prospective users will consume so much. We rarely check to make sure that their needs will continue or that the firms themselves will still be around to buy. Milton Bradley, for example, dedicated a large portion of its production to supporting Texas Instrument's video game, home computer efforts. It is now in serious trouble because TI abandoned the market after losses of nearly a quarter of a billion dollars. We make similar assumptions about the availability of the materials we require. We assume that they will continue to be available at predictable costs. We also assume that our tests of the new product have indeed been adequate. When it comes to new products, if we have made an assumption and have not questioned it, the marketplace will prove us wrong. To illustrate, in 1979 Exxon spent $1.2 billion to acquire the Reliance Electric Corporation so it could have the Reliance "Alternating Current Synthesizer," a device purporting to reduce the power requirements of electric motors. Exxon assumed the product performance claims were valid and did not subject them to any kind of verification. Exxon's current return on this investment is about one quarter of one percent.

32. *What is our decision?* When made, the decision should be a clean one and without second-guessing. If the decision is to develop and launch, then it should be implemented expeditiously. This is reasonable and generally what happens. However, when the decision is to veto, a number of problems can arise. A major source of new product ideas for any firm should be those products which were rejected at an earlier date. When a new product idea is rejected, the file should not be jettisoned. Rather, an attempt should be made to summarize the conditions which ought to exist in order for the product to succeed. Tickler files should be established to bring that idea to the surface once more when the right conditions exist.

When it comes to new products, Murphy's law applies in spades. Selecting new products to be developed and launched requires many things. But above all, it requires a kind of practical wisdom, which, for the most part, marketing people have in abundance. It is a kind of wisdom which grows with experience and which is also the same kind of practical wisdom required to manage a successful new product launch.

MANAGING A SUCCESSFUL NEW PRODUCT LAUNCH

From any point of view, a product is a success when the break-even point has been passed, the development costs have been recovered, and sales are being sustained with no more than normal effort (see

FIGURE 23–9

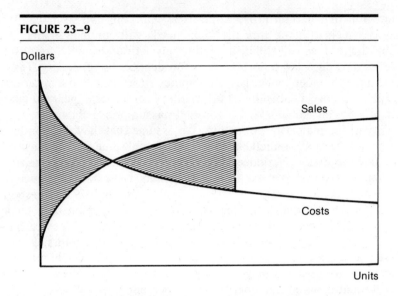

Figure 23–9). Products are more or less successful, depending upon how quickly these things happen.

Engineering and manufacturing contribute to this situation by getting the cost curve to bottom out quickly and at as low a volume figure as possible. Marketing's contribution is to get the volume up through the break-even point and moving at a rate that insures the imminent recovery of costs.

Unless we have made a horrible miscalculation about the product itself, the only thing we need fear are competitive responses. These can be merely annoying, or they can be devastating. For example, General Mills recently tried to test market a premium dog food called Speak. Consumer products, even in test markets, cannot be sold without advertising, so, everywhere Speak was advertised, General Foods dropped the price of Gainesburgers. A satisfactory test was never completed, and the product was effectively sabotaged. In most instances, me-too consumer products do not require testing, merely sufficient resources to sustain the product as it builds share and becomes profitable. Diet-Coke, for example, was introduced into a crowded market (over 18 other kinds of cola drinks) because Coke had the resources to prevail. Even so, it succeeded by stealing volume from other Coke flavors, whose sales declined by 35 percent. With a really new consumer product, it is a different ballgame. The advantage lies with the prudent producer.

Industrial products are not generally vulnerable to this kind of competitive response. We allow competition an opening only when we drag our feet and prolong a launch beyond a reasonable time. And, of course, if we drag our feet, we will also prolong the time it takes to reach break-even and begin to recover costs.

However, industrial marketers can take advantage of two characteristics of industrial selling to avoid the situation entirely. We know, for example, that 80 percent of our volume will come from about 20 percent of our prospects. Further, since our new product strategy calls for new products which tend to narrow the markets we serve, we should pretty much know who the key users of a new product will be. We also know that very few industrial sales are made on impulse, like buying a second drink or a Hershey bar. Before a purchase is made, there is usually considerable deliberation, testing, and evaluation. These two facts—the 80-20 rule and the need for testing—suggest that before we go public with a product (i.e., advertise it and hand it over to the sales force) we have it sold-in, or, at the very least, under test with key potential users.

Too frequently, those who have responsibility for developing new products have no responsibility for their sale. A new product is introduced to the sales force, its features and benefits demonstrated, its pricing explained, and its advertising and promotional support outlined. Yet, the most important attribute of a new product is not its features or its benefits, not its pricing, and surely not its advertising and promotional support. The most important attribute of a new product is its salability. This must be demonstrated.

New products should remain the responsibility of the new product development people until the break-even point has been reached, or, even better, until all the development costs have been recovered.

Getting the new product sold-in or under test with key users may require selling at the executive level. But with only a handful of new products each year and a total new product volume goal of from 3 to 10 percent of total volume, even the most distinguished CEO should be willing to make a few sales calls on his opposite numbers with potential users.

Since salespeople do best with established products, and in view of the high cost of having salespeople make sales calls, this, too, may be an idea whose time has come. The presidents of Perdue Farms and Remington Shavers have demonstrated that this is indeed so.

CONCLUSION

In the foregoing we have explored five subject areas important to the success of any new product effort.

1. From characteristics shared by successful marketers of products, we have developed 11 strategic guidelines for the initial screening of new product ideas. These guidelines, shaped to the firm that draws them up, serve as a negative screen for new product ideas. Ideas which fail to meet these guidelines are not likely to be successful for the firm considering them.

2. We have reviewed sources for new product ideas and have seen that most new products evolve from existing products and technologies. We have examined seven possibilities for the evolutionary development of new products.

3. Simplified methods have been reviewed for auditing marketplace activities and for conducting essential market research.

4. The need for a final screen for selecting those new product ideas to be developed and launched has been discussed. The requirement is an attitude of creative skepticism on the part of the new product evaluators.

5. Finally, we have proposed that some special characteristics of all markets be taken advantage of. These, together with executive selling, permit the break-even point to be achieved and development costs recovered before a new product is assigned to sales for routine sales efforts.

Each of these five discussions provide sufficient how-to information to permit new product managers to examine and improve their own new product identification, evaluation, selection, development, and launch procedures.

If success in business comes from doing a number of small things very well, these five areas provide better-than-average leverage opportunities.

24

NEW PRODUCT DEVELOPMENT

---

by
Steve Power

Thermo-Serv, Inc.

NEED FOR NEW PRODUCT DEVELOPMENT

There are many reasons why companies, industrial and consumer, large and small, are investing heavily in the development of new products.

The fact is, the world is changing and it is doing so at an increasing rate. The technological breakthroughs within the past few decades have been staggering. Home computers, for example, that cost in excess of $2,000 just three years ago, have been replaced by smaller, more powerful units at one-tenth the price. Companies *must* keep up with scientific advancements within their industry if they expect to grow and prosper.

Another reason companies must pay close attention to the area of new product development is that consumers' wants and needs are constantly changing. Until the mid-70s, the average consumer paid very little attention to the label when buying clothing. Today, not only does every woman have to own at least one pair of Gloria Vanderbilt jeans, but her children in grade school select the brands of everything from the lunch pail they carry to the sneakers they wear. And who would think of actually getting out of their car to open a garage door in this age of push-button convenience.

The combination of technological breakthroughs and the changing environment of the consumer and industrial markets has required virtually every manufacturing company to sharpen its skills and increase its dedication to new product development. But in addition, there are other reasons companies find it necessary to step up new product development activity.

Every well-managed company should have a marketing plan from which to operate. The cornerstone for all planned activities within the plan stems from the sales and profit objectives for the company. If the plan reflects a desire by management to increase sales and profits, it must be supported by some well-thought out strategies on how this growth will be accomplished. Creative new techniques to penetrate existing markets or expand into new ones can make up only a portion of the gap between current sales and projected increases. The balance must be achieved through the development of new products.

From a profit standpoint, new products are necessary to maximize plant capacity in the face of voids left by the decline of mature products.

DEFINITION

The definition of what we call new products is sometimes misunderstood. Minor revisions or embellishments to current products are sometimes mistakenly brought under the umbrella of new product development. This activity could more accurately be called "same lady . . . different dress," because the basic product itself has not changed. The product function has really remained the same, only now it has slightly different knobs or a new bell or whistle.

For the purposes of this discussion, the following definition will describe *new products:*

> A product substantially different from any produced by the *company* currently or in the past.

Implied in this definition is the understanding that, although the product is new to the company, there may be similar products in the marketplace manufactured by other companies. If this is the case, it is essential that careful attention be given to building in some proprietary features to make the finished product superior and more desirable than any other on the market.

SETTING THE STAGE

For any new product development program to be successful, it is absolutely essential for top management, all the way to the president of the company, to be committed to the program. This commitment must be reflected in the marketing plan and supported by budget and organizational staff to produce desired results.

To prepare an organization to handle new product development activities, it may require the creation of a new job function. There are several ways to organize this responsibility.

Product Manager. Although this is the area where many companies assign the responsibility of new product development, it is probably the least-effective place for it. The product manager is usually the person running in five directions at once, just keeping the current product line on track. Typically, there isn't time to devote attention to effective long-range planning and new product development.

New Product Committee. Some companies have organized new product committees to handle this task. Representatives from marketing, sales, manufacturing, and finance are usually represented. Unfortunately, each of these individuals is so tied up in his or her own areas of responsibility that, although the meetings are held, follow-up and meaningful results usually do not occur.

Director of New Product Development. A management position that is high enough in the organization to have meaningful impact to carry through on new product suggestions is perhaps the most effective approach. Ideally, an officer of the company should be in charge of the new product development function. Periodic meetings with representatives from other departments can prove more effective if this individual follows up each session with a summary of all projects under consideration, the next action required to keep them moving, the people responsible for those actions, and the estimated dates of completion. This document then serves as an agenda for the next status meeting.

THE SYSTEM

Given there is a commitment and an organization to foster new product development activity, the need exists for a well-defined system through which all new product suggestions may flow. It is generally accepted that for every 60+ new product suggestions that are considered, only one or two ever see the realization of production and distribution. Although the presence of a formalized system for evaluating and developing new products does not guarantee success, it *can* minimize the chance for failure.

The balance of this chapter is devoted to a simplified new product development system, broken down into four major steps.

   I. *Definition phase.*
   II. *Design phase.*
   III. *Development phase.*
   IV. *Production phase.*

I. Definition Phase

New product suggestions come from several places: the sales force, the marketplace (industrial users, consumers, and so on), or employees. All new product suggestions should be gathered and screened against a preestablished criteria for their general fit with the goals and objectives of the marketing plan. This initial screening process (see Figure 24–1) will eliminate several ideas. It is important that, if a suggestion does not fit, it be eliminated from further consideration so quality ideas are not diluted by their presence.

Concepts with merit should then be defined in terms of:

1. Sales forecast by quarter/year.
2. Target introduction date.
3. Target wholesale.
4. Target retail.
5. Packaging requirements.
6. Product specifications.
7. Marketing strategy.
8. Competitive data.

This information then should be reviewed with manufacturing and engineering to establish cost estimates for the development and manufacture of each new product concept.

A financial assessment is then made to determine potential sales and profits within a plus or minus 20 percent range. Viable concepts at this point should be presented to the executive committee for approval or rejection. Each new product idea that is accepted is then assigned a priority and a schedule for the remaining three phases as developed. This information should be communicated to each department head so they may schedule necessary time and budget to support these projects.

II. Design Phase

As each new product idea enters the design phase (see Figure 24–2) the necessary support functions within the company must be made aware of the design parameters:

1. Features desired.
2. Target market.
3. Expectations.
4. Product philosophy.
5. Relationship to rest of line.
6. Mandatory or optional aspects, or both.

FIGURE 24-1
I. Definition Phase

New Ideas:

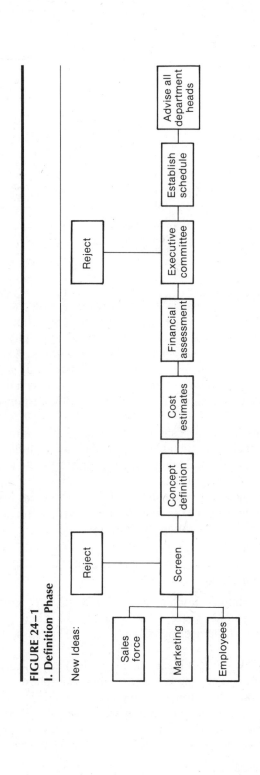

FIGURE 24–2
II. Design Phase

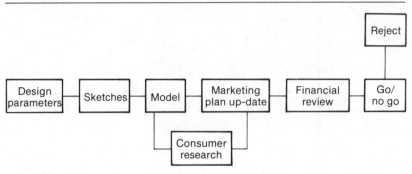

Sketches are then generated and reviewed with the appropriate marketing or product development personnel. Selection of sketches follows and a decision is made as to the need for a physical model. Depending upon the technological complexity of the new product idea, it may or may not be necessary at this point to build a breadboard model to test the feasibility of specific functions. This model can also be used to conduct consumer research and test the response to unique features.

At this point, marketing should update its plan for introduction and prepare a timetable for packaging and collateral requirements. Every element of the cost to manufacture and produce the item should then be so identified that a more complete financial review can be made.

Another go/no go decision should occur at this point. New product ideas passing out of the design phase have a very strong likelihood for survival through the remaining two phases.

III. Development Phase

For relatively simple, nonmechanical new product concepts, this should be a fairly quick phase. (See Figure 24–3.) It may require only a marginal degree of engineering effort before it is released to manufacturing.

For those new product ideas that are more mechanically or technologically complex, this is an extremely important phase.

To begin, key functional components should be identified and tested. In many cases, new products are similar to something already in the marketplace, but they apply a new technology to make it unique. Rather than take the project to the end, only to discover it can't be

FIGURE 24–3
III. Development Phase

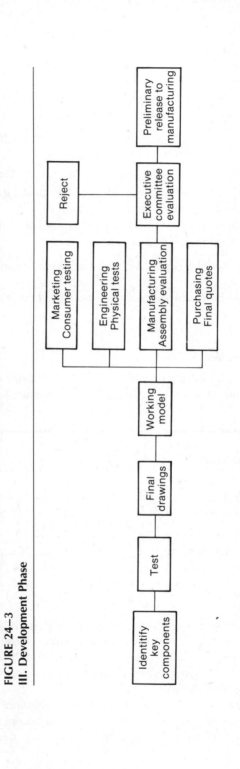

done, the unproven function should be isolated and tested. This can be accomplished either through computer simulation or may require the construction of component prototypes.

Final drawings are then generated and a complete working model can be constructed. This model can be used for:

Marketing—to verify needed information through consumer testing or reaction from the marketplace.

Engineering—to make any required changes to the final drawings.

Manufacturing—to evaluate the need for special jigs or fixtures for assembly or quality-control testing.

Purchasing—to update and finalize component quotations to establish final material cost.

A review should be made with the executive committee at this time to provide a final go/no go decision point. If approved, a preliminary release should be made to manufacturing to begin the final phase of development.

IV. Production Phase

At this point, engineering should provide a final design fix on the potential new product. (See Figure 24–4.) This is provided to the manufac-

---

FIGURE 24–4
IV. Production Phase

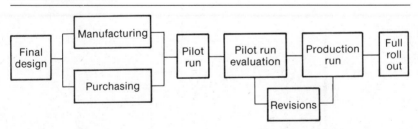

---

turing department so that plans and accommodations may be made for the manufacture of this new product, and to Purchasing so that quotes may be secured on tooling, equipment, material, and testing gauges. A final forecast and pricing information are then entered into the company's administrative network.

Necessary tooling, material, and other required equipment are then purchased and a pilot run is made. Upon acceptance of the pilot run, a full production run is made.

All necessary packaging and collateral materials prepared by the marketing department will dovetail at this final step to support a full roll-out of the new product.

SUMMARY

If a company is to grow and prosper, the need for viable new products is absolutely necessary. Once top management makes a commitment to the creation of new products and supports it with the establishment of an organization, it is necessary to follow a structured system. Since there is no such thing as a "stock" system that can be taken "as is" and work in every situation, the steps described in this chapter hopefully will provide a path to help establish a system that will work in your particular situation.

25

DETERMINING USER NEEDS FOR NEW PRODUCT DEVELOPMENT

by
Bruce S. Fisher

Lightolier, Inc.

The successful development and launching of new products in the marketplace will be vital to the growth and profitability of corporations in the 1980s. The challenge which companies face in the area of new product development can be summarized in this quote from Booz, Allen & Hamilton: "The contribution made by new products to sales growth is expected to increase by one third, while the portion of total company profits generated by new products is expected to increase by 40 percent over the next five years." In order to support these expectations, companies interviewed in this survey plan to double the number of new products introduced during the same time period. Where will the ideas come from, how will they be screened, and can we improve our batting average, are all questions which must be answered if a company is to succeed in this environment.

Booz, Allen found that those firms who have made a commitment to the following principles are most likely to be successful. These are:

Make the long-term commitment needed to support innovation and new product development.

Implement a company-specific approach, driven by corporate objectives and strategies, with a well-defined new product strategy at its core.

Capitalize on accumulated experience to achieve and maintain competitive advantage.

Establish an environment—a management style, organizational structure, and degree of top-management support—conducive to achieving company-specific new product and corporate objectives.

One other point needs emphasis: Booz, Allen reported that the success rate of new products, as measured by company financial and strategic goals, has not improved, on average, over the last 20 years. From 1976 through 1981, a 65 percent rate of success was achieved. If we assume the batting average will remain unchanged and new products will be needed to grow and increase profitability, most corporations will have their future health at stake in new product development.

TYPES OF NEW PRODUCTS

Innovation. A true innovation does something that hasn't been done before and creates unlimited opportunities. Because it is a new function, the new product becomes instantly recognizable.

Better Performance. Improved operating characteristics also can be classified as a new product. These product enhancements or modifications must be perceived by the customer as not interchangeable with earlier models.

New Uses. New applications for old products create new markets. Sometimes called "repositioning," many aging ideas find renewed vigor in alternate applications.

Added Function. Sales volume and distribution patterns can change when products perform more functions than before.

Cost Reductions. Significant reduction in cost adds new markets. Lowered cost and, therefore, selling price, may turn an old idea into a new market.

Restyling. A new way of looking at an item can also create a new product. Preferences in color, form, and shape can change, so that the existing products may continually have to be updated.

MARKET NEEDS: THE USER

What is the most effective way of researching for new products? The entire process is supposed to center around identifying the needs of the market. But many times the user, rather than the manufacturer, is actually the developer of a successful new product. Who knows better what is really needed than the individual planning to utilize the product? In summary, this technique of probing for new ideas can be very effective and less costly in the long run.

IBM, for example, created the Installed User Program (IUP) department to coordinate the effort of acquiring user-developed programs designed to run on its medium and large computers. The IUP learns of promising programs developed by either customers or their own field representatives. Those programs with potential are referred to the appropriate operating division for evaluation. IBM's approach is a proven success; approximately one third of all the software leases for use on large and medium-sized computers is developed by outside users.

In the consumer field, Pillsbury provides an excellent example of a company that knows how to find innovations from a user that is very diffuse and difficult to communicate with. Established in 1949, the Pillsbury Bake-Off is an annual contest which publicizes Pillsbury's flour and other bakery products. Consumers develop original recipes using Pillsbury products and submit thousands of entries. Winners are given prizes, and the company publishes the recipes, generating additional exposure and potential use of their product. Although started as a publicity strategy, the Bake-Off has generated one of the four cake-mix lines Pillsbury sells and several variations of another directly from recipes of Bake-Off winners.

WHEN WILL USERS INNOVATE?

1. Sometimes manufacturers are aware of a need, but the market appears to be small or high-risk. If the idea has real merit, the user may build the product itself. Later, if the idea generates a market, a manufacturer will choose to enter and commercialize the concept. Examples include the computer market of the 1950s and customized light-duty vans.

2. The consumer and manufacturer both may find a product attractive enough to develop it. But the user sometimes hides the need from the maker, because it can generate a lot of profit by having exclusive use. Examples are integrated circuits in electronic products and specialized process machinery.

FINDING INNOVATORS

1. Establish incentives and publicize them so potential users will bring their ideas to the manufacturer.

Keys to Success

A. Make sure the desired product is defined and communicated as clearly as possible.
B. Understand the importance of equating the reward with the effort required to meet the desired specification.
C. Advise only the most likely users to innovate; this saves communication expense and screening of ideas.

2. Establish a reputation for being a company which encourages user-developed products.

Keys to Success

A. Be fair, be honest. Innovators are very wary of manufacturers stealing their ideas. Create a disclosure form which should be signed by any outsider presenting a new product idea.

LISTENING TO THE VOICE OF THE MARKETPLACE

A significant trend in today's environment is the amount of human and financial resources being devoted to the "homework" phase of product development. Ten years ago, 58 new product ideas were needed, versus 7 today, to find one successful idea. Because of this, most of the money now invested in new product development is spent on winners instead of losers. Companies have developed very sophisticated market research methods, such as demographics, psychographics, and other tools to acquire a greater understanding of the potential customer's specific needs.

IN-HOUSE OR OUT-HOUSE

In the 1960s and 1970s, corporations leaned on outsiders to conduct marketing studies and consumer surveys. But something was usually lost in the translation. That "unique feel for the market" only occurs when one participates personally in the real world: as a product manager, sales manager, and now marketing manager. We don't really learn from reports by consultants, field sales representatives, or subordinates. There is no substitute for face-to-face contact with the customer.

Successful companies, such as GE, in its Video Products Division, and Matsushita Electric, in its video group, regularly talk to store owners and even visit customers at home to find out in detail what they like or don't like about their products. In early 1983, National Steel Corporation opened a product application center near its automotive customers in Michigan. The company plans to discover specific customer needs that it can serve. "We forgot how sophisticated metallurgy was," says G. Watts Humphrey, Jr., president of National's steel group. "We thought steel was steel."

Developing an "In-House" Capability

The search for new product ideas should be pursued inside and outside a company on an equal basis. To stimulate the development of new product concepts inside the corporation, the importance of innovative ideas must be made known. A real value must be placed on a total effort by all departments in the new product development process. Timeliness and the ability to react fast and take full advantage of a new product's potential requires teamwork by each operating group within the company.

Control Data Corporation recently established a technology group to concentrate not on products but rather on new ways that the company's technology could be used in products. Once a product is identified for a specific market need, the concept is given to a team of design engineers, marketers, and manufacturing people charged with focusing on the development of that product. Large companies, in particular, according to CD, should pay special attention to this technique, since it forces people to focus on a single project and avoid distractions. As long as the priorities are right, the ability to move quickly and decisively on a given opportunity is made possible.

Estée Lauder is another example of a company which uses an in-house success formula to reach the pinnacle of success in a highly competitive business: cosmetics. Lauder depends on well-cultivated relationships with research laboratories and systematic market feedback provided by highly trained department store salespeople. The firm has anticipated major trends, such as a demand for skin care products, and, unlike key competitors, has stuck to a "less is more" approach to product innovations.

The Role of the Marketing Department

A large number of new product ideas die because of certain factors within an individual company: resistance to change, not-invented-here syndrome, excessive time delays, and poor interdepartmental coordination. Enter the product manager, the backbone of any new product development program. Contrary to functional or project-oriented organization approaches, the matrix organization creates a product champion. The product manager's job is to maneuver and manipulate a particular program through all possible obstacles within the company. These may include low priority, inadequate resources, early failures, redesigns, changes in specifications, low acceptance, competitive pressures, and poor communication or unsatisfactory cooperation between departments.

This entrepreneurial aspect of the product management role within the corporation encourages creative and dynamic research of new product ideas. The "champion" acts as a catalyst, affecting all departments, as he or she leads the research and development of new products. Specific tools which the product manager uses to formalize this process include:

1. *Pro forma business plan* (Figure 25–1).
2. *New product profile* (Figure 25–2).
3. *Design brief* (Figure 25–3).
4. *Competitive product evaluation* (Figure 25–4).

Teamwork

We tend to overfocus on R&D and marketing as the two important contributors in researching for new product development. The sales and manufacturing groups not only have a large stake in this process but more often than not can make significant contributions to it. It is the responsibility of product management to act as the quarterback, making sure that all operating departments are kept informed and encouraged to give feedback on new product ideas, manufacturing processes, or competitive threats.

How to Identify Potential New Product Winners

Relatively few studies have dealt with the challenge of defining the differences between successful and unsuccessful new products. A British study, Project Sappho, found that successful innovators had a much better understanding of user needs, paid more attention to marketing, completed development work more productively, and made greater use of outside resources. In 1979, Project NewProd—funded by the Associates' Workshop on Business Research, School of Business Administration, the University of Western Ontario and the Canadian government—provided further insight into what makes a "winner" versus a loser in new product development. The 15 most important variables included:

1. Proficiently executing the launch—selling, promoting, and distributing.

FIGURE 25–1
Business Plan

Date _____

New Product Release PG _____   By   _____

Item _____ Release Date _____ 1st Shipment Date _____
Competition _____
_____

Sales Forecast: New Items: 1st 4 Months $_____ 2d year $_____
                  % Additional _____ % Replacement _____
                  Carry-over Items: Annual Rate Current $_____
                  Total, New and Carry-over, 2d year $_____
Profitability: New Items: Mfg. P/V _____%
                              Profit Contribution 2d year _____
              Carry-over: Mfg. P/V_____%
                              Profit Contribution 2d year _____
No. New Items _____   No. Carry-over Items _____
Tooling: Estimated Cost $_____
           New Machinery & Equipment Cost $_____
Literature: Estimated Cost $_____ for _____ copies
           _____ yrs. life
Other Sales Support Materials (describe, estimate cost)

Marketing Strategy:
A.   Opportunity: New market need or existing trend
B.   Leadership Edge (Innovation, Style, Performance, Value)
C.   End Use Markets (Estimate percent for each)
     Residential _____%   Commercial _____%
     Institutional _____%
D.   Sales Channels (Estimate percent for each)
                                          LOL
                    Distrib. Counter   Salesperson
     Showroom__% Distrib. Salesperson__% Spec. Job__% Others__
E.   Key Selling Concepts:

FIGURE 25-2

NEW PRODUCT PROFILE CHART

PRODUCT: _____

ANNUAL SALES (End of first year) $ _____

TARGET MFG. P·V. %: _____

DATE _____

ANNUAL PROFIT CONTRIBUTION $ _____

TOTAL CAPITAL INVESTMENT $ _____

BY _____

			MINUS		PLUS	
			-2	-1	+1	+2
FINANCIAL ASPECTS	RETURN ON INVESTMENT (BEFORE TAXES)	−2 Less than 80% +1 100 to 120% −1 80 to 100% +2 More than 120%				
	ANNUAL SALES RATE (END OF FIRST YEAR)	−2 Less than $100,000 +1 $1 to $5 million −1 $100,000 to $1 million +2 Greater than $5 million				
	TIME TO REACH MAXIMUM SALES VOLUME	−2 More than 5 years +1 1 to 3 years −1 3 to 5 years +2 Less than 1 year				
PRODUCTION & ENGINEERING ASPECTS	REQUIRED CORPORATE SIZE	−2 Can be made by any bucket operator +1 Average or larger sized companies −1 Most companies could compete +2 Only a very large company				
	RAW MATERIALS	−2 Limited supply or suppliers +1 Readily available from outside sources −1 Limited availability inside company +2 Readily available inside company				
	EQUIPMENT	−2 New plant needed +1 Some new equipment −1 Mostly new equipment +2 Present idle plant useable				
	PROCESS FAMILIARITY	−2 New process - no other application +1 Familiar process - some other uses −1 Partly new - few other uses +2 Routine process or promising other uses				
RESEARCH & DEV. ASPECTS	RESEARCH AND DEVELOPMENT TIME	−2 More than 3 years +1 1 to 2 years −1 2 to 3 years +2 Less than 1 year				
	EXISTING KNOW-HOW	−2 No experience & no other application +1 Some experience or new vistas −1 Partly new with few other uses +2 Considerable experience or potential				
	PATENT STATUS	−2 Unsettled patent situation +1 Restricted to few licenses −1 Open field or many licenses +2 Patent or exclusive license				
MARKETING & PRODUCT ASPECTS	SIMILARITY TO PRESENT PRODUCT LINES	−2 Entirely new type +1 Only slightly different −1 Somewhat different +2 Fits perfectly				
	EFFECT ON PRESENT PRODUCTS	−2 Will replace directly +1 Slight effect −1 Decrease other sales somewhat +2 Increase other product sales				
	MARKETABILITY TO PRESENT CUSTOMERS	−2 Entirely different customers +1 Mostly present customers −1 Some present customers +2 All present customers				
	NUMBER OF POTENTIAL DISTRIBUTORS	−2 Less than 100 +1 250 to 1000 −1 100 to 250 +2 More than 1000				
	SUITABILITY OF PRESENT SALES FORCE	−2 Entire new group needed +1 Few additions needed −1 Some additions necessary +2 No change necessary				
	MARKET STABILITY	−2 Volatile market, frequent price cuts +1 Fairly firm market −1 Unsteady market +2 Highly stable market				
	MARKET TREND	−2 Decreasing market +1 Growing market −1 Static, mature market +2 New potential market				
	TECHNICAL SERVICE	−2 Extensive service required +1 Slight service requirements −1 Moderate service requirements +2 Negligible service required				
	MARKET DEVELOPMENT REQUIREMENTS	−2 Extensive educational program +1 Moderate customer resistance −1 Appreciable customer education +2 Ready customer acceptance				
	PROMOTIONAL REQUIREMENTS	−2 Extensive advertising & promotion +1 Moderate requirements −1 Appreciable requirements +2 Little promotion needed				
	PRODUCT COMPETITION	−2 Several directly competitive products +1 One or two somewhat competitive −1 Several competitive to some extent +2 No competitive product				
	PRODUCT ADVANTAGE	−2 Higher price, equivalent quality +1 Competitive price but quality advantage −1 Competitive; or higher price and quality +2 Both price & quality advantage				
	LENGTH OF PRODUCT LIFE	−2 Probably 1 to 3 years +1 Probably 5 to 10 years −1 Probably 3 to 5 years +2 Probably more than 10 years				
	CYCLICAL & SEASONAL DEMAND	−2 Seasonal and subj. to business cycle +1 Subject to business cycle −1 Seasonal +2 High stability				

FIGURE 25–3

DESIGN BRIEF

To: _____   Product: _____   Date: _____
From: _____
PG: _____   Design Agenda Date/Priority _____
Target Date, Mkg. Dwg. _____

1. OBJECTIVE (market opportunity, need, trend; competitive threat)

2. APPLICATION (lighting function, architectural/decorative purpose;
    where used)

3. STYLE (form, materials, finish, detailing, sketch)

4. PERFORMANCE (light control, flexibility, maintenance, installation)

5. PARTICULARS (dimensions, lamps, finish, mounting, quantity,
    price)
    _____ _____ _____ _____ _____/yr. $_____
    _____ _____ _____ _____ _____/yr. $_____
    _____ _____ _____ _____ _____/yr. $_____

6. COMPETITION (name, cat. no., description, price)
    _____ #_____ _____ $_____
    _____ #_____ _____ $_____
    _____ #_____ _____ $_____

---

2. Having a new product that more clearly meets customers'
   needs than do competitor products.
3. Having a higher-quality new product than competitors in terms
   of tighter specifications, greater durability and reliability, and
   so on.
4. Undertaking a good prototype test of the product with the customer.
5. Having the sales force or distribution effort, or both, well targeted—at the right customers.
6. Undertaking a proficient test market or trial sell.
7. Proficiently starting up full-scale production.
8. Knowing customers' price sensitivities.
9. Executing product development well.
10. Understanding buyer behavior and the customers' purchase
    decision process.

FIGURE 25–4

COMPETITIVE PRODUCT EVALUATION
(Competitor's Sample)

To: *_____   Date: _____
      _____   By: _____
      _____
      _____
      _____
      _____
      _____

Mfgr. _____   Cat. No. _____ D/N Price _____
       Description _____
Lightolier equivalent: Cat. No. _____ D/N Price _____
1. Appearance _____
    _____
    _____

2. Function _____
    _____
    _____

3. Construction _____
    _____
    _____

4. Packaging _____
    _____
    _____

5. Comments _____
    _____
    _____
    _____

6. Disposition: Product now being held by: _____
                  Product being disposed to: _____
    * For instance: Design, Manufacturing, Engineering, Plant Manage-
                     ment, Purchasing, Sales

11. Having a product that permits the customer to reduce costs.

12. Having a good "company-product fit" in terms of sales force or distribution, or both.

13. Having a good "company-product fit" in terms of marketing research and skills and needs.

14. Doing a good job on idea-screening.

15. Understanding customers' needs, wants, and specifications for the product.

The conclusion of the research makes all the difference when it comes to separating successful versus unsuccessful new products. Market-oriented factors had the major impact on success, spearheaded by a sound product strategy.

RESEARCHING FOR NEW PRODUCT DEVELOPMENT: A "MARKET ORIENTATION"

As indicated by the NewProd study, researching for new product development must emphasize the needs of the end user. This has led many companies to reorganize by market so product managers, designers, operations personnel, and sales can be totally focused on the needs of their particular segment. Although inefficiencies and some overlap of function occur, the benefits of this type of strategic organization far outweigh a more functional approach. It is difficult in today's marketplace for one product to serve multiple end users (consumer/commercial, for example). By compromising, which many companies do to achieve internal efficiencies, the product may not be totally right for either market. The thesis remains fairly simple: Conceptualize a product for a particular market and maximize the value and benefit package for a specific end user. Be aware and attempt to coordinate common tooling, components, and factory facilities to achieve economies of scale. But don't compromise on the concept.

BIBLIOGRAPHY

Evanston, Ill.: Booz, Allen & Hamilton, Inc., 1982. *New Products Management for the 1980s.*

Buell, Victor P. *Handbook of Modern Marketing.* New York: McGraw-Hill, 1970.

Cooper, R. G. "How to Identify Potential New Product Winners." *Research Management,* September 1980.

Hippel, Eric von. "Get New Products from Customers." *Harvard Business Review,* March/April 1982.

Kolodny, H. F. "Matrix Organization Designs and New Product Success." *Research Management,* September 1980.

"Lauder's Success Formula: Instinct, Timing, and Research." *Business Week,* September 26, 1983.

"Listening to the Voice of the Marketplace." *Business Week,* February 21, 1983.

Marvin Philip. *Product Planning Simplified.* New York: American Management Association, 1972.

New Products, New Profits. New York: American Management Association, 1964.

26

ESTABLISHING A NEW PRODUCT DEVELOPMENT TEAM

by
Jim Betts

New Product Development Newsletter

There's an old story about the new product effort in the early days of the Ford Motor Company. Henry Ford had hired a consultant to evaluate the performance of his executives. The outside expert toured the company for several days and then reported to Mr. Ford.

"I understand what each person is doing," he said, "except for a man sitting alone in an office with no work on his desk. This man is just staring into space all day. He apparently does nothing."

"That may be so," Ford replied, "but the last thing he did was to develop a new feature for our cars that resulted in greater sales, easier manufacture, and a profit increase of $10 million."

Whether that man was a part of Ford's "new product team" or not, he produced the desired results.

More recently, the president of a major company was touring the R&D facility where some 800 scientists labored at benches loaded with elaborate scientific equipment. With the president was a new senior financial officer seeing the lab for the first time.

"What does all this cost?" the financial manager asked.

"It doesn't matter," the president replied, "because without this, there would be no products and no company."

THE NEW PRODUCT EFFORT IS VITAL TO BUSINESS GROWTH

The importance of new products can be summarized by quoting from a recent Dow Jones report:

> More than 52 percent of the business growth in the past 10 years was in new products. In the next 10 years, this will grow to 60 percent. Of all the goods on today's market, 71 percent were unknown 35 years ago. While established product growth was eight percent, the first-year growth of new products was 15 percent. Really new products, with little or no comparable price base to old products, tended to turn in profits 28 percent greater than established products. New products tend to enhance the image of a company as well as boosting profits.

SETTING UP THE NEW PRODUCT TEAM

It is quite obvious that every business—no matter its size—needs a new product effort. In a one-person company, the owner thinks about new products. (There is no doubt that the president of General Motors also thinks about new products, but he can afford a lot of help.)

It is easy to think that large numbers of people and giant budgets guarantee new product success. (Well, that may be true in retrospect, for, if there is no success, the people and dollars will vanish.)

In a recent survey of 1,245 companies, *New Product Development Newsletter* found that the number of persons in the new product-development program has no relationship to the number of successful new products.[1] That is, the fewer persons engaged in new product work, the fewer new products are brought forth—so the products tend to be uniquely suited to a small company, which is likely to be more certain of success, because it can't afford a failure.

At the upper end of the scale, a large company, with a giant budget for R&D, can absorb failures as part of the total program.

But, on balance, it is generally recognized that the "funnel theory" requires about 100 new product ideas into the large end of the funnel for one successful product to emerge at the small end. The more people and dollars you have to develop concepts, the greater the chance for a success.

The establishment of a new product team is, of necessity, a matter of what the company can afford and a determination of its goals. Some industries (electronics, for example) spend as much as 20 percent of sales on R&D. Others with more established markets spend as little as 1 percent. The food industry is an example. Across the board—looking

---

[1] "New versus No," *New Product*, September 1983.

at all industries—the new product/R&D budgets average 2 percent of sales, but the budgets are climbing at a rate of 15 percent each year and are also climbing as a ratio of total sales. The battle for successful new products is heating up.

BEFORE THE TEAM, THERE IS THE MISSION

No company should establish a new product development team until it knows its own mission and goal. Here are some suggestions:[2]

1. Top management must be committed to the new product program.

2. The best, most-experienced people should be on the new product team.

3. New product responsibility should be placed with line management, as well as staff.

4. Determine the company's strengths and aim the new product effort in that direction.

5. Look close to home for new product ideas. Do the things that you do best.

6. Focus on a few big ideas. Don't dilute your efforts with many small projects.

7. Good new product ideas come from people, not processes. Go for the idea, not just the company's ability to make the product. If it is a good idea and a good new product, the company can make it.

8. A successful new product must have a reason for being, not simply that the company wants it.

9. Pick a standard for new product evaluation and stick to it. (It is often said that the worst thing that can happen to a new product effort is that the company president likes it. You can't dump it—and you wind up spending too much time and money on it. Remember: The failure will be greater in the end.)

10. When you find a promising new product idea, go all-out to make it work.

11. Once the new product is in the market, stick to your guns. Selling a new product may be as tough as developing it.

SELECTION OF NEW PRODUCT TEAM MEMBERS

If you could get Thomas Edison, Henry Ford, the Wright brothers, and a few others of that calibre on your new product team, you would be in

---

[2] Morgan V. Hunter, *New Products: How to Create, Research, Develop & Market Them Successfully,* 3rd ed. (Point Pleasant, N.Y.: Point Publishing, 1984), pp. 104–5.

great shape. But, if you are starting from scratch (or rebuilding), try this group:

1. The senior nuts-and-bolts scientist (mechanic, chemist, designer, or whatever your company has as the top technician).
2. The director of manufacturing.
3. The sales manager.

But beware. The scientist sees the vision. The manufacturing director will say it can't be done and the salesperson will say it can't be sold at that cost. The challenge for the team director is to overcome the points made by each member. Beyond such a group, you may reach out for the advertising manager (or agency), product designer (internal or external), financial types, and others. In any case, the burden will fall on the group leader, chairman, or whatever you call the person with ultimate responsibility. (That's the person who must go to the company president and say that things are going well—or not so well.)

The Team's Goals

No matter the composition of the new product team, picture them in their first meeting. Someone asks, "What are we doing here and what are we supposed to do?"

A good first step might be the painting of a sign that the team would hang on the wall of its meeting room. (This is taken from a survey of 700 firms, with more than 13,000 new product introductions in their combined history.[3])

1. Build in deeper and better analysis up front, to avoid misapplying your efforts.
2. Focus new product efforts based on company goals and strategy.
3. Set rigid definitions and measurements of new product performance expectations (costs, time, sales, profits).
4. Spend more up-front—and be prepared to cut off spending earlier in questionable projects.
5. Tighten the management of new product development costs and use your experience to drive down total program costs.
6. Tailor the new product program to specific objectives.

---

[3] Booz, Allen & Hamilton, "Best Practices for New-Product Efforts," *New Products*, pp. 78–79.

The Team's Restraints

New product development "teams" seem to set, as their first "new product goal" the definition of their responsibility (or power). Such self-ordained titles as New Products Committee, Venture/Focus Force, and the like litter the corporate landscape.

In his book, *New Products Management,* Professor C. Merle Crawford, Graduate School of Business Management, University of Michigan, examines the new product function organization in realistic terms. He defines the "matrix team:"

> The matrix team, which goes by many names, is quite common today, and it is the leading candidate for growth. It may be a task force, a project team, even a venture team. It is a group of people who are actually doing the work, know what is going on, and whose support is critical. These people will expedite the project or stall it; they will achieve the necessary creative breakthroughs, or fail to. They are neither functional heads nor perfunctory representatives.
>
> All the elements of matrix management come to bear here, and industry indicates that it is still learning. From a recent study of matrix forms generally, not necessarily for new products, the following problems appeared.[4]
>
> 1. *Tendencies toward anarchy.* Having two bosses is worse, not better, than having one.
> 2. *Power struggles.* Matrix permits a balancing of interests in fast-moving or especially complex situations where conflicting interests abound. The process of achieving this balance creates obvious opportunities for power grabbing.
> 3. *Severe groupitis.* Committee-like behavior evolves in cases where the matrix is misunderstood.
> 4. *Collapse during economic crunch.* The matrix is an expensive and often slow form of management, so tough times can cause its abandonment.
> 5. *Excessive overhead.* If the matrix mode is successful, productivity recaptures the investment, but the up-front investment is heavy.
> 6. *Decision strangulation.* In a way, the matrix form is the opposite of power management, and this problem is often a consequence of too much democracy.
>
> Apparently we have a great deal yet to learn about matrix management, but certainly the basic idea of compromise, blending the interests of the individual new product project with those of the various functional groups, is here to stay.[5]

---

[4] Davis, Stanley M., and Paul R. Lawrence, *Matrix,* Reading, Mass.: Addison-Wesley Publishing, 1977.

[5] C. Merle Crawford, *New Products Management* (Homewood, Ill.: Richard D. Irwin, 1983), pp. 170–71.

Whether your company elects to have a matrix or a committee or a new product team, there are some additional guides. Stanley Katz, president of Leber Katz Partners, lists a few:[6]

1. New product development is not for new people. On your team, you need experienced people. Those who know how to feel it in their bones.

2. Don't become research dependent. You have to trust your judgment as well as your data.

3. Good new product people are generalists—entrepreneurs. They are not specifically in the area of sales, research or management.

4. It is easier to have a new idea than to implement one.

5. Clout is essential. You must persuade others in your company to follow your pattern of development. (The company president included.)

6. New product responsibility must be separate from ongoing brand management. The new product person must be an entrepreneur and a risk-taker; not a risk-avoider. Creative innovation and a pioneering spirit are essential.

7. Continuity is vital. Nothing threatens the success of a new product as much as changing the management of the new product in midstream.

While a corporate new product team should have structure and rules, it cannot be so rigid as to be inflexible. A great idea cannot be turned away because it does not fit the mold. In such a case, the team should consider setting up a separate sub-team to deal with such an opportunity.

In the case of 3M—one of the R&D giants of industry—the company addresses the development of a new product or idea in many ways and the company's various divisions have different approaches.

The Commercial Chemicals division, for example, utilizes the marketing group to spearhead new products. Each marketing manager for a product line has responsibility for new products that are related to that line. The leader of the team seeks to identify new opportunities that are either not related to a specific product line or require long-term investment, such as the development of an entirely new technology. 3M generally develops a team approach for a new product after it moves from the idea stage to actual research and development efforts. Such a "task force" is chaired by the person most involved in the project, generally the respective market manager, and will be composed of management personnel, marketing personnel, sales manage-

---

[6] Ibid.

ment personnel, and market communications people. Such a task force reports to division general management.

Such a program of small teams dedicated to specific new product efforts is now seen by most larger companies as the best approach. A major food company, for example, recently changed its new product organization chart. In the past, the company had one centralized marketing section responsible for all new product development. Individuals were assigned specific product areas of responsibility and reported to a director who subsequently reported to the vice president of marketing.

In the new organization, each business unit has new product responsibility assigned to individual brand marketing managers. In essence, this has led to approximately 12 new product managers, rather than the former organization which had only four such managers.

The advantages of such a format, says the company's corporate director of new products, are:

1. More direct interest, responsibility, and control of new product development.
2. Better team spirit, because the same corporate individuals work together on various new product endeavors.
3. Better use of business unit personnel and resources.

The company's new organization chart in the new products area is shown in Figure 26–1.

FIGURE 26–1

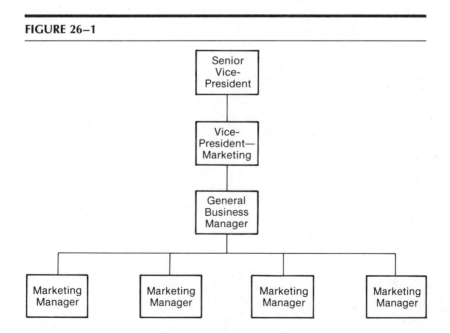

In the case of a company with many product lines, it is more practical to have new product development teams within each division. If the company produces coffee and dog food, for example, each division will have its own new product group. Each group leader will report to a corporate officer and information and guidance will flow both up and down. If the company decides that all new products will be packaged in smaller sizes, this directive will come from the top. If one division finds that a certain characteristic in a new product seems to be working well, this information is sent to corporate where it may then be redirected down to all other division new product teams.

DO WHAT WORKS BEST

There is no magic formula for new products, and none for establishing the new product team. Most successful companies have tried a variety of approaches and settled on one form of organization that works well. In time, they may experiment with other approaches. The new product organization, like products themselves, can always be improved.

27

PLANNING THE PAYBACK OF A NEW PRODUCT

by
Angelico Groppelli

Hofstra University

Effective and successful marketing of a new product is a complex decision-making process involving the selection of sound and workable strategies. One of these strategies is the careful planning of payback. Broadly speaking, the term *payback* means finding out how profitable a new product will be during its life expectancy. It means calculating how quickly a firm can recoup its original investment and determining at what point in the future it becomes advisable to replace the product with one that is more profitable. More specifically, this chapter is devoted to a discussion of approaches that can be used to develop a payback plan. Some steps a marketing manager employs to make a payback plan economically feasible are the following:

1. Estimate the initial incremental investments required to develop and market the new product.

2. Forecast the expected revenues that will be generated by a new product.

3. Calculate the normal expenses incurred during each year of the life cycle of the product.

4. Derive yearly net cash inflows by subtracting expenses from revenues.

5. Employ the discounted cash flow approach to evaluate the payback and profitability of the product.

6. Monitor the critical path of estimated outcomes to ascertain whether the expected values are on target, exceed, or fall short of the original profit and payback forecasts.

7. Adjust the original profit and payback forecasts for changing environmental and other related factors when the actual results deviate from the trends originally anticipated.

8. Determine when to replace the product.

The analytical steps outlined above indicate that planning payback is not an easy task. One of the more challenging aspects of payback planning is the generation of appropriate data. In many cases, new products require the special ingenuity of the marketing manager to come up with the right information. This might call for developing different alternatives and the application of well-grounded judgments.

This task cannot be accomplished in a vacuum. Teamwork is involved. The astute marketing manager knows how to inspire and coordinate the inputs of the product and research managers, the sales and advertising managers, as well as other responsible officials in the firm. He or she usually has a good "feel" for the forthcoming environment and knows which economic, industry, and competitive factors will have the greatest influence over the new product's life cycle. In the role of research analyst, the marketing manager has the responsibility for making the right assumptions that help in the translation of data into reasonable and attainable forecasts.

In this chapter, therefore, the discussion will center around a description of methods that can be used to estimate the payback of a new product. It will be shown that payback plans do not end with forecasting. Following the forecasting stage, the marketing manager has the assignment of monitoring and updating the results. A final step involves the preparation of alternative strategies to deal with as many unforeseen future contingencies as possible. In other words, it involves an objective and analytical approach, flexible enough to permit modification of original plans with new strategies should the plan fail to live up to expectations.

ESTIMATING THE INITIAL INVESTMENT COSTS

Once the alternative methods for marketing a product are analyzed, once the product is determined to be viable for introduction, and, more specifically, once it successfully passes the concept testing stage, the next step is to engage in business analysis. Essentially, business analysis entails an evaluation of the sales, costs, and profits estimates to determine whether they meet the company's financial objectives. This entails the calculation of initial investment costs that must be incurred to develop, advertise, market, and produce the product in order to set the stage for its successful introduction. These expenditures are called "cash outflows." Only incremental costs are relevant and should be included in this cost category.

Since any firm is faced with limited resources that must be allocated as effectively as possible among different alternatives, capital rationing analysis becomes an essential part of the initial investment decision process. Budgets, with limited amount of funds, are set up for premarket testing, advance promotion, early advertising, and capital expenditures. In the case of a new product, the justification for allocating funds to different functions depends largely on the size and growth of the anticipated market demand for the product, the profitability of the product, and the alternative opportunity costs offered by other competing products. In the final analysis, it is necessary to establish cutoff points for specific cash outflows so that they remain within the limits of budgeted dollar amounts.

Given these budget constraints, funds are then set aside for the development of a new product. These initial development costs end once the product enters the production stage. Provision must be made, however, for additional research and development funds in the latter stages of the life cycle of the product to cover improvements in the product and new package design. In other words, the marketing manager decides whether it pays to invest additional funds to extend the life of the product beyond a given period.

In order to produce the product, the firm has to invest in equipment and plant space. These capital expenditures are considered incremental cash outflows which do not recur after the product reaches the market, unless the estimated demand far exceeds the original targets and output hits the capacity ceiling at some point during the life expectancy of the product. It matters not whether the firm engages in the outright purchase of plant and equipment or whether it draws on excess capacity available from existing facilities. Excess capacity is not a free cost. It should be treated as an opportunity cost. Since this excess capacity could be used for other productive purposes, the firm must estimate the amount that would have been invested to replace the same amount of capacity. This amount, whether incurred by outright purchases of new equipment or available from unused capacity, is a cost that becomes part of the incremental investment necessary to market a new product.

The marketing manager also must spend considerable sums of money to conduct surveys, test market the product, and determine the potential demand for the product. High pre-introduction selling, promotion, and advertising expenses, over and above normal costs incurred to set the stage for the introduction of the new product, are considered part of the incremental cash outflows.

These incremental cash outflows must be recaptured in the future by a stream of cash inflows, which are defined as revenues minus expenses incurred over the life expectancy of the new product. In general, new cash inflows should cover all initial incremental cash outflows plus a required rate of return. Put differently, cash inflows adjusted for the time uncertainty of risk should at least equal the increment cash outflows and, if possible, exceed them to compensate for any error in forecasting.

FORECASTING REVENUES

Projections of the outlook for a new product ultimately rely heavily on judgment. The assumption that past trends and environmental changes will be repeated in the future is a rational assumption, as long as allowances are made for a number of unforeseen contingencies. Also, the future is subject to the risk of uncertainty. This risk of uncertainty becomes an increasing function of time. In other words, the more distant in the future one forecasts, the greater the chance that an estimate will deviate from an expected level. To minimize the risk of large errors in forecasting, the most accepted procedure is to assign weights to a range of outcomes in future years. These weights are called "probabilities."

The application of probabilities to deal with the element of uncertain risk can be described more clearly by an example. A resort owner wishes to estimate incoming reservations in order to plan food purchases and the number of employees required to run the resort. The weather plays a crucial role in the effective planning of resort business. If it rains, reservations fall off, and, if it doesn't rain, reservations increase. A good weather forecast is highly useful in planning activities and controlling costs. To hedge bets, the resort owner listens to the forecasts of 10 weather forecasters and finds out that, in general, forecasters do not agree among themselves on expected weather conditions for weekends. After monitoring the forecasts of the 10 for a time, the resort owner is able to come up with a distribution which reveals a pattern allowing him or her to arrive at an expected consensus of opinion. The owner may find out, for instance, that when 8 out of 10 weather forecasters announce no rain in the coming weekend, the chances are high that the resort will draw a good crowd. If 8 out of 10 forecast rain, then reservations will be poor in the forthcoming weekend. Put another way, experience reveals that it is possible to assign weights or probabilities to a range of different weather opinions, and, therefore, some of the elements of uncertainty are reduced. Past experience indicates that the further ahead a weather forecast, the less certain the statements and the greater the amount of hedging. This leaves the resort owner with a wider dispersion of opinions and a lower probability that the outcome will turn out as expected. Consequently, the resort manager's plans must allow for these uncertain contingencies.

The same problems face anyone engaged in forecasting the potential market demand or revenues for a new product. An assumption must be made that estimates of future revenues can be expected to deviate on the high or low side of a forecasted outcome. The idea is to make all allowances for as many unforeseen contingencies as possible. Because the risk of uncertainty increases over time, the range of high/low values, associated with the forecast, become larger. The use of probabilistic information provides valuable information on different possible outcomes and permits the planner to understand how these outcomes may vary under various sets of conditions. By knowing the extreme limits in each forecasted range, the firm can take steps to protect itself against different outcomes and, thus, develop appropriate strategies to cope with these uncertain or unforeseen contingencies.

From a practical point of view, there are two problems involved in the use of ranges. One is that ranges make decision-making indeterminate. Also, ranges cannot be easily applied to quantitative forecasting methods. The other concern is that the chances of making forecast errors increase over time because of rising uncertainty. Therefore, it is reasonable to expect that the forecasted ranges get wider the more distant into the future one forecasts. In order to overcome these deficiencies, weights or judgmental probabilities are assigned to the values in the range to narrow it to a single expected value.

Table 27–1 shows high, average, and low values of forecasted revenues for a new product in the first year and in the fifth year, and it demonstrates how these ranges are brought down to single expected and manageable values. Note that the dispersion around the expected

---

TABLE 27–1
Assigning Probabilities to a Range of Forecasted Revenues in the First and Fifth Years

First-Year Forecasts	(A) Revenues	(B) Probabilities	(A) × (B)
High	300	.25	75
Average	200	.50	100
Low	100	.25	25
Expected revenue			200
Fifth-Year Forecasts			
High	6,000	.20	1,200
Average	3,000	.30	900
Low	1,000	.50	500
Expected revenue			2,600

value increases from the first year to the fifth year, and that the fore-caster usually becomes more conservative in the fifth year by assigning a bigger weight to the low value in the range. The principle described can be translated graphically in Figure 27–1 to show how it applies to forecasting within the configuration of a life cycle of the new product.

FIGURE 27–1
Product Cycle of New Product and Corresponding Probability Curve of Expected Revenue Forecasts

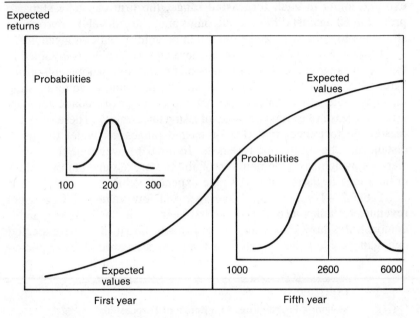

Having presented this simple theoretical discussion of the principle of probability distribution, as it applies to forecasting, we can proceed to examine various approaches employed to estimate the future poten-tial market demand for a new product.

PROJECTING CASH INFLOWS

The usual procedure in payback planning is to forecast cash flows, rather than net income. The main purpose is to justify an initial com-mitment of cash outflows with expected greater sums of inflows in the future. Therefore, the goal is to estimate cash inflows by deducting from yearly revenues, generated by the new product, the annual costs.

Typically, the life cycle of a product is divided into four stages, known as introduction, growth, maturity, and decay. In the initial year or two of the new product life cycle, the inflows may be negative or relatively small. They gradually build up and grow rapidly as customers become exposed to the product through marketing and advertising. At this stage, the inflows mushroom partly because fixed costs per unit decline as production increases and partly because the learning experience makes possible more effective use of resources. Also, as revenues increase, cash inflows benefit from an improvement in productivity and profit margins. Eventually, a maturation phase is reached when, for a number of reasons, a slowdown in revenue growth occurs. For example, increased competition gives rise to more frequent markdowns. Excess capacity emerges with a growing number of imitations and substitute products. This, in turn, reduces efficiency and profit margins. Exogeneous factors begin to adversely affect the product, such as changing demographics, environmental and other fundamental developments which have a braking action on demand. These and other trends lead to a slowdown in the growth of cash inflows. Finally, profits enter a declining or decay stage partly because marketing outlays increase in an effort to maintain share of market, competition intensifies, and the original customer-appeal of the product begins to fade. It is clear that the task of forecasting cash inflows, when faced by a life cycle, is no easy task. However, this is one of the most important parts of product planning.

Product cycle analysis, therefore, serves as a guideline in arriving at internal forecasts of annual revenues. These internal forecasts are modified by checking them against other independent external sources of analysis. External sources of information usually include projections of industry, economic, and other indicators, which are translated into revenue estimates via a regression analysis. Usual procedure calls for the evaluation of both internal and external forecasts from which a consensus forecast is calculated to obtain a single estimate of future expected revenues.

Internal and external forecasting methods fall into two main analytical categories. The first approach depends on subjective evaluations and the second method involves the use of well-known objective statistical techniques.

In many cases, new product forecasting forces marketing managers to fall back on subjective approaches, mainly because the revenues of products cannot be estimated by employing conventional regression or other quantitative techniques. Due to its unique characteristics, historical data may be inadequate to determine the future trends of revenues or share of market of a new product. One may be faced by an unknown past and an uncertain future environment. Under these circumstances, the objective approach is not feasible. Marketing managers must rely on more subjective or judgmental analyses.

One way of dealing with the lack of adequate data or published information is for the marketing manager to prepare a plan that describes the new product, assesses its potential, and suggests common assumptions. This plan is then submitted to internal respondents, such as the sales, advertising, new product, and other managers, with a request for yearly high, low, and most-likely revenue estimates. This information can then be used to develop summary frequency distributions.

Table 27–2 presents a hypothetical compilation of internal forecasts. It indicates the high, low, and most-likely outcomes of 10 managers. The objective is to translate these data into expected revenues. This is done by calculating the averages of all individual forecasts. These averages are then reduced to a single estimate by assigning the appropriate probabilities to the values of each forecast in the range.

Panel or questionnaire methods draw on the most-skilled people in the firm and supply consensus annual forecasts from internal sources. This approach should not be considered as the only input in determining the potential market for a new product. However, it does get all concerned involved and engenders their cooperation. It also establishes a sensitive sounding board by making the participants part of the payback planning process. Having submitted a forecast, everyone wants to see that their forecasts are as accurate as possible. It is a way of obtaining continuous monitoring of results from different internal sources.

An alternate subjective forecasting technique is based on external information. When an entirely new product cannot be easily related to historical data, the marketing manager may have to resort to consumer surveys, derived from questionnaires that were administered to potential users of the product. The goal in using this approach is to conduct a series of surveys over different time periods, thereby creating user reactions that measure the growing intensity of demand from one period to the next. By observing the rates of change from the respondents, as their exposure to the product increases over time, the marketing manager may be able to determine how the actual market demand for the product might develop.

It is through these kinds of subjective surveys that the marketing manager can measure user sensitivity toward prices, packaging, and other factors affecting final demand. These "product tryouts" should also provide a good insight into the more subjective factors responsible for the market development of a product. There is no reason why such subjective premarket tests cannot supplement the results obtained

TABLE 27-2
Revenues in Years after Product Introduction

Revenues
(in thousands of dollars)

Managers and Other Knowledgeable Company Officials	Period I			Period II			Period III			Period IV		
	H	ML	L	H	ML	L	H	ML	L	H	ML	L
A	70	50	40	120	100	80	290	250	200	600	500	450
B	80	60	40	240	120	90	310	290	250	800	580	500
C	70	40	50	150	90	110	350	300	250	750	600	450
D	60	55	30	170	105	95	230	210	200	750	650	540
E	65	50	35	180	110	80	270	220	190	710	630	600
F	60	40	25	190	130	85	300	250	200	700	550	500
G	60	45	35	200	120	80	350	275	235	680	530	480
H	75	50	45	180	140	75	270	230	180	850	700	650
I	80	55	35	150	135	100	340	230	220	810	610	530
J	75	60	40	130	105	90	300	260	210	820	720	670
Average revenues	69.5	50.5	37.5	171.0	115.5	88.5	301.0	256.5	213.5	747.0	607.0	537.0
Average probabilities assigned by marketing manager	.30	.40	.30	.25	.50	.25	.30	.30	.40	.15	.25	.60
Average revenues (x) probabilities	20.9	20.2	11.3	42.8	57.8	48.7	90.3	77.0	85.4	112.1	151.7	322.2
Expected revenues			52.4			149.3			252.7			586.0

Note: H = High; ML = Most Likely; L = Low.

from more rigorous quantitative approaches to improve the accuracy of revenue forecasts. An astute marketing manager draws on as many inputs as possible and then applies professional judgment to arrive at a final series of expected cash flow estimates.

There are no sure-fire methods to calculate future revenues, but it is prudent to make ample allowances for large errors that are likely to creep into the forecasts. Even when compensation is made for errors, one is still left with the constant problem of monitoring and modifying the original targets when changes in environment differ materially from the original assumptions.

There are several well-known statistical methods for estimating revenues when historical series are available. One of these consists of finding past data of a product that has similar characteristics to the new product and similar sources of market demand. For example, when color television was first marketed, producers of these sets based their forecasts largely on the growth progression of black-and-white sets.

Another objective method is to select appropriate representative micro and macro series that reflect supply and demand conditions for a new product. These so-called independent variables should be forecastable with some degree of accuracy to minimize estimating errors. The procedure then involves correlating the independent variables with the product series. The final regression equation used to forecast revenues takes the following form:

$$Y_t = a + B_{X_1} + C_{X_2} + D_{X_3}$$

The B, C, and D values indicate the relative importance of the independent variables in the forecast relationship. The equation is solved by substituting annual estimates for each independent variable (X_1, X_2, and X_3), which in turn will yield annual revenue forecasts (Y_t) over the life expectancy of the new product.

Regression analysis is a highly useful tool, because, in addition to supplying estimates of revenues, based on external factors, it lends itself to quantitative verification with such measures as the T test, or an indicator of the significance of each variable, the mean squared standard error of forecast, which measures the degree of the closeness of fit between actual and calculated values. Moreover, the coefficient of correlation provides an indicator of the overall degree of relationship between revenues and the other independent variables. Regression analysis, however, works well only when historical series are readily available.

A less-rigorous but frequently used method involves the analysis of sectors or factors which make up the final demand for the new product and then proceed to estimate the share of market. If the product can be associated with an industry, the marketing manager should estimate the share of industry sales which can be expected to be captured by the product. More specifically, the first task is to forecast the outlook for the market or industry. These data can be obtained from internal or external sources. Market or industry activity forecasts can then be calculated for each year over the life cycle of the new product by regression analysis. Once these forecasts are calculated, the marketing manager estimates a share of market which the new product can be expected to gain over its corresponding market or industry. Even when the share of market is estimated, it is necessary to acknowledge that there is a certain degree of uncertainty associated with forecasting future revenues. Because market share estimates are subject to varying forecasting errors, no single figure can adequately describe a probable future outcome. Moreover, the further into the future one estimates, the greater the chance for error. To reduce the uncertainty of the time element, the acceptable procedure is to estimate year-by-year sales in terms of high and low shares of market. Because it is difficult to work with a range, the market researcher is required to make subjective assumptions concerning the outcome, given certain expected scenarios. This calls for assigning weights or probabilities that the outcome will fall either on the high or on the low side of the range. By applying probabilities to the various values in the range, it is possible to determine a single expected value.

Table 27–3 demonstrates how the range of share of market estimates can be translated into single expected values by assigning probabilities to various outcomes. The example presented in Table 27–3 demonstrates that the further into the future sales are forecasted, the less optimistic the expected outcome, largely because the low values in the ranges of more distant estimates are assigned higher and higher probabilities.

Although estimates of revenues are essential, another important part of the payback planning analysis is a forecast of unit sales of demand. This permits the marketing manager to calculate the effect of different price assumptions on the final demand for the product, as well as its break-even point. A break-even point means that level of unit sales or production when the firm neither makes a profit or incurs a loss. At this level, total costs are equal to total revenues.

Price assumptions depend primarily on the expected intensity of competition, the assessment of the degree of substitution, and how fast other firms are able to imitate the product. Pretesting provides some insight into the behavior of the price elasticity of demand for the product (or the proportionate change in the quantity sold versus a proportionate change in the price of a product). In other words, the firm may want to know what happens to sales under different price assumptions.

TABLE 27–3
Calculating Share of Market Expected Values from Estimated Ranges (in thousands of dollars)

	Periods			
	1	2	3	4
Forecasts of market demand	$1,000	$2,000	$3,000	$4,000
Estimated ranges: share of market for new product:				
Optimistic	5%	6%	8%	8%
Most likely	4%	5%	6%	6%
Pessimistic	3%	4%	5%	5%
Probabilities assigned to the outcome:				
Optimistic	0.30	0.30	0.25	0.20
Most likely	0.50	0.40	0.35	0.30
Pessimistic	0.20	0.30	0.40	0.50
Totals	1.00	1.00	1.00	1.00
Expected share of market for new product*	4.1	5.0	6.1	5.9
Expected demand for new product (row 1 × row 5)	$41	$100	$183	$236

* An example of the method employed to calculate the expected values in the first period is:

.30 (5%) + .50 (4%) + .20 (3%) = 4.1%

The same calculation is done for periods 2, 3, and 4 to obtain their respective expected values.

In this way, it can make better revenue and cash flow forecasts. Given these conditions and taking into consideration the cost learning experience of the firm, it may be possible to observe how revenues and the break-even point will change over time as the price of the product changes.

By altering the price assumptions, marketing managers can simulate various situations and determine how flexible they can be in setting prices. Moreover, this approach can help a firm to find out how long it would take before the new product becomes profitable.

The break-even point formula in terms of units is:

$$\frac{FC}{P - VC}$$

where: FC = Total fixed cost
P = Price of the new product per unit sold
VC = Variable costs per unit sold

Let us assume that fixed costs amount to $100,000 and the unit price of the new product and its variable costs are $10 and $5, respectively. The break-even point is:

$$\text{Break-even point} = \frac{\$100,000}{\$10 - \$5} = 20,000 \text{ units}$$

In assessing potential demand, the marketing manager may find that a reduction of the price to $9 would raise the break-even point to 25,000 units—$\left(\frac{\$100,000}{\$9 - \$5}\right)$. But it may also increase demand substantially and at the same time preclude or delay competitors from entering the market. It is up to the marketing vice president to decide whether the price of $9, which yields a higher break-even point and produces greater operating leverage, will result in an improved market share or if a price of $10 in the long run produces more favorable results.

Experiments of this kind and related decisions can make the payoff plan more flexible. Strategies of this type can help the marketing manager to decide whether to shorten or lengthen the payback period or whether to shorten or lengthen the life expectancy of a new product. A great deal depends on how well costs are estimated and allocated to each expense category in the income statement. This part of the estimating procedure involves the cooperation and the inputs of the treasurer, finance vice president, and the accounting or comptroller of the firm.

PRO FORMA INCOME STATEMENT

A pro forma income statement provides the ingredients for estimating the cash inflows that should be expected over the life cycle of a new product. It entails deducting from year-to-year expected revenues the corresponding costs incurred to market a product. The residual values are the net cash inflows of the product after its introduction. Analysis of the pro forma income statement can pinpoint problems which may arise in maintaining the profitability of a new product. It can alert the marketing manager to favorable or unfavorable cash inflows originating in a short fall of revenues or within particular cost categories.

Several methods for calculating expected revenues have already been described. The next step is to determine the allocation of individual expenses. A simple method for accomplishing this is to calculate the percentage distribution of different expenses relative to revenues for a past time period. A better technique is to observe how the percent distribution of cost relative to sales has changed during the life cycle of a similar product and then proceed to assume that this change in the distribution, over time, applies to the new product.

The disadvantage with this approach is that it assumes all costs are variable. Actually, the assumption is that no operating leverage exists once the break-even point is passed. Under these conditions, cash inflows are likely to be understated, partly because they do not take into account the declining trend in per unit fixed costs as sales and production increase.

Consequently, a more effective way to develop a pro forma sales and expense breakdown for the new product is to divide both operating and cost of goods sold into fixed and variable. Make the variable costs increase in the future by a given percent of revenues while total fixed costs remain unchanged. This type of cost allocation proves useful in establishing different break-even points under various cost assumptions. Table 27–4 shows a pro forma income statement using the breakdown of costs into variable and fixed.

TABLE 27–4
Pro Forma Income Statement for a New Product Using a Variable and Fixed-Cost Format

	Periods			
	I	*II*	*III*	*IV*
Expected sales	$100,000	$200,000	$300,000	$400,000
Cost of goods sold:				
Variable costs (40%)	(40,000)	(80,000)	(120,000)	(160,000)
Fixed costs	(10,000)	(10,000)	(10,000)	(10,000)
Operating expenses:				
Variable costs (20%)	(20,000)	(40,000)	(60,000)	(80,000)
Fixed costs	(5,000)	(5,000)	(5,000)	(5,000)
Operating income	25,000	65,000	105,000	145,000
Taxes (40%)	(10,000)	(26,000)	(42,000)	(58,000)
Net profits or cash inflow	15,000	39,000	63,000	87,000

Although this is a quick way to determine cash inflows, it does not consider the large shifts in the individual operating expenditure categories, once the product goes to market. Costs of promotion, marketing, and selling usually decline after a new product is introduced. As a result, a more detailed breakdown of these expenses would prove highly useful to the marketing manager, enabling more effective budget control.

A more sophisticated and useful pro forma approach, therefore, consists of estimating individual cost categories and introducing flexible assumptions that take into account the changing behavior of these expense items at different stages of the life of the new product. A clue can be obtained from the actual cost experience encountered with similar products in the past. Using this as a point of departure, assumptions can then be modified to deal with environmental conditions when they differ from the historical ones. Whether the marketing manager has prior benchmarks or not, he or she will have to exercise judgment in forecasting and allocating the costs to each individual category.

Table 27–5 presents a hypothetical pro forma income statement of expected revenues, costs, and net cash inflows for a new product, over a six-year period. The first consideration is to determine the new product's potential life expectancy. This information can be obtained from past experience and by comparing other life cycles in the existing

TABLE 27–5
Projected Six-Year Cash Flow Pro Forma Income Statement for a New Product *($ millions)*

					Forecasted—Years			
		0	1	2	3	4	5	6
1.	Expected revenues	0	$10.00	$26.00	$41.00	$56.00	$40.00	$28.00
2.	Cost of goods sold							
3.	Variable costs	0	3.50	9.10	12.30	16.90	12.00	8.40
4.	Fixed costs	0	4.00	4.00	4.00	4.00	4.00	4.00
5.	Research and development costs	$1.00	0	0	0	1.00	1.50	0
6.	Marketing, advertising, and other related costs	6.00	3.00	4.50	5.00	7.00	6.00	3.00
7.	Overhead expenses		1.50	2.00	2.50	2.90	3.20	3.80
8.	Substitution costs		0	0	.50	.70	1.00	.50
9.	Change in working capital		.50	1.00	2.00	2.50	2.00	1.50
10.	Capital investment	6.50	—	—	—	—	—	—
11.	Total costs	13.50	12.50	20.60	26.30	35.00	29.70	21.20
12.	Profits before taxes		−2.50	5.40	14.70	21.00	10.30	6.80
13.	Taxes (46%)		0	2.48	6.76	9.66	4.74	3.13
14.	Net cash inflow		−2.50	2.92	7.94	11.34	5.56	3.67

product-line mix. The manager may also have to analyze the competitive climate which lies ahead, the effectiveness of flexible pricing, and other external factors which could either lengthen or shorten the life cycle of the new product. The assessment of all these factors will determine the number of years to assign to the pro forma statement.

Methods for estimating the expected revenues in row 1 were described previously in the section entitled "Projecting Cash Inflows." Rows 2, 3, and 4 provide a breakdown of the cost of goods sold. It is assumed that effective learning experience is likely to reduce variable costs relative to revenues later on in the life cycle of the new product. In forecast years 1 and 2, workers are still mastering the equipment and gaining experience. Material usage should decline as the rejection rate declines after the first year or two. Therefore, variable costs are estimated to be 35 percent in the first year and then fall to about 30 percent in the following years. Fixed costs in row 4 remain unchanged throughout the life of the new product. This implies that unit fixed costs should decline with rising production. The incremental research costs (row 6), to develop the product, are posted in year 0. They fall to zero in years 1 through 3 and then additional expenses are incurred to improve the product in years 4 and 5. These expenditures are required to stave off growing competition. Premarketing testing and advertising expenses prior to product introduction appear in row 6. Notice that they drop off after year 0 and rise slightly with sales until year 4, when a jump occurs in order to change the packaging design and make other product modifications.

Overhead costs, which appear in row 7, are allocated to the new product to cover its share in these expenses. Row 8 includes the deteriorating effects on income, because it is assumed that the new product will cut into the potential gains that might be lost by the existing product line.

Additional working capital requirements are taken into account in row 9. This includes costs to carry higher inventories and, initially, to fill the distribution pipeline. More cash will be tied up in accounts receivables, and the firm may well have to raise more money by borrowing from banks. In turn, this will mean higher accounts payable to finance the purchase of raw materials, carry inventories, and accounts receivables. All of these extra working capital costs are treated as a series of expenses which are recaptured after the end of the product's life cycle.

Row 10 lists the initial capital investment incurred in year 0 for plant and equipment. Although in this pro forma statement the equipment is expected to have no salvage value, provision should be made for the recapture of salvage value at the end of the product's life.

Total costs in row 11 are deducted from expected revenues (row 1), to obtain profits before taxes (row 12). When a 46 percent tax rate (row 13) is applied the residual values are net cash inflows shown in row 14. These are the cash flow estimates which will be required to calculate the payback period and to plan the growth and profitability path of the new product over its lifespan.

The marketing manager can exercise the option of constructing three pro forma income statements to observe how the net cash flows would change under optimistic, very likely, and pessimistic assumptions. Or, he or she may elect to determine the expected revenues at the onset and work with only one pro forma statement. This narrows the analysis down to a manageable single series of expected cash inflows and facilitates the monitoring of actual versus calculated values.

When the pro forma income statement is properly monitored, it can help the marketing manager to decide when a new product is no longer a viable asset to the firm. It permits the implementation of alternative strategies that may be necessary when future events unfold in a different way than was originally anticipated.

TECHNIQUES FOR PLANNING PAYBACK

A simple technique for evaluating the profitability of a new product is to measure how long it will take the cash inflows to recapture the initial investments. Obviously, firms prefer to recoup the initial cash outflows in the quickest time possible. Selection of new products for introduction should meet the time criterion set up by the firm, otherwise it may not be profitable to market the new product. Moreover, the more risky the demand or the more uncertain the market conditions, the faster the anticipated payback period. A highly risky product, whose inflows are very volatile, may require a payback period of three years, in comparison with a five-year payback for a product that is likely to generate a steady and strong demand growth in future years. Therefore, in order to determine its lifespan, the payback plan must consider various patterns of future cash inflows for a new product. A case in point appears in Table 27–6. This table illustrates alternative paths of cash flows and demonstrates how, in each case, the payback decision or period would be different.

Even though cash flows decline from the first to the fifth year, in alternative I they are front loaded so the payback period is shortened to three years. The even cash flows illustrated in alternative II produce a payback period of five years, while the rising trend of cash flows in alternative III yield a four-year payback. The main advantage of this payback approach is its simplicity and ease of calculation. The approach, however, has certain limitations. First, it ignores the time value of money. That is, early cash flows should be valued more than

TABLE 27–6
Estimating Payback Periods Based on Three Alternative Cash Flow Projections

	Alternative I	Alternative II	Alternative III
Initial Investment	−10,000	−10,000	−10,000
Year			
1.	5,000	2,000	1,000
2.	3,000	2,000	2,000
3.	2,000	2,000	3,000
4.	1,500	2,000	4,000
5.	500	2,000	6,000
Payback period	3 years	5 years	4 years

distant ones. Second, no consideration is given to cash flows beyond the payback period. Third, even though cash flows in alternative I are high in the early years, the simple payback method does not take into account the fact that there may be a noticeable acceleration of cash flow momentum in later years. The pattern in alternative III could imply that the new product requires a period of customer conditioning, and, thus, cash flows generated after the early years may turn out to be more stable—and less risky. As they gather momentum, the acceleration of cash flows in later years may lengthen the life expectancy of the new product. To ignore the possible delay in the takeoff period of cash flows does not constitute good payback planning.

The basic objections to the simple payback period approach are overcome by the employment of the more sophisticated and well-known discounted cash flow technique (DCF). The DCF method acknowledges that cash flows are less certain in distant years. It permits the marketing manager to take into account the level of risk of the product while allowing for a comparison of the expected returns against a required rate of return. In other words, the DCF approach adjusts cash flows for the level of risk associated with the product, as well as the uncertain risk expected to develop over its life cycle. Consideration, therefore, must be given to the soundness of the product demand and the confidence one can have in the fact that it will generate the estimated cash flows. The DCF method also takes into account the possibility that the product will generate relatively stable or unstable cash flows. Risk elements, such as other products making the new product obsolete, growing price competition from substitute products, and shifts in demand, as well as other contingencies, are all taken into account when the marketing manager determines the discount rate (or degree of risk) that should be assigned to obtain the present value of the expected cash flows. The present value of future expected cash flows is none other than a method for making a downward adjustment in the stream of cash flows to eliminate the element of uncertain risk over time.

Every discount rate is composed of a riskless rate (R_r) plus a premium (R_p) and can be expressed as:

$$\text{Discount rate} = R_r + R_p$$

This is also referred to as "the required rate of return." The higher the risk premium, the lower a future stream of cash flows is worth or the lower their present values. Therefore, the marketing manager must determine the riskless rate plus a risk premium associated with a new product. The decision process may take the form indicated in Table 27–7.

TABLE 27–7

Degree of Risk in New Product	Riskless Rate	Risk Premium Assigned to New Product	Discount Rate or Required Rate of Return
Low risk	5%	3%	8%
Average risk	5	5	10
High risk.	5	7	12

The assumption underlying the figures presented in Table 27–7 is that low-risk cash flows are subject to narrow dispersions (or low volatility) and there is less chance that the actual results will deviate from the estimated values. Conversely, high-risk cash flows are more volatile and the chances are greater that actual values will diverge from expected values. The way cash flows are adjusted for differences in levels of risk is presented in Table 27–8. This table indicates how high risk (high discount rates) or low risk (low discount rates) affect the present values of cash flows over time.

TABLE 27–8
Present Value of $1's Worth of Cash Flow

Year	Low Risk at 8%	Average Risk at 10%	High Risk at 12%
1.	.93	.91	.89
2.	.86	.83	.80
3.	.79	.75	.71
4.	.74	.68	.64
5.	.68	.62	.57

More specifically, Table 27–8 shows how much a current dollar of cash flow, generated by a new product, is worth in year 1, 2, 3, 4 and 5, if different levels of risk are assumed. The values in Table 27–8 indicate that the longer the time distance, the greater the uncertainty and the less a cash flow is worth at the present time. Furthermore, notice what happens to the present value of a dollar when the discount rate increases from 8 percent to 12 percent. Since this is a change from a lower to a higher-risk premium, a lower value will be given to cash flows in any given year to compensate for the higher degree of risk. As a result, the assignment of a discount rate to the cash flows which are expected to be generated by a new product is crucial to planning payback. A high discount rate, for any given series of cash flows, will raise the time required to recoup an original investment, and a low discount rate will shrink the payback period.

How does a marketing manager determine the risk premium to assign to a new product? The first step is to find out the firm's cost of capital. This is generally determined by market forces and is traceable to the yields paid for issuing bonds and equity. In the field of finance, the weighted sum of these individual security costs are referred to as the firm's "required rate of return." Given this information, the manager can establish whether the risk associated with the new product is greater or less than the firm's cost of capital. Past experience with similar products is likely to provide some answers to this question. The assumption is that the required rate of return (discount rate) assigned to a new product will probably exceed the firm's discount rate. This is because it is always prudent to make ample allowance for uncertain risk in the future.

Another technique used to determine the risk premium is to search for publicly traded companies, listed on the exchange, that produce products similar to the new one. If this information is available, then equation $K = \dfrac{D_1}{P_0} + g$ is applicable. D_1, in this equation, equals the dividend paid per share, P_0 equals the price of the stock, and g is the growth of the dividends. An actual example indicates how the formula works. For instance, if a firm pays out \$1 in dividends yearly, the price of its stock is currently \$20, and dividends are growing at 5 percent annually, then its discount rate is 10 percent.

$$K \text{ or Discount rate} = \frac{\$1}{\$20} + 5\% = 10\%$$

Companies selling similar products are assigned a 10 percent discount rate. Since this is a market measure, it is assumed to provide a good indication of the risk reflected by the new product.

In many cases, finding the correct discount rate and risk premium for a new product rests on subjective considerations. To avoid understating the degree of risk associated with a new product, the prudent decision is to pick a discount rate which is high enough to insure that it fully accounts for uncertain risk. This is referred to as "choosing a hurdle rate." Therefore, if the required rate of discount for a firm is 8 percent and the calculated value for a new product turns out to be 9 percent, the marketing manager may decide to apply a 10 percent required rate of return, as the discount factor, to cover all risk contingencies.

The marketing manager is now ready to calculate the discounted cash flow value using the pro forma cash flow estimated in Table 27–5. That table provides estimated incremental cash outflows in period 0 and the expected values of cash inflows over the following six years. Once the risk associated with the new product is determined, it is possible to incorporate these three elements into the discounted cash flow equation shown below:

$$DCF = \sum_{t=1}^{N} \frac{CF_t}{(1 + R)^t} - I_0$$

When expanded, the above equation looks like this:

$$DCF = \frac{CF_1}{(1 + R)^1} + \frac{CF_2}{(1 + R)^2} + \frac{CF_3}{(1 + R)^3} - - - \frac{CF_n}{(1 + R)^n} - I_0$$

The values in the numerator *(CF)* are the estimated cash flows over the life expectancy of the new product *(n)* and the expression $(1 + R)$ in the denominator expresses the riskless rate plus the risk premium. I_0 is the sum total of all cash outflows in period 0.

By discounting the future stream of expected cash flows, one obtains a series of present values which, when added up, yield the total present value of cash flows generated by the new product. The higher the discount rate $(1 + R)$, the lower the present value of each successive year's cash flows.

Recall that these cash flow do not reflect the initial costs of cash outflows, so they do not fully represent the true profitability of the new product. This is obtained by summing up the present values of cash flows and deducting the initial incremental cash outflows (I_0) incurred prior to the introduction of the new product. This then yields the true present worth of the product, or what financial analysts refer to as "net present value" (NPV). If the sum of present values of the cash inflows minus the original cash outflows (or NPV) equals zero, the new product is said to have achieved its required rate of return. If the sum of the present values of future returns exceeds the required rate of return, then net present value will be positive, and if it falls short of the required rate of return, it will be negative.

The same principle can be stated in relative terms and translated into the well-known concept of internal rate of return (IRR), which is the rate of return that is required to make NPV equal zero (or $PVCF - I_0 = 0$). If the cash flows produce a positive NPV, then the IRR will be higher than the discount rate (required rate of return). If NPV is negative, the IRR of the new product will be lower than the discount rate (required rate of return). The aim is to find out whether the new product meets the original return objectives.

By employing the DCF approach, the marketing manager can find out how profitable the product is and how long it is feasible to retain it in the company's product line before the net present value becomes negative. This concept is more easily understood by referring to Figure 27–2.

FIGURE 27–2
Relationship between the Discount Rate, Net Present Value, and the Internal Rates of Return

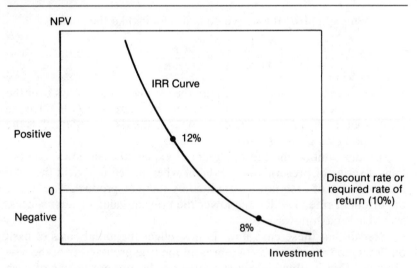

Observe that if the required rate of return is 10 percent, then a new product having an IRR of 12 percent will be profitable, whereas an 8 percent return would mean the product's returns fall short of the required rate of return. In this case, its corresponding NPV is negative and investment in and marketing of the product would not be justified. Thus, in calculating the discounted cash flows, the configuration of the product cycle implies that early cash flows are likely to exceed the return objectives of the firm, but as the uncertainty of time increases and the product reaches maturation, its IRR falls below expectations. At this point, consideration should be given to alternative product strategies.

To measure the profitability of a new product, the manager goes through the following decision process:

— When NPV is positive, IRR is greater than the firm's discount rate and the product is more than living up to expectations.
— When NPV is zero, IRR is equal to the firm's discount rate and the product just meets company profit objectives.
— When NPV is negative, IRR is lower than the firm's discount rate and the product is falling short of original expectations.

The DCF approach provides a guideline for planning the payback period. This can be demonstrated by using the cash inflows derived in Table 27–5. As indicated below, the DCF approach calculates how long it will take to recapture the initial investment if the required rate of return is 10 percent.

$$DCF = + \sum_{t=1}^{N} \frac{-2.50}{(1.10)^1} + \frac{2.92}{(1.10)^2} + \frac{7.94}{(1.10)^3} + \frac{11.34}{(1.10)^4} + \frac{5.56}{(1.10)^5} + \frac{3.67}{(1.10)^6} = 19.37$$

		Forecasted Years					
	0	1	2	3	4	5	6
Initial investment (I_0)	$-13.50						
Present values of cash flows (PV) @ 10%		-2.27	2.41	5.96	7.75	3.45	2.07
Cumulative present values (DCF)		-2.27	0.14	6.10	13.85	17.30	19.37

The payback period (PP) is approximately four years, as shown here:

PP = (Cumulative DCF − I_0 = 0) or ($13.85 − $13.50 = roughly 0)

After adjusting for the degree of risk and the uncertainty of time at a 10 percent discount rate, it is noticed that the new product has a payback period of about four years. The DCF method establishes a cutoff year but does not consider cash flows beyond that time. Unless the present value of cash flows yields a substantial return over the required rate of return beyond four years, it may not be economically feasible to continue marketing the new product. When this occurs, it may be that maturation has set in and the product is encountering stiff competition. Under these circumstances, the manager should be looking to replace the product with a more profitable one from the company's research inventory.

Cash flows of new products do not always follow a smooth upward progression over time. There may be a period of gestation, when high start-up costs and delays in introduction prevent the filling of the distribution pipeline. Moreover, initial market reception may be slow. This could generate early subnormal cash inflows and, sometimes, even initial losses. It is always possible that market tests failed to perceive the rapidity of market penetration. As a result, the early years of a new product introduction may be associated with higher risks than later years, when the product reaches its full takeoff or acceptance stage. Developments of this kind should be explored. If, in fact, the outcome is likely to turn out this way, a more appropriate procedure would be to dissect the cash flows into two distinct periods: the early years being assigned a higher discount rate than later years. Consequently, the original DCF equation becomes equation 2:

$$DCF = \sum_{t=1}^{1-3} \frac{CF_{1-3}}{(1 + R_a)^{1-3}} + \sum_{t=1}^{4-6} \frac{CF_{4-6}}{(1 + R_b)^{4-6}} \tag{2}$$

In equation 2, $(1 + R_a)$ is assigned to cash flows in years 1 to 3 and $(1 + R_b)$ is assigned to cash flows in the fourth to the sixth years. The assumption is that $R_a > R_b$. Hypothetically, cash flows in the first to the third years of the new product's existence could be discounted at 12 percent and the fourth, fifth, and sixth years at 10 percent.

Since this procedure may be somewhat cumbersome in planning payback, financial analysts have developed a more flexible method, called "the certainty equivalent approach" (CEA), for dealing with changing risk premiums over time. The suggestion is that the marketing manager assign his or her own subjective weights to future expected cash flows. For guidance in determining the certainty equivalent factors, it may be useful to refer to the present-value table. Once a required rate of return is decided upon, the manager may alter the progression of the certainty equivalent factors to make them conform to his or her judgment about the way a risk will change over time. For example, assume that the required rate of return is 12 percent, but that the risk is likely to stabilize or decrease in later years of the life expectancy of the new product. The adjustments for risk, which will be made in the expected cash flows, are shown in Table 27–9.

When these modified certainty discount values are applied to a given stream of expected cash flows, they might indicate that the payback would occur sooner than if the mechanical present value discounting procedure were applied. The implication is that, in the judg-

TABLE 27–9
The Certainty Equivalent Technique

Year	Present Value Factors at 12%	CEA Factors Which Assume That Risk Stabilizes in a 4- to 6-Year Period	CEA Factors Which Assume That Risk Is High in Early Years 1 through 3 and Diminishes in Years 4 through 6
1	.89	.89	.80
2	.80	.80	.80
3	.71	.71	.80
4	.64	.70	.84
5	.57	.70	.87
6	.51	.70	.89

Note: The CE factors adjust for the risk premium of cash flows in the numerator. Therefore, to avoid double counting, the discount rate in the denominator is represented by the riskless rate.

ment of the marketing manager, the new product would be more profitable than was expected. Consequently, original payback plans would have to be altered accordingly. As can be seen, the certainty equivalent approach suffers from lack of precision but has the advantage of being flexible enough to allow for changes in risk over time.

MONITORING THE PAYBACK RESULTS

No single approach provides all the answers in planning the payback of a new product. Whatever approach is employed, some allowance must be made for monitoring the performance of the new product once it is marketed. There is always the possibility that certain unexpected developments may arise. The question not only involves a decision to go ahead or to reject introduction; once the product is introduced it is important to evaluate whether the original assumptions were correct, whether cash flow forecasts are on target, and whether the assigned required rate of return was reasonable.

To deal with these decisions at various stages of the life cycle of a new product, financial planners employ a sequential *decision tree* concept. The decision tree approach explores different possible outcomes when probabilities are assigned to them. This approach should be used to explore how plans can be altered if demand turns out to be higher or lower than originally anticipated, and whether more or less funds should be spent on selling and marketing the product at a particular point of time. Tree decisions can draw attention to steps that should be taken under different assumptions. Although part of the decision rests on gut feeling, it is a very useful exercise.

The more crucial part of tree decisions involves the monitoring of the outcome of projected cash flows compared to the actual results. Future events are related to past events. Based on empirical studies, it has been found that expected cash flows are time-dependent. That is, the first year's cash flows correlate closely with the following year's cash flow. Accepting this premise, favorable cash flows in one year can be expected to be followed by more favorable cash flows in the next year and vice versa. This time dependence of cash flows tends to increase the risk of a new product when actual cash flows fall short of expected values and lower the risk of the product when actual cash flows exceed expected values.

This concept is illustrated in Figure 27–3, where original expected projections of cash flow trends are compared to cash flows as they are reported. As Figure 27–3 shows, the probability is that the more favorable actual results over the estimated values in the first two years will

FIGURE 27–3
Estimating Cash Flows Using the Time-Dependence Principle, and Revising Original Expected Cash Inflows Based on First Two Years' Actual Versus Estimated Values

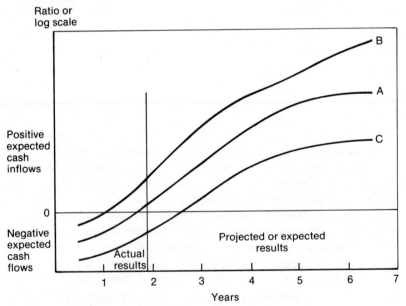

Note: A = original expected cash inflows.
B = revised cash inflows when first two years' actual results exceed the original expected cash flows.
C = revised cash inflows when first two years' actual results fall short of original expected cash flows.

continue to exceed the original expected targets in subsequent years. The reverse is anticipated to occur if the first two years' actual results fall below the original expected targets. If this is a realistic appraisal of developing trends, the marketing research manager can more efficiently analyze the payback plan and the profitability time sequence of a new product.

An example will help to illustrate this concept. Take the original cash inflow estimates presented in Table 27–5 as case A. Then assume the actual net inflows turned out to be 15 percent higher in case B and 15 percent lower in case C during the first two years of the product's life. These extrapolated or expected values for the six-year life of the product are given in Table 27–10. After discounting the cash flows at 10 percent and cumulating their present values, the results indicate that case B's payback period would be shortened to 3.7 years, while case C's would be lengthened to 4.8 years. Moreover, the net present value of case B is 61 percent higher and 61 percent lower in case C, respectively, than the NPV of the original (pro forma) cash flows estimates. The corresponding IRR indicate a similar relationship.

When time-dependence cash flows are expected to exceed the original expected values, there may be room for lowering the prices of the product to exclude competitors from entering the market or to gain greater shares of market. This pattern may also signal the need to increase capacity and the possibility of reducing selling and advertising expenditures. Furthermore, it should draw attention to certain factors responsible for this development, so the manager can prepare better forecasts in the future. A short fall in the cash flow estimates versus actual values may suggest that competition was underestimated, product imitation took place faster than anticipated, the price was too high, or costs increased too fast. There is always the possibility that market demand was inadequately forecasted from premarket testing, and that the selling campaign was less than fully effective.

Whatever the factors involved, an extrapolation of time-dependent cash flows can make for more effective allocation of selling and related expenses. It may alert the company to the need for an earlier-than-planned change in packaging or improvement of the product. Furthermore, the price may have to be lowered more quickly than anticipated. By extrapolating time-dependent cash flows of the new product, marketing managers are able to determine more accurately whether the payback period is expected to shrink or to lengthen. On this basis, the introduction of a substitute product may be delayed or advanced.

This sequential and time-dependence principle of cash flows can be highly useful for determining whether the risk of a product is increasing or decreasing over time, and whether it is feasible to continue selling the new product or replace it. By extrapolating the changing trend of

TABLE 27–10
Estimated Payback Based on Cash Flow Exceeding or Falling Short of Original Cash Flow Estimates by 15 Percent in First Two Years

	Case A			Case B			Case C		
Year	Expected Cash Inflows	PV Cash Inflows at 10%	Cumulative PV Cash Inflows	Expected Cash Inflows	PV Cash Inflows at 10%	Cumulative PV Cash Inflows	Expected Cash Inflows	PV Cash Inflows at 10%	Cumulative PV Cash Inflows
1	−2.50	−2.27	−2.27	−2.13	−1.94	−1.94	−2.88	−2.62	−2.62
2	2.92	2.41	.14	3.36	2.77	.83	2.48	2.05	−.57
3	7.94	5.96	6.10	9.13	6.85	7.68	6.75	5.07	4.50
4	11.34	7.75	13.85	13.04	8.91	16.59	9.64	6.59	11.09
5	5.56	3.45	17.30	6.39	3.97	20.65	4.73	2.94	14.03
6	3.67	2.07	19.37	4.22	2.38	22.94	3.12	1.76	15.79
Approximate payback Received:	3.95 years			3.65 years			4.82 years		
NPV	5.87			9.44			2.29		
IRR	20%			25%			14%		

Cash Flow Estimates

cash flows and then applying the discounted cash flow formula, with proper modifications for the changing degree of risk, it may be possible to find out whether the new project has a chance of meeting its required rates of returns, and whether it would take too long for the payback to justify continued selling of the product. Obviously, should extrapolating cash flows exceed the original targets, the market manager may consider extending the life expectancy of the new product, and he or she may also alter some of the initial spending and other strategies.

It is clear that the responsibility of the marketing manager does not end at the forecasting stage. Monitoring the progress of actual versus expected results is a very significant part of the payback plan. Constant monitoring permits the marketing manager to introduce modifications into the original strategies to make the plan more viable, flexible, and effective.

SUMMARY

The process of planning payback has certain pitfalls, because it is based on a subjective evaluation of risk which, in many cases, is not supported by historical experience. Although measurements of this kind cannot be avoided, they must be based on a rational step-by-step analysis of forecasting techniques, disciplined monitoring procedures, and early recognition of the need to modify original strategies.

Although the models described in this chapter suggest some guidelines to planning payback and help trace the profit time-path of a new product, there are more complex techniques that can be used to deal with uncertain and changing environments. Some help may be derived from the applications of Monte Carlo simulations, linear programming, and certain types of operations research packages. Given sufficient backup data, the employment of the powerful Box Jenkins model can provide insights into future patterns and a better comprehension of probable forecasting errors. The major drawbacks of these models are their high costs and the fact that few analysts can apply or explain the results in down-to-earth terms. In other words, sophisticated statistical techniques require complex computer programs which may not be easily understood. Moreover, complex computer models can only function effectively if the proper inputs are readily available. Ultimately, simulation approaches assume that the strategies adopted follow well-defined paths where there are no other interferences than those already considered. Still, such models have the ability to trace the results of changing developments over time while providing alternative solutions under different assumptions. A growing number of market researchers are discovering the advantages of these models. Moreover, there is a great deal to be gained by calling on the capabilities of independent internal or external consultants to aid in the construction of simulation models. Many times the results from independent sources provide objective verification of conclusions already reached, and at other times they may suggest successful strategies which may not have been considered. It is also possible that simulation model building could limit the danger of embracing "myopic solutions" arising from being too close to a given situation.

The bottom line, however, lies with the marketing manager's skills and judgments. He or she has the responsibility of developing reasonable assumptions regarding the outlook for micro and macro factors that will affect the cash flow forecasts of a new product. He or she must assign a risk premium to a new product, and he or she is also charged with the function of properly timing the introduction or withdrawal of the product.

There is no easy way to plan profit goals for a new product. Besides a great deal of hard and honest work, it is important to harness the knowledge and expertise of other departments in the firm. And there is no substitute for the learning experience built up over a number of years through the process of trial and experimentation. The important thing to bear in mind when planning payback is to explore sufficient alternatives and strategies in the event that one such strategy should fail.

28

DEVELOPMENT AND MARKETING OF A NEW NONCONSUMER PRODUCT

by
Ronald N. Paul

Technomic Consultants

BACKGROUND

To illustrate how new product introduction works in the real world, we will use as an example the development process successfully utilized by a large food company in its nonconsumer business segment. The term *industrial* is frequently used to refer to those situations in which a company is marketing its product or services to other businesses, rather than to consumers. This case will deal with how the nonconsumer organization implements a new product development program. While there are many parallels with the concepts and the processes employed in the consumer situation, there are some important differences, and these will be highlighted in this chapter.

The International Food Company of America (IFC)[1] produced a broad line of frozen and canned foods and, in addition, had interests in some nonfood operations. The bulk of the company's food products was sold to consumers in the frozen format. The company had sales of nearly $1 billion during the mid-1970s when it decided to formalize the new product function in its institutional/foodservice business unit.

---

[1] For reasons of confidentiality, certain changes have been made to disguise the identity of the company. The process, however, was in fact the one utilized by the company.

This unit had sales of approximately $100 million and had, as its primary mission, the sales and marketing of the company's retail or grocery products to commercial and institutional foodservice accounts. The commercial category included such establishments as restaurants, cafeterias, and food operations within retail drug and department stores, as well as hotels and motels. Institutional included such foodservice facilities as those found in colleges, schools, plants and offices, hospitals and nursing homes, and military bases. This portion of IFC's business was organized separate from the consumer business and was referred to as the foodservice division. With few exceptions, the foodservice division's products were manufactured in the same plants as those that produced the company's consumer products. Corporate management, however, had noticed that the food-away-from-home market was growing at a much faster rate than were consumer expenditures for food at home. To increase its participation in this business, the company took an aggressive posture towards committing resources to expanding its nonconsumer food business.

It was with this commitment that the company established its new

FIGURE 28–1
Organization Chart: International Foodservice Company's
Foodservice Division

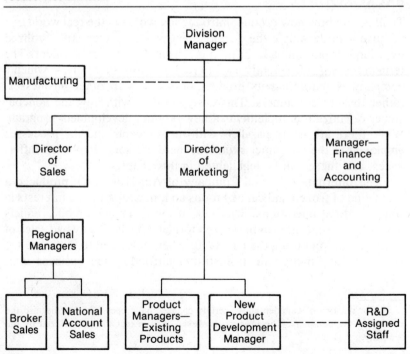

product department as part of the marketing group. The department consisted of a manager and a marketing assistant. In addition, the foodservice division had a "dotted-line" reporting relationship over two research and development staff members located at the company's central research facility. The organization of the foodservice division is shown in Figure 28–1.

ORGANIZING FOR NEW PRODUCT DEVELOPMENT

IFC had a strong commitment throughout its organization to growth through new product development. It recognized that a successful new product development program was more than the result of understanding or implementing a step-by-step process. In particular, the company's top management recognized the importance of organization and cultural factors and, thus, any discussion of the new product planning process needs to be understood in the context of these elements. Figure 28–2 illustrates the critical components as described in a presentation made by the company during an annual shareholders' meeting.

FIGURE 28–2
Critical Components of New Product Programs:
Organization + Process = Success

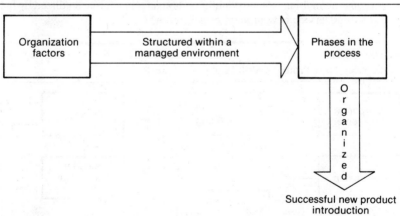

With regard to organization, the company stated that there are four requirements that need to be present in order to stimulate successful new product planning programs. These were listed as:

1. A strong commitment by corporate management to fund a new product planning program on a *sustained basis* with an adequate budget for both prototype development costs and staff costs.

2. A fundamental belief in the marketing concept. This meant, in particular, that the company would utilize a professional marketing research approach throughout its new product development process in order to meet real customer needs. In addition, the company would support both the test marketing step and the full market launch of a new product with appropriate levels of marketing spending. (Frequently the failure to make the commitments at the "back end" have negated what otherwise would have been a successful new product. Fortunately, most industrial or nonconsumer products require a much smaller financial commitment to launch than do consumer products.)

3. The creation of a distinct and separate organizational unit. This was viewed as an absolute requirement for executing a new product development program. In a sense, developing new products is a "tomorrow" type of activity, which if not separated from the "today" businesses and activities, will never get the priority and constant attention it requires. (This is true in both consumer companies and in nonconsumer firms. The legendary success of such companies as Texas Instruments and 3M, to mention just two, has frequently been attributed to these firms' ability and willingness to create a separate "entrepreneurial" type of environment in order to foster the new product development process.) IFC recognized this factor and authorized the creation of the separate new product group within the foodservice division, albeit a small one.

4. Lastly, successful new product planning and development programs require the ability to bring a multidisciplinary team together at various times during the process. Shown below is a diagram [Figure 28–3] illustrating the multidisciplinary/multifunctional team approach utilized by the IFC foodservice new product organization.

FIGURE 28–3
Foodservice New Products Multifunctional Team

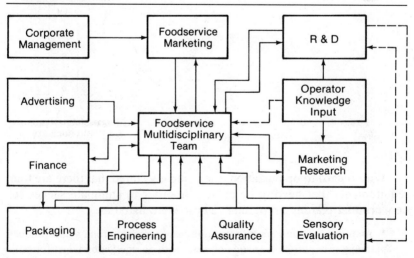

A STRATEGIC APPROACH TO NEW PRODUCT DEVELOPMENT

With these organizational factors in mind, IFC summarized the new product planning and development process as shown in the Figure 28–4.

FIGURE 28–4
International Foodservice Company's Strategic New Product Planning Program

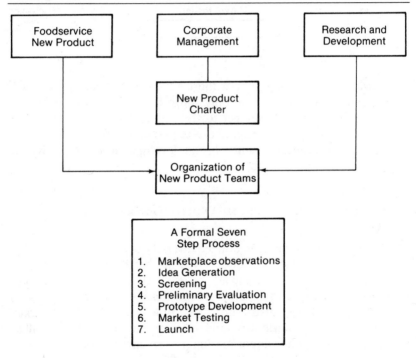

Another way to illustrate IFC's philosophy was the reference frequently made by the company that it used a "funnel approach."

Integral to the process of new product development is the requirement for developing a large flow of ideas, some of which ultimately can be translated into concepts for subsequent screening and evaluation. Further, it was recognized that only a few ideas would ever make it to market. IFC, in its planning for new products, acknowledged the nature of this funnel process. In one of the company's presentations to shareholders (referred to earlier), this was illustrated by the diagram shown in Figure 28–5.

FIGURE 28–5
International Foodservice Company's Funnel Approach to Idea Generation

Process Step	Timing required	Description	Typical results
1	Continuous	Marketplace observations	100 problems/needs
2	Continuous	Idea generation	60 ideas
3	A few weeks	Screening	15-20 potential projects
4	2-4 weeks	Preliminary evaluation	7-15 projects
5	3-12 weeks	Prototype development	5-7 prototypes
6	Minimum 3 months	Market testing	3-5 products in marketing
7	2-4 months	Launch	1-2 successful new products

It will be noted that each of these seven steps takes an idea and further refines or rejects it so only those few ideas with the highest probability for success ever get to the stage of development, where commitments of cost and capital are required. We will now see how this seven-step process resulted in the development of an innovative new foodservice product for IFC.

Steps One and Two: Marketplace Observations and Idea Generation

The IFC foodservice division utilized a variety of approaches to gather new product ideas for the foodservice market it was attempting to serve. In particular, the company believed strongly in utilizing data from the marketplace to supplement the ideas generated by company personnel, customers, distributors, and other such sources. Marketplace input came primarily from the operator interviews, which will be described below. Other important input areas are also detailed.

1. *Operator data.* To stay abreast of operator attitudes, the company periodically conducted both personal interviews and focus-group interviews with operator representatives of the various segments of foodservice. These interviews were designed both to probe "unmet needs" and to expose operators to potential new product concepts under evaluation by the company.

2. *Market data.* This area concerned itself with identifying and tracking trends taking place in the various market segments of foodservice.

3. *Environmental inputs.* The company's corporate market research department subscribed to various syndicated services that alerted the company to changes in the overall economic environment and demographic changes of interest. In addition, research input was available to

keep the company aware of changing lifestyles and provide an early identification of noteworthy trends versus those that were merely fads.

4. *Technological innovations.* An additional dimension of input came
from the company's technical personnel at the central R&D laboratory
who were responsible for monitoring and developing applications for new
technology. While the company's business was primarily in frozen foods,
the firm maintained an awareness and interest in all food processing and
packaging developments that might affect IFC, including canning, freez-
ing, aseptic packaging, and irradiation of foods, to mention just a few.

As a result of these four input sources, the company generated
numerous new product ideas during the course of each fiscal year.
What we would like to do now is to describe how one of the ideas
developed during this process moved through each of the subsequent
steps.

The Retortable Tray (or "Flat" Can) Project. The idea for a new
foodservice package resulted from a combination of inputs, including
marketplace operator needs and technological innovation. At the time
of the case, energy costs were becoming a major factor to the foodservice operator. Furthermore, the market had recognized for some products the superior quality offered by frozen foods and, thus, was willing
to pay a premium for such items. Currently, IFC offered a line of
frozen entrées to foodservice. The product available included such
items as beef stew, macaroni and cheese, chili, and lasagna—just a few
of the best sellers. Similar canned products were available in a large
foodservice size can referred to in the industry as a #10 can. Each can
held approximately 100+ ounces of product. Because the canning
process required the application of heat for sterilization, some product
deterioration took place in the canning process. The same distinction in
quality was present in the consumer product area, since the difference
in quality between a canned entrée and a frozen entrée, in large part, is
what created the success of "TV dinners." It was at this time that the
R&D personnel assigned to foodservice product development became
interested in the concept of the retortable tray, or "flat" can. The flat
can was, in fact, nothing more than a shallow tray which held the same
contents as a #10 can. However, because the dimensions and shape of
the tray were thinner, it enabled the product to be retorted in a much
shorter time, thus claiming to offer an advantage over traditional processed products and to provide product quality approaching what was
offered by frozen. Further, since the product itself was "shelf-stable,"
no refrigeration or frozen handling was required through the distribution process. To the foodservice operator, this meant the product
would not have to tie up valuable freezer space. Thus, as a result of
simultaneous inputs from the market, the operator, and the company's

R&D group, the idea for a line of retortable tray foodservice entrées was initiated. We will now trace how this new product idea moved forward through each of the succeeding steps.

Step Three: Screening Step

This step is normally accomplished by taking each of the new product ideas and "screening" them against a set of preestablished criteria. The kind of criteria utilized by the IFC foodservice division is shown in Figure 28–6.

FIGURE 28–6
International Foodservice Company's Screening Criteria

Market Factors	Population
• Size of market	• Compatibility with existing
• Growth	production skills
• Competitive environment	• Risks
• Distribution fit	
• Sales force fit	*Financial*
• Image fit	• Capital required
	• Projected profitability

The concept of the flat can passed this step with ease, so it then became appropriate to advance the product idea to the next stage of the process—the preliminary evaluation step.

Step Four: Preliminary Evaluation Step

The company had a well-established practice of having multiple ideas under consideration at the same time. Twice a year it would fund a major market research effort. Normally, this effort consisted of taking the various concepts that had passed the screening step to foodservice operators in both a focus-group and individual-interview setting. As mentioned earlier, this market research approach was also utilized to generate ideas that would later be developed into concepts. Among those concepts exposed to operators during one of these market research probes was the concept of the retortable tray. A description of the concept as it was presented to operators is shown in Figure 28–7.

These interviews, which were conducted by a consulting firm experienced in the foodservice market, were used to provide a variety of inputs useful to the company in understanding how this new product concept would be viewed by operators. During the interviews, the

FIGURE 28–7
Concept Description of Retortable Tray ("Flat Can")

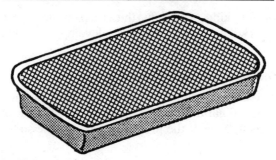

- "Tin" material
- Same guage or strength as a #10 can
- Either steam table or half steam table size

operators were probed about their attitudes toward both canned and frozen items, the reasons for using or not using such products, and, of course, their specific reactions to the concept of the flat can. Furthermore, the consultant was able to provide data on the size of the existing canned and frozen entrée market, so the company would make a judgment regarding its potential revenue opportunity from the proposed product line. In particular, these interviews contributed to refining the concept in terms of such elements as:

- Perceived operator benefits.
- Potential problems or issues relating to use of the product.
- Initial reactions to pricing.

In addition to gaining this marketplace input, during this step the company's new product development staff also began to evaluate other aspects of the potential product line. These included the gathering of information on capital requirements, time required for tooling, potential issues relating to compliance with various regulatory agencies, and a host of other nonmarketing factors. Preliminary financial pro formas were developed so estimates of likely gross margin could be made at varying proposed selling price levels. At the completion of this step, the flat can project was compared and contrasted with other potential new product ideas. This evaluation included consideration of such factors as:

- Total size of the projected market.
- Identification of likely competitive environment.
- Likely share to be obtained by the company.

- Potential profitability and return on investment.
- Degree of technical/production risk associated with the project.
- Overall assessment of financial reward to risk ratio.

Based on this kind of review, the company decided to move the product line forward into the prototype development step.

Step Five: The Prototype Development Step

Most of the activities within this step were of a production, operational, or technical nature. The company contracted for the pilot production of 10,000 cases of the proposed product line so a limited mar-

---

FIGURE 28–8
Product Features/Benefits Retortable Tray ("Flat Can") and What Various Foodservice Entrées Would Be Available

---

Preparation:
  Can be placed directly on steam table for heating or is heatable with any existing system and is fully warmed in a short time period (10 to 20 minutes).
Manufacturing process provides:
  - Better, firmer solids.
  - Avoids overcooking.
  - Less breakdown.
  - Allows larger chunks.
Features benefits:
  - *Storage:*
    — Stacking capability allows better utilization of shelf space.
    — Does not require valuable freezer space.
    — Shelf life comparable to canned.
  - *Durability and ruggedness:*
    — Resistant to puncturing/crumbling during storage handling, reconstitution, and use.
  - *Disposability:*
    — Can be compacted
  - *Size*
    — ½ steam table trays
    — Full steam table trays
    — Smaller sizes
  - *Opening*
    — Manual can opener
  - *Pricing*
    — This package would be priced at less than most frozen products but slightly higher than conventional canned goods, on a cost-per-serving basis.

ket test could be accomplished. The prototype development step also provided the company with the opportunity to refine its cost estimates and make the needed decisions concerning specific product formulation (i.e., meat to sauce ratios, and so on). In a sense, this step was used to prove the operational, technical, and cost feasibility of the proposed product. Obviously if the company could not execute the product on a prototype basis, no further development would take place. To the extent regulatory approvals are required, this prototype step provides the vehicle for submitting samples to the appropriate agencies. In IFC's case, the prototype development stage went smoothly, although a period of almost six months was required before the 10,000-case lot was available for test marketing.

Step Six: Market Testing Step

While the prior step was almost totally nonmarketing in nature, this step is almost 100 percent the reverse. Within this market test step, the company hoped to answer several important questions concerning the flat cans. Many of these same questions were dealt with in a preliminary fashion during step 4. Given the importance of "being right," these same issues were dealt with again in this step to validate the assumptions that have a major impact upon the company's commitment to the new product line. Among the important ones were the following:

- Which market segments would find this new product of greatest interest?
- What problems, if any, would be encountered in using the new product? Opening the can? Heating the contents? Disposing of the can?
- What instructions should be provided to train operators to utilize this product so neither undercooking or overcooking would take place?
- How would operators compare the taste, texture, and color of the final product from the flat can with that available from canned or frozen alternatives?
- Would a premium price higher than canned prices be justified? Would the buyers pay the same price as for frozen? Or considerably more?

To accomplish these objectives, the company utilized a two-part test approach. Part one consisted of taking small quantities to representative operators in each of the potential market segments so a first-hand market reaction could be obtained. Trained interviewers, along with company sales personnel, were present to ensure that the operator was instructed in how to use the product and also to gain a thoroughly objective understanding of their reaction. The second part of the test consisted of selecting a small geographic area (Fort Wayne) and then introducing the product line in that market in what would be described as a normal new product mode; namely, distributors were contacted and distribution arranged, and company sales personnel supported by direct mail and targeted trade advertising directly approached operators to sell them the new product line. During the first selling wave, the company priced the product based on its judgment resulting from the input received from the prior steps. It became obvious during the early stages that a price somewhere between frozen and canned might be achieved but that parity with frozen was not likely. Among the purposes for this part of the market test was to determine the difficulty of the selling tasks, the level of introductory marketing spending that likely would be required, and other such input necessary

---

FIGURE 28–9
Outline of the Marketing Plan for the Retortable Tray

---

1. Description of product line.
    — Breadth of line.
    — Quality level.
    — Pricing.
2. Target segments for the product line.
3. Projected competitive environment.
4. Statement of objectives—quantitative and qualitative.
    — First year, volume and profits.
    — Second year, volume and profits.
    — Third–fifth year, volume and profits.
5. Strategies and tactics.
    — Geographic roll-out.
    — Pricing strategy.
    — Sales program.
    — Marketing, advertising, and communication program.
    — Distribution.
6. Implementation details.
    — What, when, who.
7. Financial and organizational aspects.
    — Objectives.
    — Capital (fixed and working).
    — Staffing needs.
    — Timing.
    — Risks.
8. Appendix.
    — Supporting details.

to complete the preparation of marketing plan for the new product line. A sense of the issues can be obtained by considering the outline of the new product marketing plan shown in Figure 28–9.

Step Seven: Marketing Launch Step

The last step in introducing a new nonconsumer product typically is to go from the small market test to "national roll-out." The opportunity to go from a single market to a national program may or may not be possible as often in the consumer situation as it is in the nonconsumer one. Normally, the geographic differences that exist in the consumer situation do not apply for nonconsumer products or services. Thus, with the knowledge gained from the prior steps and the strategy and tactics outlined in the company's marketing plan, this product was successfully introduced. Because of the frequent and objective inputs received by management during the various steps, the company's expectations for this product were realistic, and, thus, while the product has not achieved volumes equal to either the canned or the frozen counterparts, it has, within the targeted operator segments, achieved its volume and profit objectives. The company continues to monitor packaging and processing technology, since this new product also provides a potentially valuable hedge against a technological threat to the company's core business, which is so heavily tied to the frozen food processing and distribution systems.

SUMMARY

As we have illustrated by this case, the successful introduction of a nonconsumer product parallels in both philosophy and execution that required for a new consumer product. The major differences are that, usually, the consumer new product process takes longer, involves more risk, requires more research, and exposes the company to a more major marketing support commitment starting with the test market step. For most nonconsumer or industrial products, the market potential is just as sizable as that available to consumer marketers. Realization of this fact, coupled with the successful experience of a growing number of industrial firms, should give input to increased interest in formalizing the new development process in an increasing number of nonconsumer organizations.

Part 3

LEGAL ASPECTS OF MARKETING

29

THE LAW'S IMPACT ON MARKETING

by
Ray O. Werner

Colorado College

Dominant among the proverbial millstones marketers must wear are government regulations. Yet while it is obvious that statutes, decisions of administrative agencies, and court decisions restrain their freedom to act, their relative inability to alter those regulations leads marketing managers to relegate them to a place of secondary importance. Only part of this attitude is valid. For while positioning of the product may be subject to more direct control than the content of regulations, knowledge of the constraints of the marketing institution is vital to the successful operation of the institutions.

Of equal importance with a working knowledge of the laws governing marketing is the recognition by effective marketers that they must have access to competent legal counsel. Access is imperative not only because of the complexities of frequently changing regulations but also because of the increasing litigiousness of the contemporary society within which marketing must operate. One case that is lost through inadvertent violation of law or ignorance of governing court precedents may prove to be far more costly than the retention of adequate counsel.

The speed with which regulatory process changes is but one of the new conditions governing the law's impact on the marketing institution. The accelerating shift of the nature of production from creation of physical goods to the provision of intangible services has required reinterpretation of the law. The rights and duties which the law impose has changed and will continue to change as the economy changes.

The basic economic doctrine underlying the legal regulation of marketing is workable competition. Legislators, administrators, and judges all adopt the premise that, if the economy can be maintained as workably competitive, the legitimate ends of the economy of low prices, high-quality products, and innovation can be so furthered that the consumer's needs and wants are effectively met. Yet while this premise is accepted, growing regulation gives the lie to the changing nature of competition in the United States.

Studies of competitive trends in the United States indicate that at least since 1939 the economy has become more competitive both in the aggregate and in every major sector of the economy. Whereas in 1939 the economy was considered to be just over 50 percent effectively competitive, by 1980 the economy was over 75 percent effectively competitive. And in the growing sectors of services, wholesale and retail trade, and finance, insurance, and real estate the growth in effective competition is as great as or greater than that for the entire economy. Only in the transportation and public utilities sector, widely granted monopoly powers by government, is the competitive share of any sector less than 50 percent.[1] What these facts emphasize is that marketers operate in an environment in which rivalry between sellers is the norm. Not only does this result *from* the law's impact, it conditions the way in which marketers may utilize legal regulations to be successfully competitive.

The significant regulations impinging on marketing do not often involve Constitutional interpretation. Advertising may give rise to questions of the scope of the First Amendment's protection of free speech; sanctions for violations of laws may present issues of the Constitutional amendments governing legal procedure and due process; statutory regulations may raise questions of enumerated Congressional powers under Article I of the Constitution. But usually the legal issues involving marketers arise under statutes or court decisions.

Because different theories may be adopted by different lawyers, judges, or scholars to determine the meaning of a statute, the interpretation of statutes can be ambiguous and confusing. First, interpretation may be based on the intention of the legislators who adopted the act. Given the diversity of rationales of most laws, and the fact that compromise predominates and unanswered questions abound, this is a tenuous—though nevertheless adopted—method of discovering what rights and duties a law imposes. Second, interpretation, ignoring legis-

---

[1] William G. Shepherd, "Causes of Increased Competition in the U.S. Economy, 1939–1980," *The Review of Economics and Statistics,* November 1982, pp. 613–26.

lative hearings and debates, may attempt to discover the accepted meaning of the words of the statute. This semantic thicket, however, may lead to distortions, such as developed in the famous *Standard Oil* case, in 1911,[2] in which legislative prohibitions of "every restraint of trade" was reinterpreted to mean "every *unreasonable* restraint of trade." Third, interpretation may be derived from what Spaeth has called "logical analysis."[3] This theory of interpretation involves a syllogism—a major premise, a minor premise, and a conclusion derived from the premises. Although tests of logical adequacy exist, there is no guarantee that the resulting conclusion will be appropriate or even sensible. Finally, there is an adaptive theory of interpretation which extends the meaning of a statute to new circumstances that develop. Illustrative of this is the current controversy about the possibility that intercorporate business practices may constitute an illegal conspiracy. Given, however, four possible theories of statutory construction, the inevitable conclusion is that even the best counsel cannot be sure what a court will hold a given statute "means" when it applies it in a specific case or controversy.

There is, then, considerable uncertainty surrounding the interpretation of a statute. In a judicial system comprised of state and federal courts with several levels of appelate jurisdiction at each level of government, this uncertainty is compounded. Different courts may apply different theories of interpretation; conflicts may arise. Courts may, upon grounds they consider adequate, reverse decisions. Final resolution can only be accomplished by appeal to the United States Supreme Court—and even here total consistency is not the rule. In addition, only a small number of the myriad of cases can be considered by the Supreme Court and the changing membership of the Court does not contribute to clarity of regulations through time. Some consolation can be derived from the Court's propensity to uphold—or at least tailor decisions to—precedents of the Court.

Yet the conclusion for marketers is inescapable. Statutes, administrative agency decisions, and court decisions, uncertain though they may be, provide the boundaries within which marketers may legally compete. The advice of a knowledgeable, aggressive, and current lawyer is a sine qua non of successful marketing. Even this can not guarantee that the dynamism of the economy and the ambiguity of the regulatory system will not clash.

---

[2] *Standard Oil Company of New Jersey* v. *United States,* 221 U.S. 1 (1911).

[3] Harold J. Spaeth, *An Introduction to Supreme Court Decision Making,* rev. ed. (San Francisco: Chandler Publishing, 1972), p. 49.

USING MARKETING LAWS TO GAIN A MARKET ADVANTAGE

Gaining a market advantage by the use of marketing laws rests on the assumption that competitors lack either the knowledge or the ability to use the laws equally well. As marketing knowledge becomes more widely understood, this assumption may become increasingly suspect. Yet there is some ability to use regulations, equally applicable to all competitors, with maximum effectiveness to attain the institution's goals.

If marketing can be described accurately as those activities that successfully relate an organization to its environment by identifying unmet needs, and then developing, pricing, distributing, and promoting those goods and services that meet those needs,[4] then legal regulations may be useful servants. For the law does provide for a variety of developmental techniques (e.g., tax incentives for research and development, the deduction of market research expenses in determining tax liability) to ascertain the unmet needs. Developing the appropriate marketing organization, be it an integrated production and distribution network or a franchising operation, is accorded wide legal latitude. Pricing is subject to many legal forms, not all of which serve equally well for each product or service. Trademarks, copyrights, and patents afford legal protections of unique elements that might otherwise be unfairly exploited in a cutthroat environment. Legal procedures, such as restraining orders issued by administrative agencies, such as the Federal Trade Commission or the Food and Drug Administration, or injunctions secured from the courts may be used to protect valid property rights.

In short, the laws relating to marketing should be thought of as facilitating the organization, the operations, and the procedures of the institution. They should not be thought of as an adversarial weapon to gain an advantage over an otherwise worthy competitor. However, once more, it should be recognized that the law is a restraining influence and may, therefore, frustrate the marketing manager who visualizes an imaginative innovation only to discover that it cannot be adopted.

HISTORY AND BACKGROUND OF LAWS ON MARKETING

Prior to 1890, the regulations governing marketing—especially contracts—were the principles of the common law. Contract law and the

---

[4] See G. David Hughes, *Marketing Management: A Planning Approach* (Reading, Mass.: Addison-Wesley Publishing, 1978), p. 3.

body of interpretive judicial precedents still remain today. But to this body of legal holdings, statutes of great importance have been added. The statutes have emerged from the Industrial Revolution in the United States in the 19th century, the growth of large business units of national scope, the political movements of the Progressive and the Populists, and the increasing role of the relatively impersonal corporate form of organization. The growth of the American economy, its expanding complexity, and more recently the development of the consumerist movement have all contributed to the laws regulating marketing in the United States. Nor should the importance of war in changing the regulatory movement in the United States be neglected.[5] Speculation about the fundamental psychological and sociological forces that underlay these movements have proliferated, but what is important here is to recognize the expansion of the laws governing marketing.[6]

The Statutes Regulating Marketing

Since marketing is an all-encompassing activity, the probabilities are high that no listing of the statutes influencing it will be totally comprehensive. Nor does this listing of the relevant acts aspire to such completeness. (This listing will indicate the major acts this author believes every marketer should know and will indicate the scope and coverage of the acts.) Five volumes of the Commerce Clearing House's *Trade Regulation Reports* can be consulted for the extensive laws, regulations, and procedures which augment this selective listing.[7]

Categorization of the basic acts affecting marketing is capricious. Many of the acts are omnibus and, therefore, do not lend themselves to placing in a single category. Other acts, though seeming to fall in a single category, have implications for other categories of acts. Consequently, a chronological listing of the basic acts provides a logical development which additionally indicates the evolving and expansionary pattern of the laws.

The Sherman Antitrust Act. Adopted in 1890 in the historical period alluded to as the "robber baron" period, this act provides that

---

[5] A voluminous background study is by Merle Fainsod, Lincoln Gordon, and Joseph C. Palamountain, Jr., *Government and the American Economy,* 3d ed. (New York: W. W. Norton, 1959).

[6] Illustrative is the interesting selection from a larger work by Joseph Schumpeter, *Can Capitalism Survive?* (New York: Harper & Row, 1978).

[7] Commerce Clearing House, *Trade Regulation Reports,* 5 vols. (Chicago: Commerce Clearing House, current). Also worth consulting is Bureau of National Affairs, *Antitrust & Trade Regulation Report* (Washington, D.C.: Bureau of National Affairs, current).

"[e]very contract, combination in the form of trust or otherwise, or conspiracy, in restraint of trade . . . is hereby declared to be illegal." Subsequently interpreted to cover only "unreasonable" restraints of trade, it was not until 1926, in the famous *Trenton Potteries* case,[8] that the United States Supreme Court modified its 1911 interpretation and held that all restraints of trade were illegal. The reinforcement of this holding, although seemingly repudiated in the *Appalachian Coals* case[9] reflecting an adaptive approach held appropriate to the economic chaos of the Great Depression, was the famous *Socony-Vacuum* case[10] of 1940. There the Court rendered its still generally definitive statement: "Under the Sherman Act, a combination formed for the purpose and with the effect of raising, depressing, fixing, pegging, or stabilizing the price of a commodity in interstate or foreign commerce is illegal *per se*." Moreover, the Court found the offense in the "character of the restraint," not in the amount of trade involved. Explicitly it declared that "the law does not permit an inquiry into the reasonableness of price-fixing agreements." Since that time the Court has uniformly held to its per se rule against price fixing, although some commentators find in the case of the *American Society of Composers, Authors and Publishers*,[11] involving blanket licenses to entertainment companies at fixed fees by copyright holders, a weakening of the per se rule. However, the unusual factual situation of that case leads to the conclusion that the *ASCAP* case, as the *Appalachian Coals* case, represents an aberration and that the current meaning of Section 1 of the Sherman Act is that no direct price-fixing will be looked upon favorably by the judicial system.

Practices other than price fixing that might be held to violate Section 1 of the Sherman Act are not treated with such an unyielding attitude. Thus, a territorial allocation system (an agreement by which one firm imposes nonpricing restraints in product marketing on the activities of a firm at another level of distribution)[12] is not uniformly held to constitute a per se violation of Section 1. In 1967, in the *Arnold, Schwinn* case,[13] the Supreme Court ruled that "where a manufacturer *sells* products to his distributor subject to territorial restrictions upon

---

[8] *United States* v. *Trenton Potteries Co.*, 273 U.S. 392 (1917).

[9] *Appalachian Coals, Inc.* v. *United States*, 288 U.S. 344 (1933).

[10] *United States* v. *Socony-Vacuum Oil Co.*, 310 U.S. 150 (1940).

[11] *American Society of Composers, Authors and Publishers, et al.* v. *Columbia Broadcasting System, et al.*, 441 U.S. 1 (1979).

[12] For an extensive analysis of the case law and the theory of territorial restrictions, see John F. Cady, "Reasonable Rules and Rules of Reason: Vertical Restrictions on Distributors," *Journal of Marketing* 46 (Summer 1982), 27–37.

[13] *United States* v. *Arnold, Schwinn & Co.*, 388 U.S. 365 (1967).

resale, a *per se* violation of the Sherman Acts results.'' (Italics in original). Territorial restrictions on wholesaling were condemned in the *Topco* case in 1972.[14]

However, in a case indicating the uncertainty that faces a market confronting the laws regulating marketing, the Supreme Court, in the *Continental TV–GTE Sylvania* case,[15] explicitly reversed its prior holdings, declaring that ''we conclude that the per se rule stated in *Schwinn* must be overruled'' and ''that the appropriate decision is to return to the rule of reason that governed vertical restriction prior to *Schwinn*.'' In its analysis of the *Sylvania* case, the Court embraced the position that the standard ''traditionally'' applied for the majority of non-price-fixing restraints under Section 1 of the Sherman Act was the rule of reason.

Tying contracts are also subject to attack under Section 1 of the Sherman Act. A tying contract is simply an agreement that, if a firm wishes to acquire one product or service, it must purchase another distinct product or service. Two requirements must be met for a tying contract to be found illegal: (1) the firm imposing the contract must have substantial power over the tying product which power may arise from either monopoly or otherwise ''sufficient'' power over it, or from the product's uniqueness and (2) the effect of the contract must foreclose the market to other sellers substantially, although courts have been very lenient in determining what constitutes substantiality.

The importance of tying contracts is closely related to franchising. Typically a franchisor provides a franchisee a license to place a trademarked or copyrighted product or service on the market. The franchisor receives, in return, fees or royalties in exchange for the right to adopt the franchisor's identity and to use its business methods. The franchisor may also provide related products used in marketing the franchised product (e.g., packaging supplies, spices, and cookers might be provided by a fast-food chicken outlet in exchange for use of the logo and tradename of the franchisor). A contract, however, that *requires* the franchisee to purchase non-unique supplies as a condition for use of the franchise constitutes a tying contract which is a violation of Section 1. Not even the franchisor's desire to preserve ''distinctiveness, uniformity, and quality of its product'' constitutes a reasonable justification for the restriction.[16]

Although marketers generally argue that marketing practices should be analyzed under a rule of reason, uncertainty about the legal-

---

[14] *United States* v. *Topco Associates, Inc.*, 405 U.S. 596 (1972).

[15] *Continental T.V., Inc., et al.* v. *GTE Sylvania, Inc.*, 433 U.S. 36 (1977).

[16] The Supreme Court's prevailing opinion is found in *Siegel* v. *Chicken Delight, Inc.*, 448 F. 2d (CA-9, 1971) *cert. den.* 405 U.S. 955 (1972).

ity of marketing practices results from this position. For the rule of reason requires judicial inquiry to answer the question of whether specific practices have either "redeeming virtue" or exert a "pernicious effect on competition." Both history and contemporary journalism provide ample evidence of the extent of the differences by which specific activities are judged to meet standards of redeeming virtue and pernicious effect. If final determination involves the definitive decision of a jury, certainty becomes increasingly evanescent.

Conclusions about Section 1 of the Sherman Act, somewhat subject to constant change, do seem subject to generalization useful to the marketer. First, activities that fix prices through joint action are per se violative of Section 1. The wise marketer simply shuns all such behavior, for the Court finds it totally destructive of a competitive system. Second, other restraints under Section 1 are generally subject to analysis of the rule of reason which contributes to uncertainty in marketing planning, especially when new procedures are under consideration.

Section 2 of the Sherman Act prohibits monopolization or attempts to monopolize. Under current law violation of Section 2, as Section 1, is a felony with fines of up to $500,000 for an individual violation and up to $1 million for firms. However, for many firms after 1890, prosecutions under Section 2 (largely because of the emasculation of the Section by the application to it of the rule of reason of Section 1 enunciated in 1911) were virtually nonexistent.

The first of several landmark decisions under Section 2 of the Sherman Act was the *Alcoa* decision[17] in 1945. Although the decision rendered by the Circuit Court of Appeals for the Second Circuit was in lieu of the Supreme Court because of a technicality, it is the leading precedent. The decision demonstrates that the first requirement in a monopolization case is the delimitation of the product and the geographic market. The definition of the product market, virgin aluminum, caused little difficulty in this case and the geographic market easily was found to be national. The significance is found in the court's broad argument that the fairness of profits and the progressiveness of the firm were irrelevant in excusing it from monopolistic control of 90 percent of production in the relevant market. The court found the intent to monopolize inherent in the fact that "[N]o monopolist monopolizes unconscious of what he is doing" and, therefore, returned the case to the district court for a consistent remedy.[18] The salient points are (1)

---

[17] *United States* v. *Aluminum Co. of America,* U.S. Circuit Court of Appeals, Second Circuit, 148 F. 2d 416 (1945).

[18] Remedial provisions were minimal because of the changes that had occurred in the industry during World War II. The district court held that new firms in the United States built to fight the war could, if jurisdiction were retained by the district court, guarantee a non-monopolistic market.

that the existence of monopoly power was found to reside in the percentage of the relevant market controlled and (2) in the court's refusal to excuse monopoly power for economic reasons observing that monopoly is undesirable "based upon the belief that great industrial consolidations are inherently undesirable, regardless of their economic results."

In 1956, the Supreme Court, in the famous *Du Pont* "cellophane case,"[19] approached the question of monopolization differently. It did not ask the percentage of the cellophane production that was controlled by Du Pont; it asked what percentage of the product sales was controlled by Du Pont. To do this, the court defined the product market in terms of the *buyer's* perceptions of substitutable products and concluded that, since buyers believed the product market was "flexible packaging materials," and since Du Pont's share was less than 20 percent, monopoly power did not exist. But the marketer must be very careful to note this argument hinges on the nature of demand, while *Alcoa* revolved about control of supply.

In 1966, the issue of monopoly received its clearest statement when the Supreme Court decided the *Grinnell* case.[20] Despite some questionable arguments about the nature of the product and geographical markets peculiar to the case, the Court outlined the essence of the monopolization offense, declaring: "The offense of monopoly under Section 1 of the Sherman Act has two elements: (1) the possession of monopoly power in the relevant market and (2) the willful acquisition or maintenance of that power as distinguished from growth or development as a consequence of a superior product, business acumen, or historic accident. . . ."

When the Clayton Act was adopted in 1914, specific definition was given to "antitrust laws" and the Sherman Act was included. This made possible individual suits under restraint of trade and monopolization provisions of the Sherman Act and, under Section 4 of the Clayton Act, "any person who shall be injured in his business or property by reason of anything forbidden in the antitrust laws" may, upon proof, recover not only cost of the suit (including a "reasonable" attorney's fee) but treble the amount of damages sustained. Hence marketers must be constantly alert to the possibility that, although the cases cited here all involved the government's prosecution of the suit, private actions are possible and violations carry a severe penalty.

The Pure Food and Drug Act. Marketers experienced a turn from the general regulation of industrial structure and coercive behavior of

---

[19] *United States* v. *du Pont de Nemours & Co.*, 351 U.S. 377 (1956).
[20] *United States* v. *Grinnell Corp.*, 384 U.S. 563 (1966).

the Sherman Act when this 1906 act was adopted. Directed at the prohibition of the marketing of misbranded or adulterated food and drugs in interstate commerce (now enforced through powers granted to the Food and Drug Administration created in 1931), this act reflects how powerful public opinion may influence marketing. Impetus for Congressional adoption of the act came, in no small part, from Upton Sinclair's muckraking book, *The Jungle*.[21] Yet autonomy of marketers has never been the same since the powerful public outcry Sinclair evoked and the pointed Congressional response.

The Food and Drug Administration has both inspection and clearance powers. Each year it inspects a large fraction of the drug establishments and the food establishments in the United States.[22] It also certifies new drugs as safe and effective after meeting the testing conditions it develops. It also monitors sales of prescription drugs and evaluates and prohibits food adulteration when found. The extent of the FDA's powers is great and, although there is extensive debate about the standards it should employ in monitoring foods and drugs, marketers who produce or distribute foods and drugs would be totally lacking in discretion if they failed to consult and comply with the FDA's applicable procedures and standards.

In 1938, the coverage of the original Pure Food and Drug Act was extended by the Federal Food, Drug, and Cosmetic Act. Definitions of adulteration and misbranding were strengthened and the act was broadened to empower the FDA to regulate medical devices and cosmetics.[23]

The Clayton Act. In 1914, Congress extended its attempt to assure a workable competitive economy when it adopted the Clayton Act. In addition to broadening the coverage of the act to include possibility of private suits, the act also increased the list of the practices which were prohibited. The result was, as had been the prevailing practice, limitation on methods that marketers could adopt.

Four practices were subjected to regulation in the Clayton Act. For marketers, probably the most important practice outlawed is the use of tying contracts and, in some specific cases, exclusive dealing arrangements. Although tying contracts and exclusive dealing arrangements

---

[21] Upton Sinclair, *The Jungle* (New York: Doubleday, Page, 1906).

[22] Shepherd and Wilcox estimate that the FDA inspects approximately half of all drug establishments and one third of the food establishments yearly. With a staff of 7,500 and a limited budget, it is not surprising to find that the FDA encounters real difficulty in enforcing all its powers fully. See William C. Shepherd and Clair Wilcox, *Public Policies Toward Business*, 6th ed. (Homewood, Ill.: Richard D. Irwin, 1979), p. 542.

[23] The definitions are found in *Topical Law Reports*, vol. 4 (Chicago: Commerce Clearing House, 1983). This volume also includes texts of the statutes discussed in this chapter and the provisions of the extensive state laws that may be applicable.

are prohibited only in those cases involving "commodities," court interpretations have extended the prohibitions to cover "services" by utilizing Section 1 of the Sherman Act and Section 5 of the Federal Trade Commission Act.[24] A tying contract, as has been noted, is a legally enforceable agreement whereby a purchaser or lessee buys or leases one commodity on the condition that another commodity be purchased or leased. The threshold question, therefore, becomes the existence of two separate commodities,[25] but this requirement does not often limit the application of the act. The additional requirement is that the agreement *may* have the effect of *substantially* lessening competition or *tending* to create a monopoly "in any line of commerce."[26] The extent to which marketers have been constrained by the denial of the use of tying contracts can readily be inferred from the earlier allusion[27] to the limitation on franchiser's ability to condition the franchise on the purchase of supplies and accessories.

An illegal tying contract requires that the marketer imposing the contract have "sufficient economic power with respect to the tying product to appreciably restrain free competition in the market for the tied product and a 'not insubstantial' amount of interstate commerce is affect."[28] Courts have found the "sufficient economic power" in the monopoly a patent conveys, in the uniqueness of a product, or in the price advantage conveyed by economic power.[29] Marketers can only infer that to condition an otherwise illegal tying contract on lack of sufficient economic power over the tying product is, at best, dubious.

Exclusive dealing arrangements, usually implemented by requirements contracts, may also violate the Clayton Act. A requirements contract provides that a supplier will deliver needed goods or services of a buyer and that the buyer will use only the specified commodities of the contracting supplier. Clearly there are marketing advantages to both the buyer and seller of such a contract—and ultimately by reduc-

---

[24] The Federal Trade Commission Act is discussed later in this chapter.

[25] *Times-Picayune Publishing Company, et al.* v. *United States,* 345 U.S. 594 (1953) hinged on the issue of two commodities.

[26] The requirement that the effect *may* be to lessen competition is commonly known as the "incipiency doctrine." Proof that lessening either *will* or *has* occurred is not required. Nor does the Court entertain proof on a post-contractual basis that lessening did not, in fact, occur. Only the probability is relevant. In the same way, marketers can take little satisfaction from the requirement that "substantial" lessening must occur. This has been very narrowly interpreted by the courts. See *International Salt Co.* v. *United States,* 332 U.S. 392 (1947).

[27] See *Siegel* v. *Chicken Delight* (footnote 16).

[28] *Northern Pacific Railway Co.* v. *United States,* 356 U.S. 1 (1958).

[29] In addition to *Northern Pacific Railway,* fn 28, and *International Salt,* fn 26, unique credit terms were held to be a tying product in *Fortner Enterprises, Inc.* v. *United States Corp.,* 394 U.S. 495 (1969).

ing uncertain and wild swings of needed commodity supplies (usually accompanied by extreme and unpredictable price variations) consumers will also benefit. These and other advantages were acknowledged by the Supreme Court in the *"Standards Stations* case."[30]

However, because these exclusive dealing arrangements may have the effect of foreclosing the product market to competitors of the firm that uses them, if the amount of commerce involved is substantial, the arrangements violate Section 3 of the Clayton Act. This economic anomaly was resolved when, in an exclusive dealing contract challenged under Section 5 of the Federal Trade Commission Act, the Supreme Court held that exclusive contracts limited to a term of one year may be permissible.[31]

Prohibition of exclusive dealing franchise arrangements, even when conditioned upon the consideration of valuable services, was effectuated in 1966.[32] In short, exclusive dealing arrangements—be they requirements contracts, franchise agreements, or other marketing techniques—are devices a marketer should adopt only with reluctance and only after careful scrutiny and approval by competent legal counsel.

The second major area in which the Clayton Act imposes limitations on the organizational discretion of marketers is the prohibition of interlocking directorates. The flagrant case in which the same person is a member of the boards of direct competitors is rare. Marginal cases in which separate members of a board (e.g., a bank) sit on boards of competing companies do exist and are suspect. The admonition of Caesar's wife of "being above suspicion" may be indicated in the marketers' compliance with Section 8 of the Clayton Act.

In the third related area of intercorporate stockholdings, the Clayton Act, as it was adopted in 1914, held that, if the effect of such stockholding might have the effect of substantially lessening competition, it was prohibited. This section prohibits acquisitions only of stock; merger of competitors by asset acquisition was not covered. Intercorporate stock acquisition which may foreclose a substantial market to a competitor is clearly prohibited,[33] and as a result of the amendment of Section 7 of the Act in 1950 by the Celler-Kefauver Act,

---

[30] *Standard Oil of California* v. *United States*, 337 U.S. 293 (1949).

[31] *Federal Trade Commission* v. *Motion Picture Advertising Service Co.*, 344 U.S. 392 (1953).

[32] *Federal Trade Commission* v. *Brown Shoe Co.*, 384 U.S. 316 (1966).

[33] The first full-blown but belated application of the prohibition of Section 7 of the original Act is found in the Supreme Court's decision in *United States* v. *E. I. Du Pont de Nemours & Co.*, 353 U.S. 586 (1957). An earlier decision, *United States* v. *Columbia Steel Co.*, 334 U.S. 495 (1948) is indicative of the way in which mergers were generally tolerated prior to the 1950 amendment of the Act.

substantial foreclosure that may result from asset acquisition is clearly prohibited.

The scope of the amended Section 7 is outlined in detail in the first major case involving intercorporate acquisition of assets.[34] Subsequent interpretations of the act extended the coverage of the act by persuasive definitions of what constituted the relevant product market and the relevant geographic markets. The state of the current interpretation of the merger prohibitions of the Clayton Act is that, whenever "in any section of the country" and "in any line of commerce" the effect has some small probability of reducing competition, it is proscribed.[35]

Enforcement of the antimerger provisions of the Clayton Act is shared jointly by the Federal Trade Commission and the antitrust division of the Department of Justice. Consequently, given the broadness and the ambiguity of the statute, the marketer needs to know when a contemplated merger is likely to be challenged. As a result of a 1976 amendment, the Clayton Act now outlines specific conditions that require persons contemplating mergers to notify the regulatory agencies and that provides for a waiting period during which the merger may not be consummated. The regulatory agencies may give clearance for the merger, may ask for additional material while the merger is held in abeyance, or may challenge the merger. Yet this does not tell the marketer if Section 7 will be utilized to prevent a merger.

In 1982, the Department of Justice and, somewhat less enthusiastically, the Federal Trade Commission issued a report designed to clarify the conditions under which antimerger action might be expected. The *Merger Guidelines*[36] replaced an earlier set issued in 1968 by the same agencies. No marketer can yet be sure what the impact of the new guidelines will be, but indications are that mergers which were prohibited in the past would, in large measure, not be prohibited today.[37]

---

[34] *Brown Shoe Co.* v. *United States,* 370 U.S. 294 (1961).

[35] The literature on the law and mergers is voluminous. The interested marketer might consult Robert H. Bork, *The Antitrust Paradox* (New York: Basic Books, 1978). The landmark cases narrowing the range of permissible mergers, in addition to the *Brown Shoe* case, include *United States* v. *Von's Grocery Co.,* 384 U.S. 270 (1966); *Federal Trade Commission* v. *Procter & Gamble Co.,* 386 U.S. 568 (1967); *Federal Trade Commission* v. *Consolidated Foods Corp.,* 380 U.S. 592 (1965); *United States* v. *Pabst Brewing Co.,* 384 U.S. 546 (1966); *United States* v. *Continental Can Co.,* 378 U.S. 441 (1964); *Ford Motor Co.* v. *United States,* 405 U.S. 562 (1972); *United States* v. *Falstaff Brewing Corp.,* 410 U.S. 526 (1973); and *United States* v. *Marine Bancorporation, Inc., et al.,* 418 U.S. 602 (1974).

[36] See *Merger Guidelines—1982,* Trade Regulation Reports Extra Edition No. 546 (Chicago: Commerce Clearing House, June 16, 1982).

[37] For a case-by-case analysis, see Eleanor M. Fox, "The New Merger Guidelines—A Blueprint for Microeconomic Analysis," *The Antitrust Bulletin,* Fall 1982, 519–92.

Until the pattern of enforcement becomes clear and court interpretation follows, only this can be concluded: Mergers which involve competitors with large percentages of the market and which involve clearly demarked product line probably are still suspect under the Clayton Act.

The fourth major area of prohibited marketing action of the Clayton Act is price discrimination, as provided in Section 2 by the amendatory Robinson-Patman Act of 1936. This statute was directed at the alleged abuses of chain stores which used their extensive buying power to induce relatively powerless sellers to grant lower prices to them than to the chain's competitors. The Robinson-Patman Act, despite Congressional unwillingness to repeal it in the face of extensive though not unanimous disenchantment, has been a legal quagmire.[38]

Price discrimination—defined merely as a difference in price between two contemporaneous buyers of a product of like grade and quality—can be justified if the marketer is simply lucky. For, although the Supreme Court prides itself in weighing "the economic realities of the marketplace," products are adjudged to be of "like grade and quality" simply on the basis of chemical and physical identity; the surrounding conditions of sale (e.g., marketing distinctions induced by branding) are irrelevant in distinguishing products.[39] Moreover, although Section 2(b) of the act provides that differences that can be cost-justified or that are made to meet the price of a competitor in good faith rebut a prima facie case of discrimination, the interpretations have been so restrictive that differences in prices become, per se, suspect. This is accentuated by the fact that a price discriminator who attempts cost-justification must undertake the burden to prove that any quantity discount classifications are legally defensible.

The price-discrimination law also prohibits the payment of brokerage, disproportional provision of allowances, and such services as advertising and other promotional aids (and requires the provision of alternate promotional aids in case firm size renders some generally provided allowances and promotions unsuitable).

The reach of the Robinson-Patman Act is frightening to the marketer. For although a seller in one market offering lower prices to buyers than to a competing buyer in a second market is covered as a "first-line injury" to competition, the interpretation of the act has been

---

[38] A definitive history of the Robinson-Patman Act that is somewhat old is Earl W. Kintner, *A Robinson-Patman Primer* (New York: Macmillan, 1970). Also relevant is Corwin Edwards, *The Price Discrimination Law* (Washington, D.C.: Brookings Institution, 1959); and Frederick M. Rowe, *Price Discrimination Under the Robinson-Patman Act* (Boston: Little, Brown, 1962, and *Supplement,* 1964).

[39] *Federal Trade Commission* v. *Borden Company,* 383 U.S. 637 (1966).

broader. Second-line injury, third-line injury (different prices to a "dis-favored buyer in his competition with customers of the supplier's buyer, three steps down the distribution chain"),[40] and even fourth-line injury (customers of customers who are disfavored by a price offered a direct-buying customer) give rise to seller's liability. The full extent to which the act may reach was revealed by the Supreme Court's approval of the finding in the *Perkins* case[41] that fourth-line injury violated the act.

The marketer is faced with the question: How can I justify price differences at different functional levels in face of such decisions as *Perkins?* There is no ready answer except to note that, since 1970, virtually no cases have been initiated by the Department of Justice to enforce the Robinson-Patman Act. Private suits still threaten the marketer; it is difficult to be sanguine that the law, if invoked, will assure a reasonable outcome.

Federal Trade Commission Act. The Federal Trade Commission Act, adopted in 1914, created a five-person commission empowered to enforce the major substantive prohibition contained in Section 5. That section provided that "Unfair methods of competition in commerce are hereby declared unlawful." The act did not define "unfair methods of competition" and, as a result, marketers did not then know—nor do they now know with any degree of certainty—what practices and organizational methods were covered. That rests on the expertise of the commission and its staff; moreover, since 1914 the coverage of the act constantly has expanded.

Marketers must recognize that the act enables the FTC to reach activities that may be reached under the Sherman Act or the Clayton Act. The definitive statement on this is found in the *Lippa* case,[42] in which the court declared: "It is clear that any activity that violates either the Sherman Act or the Clayton Act also violates Section 5(a)(1) of the FTCA." What is forbidden under those acts as interpreted by the courts is hence prohibited to marketers who may find the FTC restraining activities also broadly prohibited and subject to jurisdiction of the Department of Justice.

The Supreme Court, in 1920, gave full scope to the FTC Act when, in the *Gratz* case,[43] it held that the statute was aimed at practices

---

[40] Kintner, *A Robinson-Patman Act Primer,* p. 96.

[41] *Clyde A. Perkins* v. *Standard Oil of California,* 395 U.S. 642 (1969). The marketer should note that this was a case in which an injured buyer, having proved damages, was entitled to treble damages under Section 4 of the Clayton Act.

[42] *Lippa's, Inc.* v. *Lennox, Incorporated,* D.C. Vt., 305 F. Supp. 182 (1969).

[43] *Federal Trade Commission* v. *Gratz,* 253 U.S. 421 (1920).

"opposed to good morals because characterized by deception, bad faith, fraud or oppression." Yet, in 1931, the Supreme Court, in the *Raladam* case,[44] held that deception was not prohibited by the FTC Act, since most other sellers of obesity remedies had also practiced deception in sales and, hence, competitors had not been "injured." This loophole was closed in 1938 by the Wheeler-Lea Act, which made "unfair or deceptive acts or practices" illegal. In 1975, the Consumer Product Warranties and Federal Trade Commission Improvements Act again broadened the coverage of the act. Prior to that time, practices at the local level had been immune to FTC action. To enable the FTC to reach deceptive and unfair practices at that level, the 1975 amendment substituted "in *or affecting* commerce" (italics added) for the "in commerce" phrase.

Specific enactments that are vital to a marketer's understanding of the coverage of the FTC have been added since 1938. The Wool Products Labeling Act of 1939 empowers the FTC to protect producers and consumers from adulterated products masquerading as woolen goods. The Fur Products Labeling Act prohibiting "misbranding, false advertising, and false invoicing of fur products and furs" was added to the FTC's statutes of enforcement in 1951. In 1958, to "protect producers and consumers against misbranding and false advertising of the fiber content of textile fiber products," the Textile Fiber Products Identification Act was added to the enforcement responsibility of the FTC. A Flammable Fabrics Act was adopted in 1953 to prohibit "introduction or movement" in interstate commerce of "wearing apparel and fabrics which are so highly flammable as to be dangerous when worn by individuals." In 1966 a Fair Packaging and Labeling Act was designed to prevent unfair or deceptive methods of packaging or labeling of certain consumer commodities distributed in interstate and foreign commerce. In 1975, the Magnuson-Moss Warranty–Federal Trade Commission Improvement Act providing "minimum disclosure standards for written product warranties" and to "define minimum Federal content standards for such warranties" was added to the enforcement load of the FTC. The Webb-Pomerene Export Trade Act of 1918, providing for exemption from the antitrust acts of associations formed solely to engage in export trade, and the Lanham Trade Mark Act of 1946, requiring trade mark registration and providing protection for them, are also enforced by the FTC. The Truth in Lending Act of 1968, the Fair Credit Reporting Act of 1970, the Fair Credit Billing Act of 1975, and the Equal Credit Opportunity Act of 1975—all designed to provide for

---

[44] *Federal Trade Commission* v. *Raladam Co.*, 283 U.S. 643 (1931).

nondiscriminatory and accurate use of credit—are also enforced by the FTC.

Clearly the body of case law that has developed in the interpretation of this multitude of acts is so extensive that a review here would be so incomplete as to be deceptive. Yet generalizations about the enforcement of the acts by the FTC are possible. First—and no marketer should ever forget this fact—in disagreements about the meaning of specific provisions, the courts generally accept the expertise of the FTC and its staff on findings of fact. The widest latitude conceivable is accorded the FTC in determining such debatable issues as, for example, the meaning of "unfairness" or "dangerous flammability." Only when marketers in disagreement with the FTC can demonstrate that the findings of the agency are arbitrary, capricious, or contrary to law is it likely they can prevail. Second, marketers must look for protection against burdensome applications of FTC regulations to the sympathetic bent of the Federal Trade commissioners or their staff.[45]

Federal Trade Commission enforcement procedures. Action under the statutes it is empowered to enforce is undertaken by the FTC on its own initiative, undertaken in its Washington, D.C., office, or in one of its regional offices. These actions may be activated by private "mailbox" complaints or they may be started by the FTC.

The most common response to a formal complaint is for the party against which it is filed to reply and settle at that stage. This is manifested by the acceptance of a "consent order" which, while it does not have the legal force of a guilty decision in a court case, has the effect of agreeing to abandon the challenged activity. Consent orders are, however, issued at the discretion of the FTC. If it believes the issue is so important that a hearing should be held, it may refuse to settle by a consent action.

If a consent order is not adopted by agreement, an administrative law judge holds a quasi-judicial hearing governed by rules of evidence and procedures outlined specifically in FTC manuals. The hearing, in which the prosecution of the case is conducted by FTC employees and utilizes evidence developed by the Bureau of Competition, the Bureau of Consumer Protection, or the Bureau of Economics of the FTC, will lead to an acquittal or a finding of guilt in whole or in part. The law judge, if guilt is found, may issue a "cease and desist" order which

---

[45] Verification of the precariousness of marketing relations with the FTC is well developed in *Unfairness: View on Unfair Acts in Violation of the Federal Trade Commission Act*, Committee Print of the Committee on Commerce, Science, and Transportation, United States Senate, 96th Cong., 2d Sess. (Washington, D.C.: U.S. Government Printing Office, 1980).

may, if not followed, lead to judicial action by the FTC to enforce the order. Violations of cease and desist orders are punishable by civil penalty of $10,000 for each violation.[46]

After an administrative law hearing has reached a decision, either the FTC or the firm can appeal to the five-man commission. The commission is not obligated to hear the appeal. If it hears the appeal, it issues its decision much as an appeals court in the judicial system does. Then, unless the firm, unsatisfied with the commissioner's decision, can secure a Supreme Court hearing, the decision becomes final. If an appeal to the Supreme Court is secured, the Court will accept the FTC's findings of fact and will reverse its decision only if either an error of law or of procedure is found.

The enforcement of the FTC statutes can also be carried into effect by the issuance of trade regulation rules. Prior to adoption of the Magnuson-Moss Warranty–Federal Trade Commission Improvement Act in 1975, the status of such rules, though promulgated since 1963, was questionable, but their legality is now clear. These trade regulation rules represent a codification by the FTC of business practices that are specifically found to violate Section 5 of the FTC Act. After publication in the *Federal Register* and due opportunity for comment by concerned parties, the rules are effective. They apply ''to all persons whomsoever'' and have the effect of a statutory enactment insofar as business adherence upon penalty of civil action is required. Illustrative of the kind of rules that may be issued—although since 1980 the United States Congress has been zealous in prohibiting the use of funds to develop trade regulation rules in controversial areas (e.g., the regulation of television advertising directed toward children)—is regulation of advertising and labeling requirements for sleeping bags and of terms and conditions of franchising agreements. Twenty-eight trade regulation rules are now in effect, and several additional rules have been proposed.[47] Although the rules are often more specific than statutory enactments typically are, their extensive subjects and their force of law dictate that marketing experts become familiar with those specifically relevant to their industries.

Additional enforcement of the FTC's statutory obligations is its power to seek injunctions in district courts against potential or actual violation of those obligations.

---

[46] In the determination of what constitutes "each violation," the marketer is cautioned the penalty may become very heavy. When the *Reader's Digest* mailed letters with what was adjudged "deceptive" content, each individual letter, not the consolidated mailing, was considered a separate violation.

[47] Marketers will find the current rules and also proposals undergoing the process of comment and official formulation in "FTC Trade Rules," *Trade Regulation Reporter* 4 (Chicago: Commerce Clearing House, 1983), pp. 41, 101–248.

While it is not true that the marketer is powerless in the face of the powers of the FTC, it is true that the presumption throughout the law is that the regulatory agency has the expertise that will presumptively render its findings conclusive. To dispute the power of the FTC is to risk onerous legal fees and eventual large penalties. In the context of a specific marketing situation, knowledge and counsel are the surest protections, though not guarantees, against inadvertent violation of the laws.

CURRENT IMPACT

The impact of the administrative, legislative, and judicial control of marketing is extensive—and it has been growing. The law currently extends to the regulation of the form the marketing institution may take and the way in which it may grow. Even more important, the law operates to answer specifically what new products may be placed on the market, and thus how business may meet what it believes are the unmet needs of the consumer. Products—and in no area more clearly than pharmaceuticals—the law determines what products may be offered to meet those needs. In order to attempt to assure workable competition, the law regulates how these products may be made available to consumers. The law controls pricing practices in innumerable ways and provides strict penalties for most collective actions designed to assure orderly pricing. It even goes so far as to grant the consumer legal rights in access to information about products and services by finding that classes of consumers have a property right in such access.

In short, if marketing management, as was suggested initially, is separable into activities, successful organizations, and an environment of consumers, then not one of the components has even relative freedom from legal surveillance. The law is omnipresent and nearly omnipotent.

FUTURE IMPACT

There is an element of clairvoyance in attempting to assess the future impact of the law on marketing. Yet with firm conviction in the admonition that the past is prologue, it may be hazarded that the long-run trend of the legal regulation of marketing is an accelerating one. Much of this increased regulation reflects the growth of the consumer and public interest movement, which believes to a significant degree that the autonomy of business—and hence of marketers—should be curtailed. Debate on the desirability of this development is relatively fruitless; at least for the foreseeable future it seems likely to continue.

Other writers have ended on a "lame note" in their analyses of contemporary events. This seems an appropriate place to end on another such lame note. Even though marketers may be persons of goodwill and are honest, conscientious, and guided by a desire to meet society's own perceived needs, freedom from burdensome legal restraint is unlikely to return. The ultimate message is that marketers of both products and services must be prepared to spend an increasing amount of money and time on understanding the legal environment which will increasingly restrain their actions.

30

LAYMAN'S GUIDE TO CONTRACTS

by
Paul E. Saunders

Attorney, Private Practice

If you have ever worked for a large corporation, then you have probably encountered "the Legal Department." Rarely does one find a corporate executive who cannot tell some horrible experience he or she
had when a contract or agreement had to be cleared through the legal
department. Chances are that each story relates to the fact that things
got very complicated because the lawyers got involved. Unfortunately,
the complications arise because the lawyer does what he or she generally does best—asks questions.

Frequently, the type of questions asked by corporate attorneys will
reflect the fact that they may be more aware of other corporate activities and requirements than the manager who is involved with one or
more revenue centers of the corporation. So, rather than causing complications, attorneys may be helping you avoid all kinds of internal
problems.

It is also a fact that attorneys may be more aware of corporate
policies than the manager who is seeking assistance. Here again, they
can offer some valuable suggestions for avoiding subsequent complications. And that's all before they start doing their legal work!

Here are some basic premises:

1. Any agreement involving substantial sums of money to be paid
by or to you or your company should be reviewed by an attorney.
(Assuming it is more than a simple note or promise to pay, and requires
the parties actually to perform some functions or duties.)

2. Any agreement that involves conditions which are subject to changing circumstances, cost adjustments, or such factors as the cost of living index or another barometer of economic conditions, should be reviewed by an attorney.

3. Any agreement between competitors should be reviewed by an attorney.

4. Any agreement that has been prepared by an attorney for the party with whom you are dealing should be reviewed by your attorney.

Naturally, when dealing with an attorney outside the corporation, you need to be much more conscious of the *time* you spend with him or her. The small talk and corporate gossip should not be part of your discussion with the outside lawyer, and won't be, *if you are prepared!* How do you prepare?

1. Have with you all your facts, records, correspondence, and any other details that pertain to the matter when you attend the first session with your attorney. (And bring another set of the most important papers so you don't have to sit and watch while the papers are separated and unstapled and given to someone who disappears for a while to make copies . . . you're paying for that time.)

2. Don't assume that your lawyer understands your business and knows what you and your company do; nor that he or she understands the words of art that are peculiar to your business. The lawyer doesn't, unless he or she works solely in your industry. Like the well-known commercial slogan of the family clothing business, "An educated lawyer is your best advisor." By educated, it is meant that he or she should be thoroughly briefed about the background of a particular matter, or with any historical facts about the company that would be pertinent or helpful in making judgements. Also, your lawyer should be made aware of any industry standards that are uniformly accepted, and the source of those standards, such as a trade association, professional organization (where such standards are generally distributed in written form).

3. Be prepared to explain what you want from the agreement. Now, this sounds simple, but you would be surprised how frequently a client can be unclear in his own thinking. This is where the questioning by a good lawyer can help a client crystalize his own thinking about what he wants to achieve from a particular deal or agreement.

4. As a corollary to preparation 3, be able to explain what the other party to the deal is looking for. Trying to structure an agreement that gives that other party what she is *really* looking for can be one of the most important contributions your lawyer will make. Next to asking questions, the ability to ascertain what the other party really wants, and deliver it, is the second most important service a good contract lawyer will provide.

5. If you have some literature about your company, or about your particular operation within the company, bring it along and leave it with the lawyer.

How often have you heard a party to a potential agreement say something like: "Let's keep it simple . . . a letter will be sufficient and we can both sign it." Well my friends, it may be a letter and it may also be short and simple; *but* it is also a contract if indeed both parties signed it. And if there are any subsequent disagreements, that simple letter will be studied over and over again to look for a clue about what the parties intended. If there are ambiguities and no one can reasonably infer what the parties intended, then the law of contracts dictates that such ambiguities are resolved against the person who did the drafting of the letter. So, please, be very aware of all the pitfalls involved in those "simple letter agreements."

On the other hand, there is absolutely no reason why all agreements cannot be kept brief. There is not always the need for 30 and more pages of language that only the lawyers understand. While there are clearly major transactions, acquisitions, and the like, which clearly create a need for all the so-called boiler plate provisions, the vast majority of business deals can be recited in six pages or less. I also urge the usage of plain good old-fashioned English—so anyone reading it a few years later will have no difficulty understanding what was intended. There is no reason why an agreement cannot be written in the same language used to describe it, and there is no reason to use a legalism if plain English will say it better. Many lawyers will dictate a first draft of an agreement while you are still with them, and they will adapt your language concerning the details of the contract as they go. After all, you are the one who negotiated the deal. Who knows the terms any better than you?

This is where you can help your attorney and yourself in the process. By talking through the agreement with your attorney, you enable him or her to organize notes in an orderly manner, which makes the contract drafting much easier.

There is another important advantage you gain by doing this. Most lawyers have dealt with numerous transactions involving many different industries. They tend generally to know "a little bit about a lot of things," as the old song goes. When you talk through the agreement, it may often trigger a thought or response from an attorney, which is based on some prior experience that can then be brought to bear on your particular agreement.

Lawyers' cabinets are clogged with copies of their old contracts.

They never throw anything away. And usually, your contract needs will not be so unique that a lawyer won't be able to relate it to some other agreement he or she drafted. In other words, take advantage of that experience and those old agreements.

WHAT ABOUT FORMS?

As mentioned above, one of the more common situations involves the so-called standard contract. My experience has been that such contracts have generally been compiled over a period of years and tend to include all the clauses that favor the company offering it. It would be highly unusual for such a contract to include mutually favorable provisions. Accordingly, I tend to disregard such caveats as "They won't permit any changes." If a contract is clearly one-sided, fairness dictates that a client be protected with some new language or changes. Generally, reasonable requests for changes will be honored. Don't be afraid to ask!

Usually, such situations arise where the company offering the contract has some economic leverage and the client is faced with the decision of doing business under less than the best conditions or fighting for improved contract provisions. To choose not to ask is "getting the business" in more ways than one. It is a very sensitive situation, and one where an attorney can sometimes achieve changes and still salvage the contract. It is a situation where you can let your attorney play the "bad guy."

While on the subject of forms, every office will have a supply of clauses which were used in various agreements, and which seem to find their way from agreement to agreement. While they can represent some practical experience or have served well in some prior agreement, a word of caution is needed. Forms can frequently be misused. They must be used intelligently and not just followed blindly.

HOW TO GET THE MOST OUT OF YOUR LAWYER

The majority of business people do not know how to use the services of a lawyer, and this is unfortunate because the lawyer offers a valuable support service. Like most professionals, the lawyer comes in many types and operates in hundreds of areas of expertise. Their special training and broad experience gives them a unique ability to provide solutions to problems in all types of enterprises. Generally, the lawyer can analyze a problem without the internal constraints that tend to prevent a client from being able to gather facts, analyze the needs, and reach a sound solution.

You should be selective in your choice of attorney. No single lawyer can be well versed in all aspects of the law, and the day of the general practitioner is rapidly fading. Most lawyers will admit, if questioned, what their areas of expertise are, and are not. If you are not sure about your selection, there are some steps you can take:

— Contact the local or State Bar Association and obtain some names of lawyers who specialize in the desired area of competence.
— Do not be afraid to find the right person within a given law firm . . . the one who satisfies your requirements. The firm will be just as anxious as you are to match you with the right person.
— Evaluate the lawyer's approach to the assignment.

Once you have made your selection, you have some other responsibilities:

1. You must outline the complete scope of the assignment, and you should obtain some estimates from the lawyer about time involved and total estimated costs.

2. If you are dealing with a firm, you should ask what rates will be charged by senior and junior partners in the firm; and there will also be a paralegal rate that should be disclosed.

3. If you are dealing with a senior man, do not be bashful about asking for juniors or paralegals to do the more routine chores. It is not unusual for such senior partners to bill at rates that can be two to five times higher than the rates for juniors and paralegals.

Although your needs for legal services may be intermittent, the lawyer you select should be viewed in the context of a long-term relationship. The total use of his or her experience, skill and business knowledge will lead to a mutually satisfying experience for both client and attorney.

Unfortunately, many clients tend to overlook the valuable business experience that lawyers gain over their years of practice; in fact, some clients will stress to their lawyers that they don't want their input on the business decisions. This, in my opinion, is an overreaction by a client who wants to be sure of making all the business decisions. Beneath that outer cover of the lawyer lurks a businessman. Within reasonable limits, don't be afraid to let him out!

SOME SELF-HELP IDEAS

There are some very fine sources of help on the legal front that should not be overlooked by marketing management.

1. *General texts.* There are some fine general texts you will find useful, especially when undertaking a new campaign. Texts that deal with specific topics, such as copyrights, trademarks, or advertising, can give you a good working knowledge of the particular topic.

2. *Pamphlets and manuals.* Sometimes trade associations or bar associations will publish a paperbound treatment of a special topic. While the marketing department may not be aware of them, your legal counsel probably receives many of them and, if he or she is made aware of your interest, can send them to you.

3. *Periodicals.* These run the gamut from legal newsletters to trade association newsletters that from time to time deal with legal subjects.

4. *Government publications.* While these tend to proliferate, and it is difficult to pick and choose exact publications, there are some mailing lists you should be on. If your company is concerned with the rules and regulations of the FTC or some particular agency, then you certainly should be on that agency's mailing list. Usually, such agencies offer a wide variety of periodic releases and bulletins.

In the case of general texts, I am listing at the end of the chapter a few which I have found to be particularly helpful for the clients to whom I have recommended them.

As a final thought, let me discuss the relationship of the marketing manager and the lawyer . . . what it can be. The marketing manager and the attorney come from different training backgrounds, but each must learn the thinking of the other. While the lawyer must learn the function of the marketing department, so, too, the marketer must learn the function of the law. The understanding between the two will come with time. Confidence and trust will be established over time. Since both are seeking the same end, this understanding between the two will come with some serious effort on both sides. The conflicts that arise are usually due to misconceptions about areas of responsibility and expertise. When both sides recognize the contribution made by the other, a smooth cooperative partnership will develop. It's worth the effort.

SOME HELPFUL READINGS

Digges, I. W. *The Modern Law of Advertising and Marketing.* New York: Funk & Wagnall, 1948.

National Industrial Conference Board. *New Product Development.* New York, 1963.

New Products Marketing. New York: Printer's Ink Books, 1964.

Simon, Morton. *The Law for Advertising and Marketing.* New York: W. W. Norton, 1956.

31

USING MARKETING RESEARCH IN LITIGATION

by
Jeffery T. Wack

Marketing Sciences, Inc.
and
Steven E. Permut

Yale University
School of Management

For many companies, civil litigation has become an important management concern, not only because of the costs of mounting a defense, or of bringing a complaint, but because of the strategic business impact attributable to a win, loss, or draw. Because marketing managers have general responsibility for understanding customer needs, competitive activities, and overall marketplace dynamics, the marketing professional can often play a number of important roles in the litigation process.

This chapter has two objectives. The first is to highlight the growing use of marketing and consumer research in the world of litigation—in generating unique kinds of evidence, in assisting in the jury selection and trial process, and even in helping the corporation to minimize exposure to litigation by means of proactive research efforts.

The second is to point out several areas of the law in which marketing research has been used effectively to illuminate or clarify points at issue, particularly in matters pertaining to antitrust, trade name infringement, deceptive advertising, and products liability.

One concern is that all too often legal disputes rely on strict economic-based analysis, even though many of the points at issue have a substantial *behavioral* component. A second concern is that reliance on experts and abstract models alone ignores the reality of marketplace behaviors that are best assessed by the tools and techniques of marketing.

Marketing professionals (particularly marketing and consumer researchers) are in an excellent position to add new dimensions of understanding to augment or supplant more traditional perspectives.

This chapter suggests that the conceptual and empirical skills of marketing professionals should be integrated by corporate management as an important untapped resource in the firm's litigation activities, particularly when questions of normative or prescriptive marketplace behaviors, or both, are involved. The examples offered are illustrative of contributions to be made by using internal marketing researchers or, similarly, by relying on outside consultants as appropriate. More detailed information regarding the specific legal topics referenced here can be found in numerous textbooks, such as those by Howell, Allison, and Jentz,[1] or Reiling.[2]

ANTICOMPETITIVE PRACTICES

Most managers are accustomed to reading about legal battles in which price discrimination, price fixing, and monopolistic practices have been alleged. These are the most frequent types of actions brought under the antitrust statutes of the Sherman, Clayton, and Robinson-Patman acts. The purpose of these bodies of law is to prohibit certain practices in commerce if their effect is to substantially reduce competition in the marketplace. Consequently, in the course of antitrust litigation, a number of market and consumer issues are typically raised for which the marketing researcher's skills are particularly relevant.

Definition of the Relevant Market. In many actions brought under the antitrust laws, one of the most critical questions likely to face the court is that of determining the "relevant market" within which the defendant company's activities are to be measured. Identification of the relevant market is often necessary to determine the extent of a supplier's market power. The relevant market is defined at two levels.[3] The first is that of the product category. For example, in E.I. *Du Pont*

---

[1] R. A. Howell, J. R. Allison, and G. A. Jentz, Business Law: Text and Cases (Hinsdale, Ill.: Dryden Press, 1978).

[2] H. R. Reiling, *Business Law: Text and Cases* (Boston: Keat Publishing, 1981).

[3] E. F. Zelek, L. W. Stern, and T. W. Dunfee, "A Rule of Decision Model after Sylvania," *California Law Review* 68 (1980), pp. 13–47.

de Nemours case,[4] the government charged Du Pont with conspiring to monopolize interstate trade in cellophane. A key issue was whether cellophane represented a market unto itself, in which case Du Pont's market power was very high, or whether cellophane was part of the flexible packaging material market, in which case its share was a non-monopolistic 20 percent.

In the courts, it has been traditional to have testimony from economists regarding the definition of the product category. The usual method is to identify products with high cross-elasticities of demand—that is, products that are highly substitutable.[5,6] Specifically, substitutability has referred to the extent one product would lose or gain sales in response to a change in another product's price. When this kind of evidence of cross-elasticity is demonstrated, the Federal Trade Commission has traditionally held that it is determinative of product market issues.

From the marketer's perspective, however, there are a number of problems with this operational definition,[7] limitations that are being recognized increasingly in the courts. Foremost among these limitations are: *(a)* the economists' substitutability criterion refers to potential elasticity, which typically assumes no response by one firm to the price changes of another; and *(b)* the difficulty of obtaining valid estimates of elasticity due to changes in marketplace variables (many of which may not be measurable, controllable, or even recognized as important by the firm).

Many of these problems can be overcome by alternative measures of substitutability with which the market researcher is quite familiar, such as similarity in (1) production processes; (2) distribution channels or outlets; (3) function, performance, or technical characteristics; or (4) needs satisfied, benefits derived, or appropriateness relative to customer behavior and decision making. Interesting in this regard is that, while economic models of elasticity were part of the Du Pont litigation previously mentioned, the trial judge insisted upon doing some "market research" himself! With consent of counsel he visited the 1952 Annual Packaging Show in Atlantic City, and later he stated in his

[4] *United States* v. *Du Pont de Nemours and Company,* 351 U.S. 377 (1956).

[5] F. Schere, *Industrial Market Structure and Economic Performance* (Chicago: Rand McNally, 1970).

[6] R. W. Werth, "Determination of the Relevant Product Market," *Ohio State Law Journal* (1965), pp. 241–93.

[7] G. S. Day and A. D. Shocker, *Identifying Competitive Product-Market Boundaries: Strategic and Analytical Issues,* Report 76–112 (Cambridge, Mass.: Marketing Sciences Institute, 1976).

opinion that these personal observations confirmed his estimate of the competition between cellophane and other packaging materials.

Fortunately, the courts' sophistication vis-à-vis the introduction and use of consumer research has increased since then. Twenty years later, in the *Liggett & Myers* case,[8] for example, the question was whether there was one homogeneous dog food market or whether there were distinctive submarkets (e.g., canned, semi-moist, dry). Liggett & Myers presented evidence from a controlled field experiment designed to measure not only cross-elasticities but also buyers' *perceptions* of brand similarity and patterns of brand switching and product usage.

Attorneys and the courts are becoming increasingly familiar with, and favorable to, the argument that consumer-based measures of substitutability in use or function as they directly relate to the purchase-decision process are useful in litigation. This is true for both the identification of the relevant product market(s), as well as for assessing degrees of substitutability of, and differentiation among, products within these markets.

Behavioral analyses of purchase or usage, or decision-sequence analysis, for example, are among the demand-based methodologies used by the market researcher in the characterization of product markets.[9] Brand-switching[10,11] and the multidimensional scaling or cluster-analysis-based methods for mapping perceptions and consumer judgments[12] are among those useful for evaluating substitutability among products from the consumer perspective. It is precisely the application of these methodologies that we see as powerful contributors to a firm's litigation effort, particularly to augment or supplement strictly economic-based definitions of relevant market.

The second level at which courts have defined relevant markets is geographic,[13] the argument being that lack of competition in a market area results in monopolistic power and excessive profits. This is frequently an issue in litigation involving mergers, as when the government sought to block a contemplated merger of the Brown Shoe Com-

---

[8] Liggett & Myers Tobacco Co., Inc., *United States* v. *Federal Trade Commission* Docket No. 8938 (March 11, 1975).

[9] R. Frank, W. Massy, and Y. Wind, *Market Segmentation* (Englewood Cliffs, N.J.: Prentice-Hall, 1972).

[10] P. Kotler, *Marketing Decision Making: A Model Building Approach* (New York: Holt, Rinehart & Winston, 1971).

[11] J. Jacoby and R. W. Chestnut, *Brand Loyalty: Measurement and Management* (New York: John Wiley & Sons, 1978).

[12] J. H. Myers and E. Tauber, *Market Structure Analysis* (Chicago: American Marketing Association, 1977).

[13] Zelek et al., "A Rule of Decision Model after Sylvania."

pany and Kinney Company.[14] Since both Brown and Kinney had retail outlets in similar geographical areas, the Court's concern was that a merger would not be beneficial because it would result in a substantial lessening of competition in those areas where both firms had outlets. A major question, therefore, was where to draw market boundaries. The district court had found that the effects of the merger should be analyzed in those cities with a population exceeding 10,000 *and* the immediate contiguous territory, and where both Brown and Kinney operated retail outlets. On appeal, however, the defendants argued from a marketing perspective, claiming that central business district outlets and suburban shopping center outlets serve distinct market areas and, hence, the effects on competition in these different market areas should be considered separately.

The market research task in this type of situation is to determine effective areas of competition and to evaluate levels of competition within a trade area. These are the activities initially undertaken by most successful firms in developing and refining their product/market strategy. Thus, the researcher's analytic perspective is seen as providing an important knowledge base when such issues are being raised in antitrust litigation or other administrative proceedings.

TRADEMARKS AND BRANDS

Over 400,000 active trademarks are on the Principal Register of the U.S. Patent and Trademark Office. The fact that applications for new marks has increased to an average of 50,000 each year[15] attests to their utility and value in the marketplace. However, the crowding of the marketplace with marks, logos, and other corporate/brand symbols, and the resulting value to competitors of imitating those that have been successful, is leading to increasing trademark litigation.

Trademarks are protected by the Lanham Act because of their importance to buyers and sellers alike. Trademarks have several purposes, including (among others): indicating the source of a product, distinguishing it from similar products of other sources, and protecting the consumer from confusion or deception. Legal questions regarding trademarks are of three kinds: first, in applying for a trademark, the question is often whether the mark is distinctive or not; second, after widespread acceptance of the mark, the question may be whether it has become generic; and finally, there may be a question about whether a new mark is infringing on the rights of an existing mark.

---

[14] *Brown Shoe Company* v. *United States,* 370 U.S. 294 (1962).

[15] D. A. Burge, *Patent and Trademark Tactics and Practice* (New York: John Wiley & Sons, 1980).

The degree to which a company or other organization may use a particular mark in trade is related to its level of distinctiveness. Thus, such created "words" as Xerox or Exxon can be more broadly protected than can common words, such as Apple or McDonald which, through a particular company's use, have acquired in a market a single source-indicating significance (i.e., "secondary meaning" in legal terms).

Ironically, once a company's mark has acquired a strong trade identity, the company may have to protect the mark from becoming generic—that is, when the meaning of the mark comes to indicate the product itself, rather than to imply a unique source. This was the finding in the recent case involving Parker Brothers, which focused on whether the company could retain rights to the tradename "Monopoly." Consumer research was instrumental in showing that most consumers identified the name with only the game itself and not with the company that made it.[16,17] The Court's ruling turned on the marketplace evidence acquired by survey research, further underscoring the powerful role to be played by marketing research in this type of litigation.

Many people are surprised to hear that aspirin, cellophane, and linoleum were all once protected marks that litigation has since determined to have lost their source-indicating significance. To prevent marks from becoming generic, some firms have established trademark protection programs with staff who have responsibility for monitoring the use of the mark. Consequently, even *Consumer Reports* magazine received a letter from the company holding the Crock Pot trademark, after the magazine had inadvertently used the term without capitalizing it.[18]

The most common danger to the firm's trademark, however, is that of infringement. The courts have defined trademark infringement as the use by one party of a mark that is so similar to an existing mark that confusion between the two is likely to occur. The key issues in trademark infringement suits are the likelihood and extent of confusion between the two marks in question. Consequently, trademark law was the first to recognize the appropriateness and value of the market researcher's tool of consumer surveys for providing unique evidence of the "state of the public's mind." Prior to the use of surveys, "evi-

---

[16] "No Monopoly on Monopoly," *Business Week,* March 7, 1983, p. 36.

[17] R. L. Gordon, "Monopoly Name Doesn't Pass Go," *Advertising Age* 54 (1983), p. 3.

[18] "Letter from Rival Manufacturing," *Consumer Reports* (November 1983), p. 570.

dence" in trademark litigation was provided by expert testimony, or by the judge acting as consumer. In many cases, evidence about whether there was confusion between marks among consumers was, incredibly, a matter of the plaintiff putting a handful (or more) of people on the stand who testified that they *were* confused by the marks, and the defendant having a similar number of witnesses testify that they *were not!*

The value of a survey is that it allows the opinions of the population of interest to be represented through scientific sampling. Rather than having to rely upon experts who would presume to state what a hypothetical consumer would think, survey results provide probabilistic statements about the likelihood of a consumer's state of mind. Further, surveys are able to give the courts a more refined sense of the degree of confusion among the public in general, within specific markets (such as household versus industrial), or among different subgroups of consumers (such as heavy versus light product users).

Through the 1950s and 60s, questions were raised regarding the admissibility of survey findings due to the hearsay rule.[19] The legal question was whether survey results could themselves be relied upon, since the respondents upon whose opinions the results were based were unavailable for cross-examination in court. These concerns have largely been overcome, so competently conducted empirical studies of this type are more regularly being introduced and accepted into evidence,[20,21,22,23] not only in trademark cases but in all areas of litigation discussed in this chapter. We shall return to this topic again in our concluding remarks.

DECEPTION IN ADVERTISING

Another area in which one is likely to see an increased role for marketing and consumer research is in the development of law, policy, and rule making, particularly in administrative proceedings. The Federal

---

[19] H. C. Barksdale, *The Use of Survey Research Findings as Legal Evidence* (Pleasantville, N.Y.: Printer's Ink Books, 1957).

[20] L. Kunin, "The Structure and Uses of Survey Evidence in Trademark Cases," *The Trademark Reporter* 67 (1977), pp. 97–109.

[21] R. L. Marmer, "Opinion Polls and the Law of Evidence," *Virginia Law Review* (1976), pp. 1101–33.

[22] F. W. Morgan, "The Admissibility of Consumer Surveys as Legal Evidence in Courts," *Journal of Marketing* 46 (1979), pp. 33–40.

[23] P. N. Sherrill, "Survey Evidence in Litigation: Conflicting Doctrine," in *Review of Marketing*, B. M. Enis and K. J. Roering (Chicago: American Marketing Association, 1981), pp. 217–23.

Trade Commission provides just such a case in point. The FTC is the agency responsible for regulating commercial advertising to prevent deceptive representations. If the FTC finds an advertisement false or misleading, it either requires the seller to "cease and desist," to disclose additional information (thereby amending the advertisement), or to engage in "corrective" advertising.

The FTC is a good example of the increasing use of marketing research in administrative proceedings. Prior to the 1970s, it was generally established that the FTC was to act as a body of experts who, when faced with determining whether an advertisement was deceptive or unfair, were explicitly empowered to rely on their own intuitive understandings or perceptions—even in the face of directly opposing views from others (including consumers who had been exposed to the advertising in question). This "conventional wisdom" approach was increasingly criticized during the 1970s, however, by attorneys and by marketing and consumer researchers, who collectively argued for the FTC to incorporate consumer perspectives into these deliberations.[24,25,26,27] In the late 1970s, the commission began using consumer-based research more extensively,[28] and in the past four or five years, consumer research has been introduced by one or more parties in most FTC actions.

Research may be used at three points in the FTC's regulatory process. Copy research is conducted in the early stages of FTC interest in a particular advertisement (or campaign) to learn more about which express or implied claims consumers are likely to infer from an advertisement. In addition, such efforts enable the FTC to gauge the magnitude of deception (e.g., the proportion of the sample deceived, or the relative strength of the deceptive message), compared to other elements in the ad or to normative data. Survey research may also be useful at this stage by helping to identify the importance of particular product attributes in the consumers' purchase decision.

---

[24] D. M. Gardner, "Deception in Advertising: A Conceptual Approach," *Journal of Marketing* 39 (1975), pp. 40–46.

[25] E. E. Gellhorn, "Proof of Consumer Deception Before the Federal Trade Commission," *Kansas Law Review* 17 (1969), pp. 559–72.

[26] P. H. LaRue, "FTC Expertise: A Legend Examined," *The Antitrust Bulletin* 16 (1971), pp. 1–31.

[27] See also Vicki O'Meara, "FTC Deceptive Advertising Regulation: A Proposal for the Use of Consumer Behavior Research," *Northwestern University Law Review* 76 (1982), pp. 946–79.

[28] M. T. Brandt and I. L. Preston, "The Federal Trade Commission's Use of Evidence to Determine Deception, *Journal of Marketing* 41 (1977), pp. 54–62.

Second, if an advertisement is found to be deceptive, further research can evaluate the effectiveness of particular forms of intervention intended to correct the deception. For example, various disclosures can be evaluated experimentally to determine how best to eliminate the deceptive element while not interfering with the other components of the advertisement.

Finally, the FTC has used evaluation research to assess the impact on the public of the regulations it has issued and remedies it has required of the advertiser. Perhaps the best example of this research is that of the corrective advertising program required of Warner-Lambert after the commission successfully challenged the "cold and sore throat" claim of Listerine. In this case, two research techniques—a longitudinal mail questionnaire to members of a panel,[29] and a series of Burke day-after recall studies[30]—were conducted to assess the effectiveness of the corrective campaign. This research suggested that the corrective campaign had successfully reduced consumers' use of Listerine for colds and sore throats without reducing its use for bad breath.

Clearly, the marketing researcher has a wide variety of opportunities to apply the tools of the trade to problems of deception and unfairness in advertising, both to prevent unintended or misperceived communication from occurring, and to assist in evaluating the alternatives for eliminating or correcting its residual effects in the marketplace.

TRIAL PROCESS

In addition to providing evidence in legal and administrative cases, and input regarding the behavior of consumers to aid in the development of legislation, the market researcher's skills have also been helpful to the attorney in the trial process. This is true of two areas in particular: motions for change of venue, and *voir dire* in jury selection.

Assisting in Changes of Venue. Trial juries are drawn from the community in which the trial takes place. Changes of venue are requested of the judge when an attorney feels that it is impossible to select from the community a jury impartial to his or her client. It is most common for the attorney to seek a change of venue for one of two

[29] M. B. Mazis, "The Effects of the FTC's Listerine Corrective Advertising Order," *Report* prepared for the Federal Trade Commission, July 1981 (Washington, D.C.).

[30] Burke Marketing Research, "Listerine Corrective Advertising Evaluation Day-after Recall Testing," *Report* prepared for the Federal Trade Commission, September 1979 (Washington, D.C.).

reasons, namely, substantial pretrial publicity or widespread attitudes in the community that are prejudicial to the defendant, or both[31] The attorney is expected to offer evidence in support of a motion for a change of venue for either reason.

To assess prejudice, a community attitude survey will very often be conducted.[32] Such a survey is usually designed to reveal the extent to which potential jurors have been exposed to the case through the media and formed opinions about the case or held attitudes prejudicial to the defendant, or both. The exact nature of the questionnaire is, of course, highly dependent on the nature of the case, but generally it is structured not unlike consumer surveys conducted for other purposes: it begins with an introduction and questions to screen for persons in the population of interest (in the case of community surveys, those eligible for jury service), followed by attitudinal questions that are both general and case-specific in nature.

General-attitude questions, for example, might assess attitudes about white-collar crime, ethical beliefs, and feelings about the life-styles of high-powered executives. Opinions about the acceptability of different forms of punishment might also be sought. Case-specific questions would ask respondents about their knowledge of specifics regarding the case, and might even ask their predilection to convict the defendant. Finally, demographic and background information is obtained in order to produce more refined statistical analyses and projections.

As in any survey offered as legal evidence, close attention must be paid to sampling, interviewing procedures, and data analysis, since each stage in the process will be evaluated by the judge and opposing counsel before the survey's findings can influence the change of venue decision.

To demonstrate extensive media coverage of a case, counsel may present evidence suggestive of the effects of the coverage from a community survey, but generally one tries to impress the court with the quantity and "quality" of the coverage itself. Specifically, press clippings, TV and radio tapes, and other extant evidence pertaining to the case are accumulated. Content analysis[33] is applied in order to describe more precisely the nature of coverage and to convey its potentially prejudicial influence.

---

[31] B. Bonora and E. Krauss, eds., *Jurywork: Systematic Techniques,* 2d ed. (New York: Clark Boardman Co., Ltd., 1983).

[32] M. Pollack, "The Use of Public Opinion Polls to Obtain Changes of Venue and Continuances in Criminal Trials," *Criminal Justice Journal* 1 (1977), pp. 269–76.

[33] O. R. Holsti, *Content Analysis for the Social Sciences and Humanities* (Reading, Mass.: Addison-Wesley Publishing, 1969).

Exactly what should be the content categories depends upon the specifics of the trial. However, the National Jury Project[34] cites four content categories basic for criminal cases. These are references to the defendant, references to the victim, characteristics of the crime, and publicity generated by the government. Three different categories are recommended for civil cases. These are references to the litigant's economic importance, characterizations of the litigant's reputation, and characterizations of the litigation. Within these categories, such variables as the number of stories, number of column inches, and location within paper can be used to quantify salience. Listings of key words, biased headlines, and emotive words can also be offered as evidence of bias.

Jury Selection. The first step once the litigation has reached the trial stage is to impanel a jury. As the reader is probably aware, attorneys for both sides interview prospective jurists and make decisions about which are not acceptable to them. The criteria for these decisions are highly variable among trial teams and, until relatively recently, the basis was more art and trial experience than science. In an increasing number of cases, however, survey research is being used by attorneys to develop specific criteria to aid in selecting a "favorable" jury.[35,36,37] The use of marketing research in the jury selection process has begun to stimulate empirical study,[38] as well as prominent coverage in a wide variety of publications.[39]

Surveys conducted for jury selection are different from community attitude surveys designed to support a motion for change of venue. The purpose of a jury selection survey is to describe how demographic variables are related to attitudes and opinions thought to be predictive of how likely a jurist would vote. For example, in a case where the defendant company is charged with unfair competition and driving a small competitor out of business, the defense attorney would want to

---

[34] Bonbora and Krauss, *Jurywork*.

[35] M. J. Saks and R. Hastie, *Social Psychology in Court* (New York: Van Nostrand Reinhold, 1978).

[36] A. F. Ginger, *Jury Selection in Criminal Trials: New Techniques and Concepts* (Tiburon, Calif.: Laupress, 1977).

[37] R. Christie, "Probability vs. Precedence: The Social Psychology of Jury Selection," in *Psychology and the Law: Research Frontiers,* ed. G. Bermant et al. (Lexington, Mass.: Lexington Books, 1976).

[38] For example, see D. Chew-La Fitte, "The Use of Social Science Techniques in the Jury Selection Process," *Review of Litigation* 2 (1982), pp. 199–221.

[39] See R. Hunt, "Putting Juries on the Couch," *New York Times Magazine,* November 28, 1982.

obtain information about respondents' attitudes toward "very large companies" and the perceived unfairness of any small business competing with a much larger firm.

As a step toward identifying the characteristics of the ideal and nonideal jurors, respondents would be arrayed on their perceptions/feelings/opinions of these and other "psychographic" questions as indexed by the survey questions. Then, with a variety of demographic information used as predictor variables, one could apply standard statistical techniques, such as regression, discriminant analysis, or automatic interaction detection, to generate a multivariate model or "profile" of the ideal jurist. Having ascertained the background characteristics predictive of case-relevant attitudes, the marketing researcher is able to contribute to counsel's decisions regarding acceptability of a potential juror.

In essence, of course, what we are describing is a traditional form of marketing segmentation—but applied to a nontraditional context, namely jury selection. The choice of background questions for use in developing these profiles assumes that this information will be available about potential jurors. Consequently, it is important for the researcher to know before conducting such a survey how limited or extensive *voir dire* will be.

It is interesting to point out that the researcher's contribution need not be limited to creating jury profiles but may extend to a variety of jury-related issues. For example, marketing researchers have suggested ways to present information most effectively (particularly charts, graphs, and other information) for maximum communication impact. Pretesting different informational formats, including type size, the use of color, or graphic versus tabular presentation, can clearly add to an attorney's intuitive hunches—particularly in a complex case. The literature on information processing, information overload, and perceptual distortion are all relevant repositories of knowledge in the marketing researcher's tool bag.

Finally, any discussion of jury-related issues would not be complete without a reference to "jury simulation." By using a "shadow" jury, researchers are able to gain insight into the likely effect of each day's proceedings on the real jury. This is done by recruiting a similar group of people (the shadow jury) to sit through the proceedings and to provide feedback to the trial team regarding each day's events.[40] It would appear that important contributions can be made to trial strategy by the innovative use of these behavioral approaches.

---

[40] D. E. Vinson, "The Shadow Jury: An Experiment in Litigation Science," *American Bar Association Journal* 68 (1982), pp. 1242–46.

PRODUCT LIABILITY

The previous sections of this article have described how marketing research can be applied to yield evidence for, or assist in the process of, litigation, as well as in the development of policy and legislation. In the area of product liability, we also foresee a growing role for those with the marketing researcher's skills in minimizing companies' exposure to the threat of litigation.

The number of product liability claims due to injuries from products, as well as the burgeoning size of damage awards, has increased markedly in the past 30 years and has become a significant source of concern and expense for the corporation. In the seven years between 1974 and 1981, for example, the number of liability suits filed in federal district courts increased at a rate of 28 percent per year.[41] Unfortunately, some producers have tended to dismiss occurrences of product failure or defect as consequences of consumer misuse and abuse. However, the focus of the courts has continued to shift toward placing more, rather than less, responsibility on the manufacturer in planning, developing, and promoting safe products.

Many liability actions alleging defects in the product, or negligence in its manufacture or sale, are not stopping at the product itself but are extending to methods of marketing the product, instructions for its use, and warning information that accompanies the product to the marketplace. Consequently, corporate marketing personnel are being asked to play a larger role in minimizing company exposure to liability. In our view, marketing research needs to expand its efforts in these directions.

Product/Consumer Interactions. First, the manufacturers of many products will find it advantageous to research the actual usage situations of their products more thoroughly. Such attention may result in the identification of potential or inherent dangers in the use of the product in specific settings or by particular market segments. As a result, alterations in the product, the packaging, or the target market might be required. A vast array of unexpected usage situations, and unintended users, awaits additional attention from marketing researchers to minimize unexpected product hazards.

The Warning Process. A second area in which marketing and consumer research could be used more often to reduce the firm's exposure

---

[41] J. C. Mowen and H. W. Ellis, "Product Liability: Issues in Corporate Communications to Consumers and Jurors," paper presented at the 35th ASQC Midwest Conference, 1980, Tulsa.

to products liability is in the communication of warnings to consumers. While the firm's legal counsel should be closely involved with determining the content of any warnings, marketing research should have substantial input into the design and testing of any label or other disclosure message. For example, experimental research could compare different phrasings and wordings for understandability. Whether a consumer is more likely to see a warning if it is displayed on the package, comes as a package insert, or is written directly on the product is also a question subject to empirical test.

The magnitude of risk may even be such that other channels of communication of the warning should be experimentally evaluated, such as verbal reinforcement at the point of sale in market segments where a high percentage of users cannot read, or registered mail or telephone warnings to the purchasing agent regarding safe use of the product.

In sum, it is clear that numerous court decisions support the view that efficacious product planning includes discovering means of delivering the warning to have the desired behavioral effect.[42] This fact underscores the need for research into the content, form, and method of presentation of warnings to enhance the probability that the warning will be read and comprehended.

Product Recall. Finally, there are products that reach the market before hazards are identified and corrected. With seemingly increasing regularity, companies are having to recall products across a broad range of categories in which there exist demonstrated or potential defects. Some firms, however, have delayed recalling products because of their concern about the possible negative impact on company image.

Consumer research suggests that how the recall is managed can determine the impact on consumer perceptions, both positively as well as negatively. For example, Mowen and Ellis[43] tested experimentally how the factors of severity of injury, number of previous recalls by the company, and length of time to make the recall affected consumers' perceptions of the company. In this case, they found that company image suffered least if injuries were not serious, the company did not have a history of recalls, and the perception among the consumers was that the company had not delayed in initiating the recall.

In the instance of a recall, marketing research on consumer reactions to different scenarios for managing the recall could provide im-

---

    [42] F. W. Morgan and K. A. Boedecker, "The Role of Personal Selling in Products Liability Litigation," *Journal of Personal Selling and Management* 1 (1980), p. 34–40.

    [43] Mowen and Ellis, "Product Liability."

portant guidance to management as to how best to proceed at each stage in the recall process.

CONCLUDING OBSERVATIONS

The market researcher who offers a survey or any type of empirical research as legal evidence, and who has not previously experienced the adversarial culture of legal proceedings, should be forewarned that the process, while intellectually challenging, is rarely enjoyable.[44,45] As attention has shifted from the admissibility of survey evidence, for example, to the weight (or probative value) it should be given, the courts and opposing counsel have paid close attention to the many issues relating to the validity and reliability of research results.[46]

The researcher can be expected to be asked *in detail* about every stage in the research process, including why the population was defined the way it was, how the sample was drawn, why questions were worded and ordered as they were, the nature and extent of interviewer training, how the data were coded, what specific quality-control steps were applied, which statistical methods were chosen, and other questions that might bear on the truthfulness and accuracy of the researcher's portrayal of the data or its interpretation.

Many articles have appeared in the literature outlining the issues and concerns in using survey research in litigation and, thus, all cannot be listed here. However, those conducting their first survey for use in litigation are well advised to review the sources used in the footnotes throughout this chapter, as well as the selected works we have provided in the References section. Our own experience would lead us to highlight the following generic points relating to the use of marketing research in litigation:

1. Begin and conduct the research with a view toward the detailed adversarial evaluation the entire research process will undergo.[47] As just one example, in a recent federal district court trial, many days of expert

---

[44] H. Abelson, "My Day in Court," *Journal of Advertising Research* 13 (1973), pp. 10–12.

[45] V. Appel, "My Day in Court," *Journal of Advertising Research* 13 (1973), pp. 12–14.

[46] For a brief but cogent discussion of these issues, see Sherrill, "Survey Evidence in Litigation," pp. 220–21.

[47] We have not discussed the issues relating to the important legal process known as "discovery." Since the marketing researcher may well be subjected to this process, those becoming involved in litigation should be thoroughly briefed *prior* to beginning any research activity. See J. M. Cooper, ed., *Attorney-Client Privilege and the Work-Product Doctrine* (American Bar Association, 1983).

testimony were spent in disagreement over the coding of individual data-points—data that represented but a small percentage of the entire database and whose effect on any inferences to be drawn was likely to be negligible.

2. Be prepared to explain how your research relates directly to the case. To guide your testimony, counsel should discuss with you how your testimony fits into the overall trial strategy, and what specific linkages are to be made from your particular contribution.

3. Remember that your audience—jury or judge, or both—is not sophisticated with regard to research issues. Simplicity is highly valued. To the extent possible, presentation of research results should be limited to key points and issues, with formulas and displays of statistical wizardry held to an absolute minimum.

4. Rehearse the delivery of a concise overview of the study and a cogent interpretation of the research findings. There is no substitute for clarity in your own mind prior to your day in court.

Many legal issues revolve around what people in the marketplace think and do, questions that marketing and consumer research professionals are in a position to answer. We have offered some examples of how the marketing researcher or marketing manager can contribute to the firm's legal efforts—by providing unique kinds of evidence bearing on a case at hand, by assisting legal counsel in decisions regarding trial process, and by minimizing exposure to litigation by research that ensures the safe use of the company's products.

It is important that the marketing professional recognize how this expertise may assist in the company's legal activities, because many corporate executives and attorneys may not. Part of the marketer's role, then, is to educate. Otherwise the firm runs the risk of overlooking a resource whose value may be recognized only too late—when marketing research is used effectively by the opposing side.

REFERENCES

"Preparing for a Day in Court." *Business Week*, March 30, 1981, pp. 144–47.

Cooper, J. M. ed., *Attorney-Client Privilege and the Work-Product Doctrine*. (American Bar Association, 1983).

Dutka, S. "Business Calls Opinion Surveys to Testify for the Defense." *Harvard Business Review*, July–August, 1980.

———. "The Use of Survey Research in Legal Proceedings." *American Bar Association Journal* 68, pp. 1508–10.

Levy, S. J., and D. W. Rook. "Brands, Trademarks, and the Law. In *Review of Marketing, 1981*. ed. J. Roering. Chicago: American Marketing Association, 1981, pp. 185–94.

McElroy, B. T. "Public Surveys—The Latest Exception to the Hearsay Rule. *Baylor Law Review* 28, pp. 59–76.

Morgan, F. W. "Marketing and Product Liability: A Review and Update. *Journal of Marketing* 46 (1979), pp. 69–78.

Morgan, J. C., and H. W. Ellis. "The Product Defect: Managerial Considerations and Consumer Implications. In *Review of Marketing, 1981,* eds. B. M. Enis and K. J. Roering. Chicago: American Marketing Association, 1981, pp. 158–72.

Roettger, G. J. "Do's and Don'ts of Cross Examination." *The Expert and the Law* 2, (1981), pp. 5–7.

Roper, B. W. "Public Opinion Surveys in Legal Proceedings." *American Bar Association Journal* 51 (1965), pp. 46–47.

Smith, J. C. "My Day in Court," *Journal of Advertising Research* 13 (1973), p. 9.

Sorensen, R. C., and T. C. Sorensen. "The Admissability and Use of Opinion Research Evidence." *New York University Law Review* 28 (1953), pp. 1213–61.

_____. "Responding to Objections against the Use of Opinion Survey Findings in the Courts." *Journal of Marketing* 20 (1955), pp. 133–42.

Sprowls, R. C. "The Admissibility of Sample Data into a Court of Law: A Case History." *UCLA Law Review* 4, (1957), pp. 222–32.

Zeisel, H. "The Uniqueness of Survey Evidence." *Cornell Law Quarterly* 45 (1960), pp. 322–46.

BIOGRAPHIES

Dick Berry

Professor Dick Berry directs the Management Institute marketing and service management programs at the University of Wisconsin.

He previously worked as an engineering and marketing executive in industry. Berry has written three books and published over 75 articles and monographs. He holds degrees in engineering and adult education–business from the University of Wisconsin.

Jim Betts

Jim Betts is editor of *New Products Development Newsletter* and author of the book *The Million Dollar Idea,* and co-author of the book *New Products: How to Create, Research, Develop and Market Them Successfully.*

Stephen D. Boudreau, Jr.

Mr. Boudreau is group director, communications and marketing services, Packaging and Converted Products Group, of St. Regis Corporation in New York.

His career assignments include early training at Young & Rubicam Advertising. He established, organized, and directed the advertising/promotion department at St. Regis and the corporate account sales department. As director of corporate marketing services, he developed the marketing business planning system—the selling system and allied disciplines, such as customer service and telemarketing. In his current assignment he also is responsible for the design and implementation of education and training in these areas.

Boudreau is a contributing author of *The Sales Managers' Handbook, The Industrial Marketing Handbook,* and *Insights into Sales Effectiveness.*

John W. Burns

Mr. Burns is a principal of Rath & Strong, Inc., and is director of human resources, designing and managing strategies to improve the organization's overall climate and the effectiveness of managers.

He has firsthand experience in formulating and executing marketing plans and product strategies, in directing an industrial sales force, and in designing sales compensation programs.

Prior to joining Rath & Strong, he was director of human resources and later vice president of sales and marketing for a division of a *Fortune* 100 firm. He received a bachelor's degree, with concentrations in electrical engineering and political science, from the University of Wyoming and his master's degree from the Institute of Labor and Industrial Relations, University of Illinois.

Ardis Burst

Ardis Burst is president of Burst-Lazarus Associates, Inc., Scarsdale, New York. She specializes in applying the principles of package goods marketing to new areas, including nonprofit organizations.

She was formerly in product management in the Maxwell House division of General Foods. She holds a MBA with distinction from Harvard Business School.

Dan Ciampa CMC

Mr. Ciampa is executive vice president of Rath & Strong, Inc., and concentrates on helping top-level managers develop and implement efforts leading to overall excellence. He is one of the creators of the firm's Multidisciplinary Approach, in 1972.

He specializes in consulting in the areas of organizational change, individual management improvement, group problem solving and decision making, strategy implementation, and top-management teamwork. He also has directed long-term projects for manufacturing, service, religious, community, and educational organizations.

Mr. Ciampa is a frequent speaker and writes on topics of improving manufacturing operations, computer-integrated manufacturing, combining technical and behavioral science forms of consulting, and leadership. He is listed in Who's Who in Industry and Finance, is a member of NTL

Institute's Organization Development Network, and is an associate of the British Institute of Management.

He received his bachelor of science degree in finance and social psychology from Boston College and a master of education degree in adult education from Boston University.

Bruce S. Fisher

Mr. Fisher is vice president—markets, Residential division, of Lightolier, Inc.

At Lightolier, he has served as a product manager and as national distributor sales manager. He has also had experience in distribution at Cummins Lighting Company of Fort Worth, Texas, as vice president and general manager, and in merchandising at J. C. Penney.

Lynn Tendler Gilbert

Ms. Gilbert is principal and co-founder, with Janet Tweed, of Gilbert Tweed Associates, Inc., an executive search firm with offices in New York, Boston, Maine, and Paris.

Before establishing Gilbert Tweed Associates, Ms. Gilbert spent five years with Dunhill Personnel, which included the training of over 50 successful franchisees and the management of all engineering and technical recruiting at the New York office.

She received a BA in mathematics from the University of Florida in Gainesville. She currently serves on the board of directors of the National Association of Corporate & Professional Recruiters and is Co-chairperson of the New York chapter.

Jeanne and Herbert Greenberg

Jeanne and Herbert Greenberg are principals of Personality Dynamics, Inc., a Princeton-based personality testing firm which has, since 1961, accurately predicted the sales and management effectiveness of more than a half million individuals for over 11,000 companies throughout the world.

Angelico Groppelli

Dr. Groppelli is associate professor and chairman, Department of Banking and Finance, Hofstra University.

Dr. Groppelli was a general partner and director of research at Cowen and Company, a well-known Wall Street brokerage house. He was also vice president and associate director of Lionel D. Edie and Company, an investment and economic consulting firm.

He received a BA degree from Hunter College and MA and Ph.D. degrees from New York University.

Ann Hammer

Ann Hammer joined Gilbert Tweed Associates in 1983 and is currently responsible for managing research activities throughout the firm's five offices.

She received a Bachelor of Arts from University of Maine. After receiving her MSW from Washington University in St. Louis she spent two years as a legislative assistant to Congresswoman Olympia J. Snowe in Washington, D.C., before moving to New York City.

John F. Hartshorne CAE

Mr. Hartshorne is executive director of the Institute of Management Consultants, Inc., a nonprofit membership organization founded in 1968 to further the development of management consulting as a profession and to accredit the qualifications of individual consultants.

Previously, he had served for 18 years (from 1957 to 1975) on the administrative staff of Cresap, McCormick and Paget Inc., the international management consulting firm. As this firm's director of development, he provided planning and support services to the professional staff in a wide range of communications and practice development functions.

Mr. Hartshorne is a certified association executive. Prior to his career in consulting, Mr. Hartshorne served for nine years on the staff of *Business Week* magazine, where he held editorial and administrative positions. He is a graduate of Yale University.

Dale P. Hugo

Mr. Hugo is market manager of consumer products at Loctite Corporation's Automotive and Consumer Group in Cleveland. He is responsible for the consumer marketing of Duro, Loctite, and Permatex repair and maintenance products for the home and car.

He previously held various marketing, advertising, and sales positions with Swan Hose division of Amerace Corporation, Howard Swink

Advertising, and Westinghouse Electric Corporation. He received an MBA from Ohio State University and a BS in business from Miami University.

Mark C. Kelly

Mr. Kelly, a consultant at Rath & Strong, Inc., specializes in business planning and control, in performance measurement and productivity improvement, and in organization and human resource planning and problem solving.

His consulting experience includes developing long-range plans for small to medium-sized firms, developing and installing performance measurement systems for industrial and service companies, and addressing organization and people issues in multidisciplinary problem-solving assignments.

Prior to consulting, he was a planning assistant to the top management of McM Corporation, a medium-sized holding company. He received his BA from Wake Forest University and his MBA from the University of North Carolina at Chapel Hill.

Boris M. Krantz

Mr. Krantz formed his present company, Krantz Associates, Inc., in 1980, and has since provided strategic planning, market research, public relations and advertising services, and sales and management training to domestic and international clients. In addition, his company provides sales training designed specifically for industrial welding distributor salesmen.

He also writes a regular column ("Professional Management") for *The Welding Distributor* magazine. The first series of columns has just been published by TWD, and its title is *Sales Fundamentals*.

A graduate of Tufts and R.P.I., Krantz was product development manager and product marketing manager at Airco, and at Sandvik was general manager of the Welding Products division. In addition, he has managed a network of 12 industrial distributor locations.

Robert F. LaRue

Mr. LaRue is president of LaRue Marketing Consultants, Inc., South Plainfield, New Jersey, a firm founded in 1983 and that specializes in marketing communications strategies, feasibility studies, alternative distribution channels, and franchising and licensing.

From 1968 he operated LaRue & Associates, and earlier, marketing services organizations. Twice he has gone "inside" companies—once as vice president of marketing services and director of corporate communications and another time as president.

John T. Mentzer

John T. Mentzer is Associate Professor of Marketing in the College of Business at Virginia Polytechnic Institute and State University. He has written more than fifty papers and articles in numerous journals and is on the editorial review board of several journals. He has co-authored three books and served as consultant for over twenty corporations.

Kent B. Monroe

Kent Monroe is professor of marketing and John Mentzer is associate professor of marketing, College of Business, Virginia Polytechnic Institute and State University.

Robert A. Moskowitz

Mr. Moskowitz is a management consultant, author, and president of the Personal Productivity Center, Woodland Hills, California. He developed the Personal Productivity Audit, which provides cost-effective counselling and productivity improvement for white-collar workers by means of a computer-written and completely individualized report.

He is the editor of several national newsletters on automation, productivity, and business; author of *How To Organize Your Work and Your Life,"* published by Doubleday; and the creator/producer of eight management training programs, published by the American Management Association. Mr. Moskowitz has written and produced management training films, and has won the Silver Medal at the International Film and TV Festival of New York.

Ronald N. Paul

Mr. Paul, CMC, is president and co-founder of Technomic Consultants, a strategic market planning firm established in 1966. Its clients include more than 200 *Fortune*-listed firms. Technomic Consultants has offices in Chicago, New York, Boston, Los Angeles, and San Francisco; and an international practice with offices in Geneva, Sao Paulo, Hong Kong, and Tokyo. The firm's services relate primarily to market planning assignments, new product planning, industrial market research, and acquisition identification and evaluation.

Mr. Paul has written extensively on subjects related to marketing and new products. His articles and chapters have appeared in such publications as *Harvard Business Review* and *Management Review*. His *Handbook of Business Problem Solving*, was published by McGraw-Hill, and *Creative Marketing for the Foodservice Industry* by Wiley-Interscience.

His undergraduate degree in industrial engineering, as well as an MBA, were earned at Northwestern University.

Steven E. Permut

Dr. Permut is associate professor of marketing at the Yale University School of Management, and principal of Marketing Sciences, Inc., a New Haven, CT, consulting firm.

He is founding editor of the Praeger Series in Public and Nonprofit Sector Marketing, and co-editor of *Government Marketing: Theory and Practice*. He serves on the editorial boards of the *Journal of Marketing, Journal of Consumer Marketing, Journal of Public Policy & Marketing*, and *Journal of Business Forecasting*. Dr. Permut is a frequent participant in management education programs, with particular interest in applications of marketing research to the technology and services sectors.

Joseph T. Plummer

Mr. Plummer is executive vice president and director of research services at Young & Rubicam USA and is a member of the board of directors of Young & Rubicam USA.

Prior to Y&R, Mr. Plummer had been with the Leo Burnett ad agency, in Chicago, which he joined in 1967 as a research analyst and held a succession of research posts until 1974, when he became vice president of Worldwide Marketing Services and, in 1976, senior vice president and research director.

Mr. Plummer holds a BA degree from Westminster (Pa.) College and both MA and Ph.D. degrees in communications from Ohio State University.

He is on the editorial boards of the *Journal of Marketing, Journal of Advertising, Journal of Advertising Research, Journal of Broadcasting,*

Journal of Business Research, and *Critical Studies in Mass Communication.*

Mr. Plummer was the NAB Grant Winner in 1967. He was first listed in Who's Who in the Midwest in 1974 and 1975 and in "Who's Who in America in 1979 through 1983.

Steven J. Power

Mr. Power is vice president of marketing at Thermo-Serv, Inc. Before that he was market manager at Honeywell, manager of market research and new product development at Lehigh Products, and adjunct professor, Grand Valley State College and Aquinas College, both in Michigan.

Marvin Rafal

Mr. Rafal is president of Marvin Rafal Associates, Inc., and is a specialist in the selection, training, and development of managers. His company develops and conducts management development seminars tailored to a company's needs, and it develops competency-based performance appraisal systems.

He holds degrees in psychology and education and has served on the faculty of the department of marketing at Rutgers University.

Jim Rapp

Mr. Rapp is director of education and training for the National Office Products Association, Alexandria, Virginia. Previously, he was corporate director of education and information for Berol Corporation, where he prepared and conducted a wide variety of educational programs for divisions in the United States, Canada, Europe, and Latin America. He also held sales and marketing positions with Berol.

Prior to entering the office products industry, he held sales, sales management, and sales training positions with General Foods Corporation.

Mr. Rapp has written a number of books and training courses on sales, sales management, personnel selection, sales training, and sales compensation. He has recently written handbooks on advertising and retail store management.

Paul Saunders

Mr. Saunders is a practising attorney who, after 25 years of New York practice—both as a private practitioner and as inside counsel for two major publishing concerns—moved his practice to Sea Girt, New Jersey, a mile or so from his home at the seashore. He is still actively involved in the publishing world and represents several national trade associations.

Arnold L. Schwartz

Mr. Schwartz is founder and president of Achievement Concepts, Inc., a New York consulting firm specializing in sales training, sales management development, motivation and sales personality/aptitude testing. Mr. Schwartz conducts customized sales, leadership, and management development programs. These programs feature motivation, communications, goal-setting, creative selling skills, and the use of psychology in sales and management. Clients have included RCA Global Communications, RCA Cylix, NEC America, Lear Siegler, Dow Jones, AT&T, EF Hutton, Citibank, Sony, Seiko Time, Clairol, Bantam Books, and Beatrice Foods.

A graduate of Columbia College, Mr. Schwartz has extensive experience in sales, sales supervision, and marketing management. He has held sales and management positions with Burroughs, SCM Corp., served as national sales manager for Leasco Data Processing (now The Reliance Group), and as vice president of sales for the Data Services division of ITEL Corporation.

Charles W. Stryker

Dr. Stryker is executive vice president of Trinet, Inc., and has been involved with market planning and analysis for many industrial clients.

He has worked with over 30 of the Fortune 500 as well as other large and medium-sized businesses. He has a Ph.D. in operations research from New York University and has been a frequent author and speaker on the topic of industrial marketing productivity.

Leah S. Tarlow

Ms. Tarlow, an MBA (marketing) graduate of the University of Maryland, joined Krantz Associates as marketing consultant in early 1982 and has since been active in sales training, market research, and strategic planning.

She has designed telemarketing and computer-based systems for handling advertising leads, and she has conducted specific marketing research and planning studies in the wholesale marketing function, specialty gas marketing, and a variety of advertising and communications assignments.

Janet Tweed

Ms. Tweed is principal and co-founder, with Lynn Gilbert, of Gilbert Tweed Associates, Inc., an executive search firm with offices in New York, Boston, Maine, and Paris. Established in 1972, Gilbert Tweed has revenues in excess of $2 million and employs 23 people in its four offices. Gilbert Tweed also is a consultant, assisting corporations in the recruitment, planning, development, and assessment of their human resource needs.

She is a member of the National Association of Corporate & Professional Recruiters, the American Society for Personnel Administration, and International Association for Personnel Women, and has been elected to Who's Who of American Women.

Robert F. Vizza

Professor Vizza is dean of the School of Business at Manhattan College.

He is the author of eight books and over one hundred articles about marketing management. He also has served as consultant to major corporations.

Jeffery T. Wack

Dr. Wack is a principal of Marketing Sciences, Inc., a New Haven marketing and consumer research firm assisting a wide range of clients in the high technology and services sectors. The firm has also conducted research for use in litigation and administrative proceedings.

A graduate of Yale University's doctoral program in psychology, Dr. Wack previously served on the staff of the deputy surgeon general in Washington, D.C., and has been a senior research analyst with *Consumer Reports* magazine.

Stewart A. Washburn CMC

Mr. Washburn is recognized internationally as an authority on management of the sales and marketing functions and his work on these subjects is widely published. He is a Certified Management Consultant, a founding member of the Institute of Management Consultants, a member of the commercial panel of the American Arbitration Association and practice development editor of the *Journal of Management Consulting*. He is listed in *Who's Who in Finance and Industry*. Mr. Washburn's clients include a number of *Fortune* 500 firms and a host of smaller companies and associations.

Daniel K. Weadock

Mr. Weadock is vice president of sales at Matheson Gas Products, Inc.

He has more than 20 years of varied sales and sales management experience. He is a member of many professional societies and publishes articles regularly on the theory and practice of sales and marketing.

He holds a BS in chemistry from Manhattan College and did graduate work in chemistry at Purdue. He received his MBA in marketing from Pace University.

Ray O. Werner

Dr. Werner is professor of economics at Colorado College in Colorado Springs.

Since 1965, he has been the editor of the legal developments in marketing section of the *Journal of Marketing* and has written extensively on the legal environment of marketing.

Larry Wizenberg

Mr. Wizenberg is vice president of Yankelovich, Skelly, and White's Consumer Marketing Group. He also is an assistant professor in marketing at New York University's School of Continuing Education and is a frequent lecturer on new product development, sales, and marketing strategy.

INDEX

A

Abelson, H., 477n
Account qualification, 248–50, 268
Acme, Inc., 128
Acquisition, 341–42
Advertising and sales promotion, 38, 93
  deception, 469–71
  discounts, 115–16
  new products, 334
  product management system, 48, 49
Affirmative action programs, 61
After-sale product support, 233–43
  alternative approaches to product
    support, 241–42
  customer satisfaction, 234, 236
  insurance perspective, 235
  integrated marketing strategy, 239
  keys to growth, 242–43
  service requirements planning, 239–
    41
  service support level, 237–38
  strategic perspective, 238
After-service mix, 234–35
Allison, J. R., 464n
Allport, X. Y., 309n
Amara, Roy, 16
American Motors Company, 331
American Society of Composers, Au-
* thors and Publishers, et al. v.*
* Columbia Broadcasting System,*
  442
Americare, 232, 237
Anderson, Paul F., 118
Antitrust litigation, 464–67
  product category definition, 465

Antitrust litigation—*Cont.*
  relevant market determination, 464–
    66
Appalachian Coals, Inc. v. *United*
* States,* 442
Appel, V., 477n
Applications-support function, 234
Argyris, Chris, 159
Association of Management Consul-
  tants, 128
AT&T, 341
Automatic test equipment, 241–42

B

Baby boomers cohort group, 18–20
Bacon, Frank R., Jr., 162n
Barksdale, H. C., 469n
Base price, 114
Berry, Dick, 232, 238, 480
Betts, Jim, 383, 480
Blue collar job, 18
Bobrow, Edwin E., 212
Boedecker, K. A., 476n
Bonora, B., 472n, 473n
Booz, Allen & Hamilton, Inc., 124,
  372–74, 386n
Bork, Robert H., 449n
Boudreau, Stephen D., Jr., 244, 480–81
Box Jenkins model, 419
Boyatzes, R., 143n, 145n
Branch/district sales office management
  appraisal and evaluation, 217
  branch manager as business person,
    218–19
    personal development, 219–20
  field coaching, 216–17

Branch/district sales office management—*Cont.*
  goals and expectations, 210–11
  leadership values, 208–10
  motivation, 214–16
  recruiting and selection, 211–12
  training and development of salespersons, 212–14
Brandt, Inc., 232
Brandt, M. T., 470n
Bray, Douglas, 143n, 145n
Break-even point, 401–3
Britt, Stewart H., 33, 34, 35
Brown Shoe Co. v. *United States*, 449n, 466–67
Brown, Wilfred, 133n
Budget formulation, 37
Buell, Victor, 155, 156
Burge, D. A., 467n
Burns, John, 74, 481
Burst, Ardis, 40, 481
Business analysis, 392
Butler, Thomas W., Jr., 162n
Byham, William, 145n

C

Cady, John F., 442n
Call Planner, 255–57
Campbell, David, 312n
Campbell, Richard, 143n
Campbell Soup Company, 327, 332, 333
Capital expenditures, 393
Career path, 139–41
Carlson, Chester, 340
Cash discount, 116–18
Cash inflows
  definition, 393
  projecting, 396–403
Cash Management Account (CMA), 342
Cash outflows, 392–94
Celler-Kefauver Act, 448
Certainty equivalent approach (CEA), 414–15
Change, Management of, 14–29
Channels of distribution
  alternative, 221–31
  costs, 98
  marketing communication strategies, 227
  price decisions, 99–100
  sales force, 178–79
  use of existing channels, 222–24

Chestnut, R. W., 466n
Chew-La Fitte, D., 473n
Chief executive officer (CEO), 159–61
Christie, R., 473n
Chrysler Corporation, 331
Ciampa, Dan, 74, 481–82
Civil Rights Act of 1964, Title VII, 60
Clayton Act, 445, 446–51, 464
Clyde A. Perkins v. *Standard Oil of California*, 451
Coca-Cola Company, 357
Commerce Clearing House, *Trade Regulation Reports*, 441
Common resource problems, 111–14
Communication, 94
  creative, 170
  telemarketing, 244–66
  voice, 260–61
Computers, 282
  conference training technique, 147–48
  customer support, 301
  handling sales leads, 282–86
  list of suppliers for marketing applications, 303–7
  market analysis, 290–94
  point of sale, 286–90
  politics, 302–3
  sales calls, 297–301
  sales forecasting, 292
  sales tracking and control, 294–97
Consumer Product Warranties and Federal Trade Commission Improvements Act, 452
Continental T.V., Inc., et al. v. *GTE Sylvania, Inc.*, 443
Contract, 457–62
  lawyer's services, 457–61
  self-help ideas, 461
  standard, 460
Control Data Corporation, 376
Cooper, J. M., 477n
Corporate life cycle, 22–23
Corporate mission statement, 165–66, 169, 175–77
Counseling and appraisal training techniques, 148
Crawford, C. Merle, 387
Creative communications, 170
Creativity, 96
Crowther, John F., 119
Customer classification, 246–47

D

Dartnell, 33
Data entry, 293
Database, 283
Datsun Motor Car Company, 342
Davis, Stanley M., 387n
Davis-Standard Company, 346
Day, G. S., 465n
Decentralization, 15
Decision tree, 415–16
Della Bitta, Albert J., 119
Demographic trends, 18
Dick, A. B., Inc., 345
Discount, 99, 114–19
Discounted cash flow (DCF), 408–15
Discrimination in hiring, 60
Distributor, 35; *see also* Channels of
    distribution
  costs linked to price, 98
Donath, Bob, 160n
Doob, Anthony, 98n
Downloading data, 294
Dual-income households, 18–19
Dunfee, T. W., 464n
Dunne, Patrick M., 98n

E

Eastman Kodak Company, 332
Edwards, Corwin, 450n
Efficiency expert, 125
Ego drive, 54–56
Ego-empathy grid, 183–85
Ego strength, 54, 57
Electronic funds transfer, 287–88
Electronic spreadsheet, 291–92
Ellis, H. W., 475n, 476
Empathy, 54–55, 56, 183–86
Enis, B. M., 469n
Equal Credit Opportunity Act of 1975,
    452
Experience curve, 101
Exxon, 359

F

Face-to-face sales techniques, 187–89
Fainsod, Merle, 441n
Fair Credit Billing Act of 1975, 452
Fair Credit Reporting Act of 1970, 452
Fair employment regulations, 60
Fair Packaging and Labeling Act, 452

Federal Food, Drug and Cosmetic Act,
    446
Federal Mogul Corporation, 242
Federal Trade Commission, 449
Federal Trade Commission Act, 448,
    451–55
Federal Trade Commission v. *Brown
    Shoe Co.*, 448n
Federal Trade Commission v. *Consoli-
    dated Foods Corp.*, 449n
Federal Trade Commission v. *Gratz*,
    451
Federal Trade Commission v. *Motion
    Picture Advertising Service Co.*,
    448n
Federal Trade Commission v. *Rala-
    dam*, 452
Field sales force, 46
Fisher, Bruce S., 154, 372, 482,
Flammable Fabrics Act, 452
Ford, Henry, 347, 383
Ford Motor Company, 331, 383
Ford Motor Co. v. *United States*, 449
Fortner Enterprises, Inc. v. *United
    States Corp.*, 447
Fox, Eleanor M., 449n
Franchising, feasibility determination,
    229–31
Frank, R., 466n
Functional discount, 114–15
Functional marketing organization, 34
Fur Products Labeling Act, 452

G

Gardner, D. M., 470n
Gellhorn, E. E., 470n
General Electric Company, 242, 356,
    375
General Foods, 46, 360
General Mills, 360
General Motors, 331, 337
Gilbert, Lynn Tendler, 91, 482
Ginger, A. F., 473n
Gordon, R. L., 468n
Grant, Donald, 143n
Grant, Dwight, 117n
Greenberg, Herbert M., 53, 482
Greenberg, Jeanne, 53, 482
Gropelli, Angelico, 391, 482–83
Growth and development opportunities,
    95–96

H

Haloid Company, 340
Hammer, Ann, 91
Hansen, Jo-Ida, 312n
Hartshorne, John F., 122, 483
Hastie, R., 473n
Heterarchical organization, 15, 24
Herzberg, 214
Hierarchical organization structure, 15, 24
Hiring
   criteria, 59
   legal aspects of, 60–63
Holsti, O. R., 472n
Honeywell Company, 16
Howell, R. A., 464n
Huckabee, Bill, 21, 22, 23
Hughes, G. David, 440n
Hugo, Dale P., 164, 483
Humphrey, G. Watts, Jr., 376
Hunt, R., 473n
Hunter, Morgan V., 385n

I

IBM, 235, 237, 241, 374
Idea leadership, 28–29
Ideal Toy Company, 341
Industrial engineering, 124
Industrial product marketing, 421
Industrial selling, 360–62
Inner-directed managers, 21–22
Innovations, 322, 339–40, 373, 374–75
Installed User Program (IUP), 374
Institute for the Future, 16
Institute of Management Consultants, 128
Integrated manager, 21–22
Intel, 15
Interdepartmental creative seminars, 170
Interest inventory, 311–14
Internal rate of return (IRR), 412–13
International Salt case, 447
Interview of sales applicants
   in-depth, 71–73
   initial, 63–64
Inventions, 339–40

J

Jacoby, J., 466n
Jentz, G. A., 464n

Job rotation, 148
Johns Manville Company, 341
Johnson & Johnson Company, 341
Joint marketing conferences, 170
The Jungle, 446

K

Kelly, Mark, 74, 483–84
Keyboarding, 293
Keying in data, 293
Kinney Shoe Company, 467
Kintner, Earl W., 450n, 451n
Kotler, P., 466n
Krantz, Boris M., 3, 484
Krauss, E., 472n, 473n
Kunin, L., 469n

L

Lamb, Charles W., Jr., 98n
Land Camera Company, 340
Land, Edwin, 340
Lanham Trade Mark Act, 452, 467
Larson, Meredith, 16
LaRue, P. H., 470n
LaRue, Robert, 221, 484
Lauder, Estée, 376
Lawrence, Paul R., 387n
Leadership, 24, 26–29
Legal aspects of marketing, 437–56
   advertising deceptions, 469–71
   antitrust litigation, 464–67
   basic laws involving marketing, 441–55
   competent counsel, 437, 439
   current and future impact, 455–56
   history and background of laws, 440–55
   interpretation of statutes, 438–39
   marketing research, 463–77
   mergers, 448–50
   monopolization, 444–45
   price discrimination, 450
   price fixing, 442, 444
   product liability, 475–77
   trademarks and brands, 467–69
   trial process, 471–74
   typing contracts, 443
   using laws for market advantage, 440
Levy, Michael, 117n
Licensing, 341
Life-Long Learning, 137–39
Liggett & Meyers case, 466

Lindzey, W. Z., 309n
Lionel Trains, 356
Lippa's, Inc. v. *Lennox, Incorporated,*
    451
List price, 114
Loctite Corporation, 165–66, 169, 175–
    77

M

McGreggor, 214
McKinsey & Company, 124
Magnavox Company, 341
Magnuson-Moss Warranty-Federal
    Trade Commission Improvement
    Act, 452, 454
"Maker" style of leadership, 24
Management consulting, 122–31
    confidentiality, 130
    conflict of interest, 130
    definition, 124
    evaluation, 130
    functions, 125–26
    need for, 126–27
    origins, 124–25
    professional credentials, 131
    project planning, 129–30
    selection of firm, 127–29
Management style, 21
Management team; *see* Marketing
    management team
Management theories, 15
Managing in Diversity, 21
Managing the sale, 202
Market analysis, 290–94
Market audit, 348–50
Market planning, 8
Market research, 7–8, 350–53
    litigation; *see* Marketing research in
        litigation
Market segmentation, 345–46
Marketing; *see also* Marketing manage-
    ment
    concept, 154–55
    legal aspects; *see* Legal aspects of
        marketing
    new products; *see* New product
        marketing
Marketing Communication Research
    Center (MCRC), 160
Marketing driven approach to manage-
    ment, 6–9
Marketing intermediaries, 35

Marketing management
    advertising and sales promotion, 38,
        93
    budget formulation, 37
    channel selection, 35–36
    corporate marketing group, 158
    executing plans, 39
    forecasting, 37–38
    functions, 155–56
    multidivisional companies, 156–58
    new product development, 36
    order processing, 38–39
    organization, 31–35, 168
    pricing, 36–37
    profit, 36–37
    role of CEO, 159–61
    sales, 38
Marketing management team, 7, 74,
        158–59
    assigning responsibilities, 83–86
    eliminating turnover, 91–96
    expertise required, 79–83
    industrial teams, 76
    need for teamwork, 158–59
    selection system, 86–89
    size of, 77–78
Marketing manager, 31–39, 168–69, 308
    definition, 133
    job and responsibility, 133
    training and development, 135–52
Marketing Manager's Handbook, 33
Marketing organism, 166
Marketing organization
    establishing marketing plan, 31–35
    functional, 34
    product manager structure, 34–35,
        168
Marketing plan
    long-range, 32
    short-range, 31–32
Marketing productivity
    company philosophy, 165
    corporate mission, 165–66
    definition, 164
    financial resources allocated to mar-
        keting, 173–74
    improving, 169–73
    management style, 165
Marketing program, 7–9
    management, 154–62
Marketing research in litigation, 463–77
    antitrust litigation, 464–67
    deceptive advertising, 469–71

Marketing research in litigation—*Cont.*
  product liability, 475–77
  trademarks and brands, 467–69
  trial process, 471–74
    jury selection, 473–74
    venue change, 471–73
Marmer, R. L., 469n
Maslow, Abraham, 214
Massy, W., 466n
Matrix management, 15, 16, 40, 42
Matsushita Electric, 375
Mazis, M. B., 471n
Megatrends, 14
Mentzer, John T., 97, 117, 119, 484–85
Merrill Lynch, 342
Michael, Donald N., 16
Minute Maid Company, 344
Mitchell, Arnold, 24
Monroe, Kent B., 97, 98n, 117, 119, 485
Monte Carlo simulation, 419
Morgan, F. W., 469n, 476n
Moslowitz, Robert A., 282, 485
Motivation, 214–16
"Mover" style of leadership, 24
Mowen, J. C., 475n, 476
Multidivisional companies, 156–58
Myers, J. H., 466n

N

Naisbitt, John, 14, 15n, 16n, 23, 26
National Steel Company, 376
Nault, James P., 110n
Net present value (NPV), 411–13
Networking, 15
New nonconsumer product, 421
  market launch, 433
  market testing, 431–33
  organization for, 421–24
  strategic approach to, 425
    evaluation, 428–30
    idea generation, 426–27
    prototype development, 430–31
    screening, 428
New product, 321
  acquisition, 341–42
  advocacy approach, 327
  characteristics of successful marketing, 330–39
  competitive product evaluation, 377, 381

New product—*Cont.*
  customer requests, 347
  definition, 364
  design brief, 377, 380
  development, 36, 324–25, 363–71
  evaluation team, 355
  evolution, 342–47
  invention and innovation, 322, 339–40, 373
  managing successful launch, 359–61
  market audits, 348
  market research, 350–53, 375–77
  marketing department role, 376–81
  need for, 363–64, 373–82
  nonconsumer product; *see* New nonconsumer product
  organization for, 365, 423–24
  payback; *see* New product payback
  planning, 323
  pricing, 100, 103–5
  pro forma business plan, 377, 378
  profile chart, 377, 379
  publications, 328
  rejects and failures, 327
  selection for development, 338, 353–59
  strategic guidelines, 329–39
  system, 365–71
    definition phase, 366, 367
    design phase, 366, 368
    development phase, 368–70
    production phase, 370–71
  top management commitment, 364
New product committee, 365
New product gap, 36
New product payback, 391
  forecasting revenues, 394–96
  initial investment costs, 392–94
  monitoring results, 415–19
  pro forma income statement, 403–7
  projecting cash inflows, 396–403
  risk premium determination, 410
  techniques for planning, 407–15
New product team, 384–87
  goals, 386
  matrix team, definition, 387
  mission, 385
  restraints, 387
  selection of members, 385
New Products Management, 387
New Rules, 18
Nissan Motors, 342

Northern Pacific Railway Co. v. *United States,* 447n
Noyce, Robert, 15

O

Ohio Medical Products, 237
O'Meara, Vicki, 470n
On-line catalog, 289
Operating-line organizational structure, 193–97
Optical scanner, 289
Order processing, 38–39
Outer-directed managers, 21–22

P

Palamountain, Joseph C., Jr., 441n
Parasensory experiences, 27
Parker Brothers, 341, 468
Paul, Ronald N., 421, 485
Payback
    definition, 391
    new product; *see* New product payback
Penetration pricing, 104–5
People measurement, 311
Pepsi Cola Company, 357
Permut, Steven E., 463, 486
Perquisites, 92
Peter Principle, 219
Petroshius, Susan M., 98n
Pill Brothers, 347
Pillsbury Company, 374
Plummer, Joseph T., 14, 486
Pollack, M., 472n
Population shifts, 18
Power, Steve, 31, 363, 486
Preston, I. L., 470n
Price structure, 114–19
Pricing, 36–37
    administration, 114–19
    decisions, 99–100
    declining product, 108
    discounts, 114–19
    distribution costs, 98
    environment, 98–99
    experience curve, 101, 102
    growth product, 105
    importance of, 97–98
    marketing channel, 98
    mature product, 106–7

Pricing—*Cont.*
    new product, 103–5
    over product life cycle, 100–108
    product-line, 108–13
    structure, 114–19
    volume trap, 101–3
    who determines, 119–20
Probabilities, 394–96
Process integration, 345
Procter & Gamble, 46, 161
Product liability, 475–77
Product life cycle, 321, 326–27
    analysis, 397
Product-line pricing, 108–13
    common resources, 111–13
    determining appropriate goals, 110–11
    multiple products, 109–10
    principles for, 109
Product management
    duties and reporting relationships, 45–49
    organization and structure, 40–43, 168
    relationship to other company areas, 47–48
    selecting team, 50–52
    support groups, 46–47
    when to use system, 43–45
Product manager
    new product development, 376–81
    responsibility and authority, 42–43, 48–49, 365
    self-evaluation, 316–17
    traits, 308–17
        competency based approach, 314–16
        interest inventory, 311–14
        research findings, 309–16
        values, 309–11
Product manager marketing organization, 34–35
Product quality, 330–32
Product recall, 476–77
Product support, 233; *see also* After sale product support
Production driven approach to management, 5–6
Productivity, 336
Profit, 13
    market share relationship, 101–2
Project New Prod, 377, 382

Project Sappho, 377
Project team, 166–67
Promotion; *see* Advertising and sales
    promotion
Promotional discount, 115–16
Psychological testing, 66–70
Pure Food and Drug Act, 445–46

Q-R

Qualification of accounts, 268
    telemarketing, 248–50
Quality Circles, 15, 16
Quantity discount, 118–19
Rafal, Marvin, 308, 487
Rank, J. Arthur, 340
Rapp, Jim, 202, 487
RCA, 356
References, 65–66
Regression analysis, 400
Reiling, H. R., 464n
Relevant market definition, 464–67
Reliance Electric Corporation, 359
Required rate of return, 409
Research and development, 336–39
Research in litigation; *see* Marketing
    research in litigation
Résumé, 64–66
Return on investment (ROI), 330, 333,
    335
Reverse engineering, 342
Rewards, 92–93
Roberts, Edward B., 16
Robinson-Patman Act of 1936, 115,
    450, 451, 464
Roering, K. J., 469n
Role playing, 148
Rowe, Frederick M., 450n

S

Saks, M. J., 473n
Sales, 38
    computers, 292–301
Sales-call interview, 255
Sales driven approach to management,
    4–5
Sales force, 46
    branch/district office; *see* Branch/
        district sales office management
    channel of distribution consider-
        ations, 178–79

Sales force—*Cont.*
    competition in territory, 181–82, 192
    customer service requirements, 180
    eliminating turnover, 91–96
    hiring, 182–86
        criteria, 59
        legal aspects of, 60–63
    job descriptions, 205–6
    managing, 202–6, 192–201
    objections and goals, 179–80
    psychological characteristics, 53–59
    psychological testing, 66–70
    selection process, 63–66
    sources of productive talent, 59
    staffing requirements, 180–81
    training, 186–92
Sales leads, 282–86
Sales manager, 203–6
    duties, 205–6
Sales measurements, 268–81
    evaluation system requirements, 277–
        81
    management of system, 281
    tracking, 269–77
Sales promotion; *see* Advertising and
    sales promotion
Sanders Associates, 341
Saunders, Paul E., 457, 487
Schere, F., 465n
Schumpeter, Joseph, 441n
Schwartz, Arnold L., 207, 487–88
Sears, Roebuck Company, 341
Selchow & Righter, 341
Sensitivity, 95
Service requirements planning, 239–41
Shapiro, Benson P., 98n, 120n
Shepherd, William C., 446n
Shepherd, William G., 438n
Sherman Antitrust Act, 441–45, 447,
    464
Sherrill, P. N., 469n
Shocker, A. D., 465n
Siegel v. *Chicken Delight*, 443, 447n
Simulation as training technique, 148
Sinclair, Upton, 446
Skimming pricing, 104–5
Smale, John G., 161
Societal change, 17–18
Spaeth, Harold J., 439
Staff-line organizational structure, 197–
    201
Standard contract, 460

Standard Oil Company of California v. *United States,* 448
Standard Oil Company of New Jersey v. *United States,* 439
Stern, L. W., 464n
Straight-line organizational structure, 193
Strong/Campbell interest Inventory, 311–14
Stryker, Charles W., 268, 488
Sympathy, 54
Synectics, 27, 29

T

Tarlow, Leah S., 3, 488
Tauber, E., 466n
Taylor, Frederick W., 124
Technicon Company, 237–38
Telemarketing, 244–66
  advantages, 263–64
  Call Planner, 255–57
  combining direct mail, 262
  costs, 245, 246, 250–51, 262
  customer classification, 246–47
  customer profile and action plan, 257–59
  designation of accounts, 247–51
  equipment, 266
  limitations, 263
  organizing department, 252–53
  personnel selection and training, 253–62
  prospecting, 248
  qualification of accounts, 248–50
  setting up system, 245
Telemarketing qualification program (TOP), 248–50
Telephone, 244
Teradyne Company, 242
Textile Fiber Products Identification Act, 452
Theory X versus Theory Y, 214
Theory Y, 15
Theory Z, 15, 16
Thermo-Serv., Inc., 31
3M Company, 388–90
Tickle card, 266
Times Picayune Publishing Company et al. v. *United States,* 447n
Tracking marketing activities
  attrition file, 275–76

Tracking marketing activities—*Cont.*
  computerized, 271, 294–97
  customer file, 274–75
  methods, 268–71
  process, 271–76
  results, 276–77
Trade discount, 114–15
Trade Regulation Reports (Commerce Clearing House), 441
Trademarks and brands, 467–69
  generic, 468
  infringement, 468–69
Training and development programs
  designing program for marketing managers, 139–51
  education techniques, 147–51
  evaluating, 151–52
  need for, 135–37
  salespersons, 186–92
Truth in Lending Act of 1968, 452
Turnover in sales and marketing departments
  communication, 94
  creativity, 96
  growth and development opportunities, 95–96
  promotions, 93
  rewards, 92–93
  sensitivity, 95
Tweed, Janet, 91, 488–89

U

United States v. *Aluminum Co. of America,* 444
United States v. *Arnold, Schwinn & Co.,* 442–43
United States v. *Columbia Steel Co.,* 448n
United States v. *Continental Can Co.,* 449n
United States v. *E. I. DuPont de Nemours & Co.,* 445, 448n, 464–65
United States v. *Falstaff Brewing Corp.,* 449
United States v. *Grinnell Corp.,* 445
United States v. *Marine Bancorporation, Inc.,* et al., 449n
United States v. *Pabst Brewing Corp.,* 449n
United States v. *Socony-Vacuum Oil Co.,* 442

United States v. *Topco Associates, Inc.*, 443
United States v. *Trenton Potteries Co.*, 442
United States v. *Von's Grocery Co.*, 449n

V

Values, 25–26
Van der Horst, Brian, 16
Venture group theory, 15, 16
Vernon, A. B., 309n
Vertical integration, 336
Vinson, D. E., 474n
Vizza, Robert F., 132, 133n, 489
Volkswagen, 357–58

W

Wack, Jeffery T., 463, 486
Warner-Lambert Company, 471

Warranty, 234
Washburn, Stewart A., 326, 489
Weadcock, Daniel K., 178, 490
Webb-Pomerene Export Trade Act of 1918, 452
Webster, Frederick E., Jr., 159
Werner, Roy O., 437, 490
Werth, R. W., 465n
Wheeler-Lea Act, 452
Wilcox, Clair, 446n
Wilson, Ian, 16
Wind, Y., 466n
Wizenberg, Larry, 212, 321, 490
Women in work force, 18–19
Wool Products Labeling Act, 452

X-Y-Z

Xerox Corporation, 232, 237, 340
Yankelovoch, D., 18
Young & Rubicam, 14, 17
Zelek, E. F., 464n, 466n